The
OCCULT HILLARY CLINTON

Demon Possession, Mind Control, Witchcraft, Voodoo, Reptilian Shapeshifting, Terrorism, Conspiracies... and much more

James W. Harris

Copyright ©2016 by James W. Harris.

All rights reserved under International and Pan-American copyright conventions. No portion of this book may be reproduced, stored in a retrieval system, or transmitted in any form or by any means – electronic, mechanical, photocopy, recording, scanning, or other – except for brief quotations with attribution to the author, without prior written permission of the authors or publisher.

Published in the United States
by Amazing Temple of Miracles
OccultHillary.com

FIRST EDITION
Published October 2016

Harris, James W.
The Occult Hillary Clinton
By James W. Harris

ISBN: 978-1539766209

1. Hillary Clinton   2. Bill Clinton   3. Occult   4. Politics   5. Presidential politics   6. Antichrist   7. Shapeshifting reptilians   8.. UFOs   9. Voodoo   10. Satanism   10. Demon possession   11. Mind control   12. Conspiracy theories   13. CIA   14.. Bilderbergers   15. Council on Foreign Relations   16. Trilateral Commission   17. New World Order   18. One-world government
I. Title   II. Harris, James W.

Cover concept by James W. Harris
Cover illustration by Sheikh Salman
Cover design by Pixel Studios
Interior book design by Mahamud Hussain Noman

Manufactured in the United States of America

*To Sharon Harris:
my wife, best friend,
and love of my life.*

"Try to make sense of what you see, and wonder about what makes the universe exist. Be curious." – Stephen Hawking

"Take no part in the unfruitful works of darkness, but instead expose them." – Ephesians 5:11

"News is what someone wants to suppress. Everything else is advertising." – former NBC news president Reuven Frank

"...as we know, there are known knowns; there are things we know we know. We also know there are known unknowns; that is to say we know there are some things we do not know. But there are also unknown unknowns – the ones we don't know we don't know. And if one looks throughout the history of our country and other free countries, it is the latter category that tends to be the difficult one." – U.S. Secretary of Defense Donald Rumsfeld, February 12, 2002

"There is nothing hidden that will not be revealed, and there is nothing secret that will not become known and come to light." – Luke 8:17

"I'm not concerned about the conspiracy theories. There are so many of them I've lost track ... and so I pay no attention to them." – Hillary Clinton, Sept. 5, 2016

TABLE OF CONTENTS

INTRODUCTION AND WARNING 11

CHAPTER ONE IS HILLARY A HUMAN BEING? 16

"Be Careful to 'Be Real'" 16
Journalist: Clinton Sounds "reptilian … robotic" 17
Pulitzer Prize-Nominated Investigative Journalist: "A Spirit of Witchcraft Occultism… Fuliginous… A Curse" 17
Reptilian… Over and Over Again 19
"Like a virus or alien that needs a host body…" 20
Hillary: "I am not an alien creature…" 21
Hillary: "I am a real person!" Critics: Hillary Fails the "Turing Test" 21
Hillary: Like "a robot that is trying to become more human" 22
Hillary Shocker: "I'm really not even a human being" 23
Hillary: What If It's Worse Than We Think? 24

CHAPTER TWO HILLARY, BILL AND… VOODOO 25

Bill Clinton: Early Voodoo Experiences 28
Bill and Hillary: "The King and Queen of Haiti" 29
Did Bill's "Wanga" and Dirty Voodoo Underwear Help Him Defeat George H.W. Bush? 30
Does Hillary Use Voodoo to Create a Private Army of Zombie Slaves? 31

CHAPTER THREE COMMUNING WITH THE DEAD 34

Necromancy in the White House? 34
Is Hillary a "World Server" for the Takeover of the World by the Antichrist via the United Nations? 42

CHAPTER FOUR SATANISM AND DEMON POSSESSION: IS HILLARY POSSESSED BY DEMONS – OR THE DEVIL? 47

The Case for Demon Possession Today 47
Ivy League Psychiatrist: "Demon Possession Is Real" 51
Scientists, Exorcism and Demon Possession 53
Could Demon Possession Cost Hillary the Election? 54
Is Hillary Possessed by Demons? Examining the Evidence 55
How Hillary's Occult Activities Could Have Opened Her Up to Demon Possession 56
Does Hillary Show the Signs of Demonic Possession? 57
Witchcraft and Satanism: Clinton Insider Says Hillary Worships Satan . 68
Demon Possession and the Reptilian Conspiracy 70

REPUBLICAN PRESIDENTIAL CANDIDATES TAKE THE LEAD IN FIGHTING DEMONS.... 71
HILLARY'S DILEMMA: MILLIONS OF VOTERS WILL NOT KNOWINGLY SUPPORT A DEMON-POSSESSED CANDIDATE.. 73

CHAPTER FIVE SECRET SYMBOLS, SIGNS AND OTHER OCCULT IMAGERY AND INFLUENCES.. 74

HILLARY'S OBSCENE OCCULT "CHRISTMAS" TREE 74
HILLARY'S LUCIFERIAN LAPEL PIN 80
IS HILLARY A MIND-CONTROLLING, CHILD-ABUSING WICKED WITCH OF THE WEST? 82
HILLARY FLASHES THE SIGN OF SATAN 86
HILLARY, SAUL ALINSKY – AND SATAN 88

CHAPTER SIX HILLARY AND DEMONIC ROCK MUSIC............................ 95

HILLARY'S ROCK STAR ADVISER: "WE SEEK DEPRAVITY" 100
"WHEN THE LADY SMILES..." HORROR AND BLASPHEMY 101

CHAPTER SEVEN 666: IS HILLARY THE ANTICHRIST?............................ 107

U.S. CONGRESSMAN: "HILLARY IS THE ANTICHRIST" 107
WHAT OR WHO IS THE ANTICHRIST? WHAT IS THE BEAST? 108
THE ANTICHRIST, THE NEW WORLD ORDER, AND REAL ID 110
HILLARY = 666.. 113
HILLARY: 666... AT BIRTH 115
DID HILLARY DELIBERATELY "LOSE" TO BARACK OBAMA IN 2008 – TO GAIN OCCULT POWER?... 115
THE ANTICHRIST: FEMALE OR MALE? 116
IS HILLARY THE BEAST DESCRIBED IN THE BOOK OF REVELATION?................... 117

CHAPTER EIGHT IS HILLARY A GIANT SHAPESHIFTING REPTILIAN OVERLORD?..122

PRIME MINISTER ASSURES PUBLIC HE'S NOT A SHAPESHIFTING REPTILIAN ALIEN, HONEST 123
FACEBOOK FOUNDER: "I AM NOT A LIZARD" 124
REPTILIANS: MILLIONS OF AMERICANS BELIEVE 126
HILLARY AND THE "PENIS OF THE DRAGON" 128
TIME MAGAZINE ON THE REPTILIAN CONSPIRACY 129
THE SECRET HISTORY OF REPTILIANS AND HUMANS....................................... 130
MAINSTREAM SCIENCE OFFERS EVIDENCE BACKING THE REPTILIAN THEORY 138
SCIENCE PROVES SHAPESHIFTING IS REAL.. 144
ENTER ICKE 147
JOHN RHODES: REPTILIAN "SLEEPER CELLS" AND U.S. POLITICS...................... 150

THOUSANDS OF VIDEOS CLAIM TO SHOW HILLARY AND OTHERS SHAPESHIFTING INTO REPTILIANS 153
HILLARY, EXORCISMS… AND REPTILIAN SHAPESHIFTING 155
REPTILIAN CONTINUITY? OBAMA ADMINISTRATION EVADES REPTILIAN QUESTION 156
REPTILIAN RULE IN MASS MEDIA... 157
CONCLUSION: "IF IT IS ANYONE, IT IS HILLARY".. 159

CHAPTER NINE PROJECT MONARCH: MIND-CONTROLLED SEX SLAVES, RITUAL CHILD ABUSE, AND MURDER................................... 161

DO MIND-CONTROLLED SEX SLAVES SERVE BILL AND HILLARY? 161
EVALUATING THE MONARCH CHARGES... 167
 1. The federal government had programs to create mind-controlled agents and slaves 168
 2. The CIA and other participating government and private sector agencies knew that such experiments and activities were illegal, and continued doing them anyway.. 173
 3. Such experiments were successful in creating mind-controlled assassins and mind-controlled sex slaves, as well as "sleeper agents" (so-called "Manchurian Candidates") who carried within their minds hidden multiple personalities that could be awakened by the government when desired. 175
 4. Such experiments must necessarily have involved a vast number of players, including experts in such fields as psychology, hypnosis, drug abuse and other areas related to mind control; such experiments must also have involved the participation of some of the country's leading institutions 180
 5. U.S. government agents and contractors performed such dangerous, painful, invasive and criminal experiments on innocent unsuspecting American citizens illegally, without their consent or knowledge... 186
 6. The U.S. government forced children to participate in such dangerous, painful, invasive and criminal experiments................ 189
 7. Some alleged MONARCH victims claim to have experienced torture and abuse by Nazis, Satanists, and occultists. For this to be true there would need to be examples of collaboration between U.S. government agencies and such persons. 192
 8. Because some of these claims are recent, we would need reason to believe that such experiments and programs are going on today (or at least were active in the very recent past) 215

9. We would need evidence that the Clintons and/or other ruling elite figures could be connected to pedophile rings, sexual abuse and related matters 217

CHAPTER TEN UFOS: THE CLINTON CONNECTION 260

THE LONG CLINTON INTEREST IN UFOS 261
BILL AND HILLARY AND UFOS 267
JOHN PODESTA: CLINTON UFO POINT MAN 269
HILLARY: "WE MAY HAVE ALREADY BEEN VISITED BY UFOS" 270
PRESIDENT BILL CLINTON HIDES AREA 51 FROM INVESTIGATION – WHILE POISONING AMERICANS WITH TOP-SECRET SUBSTANCES 270
IS HILLARY'S PUBLIC UFO INTEREST PART OF A FALSE-FLAG CONSPIRACY TO TRICK THE WORLD INTO ACCEPTING A NEW WORLD ORDER? 272
CANADIAN DEFENSE MINISTER: "UFOS ARE REAL... AND THE U.S. IS PREPARING TO LAUNCH AN INTERGALACTIC WAR AGAINST THEM" 285
THE VOICE OF VRILLION: PRANK, ENCOUNTER... OR FALSE-FLAG REHEARSAL? 286
NASA AND THE OCCULT 290
THE STARGATE PROJECT: UFOS, REMOTE VIEWING AND PSYCHIC SPOOKS 299
TOP SECRET AMERICA: U.S. MYSTERY BLACK BUDGET PROGRAMS 302
SECRET AGENCIES 304

CHAPTER ELEVEN INDICATIONS OF OCCULT OR ALIEN POWER MANIFESTED BY HILLARY 307

"LASER BEAM" EYES THAT "PIERCE SKULLS" 307
INVULNERABILITY 308
HILLARY DOES NOT SWEAT 312
SUPERHUMAN POWERS OF ENDURANCE AND STRENGTH 314
OCCULT MANIPULATION OF THE STOCK MARKET? 315
MIND CONTROL / HYPNOTISM / DREAM CONTROL? 316

CHAPTER TWELVE COULD IT ALL BE TRUE? 320

CHAPTER THIRTEEN: HILLARY'S SECRET, OCCULT AND CONSPIRATORIAL SOCIETIES 322

HOW THE CIA USES THE TERM "CONSPIRACY" TO HIDE THE CRIMES OF RULING ELITES 323
CONSPIRACY THEORY – OR POWER ELITE ANALYSIS? 328
GOVERNMENT CONSPIRACY: MILLIONS OF AMERICANS BELIEVE 332
THE CLINTON CONSPIRACY NETWORK 333
BILL, HILLARY AND THE RHODES CONSPIRACY TO TAKE OVER THE WORLD 334
BILL AND HILLARY'S RELATIONS WITH THE COUNCIL ON FOREIGN RELATIONS 340
THE TRILATERAL COMMISSION 355
THE ATLANTIC COUNCIL: "CROWNING" HILLARY FOR PRESIDENT 360

THE ASPEN INSTITUTE 363
THE FELLOWSHIP (AKA THE FAMILY, THE INTERNATIONAL FOUNDATION): "YOU GUYS ARE HERE TO LEARN HOW TO RULE THE WORLD" 365
"DAVOS MAN": DAVOS WORLD ECONOMIC FORUM 370
THE NEW WORLD FOUNDATION/ INSTITUTE FOR POLICY STUDIES 372
CLINTON GLOBAL INITIATIVE (CGI) ANNUAL MEETING 378
THE BILDERBERGERS: "BILDING" A NEW WORLD ORDER................................ 385
SKULL AND BONES: DEATH, DEPRAVITY AND POWER AMONG AMERICA'S RULING ELITE 390
BOHEMIAN GROVE: DEVIL WORSHIP AND SYMBOLIC CHILD SACRIFICE CEREMONIES OF THE RICH AND FAMOUS 396

CHAPTER FOURTEEN HILLARY'S DISTURBING POLITICS: FASCISM, COMMUNISM, TERRORISM, STATISM, WAR CRIMES AND…? 407

HILLARY: A "LIBERAL FASCIST" AND "THEOCRAT" WITH "TOTALITARIAN" IDEAS .. 408
LEADING LIBERAL MAGAZINE: HILLARY IS NO LIBERAL, SHE'S A "STATIST" WHO IS HOSTILE TO CIVIL LIBERTIES – AND COULD SEND CRITICS TO "RE-EDUCATION CAMPS" 411
ECHOES OF TYRANNY IN HILLARY'S "IT TAKES A VILLAGE" 412
HILLARY'S EARLY DAYS: SEDUCED BY RADICAL POLITICS IN THE GUISE OF THEOLOGY 413
HILLARY'S COMMUNIST SUMMER INTERNSHIP 414
POST-COLLEGE RADICALISM 415
PARDONING VIOLENT U.S. COMMUNIST TERRORISTS 416
THE CLINTONS AND THE WEATHER UNDERGROUND 418
THE MAINSTREAMING OF THE WEATHER UNDERGROUND TERRORISTS?............. 420
PARDONING YET MORE COMMUNIST TERRORISTS 420
STILL MORE TERRORIST-RELATED PARDONS FROM PRESIDENT CLINTON 422
HILLARY AND THE CLINTON FOUNDATION: HELPING THE RUSSIANS ACQUIRE URANIUM? 423
HILLARY: HELPING ARM TERRORISTS, DESPOTS AND AUTHORITARIAN REGIMES?. 424
HILLARY: FRIEND OF TYRANTS AND DESPOTS AROUND THE WORLD 427
FINAL NOTE: IS RAISING SUCH ISSUES FAIR TO HILLARY? 429

CHAPTER FIFTEEN HILLARY IS COMING FOR YOUR GUNS................... 430

HILLARY'S YEARS OF ANTI-GUN POSITIONS 431
HILLARY: PUT AMERICAN CITIZENS ON SECRET WATCH LISTS TO DENY THEM THEIR CONSTITUTIONAL RIGHTS 433
HILLARY-SUPPORTED "BUY-BACKS" COULD LAUNCH A BLOODY U.S. CIVIL WAR . 434
HILLARY PROMISES "ADMINISTRATIVE ACTION" TO OVERTURN THE SECOND AMENDMENT 437
HILLARY PROPOSES THOUGHT CONTROL ON GUN ISSUES 437

HILLARY'S PRIVATE TOP SECRET ARMY WILL REMAIN ARMED 438
CHAPTER SIXTEEN HILLARY'S SECRET ARMY: TERRORISM, HARASSMENT, BLACKMAIL AND MORE 439
"THE SHADOW TEAM": HILLARY'S SECRET POLICE FORCE 439
MORE ON HILLARY'S SECRET POLICE 441
HILLARY'S "PRIVATE NSA" 442
DID HILLARY STEAL FBI FILES – AND USE THEM FOR BLACKMAIL? 444
CLINTON HIT MAN CONFESSES TO MURDERS, CASTRATION FOR BILL AND HILLARY 446
THE CLINTON DEATH LISTS 448
WRITERS AND INVESTIGATORS FEAR FOR THEIR LIVES AFTER RESEARCHING CLINTONS; JOURNALIST CHARGES HILLARY IS "PARANOID" AND HAS "PENCHANT FOR DOING ILLEGAL THINGS" 451
HILLARY VS. THE INTERNET AND FREE SPEECH 452

CONCLUSION 455

AFTERWORD 462

SOURCES 466

ACKNOWLEDGEMENTS 467

ABOUT THE AUTHOR 469

ONE LAST THING... 470

INTRODUCTION and WARNING

"The biggest mistake of the American press is thinking they know her." – Maggie Williams, Hillary's former chief of staff and one of her closest friends, New York Times, May 30, 1999

Hillary Clinton is the most polarizing, the most controversial figure in American politics today.

She is admired by millions – and feared and loathed by millions more.

Of course, the same could be said for other political figures.

However... there are those whose objections to Hillary go far beyond the usual political or personal critiques.

A startling and growing number of Americans oppose Hillary not just for the usual political reasons, but because they fear she may be:

- a witch practicing the darkest of the occult arts
- the Antichrist
- a non-human flesh-eating reptilian shapeshifter
- a blood-drinking demon-possessed Satanic high priestess
- a voodoo queen
- leader of an army of mind-controlled sex slaves and spies
- receiving and following secret instructions from evil entities from other dimensions
- a member of secret ruling elite conspiratorial societies that guide the direction of the world to achieve dark occult aims

... and more.

Such beliefs about Hillary Clinton are held not by a small fringe, but by many millions of mainstream, everyday Americans.

Their accusations can be found in books, videos, speeches, online and elsewhere.

It's easy to dismiss such seemingly outrageous charges as ridiculous and nonscientific.

However, not so very long ago, the idea that a person could be a witch, possessed by demons, practice black magic, shapeshift into beasts and alien forms, work in allegiance with Satan, exhibit supernatural or otherworldly powers, contact the dead and beings from other planets and other dimensions... would not have been thought at all unusual or controversial.

That had its negative consequences, of course. Over the centuries, tragically, many innocent people were accused of such things and harassed, persecuted, tortured, or killed.

Today we are privileged to live in more enlightened times. Science has replaced unfounded superstition in category after category. Ailments once ascribed to demons or sorcerers are now routinely treated with medicine or counseling. We should be profoundly grateful for this.

However... is it possible that we have gone too far in the other direction? Could it be that, in our efforts to understand the world in a purely rational and scientific manner, we may have neglected to fairly consider whether all allegations of supernatural powers and diabolic intent are false?

Is it possible our hyper-rational, mechanistic view of the universe may have caused us to overlook or dismiss the possibilities that there are other dimensions, other laws, that operate in our universe? Hidden forces around us that we do not yet know about or understand?

Is it possible that ESP, telepathy, black magic might actually work? That demons are real? Could strange, powerful, cunning and evil non-human beings actually live and work among us? Even rule us in secret, perhaps in concert with earthly governments, secret societies, and ruthless ruling-elite human Quislings? Could such beings be conspiring together with the ultimate goal of enslaving all of humanity via the imposition of a tyrannical New World Order?

Millions of Americans believe that mounting evidence has made such questions once again worthy of examination.

And the fact that such charges circle continually around Hillary Clinton requires us to examine them in the light of her career and political aims.

After all, as far back as 1993, Hillary Clinton declared her goal was nothing less than the "remaking of the American way of politics, government, indeed life."

Indeed, this has been a theme of her entire adult life. The college-age Hillary, in her now-famous 1969 commencement address at Wellesley College, boldly declared: "We're not interested in social reconstruction; it's human reconstruction" that she and her followers were after.

Human reconstruction...

In 2016, as Hillary approaches the White House, preparing to assume the mantle of the most powerful being on the planet (and, perhaps, as some maintain, other planets and other dimensions as well), it is vitally important that such charges be examined – carefully, honestly, and with an open and unprejudiced mind.

That is the purpose of this book.

We will examine, one by one, the occult and conspiratorial charges now being made against Hillary.

We will not simply list and detail these charges. We will go deeper. We will explore their historical, scientific and spiritual roots, in an effort to understand why growing millions of people have come to take these seemingly outrageous ideas seriously and believe that they are, or may be, true.

At first hearing some of these accusations may indeed seem, even to diehard Hillary critics, beyond the pale. Hillary, a giant shapeshifting reptile who feeds on human flesh? Hillary, a witch, possessed by hordes of demons, worshiping Satan, practicing voodoo, sacrificing human lives and drinking human blood? Hillary, leading an invisible army of government-created mind-controlled slaves? Secretly conspiring with the world's political and economic elites to run the globe?

Out of any context, such allegations may indeed sound incredible, even absurd. However, after examining the historical, spiritual and scientific arguments that lie behind them, you may well be shocked.

You may find yourself changing your mind on matters you thought were settled years – even centuries – ago.

Perhaps you will even join those growing millions who see Hillary as one of the world's most powerful practitioners of the dark arts, a threat to the very survival of the human race.

A warning: The Occult Hillary Clinton examines a body of evidence, a series of beliefs, speculations and historical facts, that in some cases challenge the very fundamentals of accepted science, history, politics and even consensus reality itself.

Some of this material is disturbing. Alarming.

This is not a book for the close-minded or the faint of heart.

What if much of what you believe about the world is a carefully constructed illusion – an hallucination, mere theater, propaganda in the service of sinister forces you didn't even know existed?

Much of what you "think" you know... may be wrong.

Or at the least, incomplete and inadequate to explain the world as it really is.

Prepare, then, to peer behind the curtain. To be entertained, enlightened, astonished – and perhaps even to have long-held notions of reality challenged, shifted, and perhaps shattered... forever.

– James W. Harris

NOTE TO READERS: We have used the name "Hillary" to refer to Hillary Rodham Clinton throughout this book. No disrespect or diminishment is intended by this. In part this is to distinguish her from her husband, former President Bill Clinton, who is also frequently discussed in this book, and thus remove any confusion that simply calling her "Clinton" might otherwise bring.

It is also the title she herself seems to prefer. Her campaign website, signs, buttons and other campaign materials all identify her simply as "Hillary."

So Hillary it is.

CHAPTER ONE

Is Hillary a Human Being?

There is, to be blunt, something very strange about Hillary Clinton.

Over the years, many people have observed that... she simply doesn't seem to be entirely human.

Her reactions, her words, her physical presence, all seem to leave people with that odd feeling.

People have struggled to put this into words. False. Acting. Reptilian. Robotic. Non-human. Cold. Occult. And more.

Before examining more specific charges, the subjects of the following chapters, let us first quickly get a sense of the widely perceived *strangeness* about Hillary that is often felt and reported on by those who encounter her in person or see her interviewed in the press.

"Be Careful to 'Be Real'"

In July 1999, at the start of her race for the U.S. Senate, one of Hillary's senior advisers sent her a private memo urging her to remember to "be real."

The odd and arguably disturbing advice – "be careful to 'be real'" – came from Mandy Grunwald, who later became head of media relations on Hillary's 2008 presidential campaign.

The private memo – kept secret for years – was finally released by the U.S. National Archives and Records Administration in 2014, after protection from Freedom of Information Act requests expired, and after what some critics charged was an unduly long delay by the Clintons in dealing with such requests.

As one conservative blog noted: "Not a great sign of authenticity when someone needs to be reminded to be real."

Note also that the words "be real" are in quotes – implying that Grunwald didn't really want Hillary to be authentically real, to be her real self – but rather, to simply *pretend* to be real. To fool people into thinking she is being "real" when she in fact is not.

Which of course makes one wonder: What would Hillary be if she actually did "be real" – without the quote marks. Would it be something far stranger than we think? Something perhaps... horrifying?

Journalist: Clinton Sounds "reptilian ... robotic"

Similarly, in a review of Hillary's Hard Choices: A Memoir, in the UK Spectator (June 21, 2014) journalist Matthew Walther notes it is written as if it is "a book for people... who don't have much experience of people..."

Noting the palpably false sound of the conversations recreated in the book, he wonders: "Does anyone, I wonder, have conversations like that? ... Pseudo-details like these and hundreds of others meant to *humanize* Clinton *end up making her sound more reptilian than she probably is.*" (Emphasis added.)

Walther further notes Clinton's "robotic equanimity."

Ultimately, Walther finds this consistent non-human tone in the book so disturbing that he actually feels driven to commit acts of evil and violence – even murder:

"It left me with the urge to be wicked. I wanted to put something menacing on the turntable and turn up the volume. I wanted to steal a child's ice-cream cone or kick a kitten. I wanted to light five or six slow-burning cigarettes and throw them in the outgoing postbox with my neighbors' postcards and utility bills. Motor vehicle theft, arson, even murder occurred to me."

It is remarkable and disturbing that her book – or any book – could have such an effect on a seasoned journalist.

Yet as we shall see, journalist Walther is hardly alone.

Pulitzer Prize-Nominated Investigative Journalist:

"A Spirit of Witchcraft Occultism... Fuliginous... A Curse"

Michael H. Brown is a Pulitzer Prize-nominated journalist who uncovered the Love Canal environmental scandal and whose work has appeared in The New York Times Magazine, Atlantic Monthly, Rolling Stone and other magazines and newspapers across the U.S. Brown left journalism to become a bestselling author of religious books.

In 1986, while investigating an environmental threat he suspected might have originated from Arkansas, he called the governor's mansion and ended up speaking to Hillary (who was at the time also a lawyer for the firm he was investigating).

She was, Brown says, "nasty, unpleasant" and "arrogant" as she dismissed his questions.

But that was the least of his worries.

"What I remember most was the incredible feeling that came upon me – and my entire apartment – after hanging up," he says.

"...I immediately felt an enormous oppression, as if the air in my apartment was preternaturally thick, oppressive, and fuliginous: a descent of darkness. I could feel it. It wasn't just to be brushed off. Even at the time, it felt, I recall thinking, like a curse. ...I immediately felt it was a 'spirit of witchcraft.'

"And as I sit here now, thirty years later, I still don't know the origin of that oppression.

"My concerns are not on politics but on the 'spirituality' – and especially any occultism – that may move into the Oval Office...

" This I can say: the sensation pervaded my apartment for a good two hours. I sat down and prayed it away from me. ...

"Has Hillary dabbled with the occult?

"I don't know that either. ... I certainly hope none of that is true, and have seen not a shred of concrete evidence for that – though, to be blunt, it would go a long way in explaining the feeling I had back in [my] Manhattan apartment. ...

"For now, I sense a turning point for these United States, and whatever the decision, real danger."

Reptilian… Over and Over Again

Journalists seem almost driven to use terms like "reptilian" to describe Hillary.

For example, an April 2015 article in New York magazine concerning Hillary's position on incarceration suddenly out of nowhere says this:

"For policy reasons and moral reasons, but also *for pure reptilian political ones*, this is a really interesting issue for Clinton to take on…"

Veteran journalist Jack Schafer, writing also in April 2015 at Politico.com about Hillary's campaign strategy of "listening tours," abruptly says:

"Listening tours (or sessions) are supposed to add a little fabric softener to a politician's starchy image, buffing *their scaly reptilian exteriors* down to kid-leather smoothness. The technique worked for Clinton in New York, where booking upstate listening stops helped her win a Senate seat in 2000."

The New York Times, writing April 14, 2015 about a series of anonymous anti-Hillary posters that appeared in the city after her announcement she was running for president, says:

"The portraits are stylized so that Mrs. Clinton's face looks almost furry, or just very wrinkled, and *her eyes almost reptilian*." (Actually, the photo of the poster accompanying the article did not look obviously "reptilian." This was a phrase of choice by the writer.)

Award-winning journalist, film and television writer and conservative pundit Burt Prelutsky, in an April 2015 column about an unusual request from Hillary's campaign that journalists not use certain words to describe her, notes that this still left plenty of other negative words journalists could use, including, he says, "devious," "cunning," "cut-throat," "nasty," "Borgia-like," "abusive," "corrupt," "vindictive," "arrogant," "snide," "power-mad" and… you guessed it… "*reptilian.*"

At the left-wing website CounterPunch Dr. Norman Pollack, a Guggenheim Fellow and professor emeritus of history at Michigan State University, offered on January 20, 2016 this startling analysis in his article "Reptilian Politics and American Leadership: The Party Debates":

"For Clinton, 'reptilian' remains apt ... in light of her creeping, slithering approach to issues, particularly involving militarism and haute capitalism (Wall Street) and her instinctive love of camouflage (a strong desire for concealment and dislike of transparency, especially in government). She too, like Cruz, goes for the jugular when it comes to perceived enemies, and is equally a vast storehouse of resentments ready to explode when given the opportunity."

Noting the increasingly "reptilian" behavior of Hillary as well as her Republican opponents, Dr. Pollack goes on to describe her as "snakelike in [her] conduct ... [a] boa constrictor...squashing the life and vitality out of democracy..."

These are but a few samples. There is much, much more

What's going on here? Are journalists and commentators actually sensing something *reptilian* about Hillary, and consciously or unconsciously expressing it in their writing?

Those who believe the mainstream media is an arm of a vast and sinister conspiracy – something we will explore later in this book – must consider even darker thoughts: Is this some form of subliminal brainwashing or mass conditioning?

Is the public being "softened up" by the media to accept the notion of a "reptilian" president, ruler, overlord? Are we seeing the mainstreaming of the "reptilian" revolution? (See Chapter 8 for far more on the theory that the concept of reptilian rule is being secretly peddled to the masses.)

Or are all of these Hillary-as-reptile remarks just... coincidence?

That of all scenarios seems too much to believe.

"Like a virus or alien that needs a host body..."

And then there is this observation from Maureen Dowd, Pulitzer Prize-winning journalist and bestselling author, in the New York Times:

"There's something so rootless and chaotic about the Clintons. *They seem like a virus or alien that needs a host body to survive.* They've invaded our national psyche and we're going to have to keep living with their weird marital problems and tangled ambitions forever and ever. Their business will never be finished. They are never going to go away because they have not any place else to go." (Emphasis added.)

Hillary: "I am not an alien creature…"

Such strange accusations – that Hillary is actually something other than human – have dogged Hillary for many years.

On September 4, 2007, Hillary went on the "Ellen" show. When asked by host Ellen DeGeneres what the biggest public misperception about her was, Hillary's response was astounding:

"You know, that I'm some kind of creature from an alien world, I suppose."

Hillary: "I am a real person!"
Critics: Hillary Fails the "Turing Test"

The Turing Test was developed by the renowned British computer scientist, mathematician, logician, cryptanalyst and theoretical biologist Alan Turing as a way of determining when a computer could be called "intelligent."

Turing's idea was both brilliant and eminently practical: a computer could be said to "think" in a human-like fashion if a human, engaged in conversation with it, could not tell, based on its responses, whether he or she was speaking to a human being or a machine.

The Turning Test today remains an active concept as we approach the age of Artificial Intelligence (AI).

Hillary, some argue, has actually failed the Turing Test on occasion. That is, she has come across as something other than human in conversations.

An early acknowledgment of this came in an October 2015 Vanity Fair article on Hillary, which noted that "This campaign is like a Turing Test of whether Hillary is indeed herself."

In her first Sunday TV news show interview of the 2016 campaign, Hillary – asked to describe herself in three words, told "Face the Nation" host John Dickerson: "I am a real person!"

Critics immediately jumped on this as exactly the way a "real person" *wouldn't* describe herself – and precisely what a non-human creature or thing, trying to pose as a human, might clumsily say. (Plus, by the way, it wasn't three words.)

Conservative satirist David Burge immediately tweeted: "Turing Test fail."

Ricochet editor Jon Gabriel similarly said: "Face the Nation's Hillary interview should have started with a Turing Test."

Other similar responses followed, fast and furious, as people expressed the feeling of millions that they had indeed witnessed a weird performance somehow disturbingly non-human:

"This is truly creepy and frightening." – Mark Shear

Eric Spencer: "Man, I thought for sure that by 2015 robots would be a lot more convincing."

"I think the Clinton Android Bot 3.5 malfunctioned again …" – The Rogue Elf

"Seconds later her head fell off, sprouted eight legs, and scurried away. The interviewer noticed during a commercial break." – Martin Cohn

On and on the comments came, a flood of them, as an amazed, and perhaps unsettled, public tried to come to grips with what they had seen.

Hillary: Like "a robot that is trying to become more human"

Hillary's "Face the Nation" Turing fail was far from the first or only time observers had noticed that Hillary seemed disturbingly like a non-human entity clumsily imitating a human.

Vanity Fair editor Graydon Carter wrote in the Nov. 2015 issue: "...you'd need to apply the famous Turing Test to see if any authentic human 'Hillary' can be distinguished from the machine version that has been in development for more than three decades."

And there was this tweet, shared by Instapundit on April 14, 2015: "Fun game: Read stories on Hillary as if they are stories about a robot that is trying to become more human."

In February 2016 in the Washington Post, political scientist Mary Nugent and computer scientist Emma Pierson joined together to summarize public opinion as expressed through a Twitter campaign that solicited words to describe Hillary:

"In addition to being criticized as untrustworthy, Clinton was frequently criticized as not likable *or human*." (Emphasis added.)

Hillary Shocker: "I'm really not even a human being"

In an October 2015 interview on the BuzzFeed podcast "Another Round," Hillary was asked about the often-reported curiosity that she doesn't sweat – and her reply was a shocker:

Another Round: "What's the weirdest thing about you?"

Hillary: "The weirdest thing about me is that I don't sweat."

Another Round "Obviously. Best argument for Hillary as a robot: zero sweat."

Hillary: "You guys are the first to realize that *I'm really not even a human being*. I was constructed in a garage in Palo Alto a very long time ago. ... I mean, a man whose name shall remain nameless created me in his garage."

Another Round "Are there more of you?"

Hillary: "I thought he threw away the plans, at least that's what he told me when he programmed me – that there would be no more. I've seen more people that kind of don't sweat, and other things, that make me think maybe they are part of the new race that he created: the robot race."

Another Round "So there's a cyborg army is what you're saying."

Hillary: "But you have to cut this, you can't tell anybody this. I don't want anybody to know this. This has been a secret until here we are in Davenport, Iowa, and I'm just spillin' my electronic guts to you."

Obviously this bizarre exchange was done in a joking manner. But as we have documented, the charge that Hillary is in fact something other than human is being made by critics around the world.

Was Hillary just trying to laugh off the growing claims that she is not human? Or – was she using humor to cover a disturbing reality? Was this a trial balloon – a hesitant first admission that, yes, she is something far different than merely human? A cyborg or alien, perhaps? Or a shapeshifting reptilian?

Hillary: What If It's Worse Than We Think?

Hillary's strangely non-human public behavior and weirdly off-target remarks continue.

Inevitably, more and more Americans are beginning to wonder if there is some horrific underlying truth hidden behind them.

As well they might.

For, as we shall see in the chapters ahead, the truth about Hillary's bizarre words and actions may be far stranger – and far more disturbing – than most people dare think.

CHAPTER TWO

Hillary, Bill and... Voodoo

Do Bill and Hillary use voodoo power and commune with strange voodoo gods to win political success?

Have they made a terrible and bloody secret political bargain with malevolent voodoo spirits?

Few Americans know it, but Bill and Hillary have a deep interest in voodoo that started well before Bill won his first political office.

In fact, Bill did not win a political race until he and Hillary – with the guidance of one of the most famous voodoo priests in the world – attended a voodoo ceremony, complete with a blood sacrifice, invoking the voodoo god "Ogou" – who voodooists believe *rules the world of politics*.

Furthermore, that was not the first of Bill's experiences with the strange, bloody and frequently deadly world of voodoo.

In his memoir My Life, Bill tells of the 1975 trip he and Hillary took to Haiti. He had lost his first political race, a 1974 bid for Congress, and was pondering his future in politics.

In Haiti he found "the most interesting day of the trip" came when he, Hillary and close Clinton associate Edwin David Edwards of CitiBank went to a voodoo ceremony – and witnessed voodoo rituals and spirit possession.

During that pilgrimage multigenerational voodoo priest Max Beauvoir instructed Bill and Hillary in what Bill describes as a "brief course in voodoo theology." This was followed by a bloody voodoo ceremony, complete with a horrific living sacrifice, in which, according to Bill, voodoo spirits seized possession of some of those present.

Bill called this an "extraordinary event" and wrote:

"Voodoo's central ritual is a dance during which spirits possess believers. ... After several minutes of rhythmic dancing to pounding drums, the spirits arrived, seizing a woman and a man. The man proceeded to rub a burning torch all over his body and walk on hot coals without being burned. The woman, in a frenzy, screamed repeatedly, then grabbed a live chicken and bit its head off. Then the spirits left and those who had been possessed fell to the ground."

If during what Bill calls this "extraordinary event" he or Hillary were themselves possessed by spirits, or if they communicated with or summoned spirits, he does not say. (Though his wording certainly leaves open the tantalizing possibility that the "man and woman" possessed by the spirits in the ceremony could, conceivably, have been... him and Hillary. Anyone having tapes of Hillary biting the head off a chicken is urged to contact this author at once.) Bill writes only that, after this "brief foray into the world of voodoo" he became further aware of "the virtually universal belief that there is a nonphysical spirit force at work in the world."

Voodoo, like Christianity, does recognize the existence of malevolent spirits ("baka"). It takes little imagination to see the possibility of demonic entities invoked by such a bloodletting session taking the opportunity to enter one or both of the Clintons.

It should be noted that Max Beauvoir, the voodoo priest the Clintons consulted, was no ordinary countryside priest. He was a major figure in the world of voodoo – indeed, perhaps the most influential voodoo priest in the world.

In his 2015 obituary, the Washington Post called him "Supreme chief of Haitian voodoo." The UK called him the "Voodoo Pope." Beauvoir founded the National Conference of Haitian Voodoo, and in 2008 was chosen by that organization as the first Supreme Spiritual Leader or Supreme Chief of Voodoo, recognizing him as a voodoo elder of great status with a vast and deep knowledge of voodoo practices.

Beauvoir lived in an elaborate voodoo temple where followers danced around totem poles to the relentless beat of drums, and animals were killed and drained of blood for voodoo rituals.

The voodoo ceremony in which the Clintons participated was held to honor the voodoo god "Ogou" – the god of iron, war and... politics. Yes, war and politics. Coincidence?

Afterwards, "the Clintons and Beauvoir sat all night by the coral-stone peristyle talking about faith and the future," said journalist Jonathan M. Katz, who interviewed Beauvoir.

Before the Haitian voodoo ceremony, Bill had waged one race for Congress, which he lost. But after the voodoo ceremony – and the personal tutoring he received in what he called "voodoo theology" – his political fortunes would abruptly change.

"By the time we got back from Haiti, I had determined to run for [Arkansas] attorney general," Bill writes in My Life.

He won that race, and that victory became the first vital step in his and Hillary's journey to the White House.

And during the years that followed, there were many more trips to Haiti.

Was this first visit to Haiti, the "brief course in voodoo theology" taught by a world-famous voodoo priest, and the direct experience of a bloody voodoo ritual just another fun stop on a honeymoon? Or was the Clintons' real purpose in going to Haiti to summon demonic entities to aid their political ambitions?

Were dark promises and terrible bargains made and sealed in blood with voodoo spirits?

We have noted that voodoo recognizes the existence of "baka" (malevolent spirits or demons). Voodoo also recognizes that individuals can make bargains with these evil spirits for worldly success via magic, spells, curses and so forth – but at a terrible price.

Of such monstrous bargains, Alfred Metraux – internationally recognized voodoo scholar and one of the most distinguished anthropologists and ethnologists of the 20th century – writes in his masterpiece Voodoo in Haiti (1959):

"This agreement – which binds him to evil spirits ... at great risk ... usually entails an obligation to feed the baka with a human being..."

Similarly, Gladys Maitres, described by the UK Telegraph as "one of Haiti's best known priestesses," told that paper in 2004: "There are some sacrifices that when you make them you pay for them very fast."

"Some of the spirits are like politicians," elaborated renowned voodoo houngan (priest) Silva Joseph. "They want something from you but they don't ask for it. And they perform a service for you to keep you in their power."

Terrible bargains indeed!

Bill Clinton: Early Voodoo Experiences

The 1975 ceremony was not at all Bill Clinton's first involvement with voodoo. He writes in My Life: "I had had some limited exposure" to voodoo and voodoo culture in New Orleans. He declines, however, to tell more about these secret experiences – which he has kept hidden for many decades. (New Orleans, it should be noted, was also the favorite U.S. city of the notorious and highly influential black magician Aleister Crowley; he visited it several times and lived in that occult-drenched city in late 1916 and early 1917. More on Crowley in upcoming chapters.)

In fact, it is quite possible that Bill Clinton could have first encountered voodoo in Little Rock, Arkansas, where he grew up. For Little Rock, and Arkansas, have a long, long history of voodoo and other occult activities.

In the 1930s the prominent Little Rock novelist, journalist, historian, and naturalist Julia Burnelle Smade Babcock, in her role as state director of the Federal Writers' Project, interviewed ex-slaves and Arkansas voodoo practitioners and attended all-night voodoo ceremonies. Her research found that voodoo was practiced among Arkansas slaves prior to the Civil War. This indicates that voodoo was active in Arkansas from the early days of the nation's founding.

And make no mistake: voodoo is still practiced in Little Rock today. A July 13, 2009 story from an ABC affiliate station, headlined "Mother of voodoo victim speaks to Action News," reported on a strange Little Rock voodoo ritual that ended in death.

From the ABC story:

"Neighbors report strange smells and strange sounds coming from the home on Loch Lomond Drive...

"'Rattles, chants, like all different stuff. You could smell the incense through the walls,' said neighbor Tina Ritz...

"After a fire next door to the voodoo priest's home two years ago, neighbors say there was disturbing findings...

"'Kids found dead chicken legs back there, after the fire, chicken heads. It's crazy,' said neighbor Malisa Crane...''

It is not hard to imagine a young Bill Clinton, footloose and intellectually curious, discovering voodoo activities in and around Little Rock... and becoming intrigued by its possibilities as he contemplated a life devoted to gaining and using political power.

And certainly he would have shared such knowledge with Hillary when they cemented their lifelong political partnership.

Bill and Hillary: "The King and Queen of Haiti"

Since that 1975 voodoo ceremony the Clintons have been deeply and intimately involved in almost every aspect of Haiti's politics, government and finances, and they are frequent visitors there.

Jonathan M. Katz, who spent three-and-a-half years covering Haiti for Associated Press, refers to the Clintons as "the King and Queen of Haiti" in a 2015 Politico article. He further notes they "repeatedly played a key role in Haiti's politics, helping to pick its national leaders and driving hundreds of millions of dollars in private aid, investment and U.S. taxpayer money toward its development.

"They've brought with them a network of friends and global corporations ... this network of power and money has left indelible marks on almost every aspect of the Haitian economy."

As president, Bill Clinton in 1994 – without congressional approval but after consulting with the United Nations – sent 20,000 U.S. troops to invade Haiti and restore the controversial deposed and exiled ex-president Jean-Bertrand Aristide to power. Aristide was widely known as "the President of Voodoo" because he gave state recognition to the religion and, some say, secretly practiced it himself. In 1991, when he became president, a voodoo banner was ceremonially placed upon his shoulders by a mambo (voodoo priestess).

Today, over forty years after his initial Haitian voodoo experience, Bill Clinton is still sometimes referred to by the Haitian press as "Le Gouverneur." And journalist Katz notes that "Hillary Clinton never took her eye off Haiti as secretary of state, even as so many geopolitical hotspots competed for attention."

Indeed, the Clinton's deep and ongoing interest in this tiny impoverished country, which is smaller than the state of Massachusetts, the seventh-smallest state in the U.S., seems obsessive. Haiti often seems the focal point of their foreign policy concerns.

Did Bill's "Wanga" and Dirty Voodoo Underwear Help Him Defeat George H.W. Bush?

U.S. historian Joel A. Ruth notes that many Haitians and other observers believe that Bill Clinton used voodoo powers to defeat George Bush and win the presidency in 1992.

Ruth told the strange story at the conservative World News Daily site in 1998:

"Acting on the advice of a 'houngan' or sorcerer...Clinton did not change his underwear the last week of the 1992 campaign, voodoo practitioners say.

"The same houngan also cast a 'malediction' on President Bush by manipulating a doll made in the president's image, goes the story. The torment climaxed when the houngan caused Bush's projectile vomit into the lap of the Japanese prime minister as the world press looked on, disgracing him with the public.

"Those and other bizarre stories were being told the Haitian people through the Lavalassien, a newspaper published by [the] ruling Lavalas party. ...

"[It was] claimed that [exiled Haitian president] Aristide had developed a powerful grip on Clinton's psyche through the power of voodoo. ...

"As told in Lavalassien, in the Haiti Observateur, another popular paper, and in private interviews by participants,

Clinton staffers first got the idea of invoking voodoo during conversations with Aristide who was living in exile in Washington, DC. The aim was to learn what the future held for then candidate Clinton, and to cast spells to help influence the election.

"In return for what [was] called a 'large sum of money,' a houngan was retained by the Clinton campaign, the story goes, and a 'wanga' or malediction was cast upon Bush to cause his electoral defeat.

"Clinton, for his part, agreed to wear the same pair of underpants the last week of the campaign.

"Both Haitian officials and the Haiti Observateur stated that Clinton reaffirmed his faith in voodoo during his March 31, 1995 visit to the island. The official purpose of the visit as told by the American media was to celebrate Haiti's supposed 'return to democracy.' However, the Haitian press had a much different story. The headlines of the March 29, 1995 issue of the Haiti Observateur read: 'CLINTON ASSISTERA A UNE CEREMONIE VAUDOU EN HAITI' ('Clinton to assist in a voodoo ceremony in Haiti').

"The story, confirmed by Haitian officials, stated that initiating Clinton under the power of voodoo had two purposes – to render him impervious to the attacks of his Republican enemies in Washington, and to guarantee his re-election."

Haiti, like the United States, has many secret societies. Among them is the dreaded Bizango, whose membership includes Haitian elites, is deeply and clandestinely involved in Haitian politics, and has been accused of ritual murder, black magic, zombification, and other horrors.

It is known that Bill personally owned a Bizango statue. Is this indicative of a deeper involvement with the murderous secret Bizango cult?

Does Hillary Use Voodoo to Create a Private Army of Zombie Slaves?

Bill, in his autobiography My Life, writes with obvious fascination about the ways voodoo priests are believed to have created zombie slaves by the use of secret chemicals – something right out of the CIA's infamous MK-ULTRA mind-control program. (See Chapter 9).

In fact, Bill says that voodoo leader Max Beauvoir, who taught him about Haitian voodoo, told him in 1975 about secret voodoo poisons that can paralyze victims and lower their breathing to the point that they seem dead – obviously knowledge that could have considerable political uses.

Beauvoir, it should be noted, spoke from authority: not only was he an acknowledged master of voodoo, he studied chemistry at the City University of New York and biochemistry at the Sorbonne.

This claim parallels the investigations of Dr. Wade Davis, author of the acclaimed book The Serpent and the Rainbow: A Harvard Scientist's Astonishing Journey into the Secret Societies of Haitian Voodoo, Zombis, and Magic. Dr. Davis, who received his doctorate in ethnobotany from Harvard University and is an Explorer-in-Residence at the National Geographic Society, spent considerable time in Haiti with voodoo priests and zombified humans, concluding that voodoo priests use secret poisons and other substances to create and control zombies.

In his autobiography Bill sums up his and Hillary's voodoo experiences by saying, perhaps cryptically: "The Lord works in mysterious ways."

Which inevitably begs the question, as such statements by the ruling elite often do: Which "Lord" is Bill Clinton referring to? Could it perhaps be... the voodoo spirit "Ogou" – voodoo god of war and politics – that the Clintons summoned forth at the strange and bloody 1975 voodoo ritual that marked the beginning of their meteoric political ascension?

Does Hillary – who many charge, as well documented in this book, with being deeply involved with the occult – use dark voodoo power today to advance her personal and political causes? Were the many thousands of people who have died in political actions in which Hillary took part in America and around the globe some kind of mass sacrifice to bloodthirsty voodoo spirits?

Is Bill and Hillary's obsession with Haiti part of a darker supernatural scheme? Does Hillary cast voodoo spells against her political enemies?

Bill and Hillary Clinton's inner circle of activists and advisers are often portrayed as fanatically loyal and almost eerily close-mouthed. In October 2015 Vanity Fair described them as "protectors: a tightly knit Praetorian Guard, mute and loyal. ... To get into her circle, one must behave with extraordinary loyalty. ... Try to penetrate...and you'll come face-to-face with people who are authorized to speak but deliberately say nothing; people who know everything but deliberately never speak..."

Are they, or some of them, zombie slaves? Do Bill and Hillary command an army of mind-controlled zombie slaves?

Such are the disturbing questions that inevitably come to mind when pondering the strange conjunction of voodoo, blood sacrifice, and ruthless take-no-prisoners brutal politics in the lives of Bill and Hillary Clinton.

CHAPTER THREE

Communing with the Dead

Necromancy in the White House?

In his bestselling 1996 book The Choice: How Clinton Won, Pulitzer-Prize-winning journalist Bob Woodward of Watergate fame shocked the nation by describing Hillary's apparent contacts and conversations with dead spirits and her regular meetings with Jean Houston, a controversial mystic who taught doctrines derived from ancient "mystery schools."

Nor was this a casual relationship. According to Woodward, Houston "virtually moved into the White House" for many days while helping Hillary write her highly controversial 1996 book It Takes a Village: And Other Lessons Children Teach Us.

Houston has a lengthy and fascinating background in such matters. While participating in a research project on the effects of the mind-altering drug LSD (before LSD use was outlawed), she met her future husband, the sexologist and novelist Robert Masters.

Robert Masters was the author or co-author of numerous books on sexuality and mysticism, among them Eros and Evil: The Sexual Psychopathology of Witchcraft (1974), described by its publisher as "the first systematic modern study of the sexual behavior of witches"; Sex Crimes in History: Evolving Concepts of Sadism, Lust-Murder, and Necrophilia, from Ancient to Modern Times (1963); Sexual Self-Stimulation (1967); Sex-Driven People (1966), described by its publisher as "a decisive contribution to the better understanding of human and animal sexuality."

There was a strong occult aspect to Masters' work, as we shall shortly see. In fact, Masters was praised for his occultic insights by no less than Kenneth Grant, one of the most important occultists of the twentieth century and widely considered to be heir to the infamous black magician Aleister Crowley. Said Grant: "Masters provides valuable insights and *practical formulae for establishing contacts with other worlds...*" (Emphasis added.)

(It should be noted, coincidence or not, that Masters' book Eros and Evil: The Sexual Psychopathology of Witchcraft begins with Aleister Crowley's "Hymn to Pan" – a strange and disturbing chant we shall encounter again in Chapter 10.)

Together Masters and Houston wrote The Varieties of Psychedelic Experience: The First Comprehensive Guide to the Effects of LSD on Human Personality (1966) and established The Foundation for Mind Research.

As NPR journalist Scott London described their work:

"At 21, she was one of the few people in the country with a legal supply of LSD. She used the controversial hallucinogen to take 'depth soundings' of more than 300 people.

"From LSD, Houston moved on to lead thousands of people through the mysteries of the mind without drugs. Among her tools was a sensory deprivation chamber built by her husband, Robert Masters. This device, and others like it, encouraged hallucinations by leaving subjects in total, silent darkness, starved of normal sensory input.

"In the 1980s, Houston, turning more and more toward ritual, founded The Mystery School, where students embark on a year-long study of mythic stories which are meditated upon and enacted."

Houston describes The Mystery School as "my 20th Century version of an ancient and honorable tradition, the study of the world's spiritual mysteries. Once upon a time there were such schools in Egypt, Greece, Turkey, Afghanistan, Ireland, England, France, Hawaii, India, China, Japan and many other places on the globe. We harvest what is available (or can be imagined) of the knowledge and traditions, rites and rituals of these ancient studies, imbuing them with new realities and applications in order to live more freely and more fully. ... Exercises include psychophysical work, psychospiritual exploration, creative arts, energy resonance, movement and dance, altered states of consciousness..."

Houston says The Mystery School "provides practices which have the effect of both rewiring your brain, body and nervous system, and eliciting the evolutionary latencies in your physical instrument. These latencies have been there like a fetal coding for perhaps tens of thousands of years, but could not be activated until various aspects of complexity emerged, joined to crisis." Further: "As we encounter the archetypal world within us, a partnership is formed whereby we grow as do the gods and goddesses within us."

According to journalist and New Age critic Lee Penn, the worship of a strange ancient Egyptian goddess lies behind much of the work of Robert Masters:

"Dr. Robert Masters, Jean Houston's husband and co-founder of her Foundation for Mind Research, describes himself as one who has 'devotedly followed the Way of the Goddess Sekhmet for more than 30 years.' The online bookstore at Jean Houston's website sells two article reprints and one book that honor 'Goddess Sekhmet.'"

Masters wrote "Invocation of Sekhmet" which celebrates and summons this bloodthirsty Egyptian goddess. Excerpts:

> Sekhmet,
> Goddess of Pestilence,
> Sekhmet,
> Goddess of Wars,
> Sekhmet,
> Queen of the Wastelands,
> Sekhmet,
> Terrible Is Thy Name...
> O, Come to me!
> Thou art the Terror Before Which fiends tremble!
> Thou art Lust!
> Thou Art Life!
> Ever-Burning One!

(Note: For clarity this excerpt has been rearranged, while leaving the wording the same.)

There are striking similarities between this invocation of the strange and bloody Sekhmet and Crowley's "Ode To Pan" mentioned a few paragraphs above.

Masters, it should be pointed out, emphasizes in his writing that Sekhmet is a real entity, not a mere metaphor, and that Sekhmet can descend upon people and literally possess them. In fact, he states bluntly in his writings that he himself is possessed by Sekhmet and has served her for decades.

Indeed, Masters warns that merely *reading* one of his books can open one to being "seized by Sekhmet, and then unspeakable horrors as well as indescribable delights are among the possibilities. It is always so when one 'falls into the hands of the Living God.'"

The book he is referring to is The Goddess Sekhmet: Psycho-Spiritual Exercises of the Fifth Way (1988), which, he says, "initiates readers into a direct experience of the lost feminine mysteries."

That book, Masters says, helped set off a worldwide revival of worship of Sekhmet, and he writes that he personally has heard from hundreds of people who, like him, were "seized" by this entity.

It is true that worldwide interest in Sekhmet is rapidly growing in America and worldwide. Once obscure, references to the bloody goddess are now found in popular culture, including television shows, movies, novels, songs, even children's literature and video games. A desert temple dedicated to Sekhmet has been erected in Nevada.

Masters says his book The Goddess Sekhmet was transmitted to him telepathically as he sat before a statue of Sekhmet – one of the surprisingly numerous works we will see cited throughout this book that were allegedly transmitted telepathically by alien entities.

Masters viewed Sekhmet as a "Gateway to alien realms..." This too is strikingly reminiscent of stories later in this book of people who have sought "gateways" to reach alien entities and allow them entrance to this world.

This fervid devotion to Sekhmet may be disturbing to some. Around 1500 BC in Egypt, Sekhmet was worshiped by night-long drunken sexual orgies accompanied by blaring music. According to award-winning NBC News science writer Alan Boyd:

"Archaeologists say they have found evidence amid the ruins of a temple in Luxor that the annual rite featured sex, drugs and the ancient equivalent of rock 'n' roll. ... Drink huge quantities of beer, get wasted, indulge in gratuitous sex and pass out."

Perhaps this history of worship via blood, destruction, drunkenness, loud music and orgiastic sex explains why Sekhmet has recently been referenced by several death metal bands.

Sekhmet was a bloodthirsty goddess who, according to legend, nearly destroyed the entire human race.

Writes Masters of the ancient history of the entity he worshiped and said had taken possession of him:

"Then Sekhmet walked among men and destroyed them and drank their blood. Night after night Sekhmet waded in blood, slaughtering humans, tearing and rending their bodies, and drinking their blood. ...

"She has the power to completely destroy not only human bodies, but also their souls – total destruction. ... Sekhmet's demons were dispatched to send disease, chaos and pestilence. ... Celebrations for Sekhmet included wild orgies, which earned her the additional titles of Great Harlot and Lady of the Scarlet-Coloured Garments."

Those pondering the recurring theme of the reptilian conspiracy in the Hillary saga may find it intriguing that one of Sekhmet's many nicknames is... "Ruler of Serpents and of Dragons."

In the 2002 Afterward to The Goddess Sekhmet, Masters describes Jean Houston's help with his Sekhmet work: "While she [Jean Houston] has never been involved in the Sekhmet or Fifth Way Work directly – her own soul marches to a different Drummer! – it would be quite impossible for me to overstate her supportive contribution to it."

Thus, based upon her husband Masters' own words and practices, there can be no doubt that Jean Houston is intimately familiar with the concept of strange ancient gods, spirits, and other such entities entering into, and seizing control of, the bodies, minds and souls of humans.

But back to those White House sessions with Hillary and Jean Houston.

According to the Pulitzer Prize-winning Woodward, Jean Houston was "controversial... a believer in spirits, mythic and historic connections to the past and other worlds... she believed in spirits and other worlds, put people into trances and used hypnosis..." though he points out that Houston says she intentionally did not use hypnosis and trance inducement with her work with Hillary.

However, exactly what did happen during those secret sessions in the White House solarium (sunroom) and the other long hours and days Hillary spent with Houston remains a mystery – at the request of the White House itself.

Woodward writes:

"Houston asked Hillary to imagine she was having a conversation with Eleanor. In a strong and self-confident voice, Houston asked Hillary to shut her eyes in order to eliminate the room and her surroundings..."

"'You're walking down a hall,' Houston said, 'and there's Mrs. Roosevelt...'"

Houston then instructed Mrs. Clinton to speak to Mrs. Roosevelt, according to Woodward.

After a long "conversation" with the long-dead former First Lady, Hillary did the same for Gandhi. Houston also asked her to try to channel the teachings of Jesus, but Hillary refused, saying it was too personal.

Woodward's revelations of this set off an international explosion of controversy over what some called "Guru-Gate" or "Eleanor-Gate."

Some critics described the sessions as "séances" or "necromancy" or "channeling" or other occult practices.

But Hillary denied there was any occultism or spiritualism involved, saying that the talks were merely an "intellectual exercise" without psychic or religious overtones.

Houston, despite her mystic interests and her work with her husband – who, recall, actively promoted the possession of the living by the violent and bloody ancient goddess Sekhmet – also insisted there was no occultism involved in her sessions with Hillary. What had taken place, she said, was only an exercise of the imagination – creative visualization, brainstorming, etc.

It was simply "a classic role-playing game," Houston protested. "It's done every day, everywhere, at every corporation around the world."

Some therapists backed Houston by pointing out that the use of guided imaginary conversations was a conventional therapy tool.

If that was all that happened, it would have been quite easy to prove: according to the Los Angeles Times, the sessions were taped. But the tapes have never been made public.

Houston herself went silent about the event – at, she says, the request of the White House.

So we are left without final answers to the question of what, exactly, went on in those mysterious sessions. (And inevitably, to wonder if the bloodthirsty Sekhmet or other ancient entities could have been invoked – or, yes, even secretly guided to take possession of Hillary...)

However, according to Dr. Paul Kengor, New York Times bestselling author, professor of political science and director of the Center for Vision and Values at Grove City College of God, and author of Hillary Clinton: A Spiritual Life, what Hillary says she participated in, by her own description, was – at the very least – a distinct form of spirit channeling with great potential for danger – and which goes directly against mainstream Christian teachings.

Kengor says Hillary was doing "clairaudient channeling," which "involves relaxing oneself in either a fully conscious or mildly altered state of consciousness and then listening to one's 'inner-self.'

"...what Hillary was involved with *had the potential to be dangerous, and is widely condemned by the vast majority of Protestant denominations."* (Emphasis added.)

He adds that "these sessions...were indeed very strange... they were definitely bizarre..."

Kengor notes that Houston and Masters did do channeling in the past. Masters, not surprisingly, had his patients channel Sekhmet. In her book, Public Like a Frog: Entering the Lives of Three Great Americans, Houston introduced three individuals that she said were available to be contacted through a trance or altered state of consciousness: Thomas Jefferson, Emily Dickinson, and Helen Keller. Somewhere along the line, Eleanor Roosevelt also presumably made herself available.

Rev. Eric Barger, a former occult practitioner turned popular Christian pastor and author of numerous books including Entertaining Spirits Unaware: The End-Time Occult Invasion expressed similar concerns:

"So Eleanor Roosevelt was giving [Hillary] advice about running the country. This is what the Bible calls necromancy.

"This is speaking to any entity in the spirit realm except God. Necromancy is the attempt to speak to a being in the spirit realm or the successful communication with a being in the spirit realm.

"It isn't Eleanor that Hillary is communicating with – *it is actually a demon masquerading as Eleanor Roosevelt*. (Emphasis added.)

"Deuteronomy 18 forbids this kind of thing in the strongest possible terms used anywhere in the Bible."

Specific Bible verses are often cited by mainstream Christian denominations to condemn such practices:

"When thou art come into the land the Lord thy God giveth thee, thou shalt not learn to do after the abominations of those nations. There shalt not be found among you anyone that maketh his son or his daughter to pass through the fire, or that useth divination, or an observer of times or an enchanter, or a witch, or a necromancer, for all that do these things, are an abomination unto the Lord." – Moses in Deuteronomy 18:9–12.

"Do not turn to mediums or necromancers; do not seek them out, and so make yourselves unclean by them: I am the Lord your God." – Leviticus 19:31.

"A man or a woman who is a medium or a necromancer shall surely be put to death. They shall be stoned with stones;

their blood shall be upon them." – Leviticus 20:27

And there are still more questions. Some have wondered if the choice of the sunroom for the sessions was far more than coincidence. Sun worship is ancient and can be traced back to Babylonian/Egyptian/Canaanite beliefs. The Bible, in Deuteronomy 4:19 and Deuteronomy 17:3, explicitly warns against sun worship. And of course, Satan is often described as Lucifer the "Light Bearer."

The choice of Eleanor Roosevelt is also interesting, as Eleanor Roosevelt and President Roosevelt were both known to engage in occult practices. Eleanor visited a palm reader; FDR consulted with psychics and astrologers during World War II, including the famed Jean Dixon. FDR was a 33 Degree Freemason and a member of several Masonic lodges and organizations; on October 30, 1931, shortly before his first presidential run, he was made a Prophet at Sight in the Mystic Order Veiled Prophets of the Enchanted Realm, originally known as the Fairchild Deviltry Committee; one of its female auxiliaries was the Mysterious Order of the Witches of Salem. We are assured that such references to seers and devils and witches was just good fun.

Perhaps the question of whether or not Hillary engaged in actual occult behavior during those secret sessions – and whether she continues to do so to this very day – was settled by no less an authority than Bill Clinton.

In a 2012 speech Bill declared: "As all of you famously learned when I served as president, my wife, now the secretary of state, *was known to commune with Eleanor [Roosevelt] on a regular basis.*" (Emphasis added.)

Bill went on to say that Mrs. Roosevelt – who left this earthly plane on Nov. 7, 1962 – had in fact sent Hillary a message... *that very week.*

Is Hillary a "World Server" for the Takeover of the World by the Antichrist via the United Nations?

According to journalist Bob Woodward, "[Jean] Houston

... called Hillary a 'world server,' someone who would help all humanity."

It should be noted that the term "world server" has a very specific meaning in the controversial occult writings of Alice Bailey (1880-1949), one of the most influential occultists of the twentieth century.

We don't know if Jean Houston was using the word in a Baileyan context, but it is a very specific phrase, and is worth exploring further.

"World Servers," wrote Bailey, are "the people who are beginning to form *a new social order* in the world. They belong to no party or government, in the partisan sense. They recognize all parties, all creeds, and all social and economic organizations; they recognize all governments.

"They are found in all nations and all religious organizations, *and are occupied with the formulation of the new social order. ...*

"They are occupied with the task of inaugurating the new world order, by forming throughout the world – in every nation, city and town – a grouping of people who belong to no party, take no sides either for or against, but who have as clear and definite a platform, and as practical a programme, as any other single party in the world today." (Emphasis added.)

Alice Bailey's political and spiritual beliefs remain highly controversial. Dr. Robert A. Herrmann, author and retired professor of mathematics at the United States Naval Academy, has written a lengthy and highly critical analysis of Bailey's writings from a Christian perspective, entitled "A Scientific Analysis of the Writings of Alice A. Bailey and their Applications."

Dr. Herrman concludes:

"Bailey 'theology' ... is, in all of its variations, absolutely occult in character and *leads to one of the most evil forms of demonic possession*. This theology is designed to prepare humankind for the 'appearance,' in one form or another, of the Antichrist. ... Bailey's god...is the Scripturally defined Adversary (Satan) and...the [widely publicized Bailey] 'prayer' entitled 'The Great Invocation' is actually *a Satanic invocation designed to call forth the Antichrist*." (Emphasis added.)

The program that Bailey's World Servers are working to manifest, said Bailey herself, is "the new world order" – a phrasing that will be heard often in chapters ahead.

Bailey said that most of her two dozen or so books were telepathically dictated to her between 1919 to 1949 by an otherworldly entity named Djwhal Khul. Khul, she said, was one of a group of secret and super-powerful Masters, the Hierarchy, who attempt to influence world events through occult means. (As we shall see throughout this book, books and ideas transmitted by alien entities to various occultists and political activists have played a significant, if little-known, role in American politics.)

The Bailey / Djwhal Khul books are printed today by the Lucis Publishing Company, which was formed in the early 1920s as the Lucifer Publishing Company. That original name was, the company acknowledges, chosen to honor Lucifer. The name was changed in 1925, for rather obvious public relations reasons. However, they also note: "Both 'Lucifer' and 'Lucis' come from the same word root, lucis being the Latin generative case meaning of light."

The Lucis Trust oversees the publishing of Bailey's books today and works in many other ways to spread her ideas. In accord with Bailey's long-stated plan that the United Nations advance the New World Order and her other occult and political goals, Lucis Trust is very active in United Nations activities. Indeed, the Lucis Trust was for many years based within the United Nations headquarters in New York. Today the Lucis Trust has consultative status with the Economic and Social Council of the United Nations (ECOSOC) and its sister organization, World Goodwill, is recognized by the Department of Public Information at the United Nations as a non-governmental organization (NGO). It is frequently reported that the Lucis Trust played a significant role in maintaining the symbol-laden United Nations Meditation Room at the UN world headquarters.

The Bailey / Djwhal Khul books outline what many critics interpret as an ominous political program. Some critics say that a careful reading of her books shows that she is calling for the creation of a worldwide army to manifest the arrival of the Antichrist, who will use a United Nations-dominated New World Order, armed with nuclear bombs and armies, to impose and enforce the rule of Satan upon all mankind.

For example:

The Bailey / Djwhal Khul book The Reappearance of the Christ declared support for a powerful United Nations: "...when the United Nations has emerged into factual and actual power, the welfare of the world will then be assured."

The Bailey / Djwhal Khul book The Externalisation of the Hierarchy argues that the atomic bomb that devastated Hiroshima and Nagasaki was "the greatest spiritual event which has taken place since the fourth kingdom of nature, the human kingdom, appeared..." The Second World War, "with all its unspeakable horrors, its cruelties, and its cataclysmic disasters – was but the broom of the Father of all, sweeping away obstructions in the path of His returning Son."

According to Dr. Robert A. Herrman, Bailey and the entity Djwhal Khul saw nuclear weapons, in the hands of a New World Order-dominated United Nations, as a tool for enforcing their will on the rest of the world, including religious groups who resist the coming New World Order.

Again from The Externalisation of the Hierarchy:

"The atomic bomb emerged from a first ray Ashram, working in conjunction with a fifth ray group; from the long range point of view, its intent was and is purely beneficent.

"As a means in the hands of the United Nations to enforce the outer forms of peace and on the growth of goodwill to take effect ... [the atomic bomb] belongs to the United Nations for use (or let us rather hope, simply for threatened use), when aggressive action on the part of any nation rears its ugly head. It does not essentially matter whether that aggression is the gesture of any particular nation or group of nations or whether it is generated by the political groups of any powerful religious organization, such as the Church of Rome..."

We have already witnessed the incineration of one religious group by Hillary and Bill, the Branch Davidians in Waco, Texas. We have also seen the aggressive militarism that has defined Hillary's foreign policy thus far. Hillary is also a firm supporter of the United Nations.

If Hillary is indeed a Bailey / Djwhal Khul "World Server," one must shudder at the thought that she will be given total control of the most powerful nuclear arsenal in the history of the world.

The Bailey / Djwhal Khul book Telepathy and the Etheric Vehicle says that *telepathic communication* is used between the otherworldly beings who are guiding the creation of this New World Order movement and the "World Server" earthly leaders.

Wrote Bailey / Djwhal Khul: "Telepathic communication is also [used]: ...

> d. Between the occult Hierarchy and groups of disciples on the physical plane.

> e. Between the Hierarchy and the New Group of World Servers in order to reach humanity and lift it nearer the goal."

All this must lead us to ponder such questions as:

Is Hillary part of an occult group of "World Servers" – secretly preparing the world for mass demon possession, the arrival of the Antichrist, and the rule of Lucifer enforced by nuclear bombs and the United Nations?

Has Hillary gone through the kind of Baileyan process, described by Dr. Robert A. Herrmann in his paper cited above, that opens one up to demonic possession?

Does Hillary use occult telepathic powers to communicate with a secret group of otherworldly alien beings or entities, to discuss and carry out their plans to create a Luciferian "New World Order"?

(We should note that many people do not see Alice Bailey's writings in nearly so negative a light as the critics referenced in this section. We present these particular interpretations because of the serious questions they raises concerning Hillary.)

CHAPTER FOUR

Satanism and Demon Possession: Is Hillary Possessed by Demons – or the Devil?

"The devil's in that woman." – Miss Emma, cook for the Clintons in Arkansas, after witnessing Hillary in a cursing rage, as reported by Arkansas state trooper Larry Patterson

Is Hillary Clinton actually possessed by demons? Over the years many people have said exactly that. Some, of course, were speaking metaphorically.

But many were not. They meant it quite literally.

In this chapter we will examine such claims. Because many people today do not believe in demon possession, we will first briefly examine some startling evidence that the phenomenon of demonic possession is in fact... real.

The Case for Demon Possession Today

Throughout most of the history of mankind, few would have found unthinkable the idea that a political figure could be possessed by demons, Satan, or other malevolent forces.

Indeed, the belief that demons or otherworldly beings can take possession of people has existed for thousands of years, in virtually every culture in world history.

Today belief in demon possession is dismissed by some as merely a superstitious holdover from less enlightened times.

Yet as researchers know, this belief is widely held around the globe – today.

"The belief that demons exist and can possess people is of course the stuff of fiction and horror films – but it is also one of the most widely held religious beliefs in the world," writes science journalist and professional skeptic Benjamin Radford, deputy editor of Skeptical Inquirer magazine. "Most religions claim that humans can be possessed by demonic spirits...and offer exorcisms to remedy this threat."

Indeed, exorcism rituals are found in religions around the globe – Abrahamic, Eastern and others – including Christianity, Judaism, Islam, Hinduism, Buddhism, Taoism, and Shintoism.

Many people today, including scientists, medical professionals, intellectuals and religious leaders – and many U.S. and world politicians – strongly believe in demon possession.

Consider:

- The Bible makes numerous references to demons, demon possession, and exorcism. In the New Testament there are six incidents where Jesus cast out demons (for example, Matt. 4:24, Luke 4:35) and was accused by his opponents of being possessed himself (Mark 3:22, John 8:48-49). In Ephesians 6:12 Paul wrote: "For we wrestle not against flesh and blood, but against principalities, against powers, against the rulers of the darkness of this world, against spiritual wickedness in high places."

- Every Catholic diocese has an exorcist, or is supposed to have one.

- The International Association of Exorcists (IAE) is a Roman Catholic organization with a worldwide membership. It was founded in 1990 by six priests, among them the internationally renowned exorcist priest Father Gabriele Amorth, author of the worldwide bestselling book An Exorcist Tells His Story. Father Amorth claims to have freed tens of thousands of people from demonic possessions.

  "I have seen many strange things," says Father Amorth. "The devil told a woman that he would make her spit out a transistor radio, and lo and behold she started spitting out bits and pieces of a radio."

- Catholic exorcists report a startling rise in demonic possession in recent years.

  "Diabolical possessions are on the increase as a result of people subscribing to occultism," said Father Francesco Bamonte, president of the International Association of Exorcists, in 2014.

  Similarly, International Association of Exorcists spokesman Valter Cascioli warned in 2014 of an "extraordinary increase in demonic activity."

  In 2014 Pope Francis formally recognized the International Association of Exorcists.

  In 2010 the New York Times reported that Catholic exorcists were "overwhelmed with requests from people who fear they are possessed by the devil."

  "[D]emonic activity is real," says Father John Bartunek, LC, who has contributed news commentary about religious issues on NBC, CNN, Fox, and the BBC. "The Church teaches this clearly, and it is obvious in the Gospels."

Exorcism is found not just in Roman Catholicism but in numerous Christian denominations.

In the Eastern Orthodox Church exorcisms are quite common. In the 1970s the Church of England equipped every diocese in the country with persons trained in both exorcism and psychiatry. The Book of Occasional Services of The Episcopal Church discusses exorcism. Many Mennonite seminaries include exorcism training.

In charismatic Christianity worldwide the fast-growing practice of "deliverance ministries," while differing somewhat from exorcism, consist of activities aimed at delivering individuals from demonic possession of body and soul, as well as other problems attributed to demon and spirit activity.

In 2010 a Pew survey found that in Ethiopia, according to the BBC, "74 percent of Christians say they have experienced or witnessed the Devil or evil spirits being driven out of a person."

Exorcism is mainstream in America. A 2013 YouGov poll of 1,000 U.S. adults found over half – a majority – believed in possession. And that belief is growing. A late 2012 Public Policy Polling survey found a whopping 63 percent of young Americans 18-29 years old believe that demons exist and can take control of human beings.

TV superstar journalists Oprah Winfrey, Diane Sawyer, and Barbara Walters have all featured exorcists on their top-rated shows.

"Exorcism is more readily available today in the United States than perhaps ever before," writes Michael Cuneo, a sociologist at Fordham University, in his 2001 book American Exorcism.

Figures for how many exorcisms are performed in the U.S. annually are obviously difficult to come by, but rough estimates indicate there may be thousands.

The well-documented 2012 Latoya Ammons possession and exorcism case in Gary, Indiana captured international attention. A family of four was tormented by mysterious and horrifying voices, flying objects, strange materializing oozing liquids, terrifying sounds and smells, inexplicably malfunctioning electric devices, and what seemed to be malevolent spirits possessing a mother and her children.

A Department of Child Services (DCS) case manager and registered nurse testified they saw a nine-year-old boy walk backward up a wall all the way to the ceiling, at a hospital. They also watched as the boy was "lifted and thrown into the wall with nobody touching him." The terrified DCS case manager fled the room. Note that these descriptions come from official DCS reports; it is a crime to lie in them. In fact, it was a trained medic who, after witnessing such sights, in desperation contacted a Catholic priest and requested an exorcism.

Ultimately the Latoya Ammons possession case generated nearly 800 pages of official documentation, including testimony from police, social workers, medics, priests, and other such reliable sources.

As the UK Daily Mail summarized the Latoya Ammons case: "...today, the veteran police officers, experienced physicians, paramedics, nurses, social workers and clergy linked to the case speak of being 'attacked' by demons, profoundly shaken and left with little choice but to believe that 'something' possessed the 32-year-old mother of three and the rented home in which she, her children and her mother, lived from November 2011 until May 2012."

The first known U.S. court case in which the defense claimed innocence due to demonic possession was the 1981 murder trial of Arne Cheyenne Johnson. Johnson argued that, while witnessing the Roman Catholic exorcism of a young boy allegedly possessed by over 40 demons, he taunted the demons and dared them to enter his body instead. One or more demons, witnesses say, did exactly that. Later these demons drove Johnson, against his will, to stab his landlord to death. Johnson was convicted of first-degree manslaughter, but served only five years of his 10- to 20-year sentence.

To some, this universal recognition of a need to expunge demons from tormented souls indicates the truth of exorcism and demonic or Satanic possession.

Ivy League Psychiatrist: "Demon Possession Is Real"

Dr. Richard E. Gallagher is a board-certified psychiatrist, trained at the Yale University School of Medicine, a Phi Beta Kappa graduate of Princeton University, and a professor of clinical psychiatry at New York Medical College.

He describes himself as "a man of science and a lover of history; after studying the classics at Princeton, I trained in psychiatry at Yale and in psychoanalysis at Columbia."

Dr. Gallagher is also experienced in... diagnosing demonic possession.

"As a consulting doctor, I think I have seen more cases of possession than any other physician in the world," he said in an astonishing 2016 Washington Post article entitled "As a psychiatrist, I diagnose mental illness. And, sometimes, demonic possession."

Dr. Gallagher tells how, in the late 1980s, he was introduced to "a self-styled Satanic high priestess" by a Catholic priest. The priest was "the most experienced exorcist in the country at the time, an erudite and sensible man" and he was seeking a scientist's opinion on this bizarre case. He turned to Gallagher for this.

Dr. Gallagher was highly skeptical. But the Satanic high priestess's behavior "exceeded what I could explain with my training. ... This was not psychosis; it was what I can only describe as paranormal ability. I concluded that she was possessed."

Since then, he says, "For the past two-and-a-half decades and over several hundred consultations, I've helped clergy from multiple denominations and faiths to filter episodes of mental illness – which represent the overwhelming majority of cases – from, literally, the devil's work. It's an unlikely role for an academic physician, but I don't see these two aspects of my career in conflict. The same habits that shape what I do as a professor and psychiatrist – open-mindedness, respect for evidence and compassion for suffering people – led me to aid in the work of discerning attacks by what I believe are evil spirits and, just as critically, differentiating these extremely rare events from medical conditions. ...careful observation of the evidence presented to me in my career has led me to believe that certain extremely uncommon cases can be explained no other way. ... I believe I've seen the real thing... skills that cannot be explained except by special psychic or preternatural ability. ... "

Gallagher has seen the possessed display such supernatural traits as: "hidden knowledge" of persons, places, history, and other subjects they could not know by non-supernatural means; enormous strength; speaking in languages unknown to them, including patients who abruptly begin speaking in "perfect Latin" without any such training. In the first case he explored, objects inexplicably flew off shelves and the temperatures rose and fell wildly. Gallagher says he knows "half a dozen" people he trusts who have seen levitation.

Support for the demonic possession hypothesis is growing among medical professionals, he writes.

"I've been pleasantly surprised by the number of psychiatrists and other mental health practitioners nowadays who are open to entertaining such hypotheses. Many believe exactly what I do, though they may be reluctant to speak out."

Dr. Gallagher notes that "anthropologists agree that nearly all cultures have believed in spirits, and the vast majority of societies (including our own) have recorded dramatic stories of spirit possession. Despite varying interpretations, multiple depictions of the same phenomena in astonishingly consistent ways offer cumulative evidence of their credibility."

Scientists, Exorcism and Demon Possession

Though certainly not all scientists endorse the reality of demon possession (just as not all religious leaders do), there is strong support for the idea in parts of the scientific community.

In fact, many top exorcists say that the best exorcisms are conducted hand in glove with mainstream science and medicine.

The renowned psychiatrist and bestselling author M. Scott Peck – whose books have sold over 14 million copies worldwide – believed strongly in demonic possession and sometimes practiced exorcism.

"Because I was a scientist I was perhaps more stringent than most people would be in diagnosing," Peck said. "But it is a real condition and one of the things that I would argue, as a psychiatrist, is that it [demonic or Satanic possession] ought to be recognized as a psychiatric diagnosis. ... I think it should be in the DSM-IV and have equal status with multiple personality disorder... I consider multiple personality disorder to be a less common condition than possession."

Such cases led Dr. L. Stafford Betty, Professor of Religious Studies, to write "The Growing Evidence for 'Demonic Possession': What Should Psychiatry's Response Be?" in the scholarly Journal of Religion and Health, Spring

2005 issue. Dr. Betty argues that "Evidence of evil spirits is voluminous and comes from many cultures, both ancient and modern... there is mounting evidence today that evil spirits do oppress and occasionally even possess the unwary, the weak, the unprepared, the unlucky, or the targeted."

Indeed, believers argue, scientists who reject out of hand the demon possession hypothesis and the exorcism treatment may be guilty of continuing a kind of arrogant close-mindedness that, just a few decades ago, led to barbaric and abusive treatments for the mentally ill. Examples of standard medical procedures that civilized people shudder at today include imprisonment in filthy and dangerous "hospitals" that were more like medieval dungeons, the turning of patients into vegetables through lobotomies and high voltage electrocution, the use of powerful psychotropic drugs that wreaked havoc with already-tortured minds, the stripping away of civil liberties, and so on. All of this was, not long ago, standard psychiatric procedure. (See the writings of psychiatric reformers Thomas Szasz and Peter Breggin for much more on this.)

Today, as in times past, there are people whose mental and physical disorders cannot be explained away or treated by conventional means. Just as today we shudder at the ignorance and barbarity of some treatments of the past, exorcism advocates say that, in the near future, scientists and reformers may wonder why the psychiatric and medical professions ignored the centuries-old practice of exorcism as a possible tool in their arsenal.

"Just how long can we go on like this until we admit that there is real data, and that we haven't the slightest idea where to put it?" asks Jeffrey Kripal, head of Rice University's religious studies department, in his 2011 book Authors of the Impossible: The Paranormal and the Sacred.

Could Demon Possession Cost Hillary the Election?

Demon possession and other evidence of occult involvement are vital political issues to a majority of U.S. voters.

A 2012 poll by the highly respected Public Policy Polling firm found 57 percent of registered voters – both Democrat and Republican – believe in demonic possession.

Plus, fully 68 percent – over two thirds – of registered Republican voters believe demon possession is real. A whopping 26 percent of all voters say they've seen a ghost. More than half of voters believe it is possible for a house to be haunted.

Further, the same survey indicated that belief in demon possession seems to be growing. 44 percent of Americans over 65 years of age believe in demon possession. Of Americans aged 47-65, 57 percent do. And most tellingly, among the Americans aged 18-29, a whopping 63 percent believe in demon possession.

In short, American belief in demon possession is not just a majority belief, it is growing rapidly – and fastest and most rapidly among America's rising generation of voters and leaders.

It is highly unlikely that most of these voters would vote for someone they believed is, or could be, possessed by demons.

Thus demon possession could well become a major issue in future American elections – starting, perhaps, with 2016.

Is Hillary Possessed by Demons?
Examining the Evidence

Given such powerful evidence, demonic possession and its cure, exorcism, should arguably be taken very seriously.

And given the activities of many elected leaders, politicians would certainly seem to be high on the list of possible suspects of demon possession.

So the oft-heard charge that Hillary Clinton could be possessed by demons – or even by Satan himself – is certainly something that is worthy of further examination.

A caveat: First, it must be stated that exorcism experts, including scientists and psychiatrists as well as many priests, strongly advise that it is simply not possible for a lay person to accurately diagnose demon possession, any more than he or she might diagnose a tumor or rare disease.

So let us be clear: this author is not qualified to accurately diagnose whether Hillary Clinton is possessed by demons or Satan. I do not have the religious or medical or scientific background to do so.

However, it is equally unlikely that Hillary will allow herself to be examined by professional exorcists to see if she is demon-possessed – though it is certain that many millions of Americans would welcome such a good-faith offer from her.

So, those of us who feel the need to pursue this vital question are left to do so ourselves, as best we can.

How Hillary's Occult Activities Could Have Opened Her Up to Demon Possession

Scientist and psychiatrist M. Scott Peck sums up in his landmark book People of the Lie how, in his opinion and that of many other experts, a person can become possessed by demons: "It seems clear from the literature on possession that the majority of cases have had involvement with the occult..."

This book documents many such examples of Hillary's involvement with the occult.

We have written of her and Bill's involvement in Haitian voodoo, where spirits – sometimes sinister and malevolent – are specifically summoned in bloody ceremonies to enter human bodies

We have explored Hillary's controversial attempts to, by some descriptions, contact and channel the spirits of the dead – activity that is, say many theologians and occult experts, extremely dangerous, a virtual invitation for demons and other entities to enter and take possession of the experimenter.

In upcoming chapters we will examine Hillary's association with occult talismans, blasphemous music and more.

Again, according to experts, any and all of these activities are extremely dangerous and open one to demon possession.

And that could be just the beginning. Other sources quoted in this book, such as occult expert Doc Marquis, say that Hillary clearly shows the signs of being a high witch or occult priestess. If so, says Marquis, she would have actively solicited demons to possess her. She could be possessed by hundreds, thousands, perhaps even an infinite number of demons, in the hope that she might use their power for earthly gain even as they use her for their own dark ends.

Given such arguments, and given that she is seeking the most powerful office in the world, the possibility that Hillary is possessed by demons deserves our closest and most careful attention.

Does Hillary Show the Signs of Demonic Possession?

What are the signs of demon possession? And does Hillary exhibit them?

Let us examine some of the well-known signs of demon possession that are repeatedly cited in the scholarly and popular literature on this subject.

1.) **Cursing:** Hillary is legendary for her foul-mouthed cursing. So is Bill.

"You heard so much foul language" in the Clinton White House, said White House florist Ronn Payne.

L.D. Brown, a member of Clinton's security staff in Arkansas, said Hillary is "as foul-mouthed as any sailor you'd ever meet."

"She has a garbage mouth on her," agreed state trooper Larry Patterson, a thirty-two year police veteran who guarded the Clintons for six years.

Numerous Clinton employees and associates, from Arkansas to Washington DC, have said the same.

Bill's cursing eruptions – described as "profanity-fortified rages" by the UK Guardian, described as "cuss words for five minutes," by White House counsel Abner Mikva, described as "purple fits" by White House staff – are widely known and documented, and are set off by the slightest offenses.

Hillary "was not able to express [her] thoughts, or make a point, without the use of obscene language and rage," says FBI agent Gary Aldrich in Unlimited Access: An FBI Agent Inside The Clinton White House. His comment, he says, applies also to Bill and to many in their staff, "young or old, male or female."

"This type of rage is ... very typical of a person who is a practicing witch, or one who is an Illuminist witch," says occult expert Rev. David Bay, director of Cutting Edge Ministries. "Therefore, we have one more bit of proof that Bill and Hillary are practicing Illuminist witches...

"When a person wants to become a powerful witch, *he or she invites numerous demons to indwell them*. What separates a person who is a powerful witch from a less powerful witch is the number, type, and power of the demons indwelling. Therefore, the most powerful witch will be the one who has called into himself or herself the greatest number of demons and/or the most powerful."

If the Clintons are indeed witches, as Rev. Bay theorizes, so might be many of their advisers and allies.

Agent Aldrich writes of one close associate of President Clinton: "This man works in close proximity to the president, and he can't seem to moderate his anger. He can't seem to control his emotions. ... out-of-control screaming, his explosive temper, his vulgarity, his disrespectful attitude to religion, and his obscene references to biological, scatological, and sexual acts, and perversions, all of which seem to be an important part of this man's vocabulary."

Here are a few examples of Hillary's seemingly demon-inspired cursing fury from eye-witness sources, some taken under oath. The list was presented by world-renowned cursing scholar Reinhold Aman, Ph.D, perhaps the world's leading expert on obscene language and editor of the scholarly journal Maledicta, the International Journal of Verbal Aggression, where it appeared. TIME magazine calls Dr. Aman "the name in pejoration, not to mention invective, vituperation, obloquy, opprobrium, objurgation, abusive epithets and billingsgate" and notes "He can curse in 200 languages..."

WARNING: the following quotes contain extremely explicit words that are offensive to many people. If such language offends you, you are urged to skip this section. The author regrets any disturbance this section may cause some readers, but it was deemed necessary in order to make clear the shocking nature of the language we are reporting upon.

- "Where is the goddamn fucking flag? I want the goddamn fucking flag up every fucking morning at fucking sunrise." (From Inside The White House by Ronald Kessler – Hillary to the staff at the Arkansas Governor's mansion on Labor Day, 1991.)
- "You sold out, you motherfucker! You sold out!" (From Inside by Joseph Califano – Hillary yelling at Democrat lawyer.)
- "Fuck off! It's enough that I have to see you shit-kickers every day, I'm not going to talk to you too!!! Just do your goddamn job and keep your mouth shut." (From American Evita by Christopher Anderson – Hillary to her state trooper bodyguards after one of them greeted her with "Good Morning.")
- "You fucking idiot." (From Crossfire: Witness in the Clinton Investigation by L. D. Brown – Hillary to a state trooper who was driving her to an event.)
- "If you want to remain on this detail, get your fucking ass over here and grab those bags!" (From The First Partner – Hillary to a Secret Service agent who was reluctant to carry her luggage because he wanted to keep his hands free in case of an incident.)
- "Get fucked! Get the fuck out of my way!!! Get out of my face!!!" (From Hillary's Scheme by Carl Limbacher – Hillary's various comments to her Secret Service detail agents.)
- "Stay the fuck back, stay the fuck away from me! Don't come within ten yards of me, or else! Just fucking do as I say, Okay!!!?" (From Unlimited Access by Gary Aldrich – Hillary screaming at her

Secret Service detail.)
- "Where's the miserable cock sucker?" (From The Truth About Hillary by Edward Klein – Hillary shouting at a Secret Service officer.)
- "Son of a bitch." (From American Evita by Christopher Anderson – Hillary's opinion of President George W. Bush when she found out he secretly visited Iraq just days before her highly publicized trip to Iraq.)
- "Come on Bill, put your dick up! You can't fuck her here!!" (From Inside The White House by Ronald Kessler – Hillary to Gov. Clinton when she spotted him talking with an attractive female at an Arkansas political rally.)

Such examples could go on and on. "I remember one time when Bill had been quoted in the morning paper saying something she didn't like," recalled Arkansas state trooper Larry Patterson in the 1990s. "I came into the mansion and he was standing at the top of the stairs and she was standing at the bottom screaming and she was calling him motherfucker, cocksucker, and everything else."

Some people have said that Hillary's and Bill's considerable vocabulary of obscenities included racist remarks, including anti-Semitic language and the use of the incendiary racial hate term commonly referred to as "the N word."

We have no recorded evidence of this, and therefore no proof – though there is a tape of Clinton's brother Roger using the "N word" several times in a few seconds – but there is a considerable amount of allegedly eye-witness testimony from different sources that is consistent over the years.

Former Dallas lawyer Dolly Kyle was a childhood friend of Bill. She met Bill when she was 11 and he was 12, was his girlfriend in high school, and claims to have had a sexual affair with him from the mid-1970s until roughly 1991.

In her 2016 book Hillary: The Other Woman, she describes Bill's and Hillary's obsessive cursing.

Kyle says Bill frequently used the phrase "goddamned niggers" in high school and afterward. She says both Bill and

Hillary privately called civil rights icon Rev. Jesse Jackson a "goddamned nigger" and, when governor, Bill used the phrase to refer to prominent Arkansas black activist Robert 'Say' McIntosh. Kyle says they used similar language to refer to other prominent African Americans.

She further charges that Bill and Hillary are racists, pointing out not only the use of offensive racist language, but racist policies implemented by Bill as governor. She notes racial discrimination lawsuits filed against Bill by blacks and Hispanics; the incarceration of vast numbers of Arkansas blacks; and Bill's notorious racial-profiling order to state troopers to pull over and search any car in Arkansas containing Hispanics – a program he continued in a modified form (giving troopers discretion to pull over whoever they wanted) even after a federal judge ruled it unconstitutional.

Hillary, Kyle says, was caught on tape using the terms "stupid kikes" and "fucking Jew bastard" and once called disabled children at an Easter egg hunt "fucking retards."

Arkansas state trooper Larry Patterson is on record as saying he heard both anti-Semitic terms and "the N word" from Hillary. Patterson said he estimated as many as 15 other Arkansas state troopers had heard such language.

"It was fairly common for both Clintons to tell ethnic jokes and use ethnic slurs about Jews," Patterson said, as reported by the conservative NewsMax.com.

"If she disagreed with Bill Clinton or she disagreed with some of the Jewish community in Little Rock – or some of the ethnic community – she would often make these statements."

Patterson said he heard Hillary say "nigger" "...probably six, eight, ten times. She would be upset with someone in the black community and she would use the 'N' word..."

Patterson and others say Bill used these racial epithets in the same way.

State of a Union: Inside the Complex Marriage of Bill and Hillary Clinton by Jerry Oppenheimer makes the same accusation that Hillary used anti-Semitic language. Most notably the book details the widely publicized charge that Hillary called Bill's campaign manager Paul Fray a "fucking Jew bastard" during Bill's 1974 congressional race.

Oppenhimer cites three witnesses: Fray, his wife, and Neill McDonald, a campaign worker.

Indeed, Fray's wife Mary Lee Fray said that Hillary not only said the slur, she yelled it so loudly "it rattled the walls." Campaign worker McDonald said he heard the anti-Semitic slur while outside the room.

It should be noted that Hillary and Bill have vehemently denied the charges that they have ever in their lives used anti-Semitic and/or racist language. In 2000 Hillary said that such language had never even entered her thoughts – not even once:

"I have never used ethnic, racial, anti-Semitic, bigoted, discriminatory, prejudiced accusations against anybody. I've never done it. I've never thought it," she told the New York Daily News.

2.) Violence and fury: Hillary has been known to engage in physical violence, as well as screaming and threatening fits, aimed at those around her.

Indeed, at one point Secret Service agents reportedly feared that she might seriously injure or even assassinate President Bill Clinton during one of her rages. Again quoting top FBI agent Aldrich, who had a unique perspective from his years of involvement with the Clintons:

"After taking the oath, Bill and Hillary Clinton were taken to a holding room in the Capitol building. Minutes passed ... Hillary Clinton was screaming at her husband in what was described as *'uncontrolled and unbridled fury.'* ... The Capitol Hill police and the Secret Service quickly conferred about intervening if it *appeared the president's life might be threatened by the First Lady*! The question before them, was *'How much physical abuse is too much physical abuse?'*" (Emphasis added.)

Other accounts speak of similar violence, almost demonic or superhuman at times: such thing as furniture scattered and doors ripped off cabinets. Bill has been seen with scratches and wounds attributed to Hillary.

White House Secret Service agent Gary Byrne has written that "She'd explode in my face without reservation or decorum..." He notes during one of her rages she threw a Bible at an agent assigned to protect her life, hitting his head from behind.

Former White House reporter Kate Andersen Brower's 2015 book The Residence: Inside the Private World of the White House recounts three times Hillary reportedly threw dangerous objects at Bill, at least once drawing blood and requiring stitches.

"There was blood all over the president and first lady's bed," writes Brower. "A member of the residence staff got a frantic call from the maid who found the mess. Someone needed to come quickly and inspect the damage. *The blood was Bill Clinton's.* The president had to get *several stitches* to his head." (Emphasis added.)

Such extreme and bizarre violence continues to this day, as an article entitled 'Clinton's Camp Says She 'Could Have a Serious Meltdown'" by Edward Klein in the New York Post, October 10, 2015, makes clear:

"Hillary's been having screaming, child-like tantrums that have left staff members in tears and unable to work," says a campaign aide. "She thought the nomination was hers for the asking, but her mounting problems have been getting to her and she's become shrill and, at times, even violent."

3.) Violent and abusive sexuality: Bill's hyped-up and (according to some accusations) violent sexuality, described in Chapter 9, is a classic sign of demonic possession.

Hillary's endless cover-ups of his actions – sometimes allegedly employing the private Clinton secret police force (see Chapter 16) to threaten, harass, or even commit acts of violence – indicate her deep complicity in this.

4.) Lying: John 8:44 says: "You are of your father the devil, and your will is to do your father's desires. He was a murderer from the beginning, and has nothing to do with the truth, because there is no truth in him. When he lies, he speaks out of his own character, for he is a liar and the father of lies."

Satan's nickname is the Father of Lies. It is simply undeniable that the Clintons lie in extraordinary ways, and lie constantly. It is one of their most notable characteristics.

Indeed, more than ideology or political affiliation, it may be this constant never-ending flood of lying that best describes their modus operandi, their very personalities.

This is so widely recognized that the prominent political website Politico.com ran an article in August 2015 entitled "Can Hillary overcome the 'liar' factor?" The article summarized the results of a Quinnipiac University poll:

"More than 3-in-5 voters, 61 percent, think [Hillary] Clinton isn't honest and trustworthy. ...

"When voters were asked the first word that came to their mind about Clinton, the top three replies were indictments of her trustworthiness. The No. 1 response was 'liar,' followed by 'dishonest' and 'untrustworthy.' Overall, more than a third of poll respondents said their first thought about Clinton was some version of: She's a liar."

This is nothing new. As far back as January 8, 1996 the conservative columnist William Safire wrote for the New York Times an essay entitled "Blizzard of Lies," which began:

"Americans of all political persuasions are coming to the sad realization that our First Lady – a woman of undoubted talents who was a role model for many in her generation – is a congenital liar. ...she is compelled to mislead, and to ensnare her subordinates and friends in a web of deceit."

Washington Post and TIME investigative reporters Susan Schmidt and Michael Weisskopf, in their 2000 book Truth at Any Cost: Ken Starr and the Unmaking of Bill Clinton, noted about the Whitewater scandal: "Virtually everybody concluded that the First Lady had lied but that the evidence was not strong enough to convict her."

Writing in the conservative American Spectator on August 20 2015, journalist, author and former White House associate political director (1987–1988) Jeffrey Lord noted: "...it is now apparent that her inability to tell the truth is an ingrained personality trait. ... Time after time after time, like clockwork, this 'essential characteristic' of deliberately and willfully lying surfaces with Hillary Clinton."

Both Clintons have been caught lying so many times that it would take an entire book – and a massive one – to compile all of the lies. Conservative journalist Jonah Goldberg memorably described Bill in 2015 as "a prodigy at deceit, a renaissance man of lying. If football were a game of lies, he could play every position on offense and defense."

David Schippers, a lifetime Democrat and Chief Investigative Counsel for the 1998 U.S. House Judiciary Committee inquiry on whether President Bill Clinton had committed impeachable offenses in his handling of the Paula Jones sexual harassment suit, famously summed up his investigation of that case:

"The president, then, has lied under oath in a civil deposition, lied under oath in a criminal grand jury. He lied to the people, he lied to his Cabinet, he lied to his top aides, and now he's lied under oath to the Congress of the United States. *There's no one left to lie to.*" (Emphasis added.)

In February 2016, the Washington Post summarized public opinion: "public opinion polls ... show that 60 percent of voters do not believe [Hillary] Clinton is trustworthy."

Lying – condemned by the Bible in the Ten Commandments and elsewhere, and one of the defining traits of Satan himself – is, quite simply, a way of life for Hillary and Bill.

We might well quote 1 John 2:4 and say of Hillary and Bill that "there is no truth in" them.

Needless to say, Bill and Hillary are hardly the only persons in political life to lie; indeed, one might well say that it is lying, rather than money, that is the mother's milk of politics. Still, such constant lying can indicate a closeness to Satan or demonic possession, according to experts – especially when accompanied by other symptoms as described in this chapter.

5.) Child sacrifice. It seems hardly worth noting that engaging in child sacrifice could well be a strong sign of demonic possession. Experts are in wide agreement on this.

Concerning child sacrifice, here is an interesting point to ponder from Tom Cooney of the Foundation for the Study of Paranormal Phenomena:

"Now, suppose I told you that there are 1.4 million sacrifices each year to Satan? That would shock you beyond belief, as it should. Most people would shake their heads and say that 'this guy is nuts.'.. but there are that many sacrifices on a yearly basis in this country. However, being a politically correct country, we do not call them sacrifices to Satan. We have a better term: we call it abortion."

Similarly, Troy Newman of Operation Rescue argues in his book Their Blood Cries Out that abortion is simply, for many practitioners of the dark arts, a disguised modern means of sacrificing children to Satan and to ancient evil entities like Baal, to whom children were sacrificed ages ago.

"...abortion is...a form of idolatry. ... The argument can logically be made that abortion is a sacrifice to demons. The evil spirits to which children were sacrificed in the Baal groves are probably the same ones hanging out down at the Planned Parenthood offices! ...

"Throughout history the Enemy has been known to take the innocent blood of every boy or girl he can get, whether it is through Baal worship or abortion..."

Hillary is a well-known and enthusiastic advocate for abortion on demand. Perhaps she simply takes this position, as many millions of other Americans do, because she honestly believes it is politically right and a matter of civil liberties. If so, there is certainly nothing demonic about that, regardless of one's views on the issue itself.

If, however, she secretly encourages government funding and promotion of abortion specifically as a way of sacrificing babies to Satan or ancient foul deities, then that most likely would indicate demon possession (or some other form of hideous evil). Here, intent is key.

6.) Lack of empathy: Many people have spoken of Hillary public and private displays of lack of empathy for the suffering of others. Many of the professional government agents assigned the dreaded task of guarding her have noted her coldness and cruelty.

Her spontaneous ghoulish reaction during a CBS interview when informed of the death of Libya dictator and former U.S. ally Mohmmar Khadaffi – "We came, we saw, he died," she crowed, followed by peals of harsh mocking laughter and self-applause – shocked many people. Writer Mike Krieger noticed her "characteristic sociopathic giddiness"; Irish journalist Bryan MacDonald noted her "near-psychopathic glee." The self-congratulation of Hillary and her Obama administration cohorts continued even as their intervention in Libya turned that state into a nightmarish region, with roughly half a million citizens fleeing their homes and the once-prosperous country overrun with violence, chaos, torture and terror. Even President Obama eventually called the debacle a "mess... a shit show" while also noting that Hillary's arguments tipped him into favoring the intervention.

7.) Engaging in Satanic practices: Of course, if stories discussed elsewhere in this book – that Hillary worships Satan at Black Masses, sacrifices children to evil forces to gain power, feeds on human flesh with reptilian shapeshifters, and so forth – are indeed true, then those would be also very strong signs that Hillary is possessed by demons.

Self-proclaimed ex-witch and widely recognized occult authority Doc Marquis says that all Illuminati witches are demon possessed; indeed, they avidly cultivate these demons and invite them into their lives. Therefore, if Hillary is, as Marquis charges, a high-ranking witch, she is, by definition, also demon possessed.

8.) Demonstration of unexplained or supernatural powers: The manifestation of occult-derived powers beyond those of non-demon-possessed humans would likely accompany demon possession. We have devoted an entire chapter, Chapter 11, to the evidence for this.

9.) An amoral lust for worldly power: This seems to be a near-universal trait of many seeking political office today. But such ambition has been particularly widely noticed and remarked upon concerning the Clintons.

FBI agent Aldrich: "The White House has a completely amoral worldview. ... The Clinton crowd justified their behavior by their power – and the limits of their power and behavior were, in their own eyes, nonexistent."

* * *

After examining the evidence above, we cannot say definitively that Hillary is possessed by demons; only an expert can do that. And to our knowledge Hillary has never been examined by an exorcist.

However, we can examine her life and actions and look for the classic signs of demon possession that have been noted by experts in this field for many centuries – always being aware, as professional exorcists urge, that these could be instead signs of mental illness, physical trauma, emotional instability, or simple human vanity, cruelty, selfishness, hubris, egotism and other such vices.

We can safely say this: there can simply be no doubt that **Hillary clearly does exhibit many of the classic signs of demon possession.**

Witchcraft and Satanism: Clinton Insider Says Hillary Worships Satan

In Chapter 5 we discussed occult expert and professed former witch Joseph "Doc" Marquis' charge that Hillary is a high-level practicing witch. Marquis says that a genuine witch would be possessed by, indeed, infested with, demons.

A decades-long intimate associate of the Clintons has also accused her of witchcraft – and worshiping Satan.

Larry Nichols' complex relationship with Bill and Hillary goes back to the late 1980s when Bill was Arkansas governor. In fact, as we discuss further in Chapter 16, in 2013 Nichols – a former Green Beret – stated he had acted as the Clinton's personal hit man, actually beating and murdering people upon their orders.

After breaking with the Clintons, Nichols was one of the creators of the 1994 film "The Clinton Chronicles: An Investigation into the Alleged Criminal Activities of Bill Clinton."

On June 24, 2015, interviewed by renowned conspiracy investigator Alex Jones, Nichols said:

"Back when Hillary was first lady, she would go home on the weekends to California with Linda Bloodworth-Thomason and some of the [inaudible] women, and they went to a church for witches. Witches, witches, witches... Hillary went to a church and worshiped Satan."

Linda Bloodworth-Thomason is a television producer who, with her husband Harry Thomason, is best known for creating, writing, and producing the TV series "Designing Women," a popular TV show infamous for its blatant pro-Clinton, liberal views. Like Nichols, the couple have a longtime and close connection with the Clintons dating back to Bill's regime as governor of Arkansas. The Thomasons created political propaganda films for Bill and Hillary, among them "The Man from Hope" which introduced Bill at the 1992 Democratic Convention.

On September 17, 2015 Nichols, again on the Alex Jones show, repeated the claim – and said that Bill Clinton himself was his source:

"[A]bout once a month Hillary would go out to Los Angeles. And she did it so regular that it became a bit of an issue trying to... 'Why's she always going?'"

"Bill told me that she was going out there, she and a group of women, and she would be a part of a witch's church. Man, when Bill told me that, he could have hit me with a baseball bat.

"I tried to point out to him, 'Do you realize what would happen if that got out?' Of course my job was to make sure it didn't get out."

"Now I don't know the day, if Hillary still partakes in the witch ritual, I don't know that I even know what the ritual was. But for the better part of many years, Hillary would go quite often, whether it was regularly once a month, or maybe once every couple of months, she would go out on the weekend simply to be a part of it."

We should note, however, that Nichols cannot be viewed as an always reliable witness, having made some questionable and contradictory statements in the past.

Indeed, in a startling turnabout, in early 2015 Nichols told the left-wing magazine Mother Jones that statements he had made in 2013 about murdering people for the Clintons was not true; he had made them, he said, under the influence of pain pills. Further, he declared he now... supported Hillary for president!

Of course, this reversal, this sudden embracing of Hillary's candidacy inevitably has led some to wonder if Nichols was not intimidated into repudiating his earlier claims and then forced into the further humiliation of endorsing his decades-long enemy Hillary – threatened, perhaps, by another Hillary hit-person? Or by a terrifying display of Clintonic demonic powers?

Certainly Nichols has long feared possible retribution from the Clintons. In a 1997 interview, Nichols said bluntly: "They may just kill me. You'll read one day that I got drunk and ran into a moving bridge. Or Larry Nichols got depressed over everything and blew his head off."

Demon Possession and the Reptilian Conspiracy

In Chapter 8 we will explore in detail the charges that Hillary is, in reality, a reptilian: a giant shapeshifting lizard being in human guise.

But could there be a reptilian-demon connection?

Some say yes.

World-renowned psychiatrist and author M. Scott Peck, discussed earlier, told Beliefnet.com of a surprising possible reptilian connection to demonic possession, suggested by videotapes of two exorcisms he conducted.

"With one we have close to 40 hours of tape. The other, close to 30. One of the most extraordinary things for me was the facial expression of these patients. In the first case, none of these facial expressions were captured on the video tape. The patient did not show any facial changes which were paranormal, except on one occasion when she had actually been trying to hide her face from the camera. It was just a few seconds long, when *her face underwent a profound change. The second patient had this snake-like appearance which was evident to everybody on the team*, but again, not picked up by the video camera. Now in following up that patient there were moments where I also saw in her – and maybe this is translated into some kind of intuitive kind of vision – but *flashes of her looking like an amphibian or a lizard.*" (Emphasis added.)

We are unaware that Peck, who believed in demon possession, ever claimed to believe in the reptilian theory, which makes his observations here all the more intriguing.

Republican Presidential Candidates Take the Lead in Fighting Demons

Republican candidates for the White House have taken the lead in fighting demons. A few examples:

- Presidential candidate Pat Robertson, a renowned television evangelist, entrepreneur, and bestselling author, regularly cast out demons before and after his White House run. "Like it or not, demons are real … they will possess and they will destroy" he said in 2015 on his television show.

- Louisiana Governor and 2016 presidential candidate Bobby Jindal – a convert from Hinduism to Catholicism – wrote in a 1994 article for New Oxford Review, a Roman Catholic magazine, about his first-hand experience of the "physical dimensions of spiritual warfare" while witnessing the casting out of demons while he was in college.

  "Kneeling on the ground, my friends were chanting, 'Satan, I command you to leave this woman.' Others exhorted all 'demons to leave in the name of Christ,'" Jindal wrote.

- Texas megachurch pastor John Hagee, CEO of Global Evangelism Television, is an enormously influential figure in the political/evangelical movement. Hagee's numerous books have sold in the millions; his sermons are broadcast around the world. His endorsement has been eagerly sought by powerful political figures including 2008 GOP presidential candidate John McCain.

In his bestselling 1973 book Invasion of Demons: The Battle Between God and Satan in Our Time, Rev. Hagee warns that America is facing nothing less than "an invasion of demons, and [it] is being spread like wildfire through the occult practices sweeping America in a Satanic revival with demons for evangelists." In 2015, Hagee said Christians must "storm the voting booths and vote the Bible!"

- John McCain's 2008 vice-presidential candidate Sarah Palin was an associate of at least two prominent witch hunters. She attributed her victory in her race for governor of Alaska in part to an anointing and a laying-on-of-hands ceremony conducted by Rev. Thomas Muthee of Kenya, director of the New Apostolic Reformation (NAR) East Africa Spiritual Warfare Network; the ceremony was specifically performed to protect Palin from witches and demons.

  Rev. Muthee told Palin's church that he fought "against all forms of witchcraft – all the python spirits that are released against the body of Christ."

  Alaska evangelist Mary Glazier says Palin joined her spiritual warfare network at age 24. Glazier was renowned for, among other things, organizing prayer groups against an Alaska witch active in the state's prison system, with remarkable results:

  "As we continued to pray against the spirit of witchcraft, her incense altar caught on fire, her car engine blew up, she went blind in her left eye, and she was diagnosed with cancer."

- Former Republican Colorado state representative

Gordon Klingenschmitt, Ph.D., D.D. says he has advised or served six U.S. presidential candidates. He is an exorcist and television evangelist, as well as an ordained minister, former Air Force officer and former Navy chaplain. He is the founder of the Pray in Jesus Name Project.

In his controversial 2012 book The Demons of Barack H. Obama: How the Gift of Discerning of Spirits Reveals Unseen Forces Influencing American Politics, he argues that President Obama is ruled by at least fifty demons.

Rep. Klingenschmitt also argues in the same book that demons are using and speaking through... Hillary Clinton.

In short: Many GOP presidential contenders and their trusted advisers have been publicly engaged in battling demons – something that the two-thirds of Republican voters who believe in demon possession likely see favorably.

Hillary's Dilemma: Millions of Voters Will Not Knowingly Support a Demon-Possessed Candidate

There is little doubt that tens of millions of voters – Democrats, Republicans, Libertarians, Greens and independents alike – would never support Hillary – would, in fact, campaign vigorously against her – if they thought she was possessed by demons.

Indeed, because such rumors, long a part of the Hillary story, are spreading rapidly, this – along with related issues explored throughout this book – could be the death-knell for her hopes to win the U.S. presidency – and become the most powerful person on Planet Earth.

It is up to Hillary to refute them – or suffer potentially devastating political consequences.

CHAPTER FIVE

Secret Symbols, Signs and Other Occult Imagery and Influences

Hillary's Obscene Occult "Christmas" Tree

As we have noted earlier, former FBI agent Gary Aldrich has an impressive background and has led a remarkable life that has given him an up-close and intimate look at the White House and the Clintons from many perspectives. He served in the FBI for 26 years and was assigned to the White House in both the Reagan and Clinton administrations. At the White House he was, among other things, responsible for background checks for key positions including White House counsel, chief of staff, secretary of state, attorney general, FBI director, and more. Before this, Aldrich had worked in both the U.S. House of Representatives and the U.S. Senate. After retiring from the FBI he wrote bestselling books and founded the Patrick Henry Center for Individual Liberty, whose mission is "promoting the U.S. Constitution and Bill of Rights and supporting the right of citizens to engage in ethical dissent."

In his #1 New York Times bestseller Unlimited Access: An FBI Agent Inside the Clinton White House (1996) Aldrich reported that in 1993 Hillary ordered the White House Blue Room Christmas tree to be festooned with what one frustrated and outraged permanent staff member described as "carved dark wood... like fertility gods or something... carvings [that] look kind of obscene... On top of the tree, there was a large stainless steel ball pierced by colored shafts..."

"Nowhere can we find anything that resembles *Christmas*," the staffer said. "Nowhere."

In 1994 Hillary asked Aldrich to assist with the decoration of the tree. Hillary sent boxes of ornaments, some solicited by her from art students. Aldrich describes some of what he and White House permanent staffers found when they opened the boxes:

"...a mobile of twelve lords a-leaping [where] each was naked and had large erections... ornaments constructed out of various drug paraphernalia, like syringes, heroin spoons, or roach clips... crack pipes hung on a string... three French hens were kissing in a ménage a trois... sex toys known as 'cock rings'... condom ornaments [including inflated condoms] 'blown' into balloons and tied to small trees... other condom ornaments, some still in the wrapper, some not... sex toys and self-mutilation devices..."

Aldrich was shocked by the pornographic, blasphemous, and drug-oriented nature of these "ornaments."

"I couldn't believe what I was looking at," he writes.

To the other decorators he said: "This stuff is just childish garbage! We can't hang this stuff on any White House Christmas tree!"

However, he was told it was Hillary's orders to do exactly that.

What is particularly fascinating is that Aldrich – an FBI-trained professional observer – did not realize the true occult significance of the ornaments he saw – yet his observer skills describes them in such detail that an expert in occult symbolism was quickly able to see them for what they actually were.

That expert is occult researcher and self-professed former Illuminati witch Joseph "Doc" Marquis, now a born-again Christian and leader of the organization Christians Exposing The Occult.

Marquis was named "the foremost leading expert in the nation on the occult world, possibly the whole world" by Ted Gunderson, former Senior Director of the FBI.

Doc Marquis – the "Doc" comes from his past as a U.S. Army medic – is author of nearly a dozen books, including Secrets of the Illuminati, The Illuminati's New World Order,

Signs and Symbols of Satan, and Memoirs of a Former Illuminati Witch. He has appeared on and has consulted for TV shows around the world, including the "Oprah Winfrey Show," "20/20," "Geraldo Rivera," "Hard Copy" and "Inside Edition."

Marquis says Hillary's "Christmas ornaments" were actually powerful occult symbols that confirm beyond doubt that Hillary is a practicing witch.

Here is how Doc Marquis explains the symbolism of these occult ornaments, excerpted from a detailed examination at the website of Cutting Edge Ministries.

Marquis' comments follow Aldrich's descriptions from Unlimited Access:

Aldrich: "carved dark wood... like fertility gods or something"...

Doc Marquis: "The male fertility god is in authority during this time of the year. Sex is paramount in the religion of the occultist, and its celebration is one of the highest activities in which occultists can participate. From September 21 to March 21, the male fertility god is in control of the earth. From March 21 to September 21, the female goddess assumes supreme leadership. Therefore, the occultist will celebrate either the sex act or the male sex organs at this time of year, preponderantly."

Aldrich: "...twelve lords a-leaping. The ornament consisted of tiny clay male figurines. Each was naked and had a large erection."

Doc Marquis: "This associates directly with the male fertility god, above. Human sacrifice is also required on December 21, Yule."

Aldrich: "Two turtle doves, but they didn't have shells this time – they were joined together in an act of bird fornication."

Doc Marquis: "This represents the sexual union of the god and goddess. Usually the two preferred times of sexual union are during the two times of the Equinox when the transfer of authority is occurring. This act is also a symbol of the sex rite."

Aldrich: "Five golden rings... sex toys known as 'cock rings'"

Doc Marquis: "This is emblematic of the phallic god. Sex worship is a major part of the occult religion."

Aldrich: "Another mystery ornament was the gingerbread man. ... There were five small, gold rings: one in his ear, one in his nose, one through his nipple, one through his belly button, and, of course, the ever-popular cock ring."

Doc Marquis: "These are the five places where the occult Five-Fold Kiss is given during a ritual. This kiss is a simple blessing in the occult, a recognition, and a welcoming. During an occult ceremony, a man gets his penis kissed; this is part of the legend, or myth, of the god and goddess of witchcraft. The goddess had never loved, but she wanted to solve all mysteries, even death, and so she journeyed to the Netherworld. When she was challenged by the guardians of the Netherworld, she was forced to disrobe and give up all her jewelry. But, since she was so beautiful, the god of the Netherworld fell in love with her, and kissed her. He wanted her to abide with him in death, but she would not. Because she refused, she was made to suffer the symbolic scourge of death. Her beauty remained, so the god of the Netherworld taught her all the mysteries. He then gave her the 'Five-Fold Kiss,' which is still practiced among the occult today."

Aldrich: "Here was another five golden rings ornament – five gold-wrapped condoms. ... There were other condom ornaments, some still in the wrapper, some not. Two sets had been 'blown' into balloons and tied to small trees."

Doc Marquis: "This is emblematic of the fertility rites of 'Sexual Magick.' Sexual Magick is defined as that part of the occult belief that the energy of the sexual organism can be used for spell casting. "

Aldrich: "On top of the tree, there was a large stainless steel ball pierced by colored shafts."

Doc Marquis: "This is the 'orb' of the 'Sun god.' The Winter god is a personification of the god of the dead. This is because this god is a successor to the Celtic god of the dead – Samoan – worshiped during Halloween. The male Winter god begins his reign during the Autumnal Equinox, Mabon [Sept

21], and ends March 21, when the goddess comes to life during the Spring Equinox. March 21st is manifested as the Spring goddess at first, and then on May 1st, the night of Beltain, she is fully manifested as the Earth Mother, called among other names, Diana, and Gaia. Both March 21 and May 1 call for human sacrifice. The third manifestation of the goddess is Sept 21st and she is called the Crone. Human sacrifice is called for on Sept 21, March 21, and May 1. When Hillary put up this Sun Orb, she is passing her supreme authority to the male Sun god, until March 21st when the goddess takes this supreme authority back. This means that, throughout the occult year, the male god rules for six months, and the female goddess rules for the other six months, another example of the Duality of Nature principle.

"When Hillary placed the orb on top of this tree, she is yielding to the male god until March 21. I find it interesting, also, that Hillary placed a similar stainless steel orb on top of the traditional Christmas tree on the lawn of the White House. Thus, she was flashing a signal to the entire occult world that the Illuminists control the White House."

Aldrich: "Crack pipes hung on a string."

Doc Marquis: "Crack pipes are indicative of Lucifer's built-in vocal cord pipes, cracked when he fell, when he was defeated by God; Lucifer was created as God's angel of Music, even to the point of being created with 'tabrets and pipes' being built into his vocal cords [Ezekiel 28:13] so he could sing the more beautifully for God's glory. When Lucifer fell, his beauty and his wisdom were corrupted. These pipes were actually cracked, because his former glorified body was destroyed. Therefore, the Illuminist envisions the 'crack pipes hung on a string' as being representative of Lucifer."

Aldrich: "Three French hens were French-kissing in a menage a trois."

Doc Marquis: "This represents the three faces of the goddess, the Spring Maid, the Earth Mother, and the Fall Crone."

Aldrich: "Some ornaments were constructed out of various drug paraphernalia, like syringes, heroin spoons, or roach clips..."

Doc Marquis: "This is classic for an occultist. The drug paraphernalia is commonly used by an occultist. Illuminists can use all kinds of drugs except mind-altering drugs. Drugs are used to close the Conscious Mind, open the Subconscious Mind, and allow them to maintain communication with their Spirit Guides."

Aldrich also describes a huge – twice-life-sized – statue of a naked woman with "enormous buttocks, far out of proportion to the rest of her body" that Hillary demanded be placed along the public tour line. The agents were appalled that such a garish statue would be chosen to greet the general public at Christmas. However, Doc Marquis recognizes it from Aldrich's precise description:

"This statue is obviously Lilith, whom occultists believe was Adam's first wife. Lilith is thought of as the Hebrew female devil. It is she who taught Adam all about witchcraft, since she was a sorceress."

Doc Marquis and Rev. David Bay, director of Cutting Edge Ministries, go into much greater detail about all this at The Cutting Edge website, from which the above is excerpted.

Rev. Bay, it should be noted, says he spent four years in Army intelligence; his security clearance was Top Secret Crypto.

What is remarkable is how Aldrich's expert FBI-trained observation skills allow him to report what he sees – even though he himself does not fully understand what he is seeing – so carefully and accurately that an occult expert like Doc Marquis, based on his knowledge of the dark arts, is able to see these objects for what they really are.

Thus agent Aldrich's complete lack of knowledge of occult symbolism gives far more power to the idea that these were, in fact, occult symbols knowingly displayed.

It should be further noted that Christmas decorations were overseen by Hillary's social secretary, Ann Stock, who came down to inspect the tree with Aldrich and pronounced it "perfect... delightful... neat."

In her book Target: Caught in the Crosshairs of Bill and Hillary Clinton, Kathleen Willey describes Stock in this way:

"She cussed like a sailor, dropping the 'F bomb' every other minute."

As we have explained in Chapter 4, such obsessive cursing – common in Hillary's and Bill's associates at the time – is a well-known sign of possible demon possession.

Hillary's Luciferian Lapel Pin

In early 1998, during the Bill Clinton administration, some critics began to note a prominent lapel pin with a bird on it that Hillary was wearing. The same lapel pin was photographed on Bettie Currie, Bill Clinton's personal secretary and on Donna Shalala, Bill Clinton's Secretary of Health and Human Services. It was also later photographed on prominent Republicans: on Socialist Party member-turned-Republican and U.S. Ambassador to the United Nations Jeanne Kirkpatrick, who was dubbed "Chief sadist-in-residence of the Reagan Administration" by left-wing social critic Noam Chomsky for her support of dictatorships and authoritarian regimes; and on Senator McCain's wife Cindy Lou (McCain has praised Hillary for her militaristic foreign policy). In 2001, President Bush's wife Laura sent a Christmas card to Texas GOP supporters including a photograph of what appeared to be the Bush home. Prominent on the Bush wall was... the same or a similar bird.

At a casual glance there seems to be nothing unusual about the pin. It appeared to be a golden flying eagle carrying a round pearl. The eagle, of course, is a familiar symbol of the United States.

However, according to some occult experts, the pin is something else entirely, something far more sinister – even Luciferian.

Indeed, a closer look seems to show that the "eagle" is no eagle at all. Its neck is too long and thin.

So what is it? And why were so many prominent U.S. political leaders suddenly seen wearing it?

Rev. David Bay of Cutting Edge Ministries, who has written extensively on the hidden influence of the occult in

American politics, was among those who identified the creature on the pin.

Says Bay: "You will notice that this bird is not an American Eagle, because its neck is far too thin and is stretched well out. In fact, you might even say it is 'scrawny.' This bird is the occultic Phoenix Bird of Ancient Egyptian legend. ...an ancient symbol used by the Masters of the Illuminati...as one of their symbols of the coming New World Order of [the] Antichrist."

Warns Rev. Bay: "Do not ever forget that this goal is paramount for the New World Order. They plan on staging the False Christ, whom we will know is [the] Antichrist. Thus, the symbol of the Phoenix Bird perfectly fulfills their plan and can perfectly serve as the symbol of that Man of Perdition."

Manly P. Hall, the immensely influential 20th-century "mystery school" occultist, was author of The Secret Teachings of All Ages: An Encyclopedia Outline of Masonic, Hermetic, Qabbalistic and Rosicrucian Symbolic Philosophy, which has sold over a million copies since first privately printed in 1928. Along with his other writings it is still studied by those interested in occultism today; indeed, according to the Washington Post, President Ronald Reagan, whose interest in occultism was quite deep (the Post noted Reagan's interest in numerology and astrology, and also that his "reading tastes ran to some of the outer reaches of esoteric spiritual lore"), clearly shows the influence of Hall in some of his speeches.

Hall writes of the Phoenix: "All symbols have their origin in something tangible, and the Phoenix is one sign of the secret orders of the ancient world, and of the initiate of those orders, for it was common to refer to one who had been accepted into the temples as a man twice-born, or re-born." It should be noted that this "re-birth" is very different than the Christian notion of being born again: it involves initiation and oaths of loyalty to occult organizations and movements.

The controversial William Schnoebelen is a minister, prolific author, and occult expert who says that before he found Jesus he was a witch, a Second Degree Member

(Warlock) of the Church of Satan, a member of Aleister Crowley's Thelema cult, a Voodoo High Priest, a Spiritualist minister, a channeler, a 90th degree Mason, a Druid High Priest, and, near the end of his wide-ranging career in the occult... a practicing vampire who could consume only human blood and communion wafers. (Rev. Schnoebelen backs up these seemingly unlikely claims with a plethora of documents and dates.) A member of the National Investigations Committee on Aerial Phenomena (NICAP), he has studied UFOs since the 1960s, personally seen over 100 UFOs, and interviewed numerous alien abductees. He is listed in Who's Who in Religion.

About the Phoenix Rev. Schnoebelen says: "The Phoenix ... is believed to be a divine bird going back to Egypt ... This Phoenix destroys itself in flames and then rises from the ashes. Most occultists believe that the Phoenix is *a symbol of Lucifer* who was cast down in flames and who they think will one day rise triumphant." (Emphasis added.)

One can find other references to the Phoenix throughout occult literature.

The ball the Phoenix is carrying in Hillary's pin symbolizes the earth. Thus the pin shows the Phoenix – perhaps Lucifer or the Antichrist – has captured the world, and is ready to impose a New World Order. Earlier occult versions of the Phoenix emblem similarly show it clutching a round object symbolizing our world.

Rev. Bay and other experts on the occult say that the pin is proof that Hillary is a practicing occultist and witch, and by wearing it she is sending a message to other occultists: the New World Order is near.

Rev. Bay notes yet another ominous aspect of the strange pin: "...this Hillary Pin has the Phoenix Bird looking left, which means he is looking with evil; left is the evil side in the occult."

Is Hillary a Mind-Controlling, Child-Abusing Wicked Witch of the West?

Around the time of Bill Clinton's 1992 presidential race, at least two incidents associated Hillary with the fictional

Wicked Witch of the West from the Wizard of Oz books and film.

This may have great significance, as we will shortly see.

In early 1993 Newsweek noted: "At a private dinner party with friends in Washington, Hillary was toasted with a joke gift: a witch's hat in anticipation of all that she would be accused of as the wicked witch of the West Wing." In a widely publicized photo, Hillary, dressed in all black, laughed delightedly as she placed the hat upon her head.

And in 1992 it was widely reported that GOP campaign adviser Mary Matalin (who later married Clinton's top campaign adviser James Carville) had a retouched photograph of Hillary Clinton as the Wicked Witch from the Wizard of Oz on her wall, with the caption "I will get you, my pretty, and your little dog too!"

Newsweek dismissed the witch costume as a "joke gift," and Matalin's picture was laughed off as simply an amusing campaign anecdote.

Yet some observers with deep knowledge of occult symbols and other esoteric knowledge saw these two incidents as examples of the many powerful occult symbols, garments, secret hand signs, coded language and the like that have been reported around Bill and Hillary.

The Oz/Wicked Witch of the West symbolism is, many say, powerful and filled with disturbing meaning.

The controversial Fritz Springmeier, author of Bloodlines of the Illuminati, who has written extensively about secret societies and their influence in modern America, has said this of the rich symbolism in The Wizard of Oz:

"The man who wrote the book The Wizard of Oz was a member of the Theosophical Society. L. Frank Baum... created The Wizard of Oz book as a theosophical fairy tale incorporating the 'ancient wisdom' of the Mystery Religions. The moral of the book is that we must rely upon ourselves, for we alone have the power to save ourselves. This was part of the original lie of Satan in the garden. Satan has simply dressed up the same original lie into different packaging and is distributing it worldwide as the most popular American fairy tale."

In their book The Illuminati Formula to Create an Undetectable Total Mind Control Slave, Springmeier and self-described government mind-control victim (see Chapter 9) Cisco Wheeler elaborate on this, and tie the imagery used in the book and film The Wizard of Oz to the federal government's monstrous MK-ULTRA mind-control programs (again, much more on this in Chapter 9), which they and many others believe is still going on today under the name Project MONARCH and in other forms as well:

"The occultist L. Frank Baum, a member of the Theosophical Society, was inspired by some spirit who gave him the 'magic key' to write the Wizard of Oz book, which came out in 1900. The book's story is full of Satanic activity and Satanic thinking. The story was chosen in the late 1940s to be the basis for the Illuminati/Intelligence community's trauma-based total mind-control programming."

Some of those who argue that MK-ULTRA continues today in the form of MONARCH believe MONARCH creates sex slaves and spy slaves by what Springmeier above describes as "trauma-based total mind-control programming": generating multiple personalities in young children via extreme violence and sexual abuse and then using the same techniques to condition and control them. Key words and images are supposedly implanted in the minds of such victims and used to reinforce this programming, to trigger the appearance of alternate personalities when desired, and otherwise command and control the victim.

Some of the symbolism used in this horrific process is said to be taken from the Oz books and film. Although the books was written long before MK-ULTRA, MONARCH researchers say the widespread popularity of the books and film, coupled with its buried and little-known occult meanings, makes its imagery ideal for such mind-control techniques.

Springmeier quotes L. Frank Baum on how The Wizard of Oz came to be written. Said Baum: "It was pure inspiration... It came to me right out of the blue. I think that sometimes the Great Author has a message to get across and He has to use the instrument at hand. I happened to be that medium, and I believe the magic key was given me to open the doors to sympathy and understanding, joy, peace and happiness."

Throughout this book we will see numerous references to important, history-altering manuscripts allegedly dictated from other worlds or dimensions, or spirits, or unearthly beings.

Springmeier is correct about Baum's occult interests. Though it is not widely known, Baum joined Madame Blavatsky's occult Theosophical Society in 1892, eight years before The Wizard of Oz, the first of 14 Oz books he would write, was published. His mother-in-law, a prominent political activist, had been a Theosophist years earlier and introduced Baum to Theosophy. Baum became very interested in the occult, including spiritualism and mediumship, and wrote on these subjects prior to joining the Theosophical Society.

According to Dr. John Algeo, professor emeritus of English at the University of Georgia and past president of the Theosophical Society in America: "...Theosophical ideas permeate [Baum's] work and provided the inspiration for it. Indeed, The Wizard [of Oz] can be regarded as Theosophical allegory, pervaded by Theosophical ideas from beginning to end."

Although Baum was, like Hillary, raised a Methodist, critics have noted that the only mention of a church in the Oz books is a porcelain model in the first Oz book – which the Cowardly Lion accidentally smashes "all to pieces." Some critics say this pointedly symbolizes an anticlerical theme in the book.

It is outside the scope of this book to explore the many occult and political interpretations, sometimes conflicting, of the classic book and film The Wizard of Oz. But just being aware that some claim there are indeed occult messages hidden in this allegedly telepathically transmitted book, and that some charge that the book is used in MK-ULTRA-type mind control today, certainly brings a new light to Hillary's association with, and joking references to, the Wicked Witch of the West.

Hillary Flashes the Sign of Satan

Hillary, like Bill, has been seen publicly making the Sign of Satan hand gesture, made by lowering the two middle fingers while the first and pinkie finger are upright, representing the horns of Satan.

In recent years, because of the mass use of phone cameras, so many politicians and other prominent figures have been caught making this ancient and notorious sign that mainstream media apologists have found it necessary to offer the public an acceptable explanation.

It's not at all the Sign of Satan, we are told. What a silly idea! No, it is merely the "hook 'em horns" symbol of the Texas Longhorns football team of the University of Texas at Austin.

How odd. Whoever knew that so many politicians, from all across America – indeed, from around the world – were such big fans of this particular college football team? Such big fans, in fact, that they feel compelled to show their allegiance to it in public appearances far from Texas, year after year after year?

Indeed, a very incomplete list of politicians and other prominent persons photographed using this sign includes not just Hillary and Bill but Barack Obama, George and Laura Bush, Barbara Bush, Dick Cheney, George W. Bush's senior adviser Karl Rove, Sarah Palin, Ronald Reagan, Homeland Security Director Tom Ridge, Rep. Nancy Pelosi, Sen. Dan Quayle, Prince William of Britain's royal family, Silvio Berlusconi (Italian billionaire and politician), French president Sarcozy, Maria (Kennedy) Shriver, King Abdullah, Yasser Arafat, Iranian president Mahmoud Ahmadinejad, Mario Cuomo, disgraced Washington DC mayor Marion Berry... we could go on and on.

We might also add to that distinguished list Anton Lavey, founder of the Church of Satan, who describes its proper use in Satanic ceremonies in his book The Satanic Rituals. Indeed, LaVey can be seen making the same "horned hand" or "Satanic salute" with his left hand on the back cover of his infamous book The Satanic Bible – a book that, most assuredly, has nothing to do with Texas college football.

Add, too, serial killer and self-proclaimed Satanist Richard Ramirez aka "The Night Stalker," not publicly known as a big UT football fan. Add also members of innumerable occult-drenched black metal bands.

If this symbol does denote Texas football or the University of Texas at Austin, why are people like these – American and foreign political leaders with no Texas connections, serial killers, and avowed Satanists – constantly using it?

Is this Austin, Texas college football team really *that* popular around the world?

No, the absurdity of that explanation is enough to disprove it.

According to award-winning Canadian journalist Judi McLeod, "The Horned Hand or Mano Cornuto is a Satanic salute, a sign of recognition between and allegiance of members of Satanism or other unholy groups."

In her book Masonic and Occult Symbols Illustrated, Dr. Cathy Burns further explains: "The devil horns sign (also known as il cornuto, cornuto, the horn, horned devil, twin-horned salute, horned hand, devil salute, and devil horn salute) is a recognition sign among Satanists and witches. Remember that Satan is called 'The Horned God,' so the hand signal is formed so as to resemble horns."

For centuries, around the world, the notorious horned salute has been understood as the sign of Satan.

Certainly there are alternative interpretations of the sign. In some contexts it may represent various obscure non-Satanic pagan entities. In some cultures it is a curse, a blasphemy, a sign of adultery and other evil.

But these alternative non-Satanic explanations, too, beg the question: why would scores of prominent figures in politics and media constantly salute near-forgotten ancient pagan creatures, or signal hexes or blasphemy to crowds at large public events?

No, the idea that Hillary and hordes of other political and cultural leaders around the world are flashing the devil horns in order to express solidarity with a college football team or as a friendly nod to some long-obscure pagan entity is beyond absurd.

Writing of Bill Clinton's use of the sign at his inauguration, researcher Fritz Springmeier, in his controversial book Bloodlines of the Illuminati, gets to the point:

"People that are Christians now, but were Satanists, recognized President Clinton's signal at his inauguration as a sign of Satan. That seems fairly cut and dried, and it is. Clinton communicated what he wanted to the people to whom he wanted to communicate. The whole affair with him flashing the Satanic hand signal took only a couple of seconds."

Let us grant that it is unlikely that Hillary, who has made the sign for years across the nation and around the world, is constantly signaling her support for the football team of a Texas university she never attended.

What, then, is she really saying when she makes the centuries-old Sign of Satan?

Perhaps even more important: to whom is she saying it?

Hillary, Saul Alinsky – and Satan

"Now, one of the things that I have learned about Hillary Clinton is that one of her heroes, her mentors was Saul Alinsky. ... Are we willing to elect someone as president who has as their role model somebody who acknowledges Lucifer? Think about that." – Dr. Ben Carson, 2016 Republican National Convention

Hillary first met with the radical political activist Saul Alinsky as a high school student, when her left wing Methodist youth minister took her and other church youth to meet Alinsky in Chicago.

Alinsky must have made a considerable impression, for, as we shall see, Hillary went on to have a long and close relationship with Alinsky – far closer than, until recently, was publicly known.

In his most famous book, Rules for Radicals (1971), Alinsky actually salutes Lucifer – Satan – as a role model and inspiration.

At the beginning of the book there is a page of three quotes, just before the table of contents. The last is from Alinsky himself:

"Lest we forget at least an over-the-shoulder acknowledgment to the very first radical from all our legends, mythology, and history (and who is to know where mythology leaves off and history begins – or which is which), the first radical known to man who rebelled against the establishment and did it so effectively that he at least won his own kingdom – Lucifer."

That "kingdom," of course, was Hell. And Lucifer didn't rebel against "the establishment" but against the biblical God.

That is not the only mention of Satanic influences in the book. On page 71, writing of his training program for political organizers, which Hillary studied, Alinsky says:

"The qualities we were trying to develop in organizers in the years of attempting to train them included some qualities that in all probability cannot be taught. They either had them, or could get them only through a miracle from above *or below*." (Emphasis added.)

Shortly before his death in 1972, Alinsky told Playboy magazine that if there was life after death, he wanted to go to hell, not heaven, because "Hell would be heaven for me" and in hell he would find "my kind of people":

Alinsky: ...if there is an afterlife, and I have anything to say about it, I will unreservedly choose to go to Hell.

Playboy: Why?

Alinsky: Hell would be heaven for me. All my life I've been with the have-nots. Over here, if you're a have-not, you're short of dough. If you're a have-not in Hell, you're short of virtue. Once I get into Hell, I'll start organizing the have-nots over there.

Playboy: Why them?

Alinsky: They're my kind of people.

Alinsky was raised a religious Jew until age 12, when, he said, he "kicked the habit." Solidly on the radical left his entire adult life, Alinsky says he was never a Communist Party member, but also said that in the 1930s "their platform stood for all the right things."

Indeed, conservative journalist Stanley Kurtz notes that Alinsky "worked closely for years with Chicago's Communist Party and did everything in his power to advance its program. Most of his innovations were patterned on Communist-Party organizing tactics. Alinsky was smart enough never to join the party, however. From the start, he understood the dangers of ideological openness. ... Working effectively, Alinsky believed, requires ideological stealth, gradualism, and pragmatic cover." In this, Alinsky echoes the tactics of the earlier Fabian Socialists, mentioned elsewhere in this book.

Some Satanists today are well aware of Alinsky's leanings. Diane Vera is an outspoken "theistic Satanists." A theistic Satanist, she explains, is "anyone who reveres Satan as a deity." This is as opposed to non-theistic Satanists who merely view Satan as a metaphor or symbol of various desired traits, not an actual entity.

In her 2005 article "Saul D. Alinsky: A role model for left-wing Satanists" Ms. Vera says Alinsky is "an excellent role model for politically left-leaning Satanists, whether theistic or symbolic... he espoused a lot of values that are familiar to today's Satanists, such as his emphasis on power, self-interest, creativity, and practicality."

After her high school meeting with Alinsky, Hillary stayed in touch with the radical Lucifer-admiring social agitator.

In 1969 she wrote her Wellesley College senior thesis on Alinsky. The White House considered the contents of this thesis so threatening to Bill's presidency that in 1993, in the very early days of the Clinton administration, the thesis was sealed from the public for several years by Wellesley – at the request of the Clintons. Wellesley had never before (or since) sealed a thesis paper, but it did so for Bill and Hillary.

Alan H. Schechter, Hillary's political science professor and thesis adviser, said the request was based on a lie, which he described as "some mumbo jumbo" about the paper possibly hurting the administration's healthcare reform ideas because it criticized Sen. Daniel Moynihan. In truth, there is nothing negative about Moynihan in the paper.

The thesis was finally revealed in 2001, and it turns out that, while not so damaging as one might have thought, considering the Clinton-initiated ban, it indeed could have damaged Bill and Hillary's White House agenda.

Entitled "'There Is Only the Fight...': An Analysis of the Alinsky Model" the 92-page thesis centered on Alinsky's theory of community organizing.

In the thesis Hillary notes: "If the ideals Alinsky espouses were actualized, the result would be social revolution. ... Alinsky is regarded by many as the proponent of a dangerous socio/political philosophy. As such, he has been feared – just as [five-time Socialist Party presidential candidate] Eugene Debs or Walt Whitman or Martin Luther King have been feared, because each embraced the most radical of political faiths – democracy."

No doubt many Hillary critics would have charged her and Bill with trying to "actualize" the Alinsky ideals and "social revolution" she speaks of.

During the writing of her thesis Hillary met with Alinsky several times, and the two became quite close. Indeed, Alinsky offered her a job. Hillary declined, saying she wanted to work within the system for radical change.

As she explained in Living History, her 2003 autobiography: "I agreed with some of Alinsky's ideas, particularly the value of empowering people to help themselves. But we had a fundamental disagreement. He believed you could change the system only from the outside. I didn't."

In fact, their relationship was closer than was known, as was revealed September 2014, when two letters obtained by the Washington Free Beacon show Clinton's relationship with Alinsky, and her support for many of his ideas, continued for several years after she entered Yale Law School in 1969.

The letters indicate that Alinsky had discussed student activism with her.

Hillary wrote: "If I never thanked you for the encouraging words of last spring in the midst of the Yale-Cambodia madness, I do so now." (The reference is to campus strife over the Vietnam War.)

Hillary said she missed talking with him, and wondered if Alinsky could meet her in California.

"I am living in Berkeley and working in Oakland for the summer and would love to see you," Hillary wrote. "Let me know if there is any chance of our getting together."

In Oakland Hillary, then 23, was interning for the self-described (by founder Robert Treuhaft) communist law firm Treuhaft, Walker and Burnstein. Treuhaft was a former Communist Party USA member and husband of ex-Communist Jessica Mitford. Both remained ideological communists after leaving the Party. Pulitzer Prize-winning journalist Carl Bernstein of Watergate fame notes that, of the law firm's four partners, "two were communists, and others tolerated communists." The firm was one of the most radical law firms in America, infamous for its radical left-wing politics and participation in radical leftist legal battles. Almost certainly Hillary was aware of this when she chose to travel across the continent to intern with them. (See Chapter 14 for more on Hillary and this law firm.)

The letters also suggest that Alinsky, who died in 1972, had a deeper influence on Clinton's early political views than previously known.

David Brock wrote in his 1996 book The Seduction of Hillary Rodham that "Hillary was like Alinsky's daughter."

Alinsky wanted Hillary to work for him in his Industrial Areas Foundation. In Hillary's autobiography Living History she writes that she rejected Saul Alinsky's offer, instead choosing to go to Yale law school, "to follow a more conventional path."

However, she remained sympathetic. As noted in March 2007 in the Washington Post: "As first lady, Clinton occasionally lent her name to projects endorsed by the Industrial Areas Foundation (IAF), the Alinsky group that had offered her a job in 1968. She raised money and attended two events organized by the Washington Interfaith Network, an IAF affiliate."

On July 8, 1971 Hillary wrote to Alinsky: "Dear Saul, When is the new book [Rules for Radicals] coming out or has it come and I somehow missed the fulfillment of Revelation?

"I have just had my one thousandth conversation about Reveille [Alinsky's book Reveille for Radicals] and need some new material to throw at people."

Note that in Reveille for Radicals, of which the young Hillary speaks so admiringly, Alinsky defines his politics:

"Radicals want to advance from the jungle of laissez-faire capitalism to a world worthy of the name of human civilization. They hope for a future where the means of economic production will be owned by all of the people instead of the comparative handful."

Government ownership of the means of production is, of course, a key Marxist tenet.

Alinsky expressed his ruthless outlook in these chilling words from Rules for Radicals: "The man of action... ask of ends only whether they are achievable and worth the cost; of means only whether they will work."

According to Carl Bernstein, Alinsky's most famous mantra was "Whatever works to get power to the people, use it." Again, the end justifies the means.

Hillary was not the only bright student to be intrigued by Alinsky and study his methods and model for social change. In 1985 a promising young leftist lawyer named Barack Obama began three years of work in Chicago with the Developing Communities Project, part of the Alinsky network. He later described the experience as "the best education I ever had..." Afterwards, Obama attended Harvard, then began teaching the Alinsky philosophy and strategy. Obama's presidential campaign was noted for use of Alinsky-inspired tactics. Even Michelle Obama's speech at the 2008 Democratic Convention noticeably echoed Alinsky's words and themes.

Thus, astoundingly, the two candidates for the

Democratic Party's presidential nomination in 2008 were both Alinsky disciples.

Disciples of a man who saluted Lucifer in his most famous book.

CHAPTER SIX

Hillary and Demonic Rock Music

"It turns out all those nutty Christian evangelists who warned that rock and roll is demonic were right ...pop music is soaked in the occult." – philosopher Jules Evans

L. David Mitchell – author of Liberty in Jesus: Evil Spirits and Exorcism Simply Explained (1999) – warns that people can open themselves to occult possession and control by:

"...inviting seemingly 'good' but obviously strange spirit manifestations (2 Corinthians 11:14); being at the receiving end of a curse; practicing Eastern-style or New Age meditation; using drugs; playing spirit 'games'; being involved in abortion or incest; having a dependency of any kind, *including rock music*." (Emphasis added.)

As we have already seen, Hillary arguably has met most of the above criteria for inviting demonic/spirit possession listed in the previous paragraph, along with other widely recognized signs. She has also continually used rock music, with its hypnotic rhythms, pounding volume, and sometimes near-subliminal lyrics, to advance her candidacies and promote her message.

In 2015, Hillary's campaign paid $9,000 to a Portland, Oregon "boutique music agency" for "music supervision and creative support" in music choices. Thus her Spotify playlist, shared publicly as part of her presidential campaign, is bland, soulless and utterly inauthentic, just another campaign branding/public relations tool. (Indeed, the list is so corporate/boring it seems like another Hillary Turing Test fail.)

But an examination of Hillary's earlier, ungated campaign music choices is very revealing indeed.

Recall earlier in Chapter 3 that Dr. Robert Masters, the husband and partner of Hillary's White House mystic consultant Jean Houston, described himself as one who has "devotedly followed the Way of the Goddess Sekhmet for more than 30 years." Jean Houston has also written favorably about Sekhmet. Recall also how this same goddess Sekhmet, known to some worshipers as "Ruler of Serpents and of Dragons," was worshiped in nighttime drunken sexual orgies accompanied by the relentless beat of what award-winning NBC News science writer Alan Boyd has described as "the ancient equivalent of rock 'n' roll."..

It is well documented that many rock-and-roll musicians openly practice black magic and are Satanists. Examples abound. How many parents, dropping off their youngsters to enjoy an evening of music and dancing with the popular chart-topping and four-time Grammy Award-nominated musician Marilyn Manson, know that Rev. Manson is an ordained minister in the Church of Satan who reportedly purchased a child's skeleton and several masks made of human skin – and that he entertains his young audience members by preaching Satanism, tearing a Bible apart, using the American flag as toilet paper, and screaming obscenities?

How many parents are aware that black metal bands and their fans have set more than 50 churches on fire – or that one of the most popular of such bands even used a photograph of a church they burned as an album cover? Lead singer Gaahl of the world-famous black metal band Gorgoroth – whose founder describes himself as "Satan's minister on Earth" and whose albums include "Antichrist" and "Incipit Satan" ("Satan Begins") – has bluntly declared: "Church burnings and all these things are, of course, things that I support 100 percent and it should have been done much more and will be done much more in the future. We have to remove every trace from what Christianity and the Semitic roots have to offer this world."

Indeed, references to Satan and the occult permeate the whole history of modern rock music. In particular, the influence of Aleister Crowley, the leading occultist of the 20th century, who proudly dubbed himself "The Beast 666," is simply everywhere.

Consider the biggest and most influential bands of the 1960s and 1970s, still wildly popular today. A photograph of Crowley appears on the cover of the Beatles' "Sgt. Pepper's Lonely Hearts Club Band" album. The back cover of the Doors' album "Doors 13" (note the occult number 13) is devoted to a large photo of the Doors gathered reverently around a statue of Crowley. (The Doors originally wanted this photo to be the front cover.)

Crowley's motto "Do What Thou Wilt" was cut into the vinyl of "Led Zeppelin III" – thus bringing it into millions of homes around the world – and Led Zeppelin guitarist Jimmy Page bought and lived in Crowley's Loch Ness home, Boleskine House, where Crowley had performed numerous black magic rituals and ghostly figures were often seen. Some claim the home is named after the demon Ba'al, believed by some to be the same entity to which ritual human sacrifices are offered today at the annual ruling-elite Bohemian Grove ceremonies, attended by U.S. political and cultural leaders, as described in Chapter 13.

The Rolling Stones got into Crowleyan black magic in the late sixties as Mick Jagger and Keith Richards befriended filmmaker and Crowleyan occultist and black magician Kenneth Anger; indeed, Anger lived for a while with Jagger and Richards, and was an obvious influence on "Sympathy for the Devil" and other Stones work. (See Chapter 10 for more on Anger and Crowleyism.) Jagger was intrigued by Anger and by Crowleyan occultism; Jagger acted in and created original music for Anger's film "Invocation to my Demon Brother" (1969), which also features Church of Satan founder Anton Lavey and stars Charles Manson associate and future murderer Bobby Beausoleil as Lucifer (a role Jagger also considered). "Invocation of My Demon Brother" also features footage of a Stones concert. Jagger's popstar girlfriend Marianne Faithful acts in Anger's "Lucifer Rising," which also featured a Manson family member and dealt with similar occult themes and personalities. Anger also hung out for a while with John Lennon and Yoko Ono. Anger, it should be noted, is widely credited for having virtually invented the music video that has so dominated American pop culture since the 1980s.

David Bowie is another pop star who became obsessed with Crowleyism and the occult, with frightening consequences. Bowie biographer Marc Spitz writes that during the mid-1970s Bowie became "obsessed with using occult magic to attain success and protect himself from demonic forces." This eventually took a terrifying turn. Bowie lived for a while very close to the house where Manson Family members killed Leno and Rosemary LaBianca just two days after murdering Sharon Tate and several others. According to Spitz: "Increasingly Bowie was convinced there were witches after his semen. They were intent on using it to make a child to sacrifice to the devil…" Bowie hired a witch to protect him against this and other manifestations of the occult evil he felt growing around him. Shortly after that, according to his then-wife Angela, Bowie saw Satan rising from a pool in a house he'd bought, and Bowie contacted his witch to perform an exorcism.

We could go on and on with other examples right up to the present day, when Crowleyan symbols are frequently seen in music videos and concerts, and sights like rapper Jay-Z wearing a "Do What Thou Wilt" hoodie and the mononymous singer/actress Ciara wearing a jacket with nothing less than "Hermetic Order of the Golden Dawn" printed on the back in huge letters are so common as to hardly be remarked upon. When Lady Gaga, who has performed onstage costumed as the Satan figure Baphomet and whose video for her hit song "Alejandro" was declared blasphemous by the Catholic League, announced she would do a tribute to the late David Bowie at the Grammy Awards, the mainstream website sheknows.com's article asked in its headline for the story: "Is Lady Gaga planning to summon the Antichrist at the 2016 Grammys?" Meanwhile Kenneth Anger's explicitly occult films are now seen as major cultural artifacts and shown at such mainstream Establishment venues as the Museum of Modern Art.

"It turns out all those nutty Christian evangelists who warned that rock and roll is demonic were right," writes the world-renowned philosopher and author Jules Evans. "…pop music is soaked in the occult, particularly in Aleister Crowley's highly egotistical version of it."

Crowley's considerable influence in current music, film and literature is well documented. One could expand the list to other areas. (For example, in the late 1940s filmmaker and Crowleyan Kenneth Anger began a lifelong friendship with the notorious and enormously influential Rockefeller-funded sexologist Alfred Kinsey, and aided Kinsey in his controversial research; Kinsey shared Anger's deep fascination with Aleister Crowley and visited the deceased Crowley's temple in Sicily shortly before his own death.)

Indeed, one could well argue that Aleister Crowley is one of the most dominant cultural figures of our time, a major shaper of today's world. Certainly we are living in very Crowleyan times: today's widespread drug abuse and addiction, sexual libertinism, mind control, violence, blasphemy, Satanism, black magic, Anti-Christianism, and highly ritualistic occult-themed music concerts all could have sprung directly from the depraved mind of Crowley, who doubtless would have cheered it all on.

Lest any reader think we exaggerate Crowley's influence, in 2002 the BBC broadcast a program entitled "100 Greatest Britons," based on a poll conducted to discover who the United Kingdom public considered the greatest British people in all history. In a list that included Shakespeare, Chaucer, Sir Isaac Newton, Charles Darwin, William Blake, Charles Dickens, Jane Austen, Winston Churchill, Ernest Shackleton, Thomas Paine, John Wesley and other luminaries was also... the Beast 666, Aleister Crowley.

As philosopher Jules Evans notes: "...Crowley's 'Do What You Wilt' philosophy has become one of the ruling philosophies of our time."

(And one must wonder: given the extraordinary influence of Crowley in the world of entertainment, might he not have an equal, or even greater, if far lesser known, influence upon the worlds of finance and politics? Wouldn't that, in fact, seem almost inevitable? Keep that in mind while perusing Chapter 10, devoted to the powerful secret organizations associated with Hillary that, many allege, covertly set the agenda for much of the world.)

Perhaps we should all be more careful as to what our children listen to – and what we ourselves listen to and share with the world.

And now, back to Hillary's rock music choices.

Hillary's Rock Star Adviser: "We Seek Depravity"

Of course, most presidential campaigns today use some rock music in their public appearances. But Hillary's distinctive use of it deserves special attention.

First, note that Hillary's 2014 2.4-pound "autobiography" Hard Choices was ghost-written in part by one Ted Widmer. To rock-and-roll fanatics, Widmer is far better known as… "Lord Rockingham," singer and guitarist of the bizarre and perverse Boston hard-rock band The Upper Crust. (Widmer was in the band from 1993 to 1997.)

The Upper Crust – men who perform in 18th century-style powdered wigs – summed up their philosophy in a 1999 interview in Ear Candy magazine as "If not great and excellent, then debauched…" and said the problem with today's rock music is that "Depravity is missing. … we seek depravity in all its delicious forms." One of the band's recent (post-Widmer) albums is entitled "Horse and Buggery."

Lord Rockingham aka Widmer left the band in 1997 to become… a speech writer and senior adviser for President Bill Clinton, and later, as noted, he became a Hillary ghostwriter and a senior adviser to Hillary while she was secretary of state. After ghosting Hillary's autobiography he wrote Ark of the Liberties, a history book which praises arch-globalist presidents Wilson and Roosevelt and, as a Washington Post review noted, hails the "latticework of multilateral institutions, including the United Nations, the World Bank, the International Monetary Fund, General Agreement on Tariffs and Trade (which later morphed into the World Trade Organization) and NATO." (See Chapter 13 for Hillary's affiliations with such globalist organizations and the sinister nature of their agenda.) In 2014 Widmar wrote an article mocking and criticizing "The Star-Spangled Banner," the U.S. national anthem, entitled "Is It Time to Ditch the Star-Spangled Banner?"

Ironically, one of the Upper Crust's Widmer-era songs, "Let Them Eat Rock," could serve as a summary of one of the oft-heard criticisms of Hillary, that she is a tool of the corporate globalist wealthy one percent ruling elite who, in reality, care nothing for the average citizen:

> They say there's people starving,
> dropping down dead in the streets
> The lazy slobs, they ain't got a job,
> They say they ain't got enough to eat...
> Let them eat rock!

A cold-hearted credo indeed – made all the more so when preached by men dressed as 18th-century aristocratic elites.

The Upper Crust have taken their messages of depravity and cold-heartedness to the world in several albums, countless concerts, and a documentary film, "Let Them Eat Rock."

To cap things off, one of the record labels on which The Upper Crust appears is, incredibly... Reptilian Records! Just a coincidence, no doubt. (See Chapter 8 for much more on Hillary's alleged connection to the reptilian agenda.)

"When the Lady Smiles..."
Horror and Blasphemy

But things get far weirder – and far worse. Around early 2008, the Hillary for president campaign used as campaign music the notorious 1984 song "When The Lady Smiles" by the hard rock group Golden Earring, best known for their 1970s hit song "Radar Love."

If you consider the accusations of demon possession and occult hypnotic mind control that have circulated around Hillary for so many years, the lyrics are disturbing in the extreme. Excerpts:

When the lady smiles,
You know it drives me wild...

And I love it, yeah I love it
It's the answer to all my dreams...

When the lady smiles,
She holds me in her hand...
I can't resist her call...
As a matter of fact,
I don't resist at all
'cos I'm walking on clouds
And she is leadin' the way

My friends tell me,
She's the beast inside your paradise
I guess you've heard it all before
A fallen angel,
That has got you hypnotized
And that always needs some more...
And I love it, yeah I love it

Oh no, oh no, oh nooooo......

These lyrics are quite terrifying in the context of the song as a theme for a political rally, especially in the light of the issues discussed in this book. The lyrics picture someone – presumably, in the context of its use at a political event, someone symbolic of the American citizenry – who is totally hypnotized, totally under control, unable to resist the siren call of the person – "the lady" – who is "the answer to all my dreams."

Note the eerie descriptions of hypnotic mind control, which we have discussed in relation to Hillary in chapters 9 and 11:

I can't resist her call...

I don't resist at all...

she is leadin' the way...

[she] has got you hypnotized...

And who is this "the lady," this controlling hypnotic being? The lyrics give us still more clues: she is "the beast inside your paradise... a fallen angel..."

These are terms that are commonly used to refer to Satan and/or the Antichrist. The Beast is commonly used to refer to the two beasts described in the Book of Revelation. The first beast is mentioned in Revelation 11:7 and it comes "out of the sea" and is given power by the second beast, Revelation 13:1-18, believed by many to be Satan himself. Both come to oppose God in this world.

Clearly, "The beast inside your paradise... a fallen angel..." can only refer to Satan. It is Satan, the Beast, who in the Garden of Eden ("paradise" in the song) seduces Eve to break God's law. Satan is commonly referred to as a "fallen angel."

So, returning to the song, a Beast – a monstrous demon or even Satan him (or her) self – has you helplessly under control and you must obey her every command!

In the context of a campaign song, this demon, this "beast inside paradise," this being who may be Satan or Satan's servant, simply can be no one else but... Hillary.

The knowledge of the eternal damnation that "the lady" brings to those trapped by her spell is made clear in the wailing of the singer at the end:

"Oh no, oh no, oh nooooo......"

But there are yet far more sinister overtones to this song.

The music video for the song begins with the singer of the band as a *rapist*, viciously attacking a nun on a subway train, tearing off her habit and exposing her brassiere. The scene abruptly shifts to heaven, where the nun – suddenly transformed into a seductive angelic-appearing being clothed in flowing robes – embraces and kisses the man who we've just seen assaulting the nun. Not only is this outrageously and deliberately blasphemous – a nun raped, then reappearing as a sexually provocative angel – it is profoundly anti-woman: as if sexual assault and rape can be instantly transformed into romantic love.

A central act in Satanic Black Masses is the defilement of religious symbols. In a very real way, this film is itself a kind of video Black Mass.

The video makes another scene switch, and the leader of the band now violently attacks the same woman, now a secretary in an office. He knocks over furniture and chases her down a hall, finally falling upon her trapped in an elevator. The scene again switches to heaven, where the same angelic-appearing being appears.

Again, savage rape is translated into romantic love.

Because the victim is also the same actress who portrays the seductive angel, the obvious message is that the nun/victim actually "asked for it" and wants to be raped.

In the next scene the rapist is pulled off the victim in the elevator. The victim is shown slumped on the floor, her legs spread apart.

In the next scene the lead singer/rapist is found guilty by a court, is bound to an operating table, surrounded by highly sexualized nurses doing provocative erotic dances and gyrations – while part of the rapist's brain is cut out by surgeons... and thrown to a dog, who happily devours it! This is a scene right out of the monstrous MK-ULTRA mind experiments conducted by the CIA, which some have associated with the Clintons. (See Chapter 9 for much more on this.)

This video was so over the edge, such an assault on decency, that even MTV – notorious for its highly sexualized and anti-social videos aimed at youth – banned it, allowing only an edited version to be shown – and even that only after midnight.

That's right, it was too much even for MTV, a channel infamous for what Jim Daley, president of Focus on the Family, has described as "sexually suggestive, near-pornographic music videos..." and for other controversial programming Daley denounces as "nothing short of technological child abuse."

All this – particularly the video – becomes even more disturbing when one recalls that Bill Clinton has been accused of rape for decades, based on charges by several women, and, while he has not been convicted, some journalists and commentators believe the evidence for these charges is compelling. (This is explored further in Chapter 9.)

Indeed, as the savage rapist in the video charges at women, raping and assaulting them, then trying to sooth and charm them, we cannot help but be reminded of... Bill Clinton himself, as described by women who allege he assaulted them.

And we may also be reminded while watching that Hillary has been accused – again, we must note, without proof – of ruthlessly protecting Bill (and her own political aspirations) from the charges of women who claim he raped or otherwise sexually assaulted them.

Obviously, it could be argued that the Hillary campaign didn't know of this video, or the – literally – diabolical lyrics of the song.

However, the lyrics are clear in the song – anyone listening can understand them.

And the video aired on MTV, with its millions of viewers, in 1984, in a censored though still shocking form, to be seen by anyone interested in popular rock music. It is easily found on YouTube today with just a moment's search.

And there is this final disturbing note. While touring the U.S. in 1984, Golden Earring played at the Six Flags theme park in New Jersey on May 11. In the midst of their set a fire erupted at the park's Haunted Castle. Eight teenagers were killed.

This tragedy at a "Haunted Castle" has obvious occult overtones. Was this the reason that the band refused to ever again tour America? Were they afraid, perhaps, of demonic forces they may have conjured up and set loose as they played blasphemous music, music whose accompanying video was, as we have noted, reminiscent of a Black Mass, near a "Haunted Castle" as eight young people were "sacrificed" in fire?

As this is written the band's latest studio album is entitled

"Tits 'n Ass." Their 1999 song "Paradise in Distress" was described by their lead singer as "rather blasphemous. I sing about the Devil having bought a penthouse in heaven."

And the notorious video to "When the Lady Smiles" can be found on their DVD compilation, entitled... "The Devil Made Us Do It."

Ironically, in her controversial child-rearing book It Takes a Village, Hillary praises Tipper Gore and her Parents Music Resource Center, and warns readers about the dangers of violence in rock music and television.

Yet Hillary used this vile song to promote her campaign, blasting its strange, occult and obscene message, linked to an incredibly depraved, violent and blasphemous video, to her audience, including young children.

CHAPTER SEVEN

666: Is Hillary the Antichrist?

"And he causeth all, both small and great, rich and poor, free and bond, to receive a mark in their right hand, or in their foreheads: And that no man might buy or sell, save he that had the mark, or the name of the beast, or the number of his name.

"Here is wisdom. Let him that hath understanding count the number of the beast: for it is the number of a man; and his number is Six hundred threescore and six (666)." – Revelation 13:16-18

"Little children, it is the last time: and as ye have heard that Antichrist shall come, even now are there many Antichrists; whereby we know that it is the last time." – I John 2:18

"[H]ave you noticed that Hillary Clinton and the Antichrist are never seen together? Coincidence? You be the judge!" – George Case, History News Network, Feb. 7, 2016

U.S. Congressman: "Hillary Is the Antichrist"

"We need to focus on the real enemy. ... [Hillary Clinton is] the Antichrist."

So declared U.S. Congressman and former U.S. Navy Seal Ryan Zinke (R-MN), January 27, 2014.

Congressman Zinke is hardly alone in believing that Hillary is in fact the biblical Antichrist, or is working in league with the Antichrist.

Dr. Don Colbert is a New York Times bestselling author of over 40 books who has been featured on The Dr. Oz Show, Fox News, ABC World News, the BBC, Readers Digest, News Week, Prevention Magazine, and many others.

On the "The Jim Bakker Show" televangelist TV show in September 2016, Dr. Colbert warned viewers that "the spirit of Antichrist" is in, or on, Hillary: "That spirit of [the] Antichrist is majorly on...Hillary Clinton. Jesus even said there will be many Antichrists in the world [I John 2:18]..."

That same month, also on "The Jim Bakker Show," Fox News contributor Alveda King, a niece of civil rights leader Martin Luther King, Jr. and a former Georgia state legislator, warned that Hillary is preparing America for the Antichrist. King warned that Hillary "said basically, Christians and religious people in America need to set aside their religious beliefs and serve secular humanism. ... She really has said that we are going to have to learn in America to set aside our religious beliefs. And so I was saying, what she's really saying is, *usher in the Antichrist*. She actually did say that."

American Family Association radio host Bryan Fischer declared in August 2016 that "Hillary Clinton is motivated by the spirit of the Antichrist because she is against Christ, she is against Christianity, she is against the free exercise of the Christian faith, she doesn't want the Christian faith to be a part of the public square, to influence public policy in any way, she is against everything that Christianity stands for...She is an opponent of all that is good and right and noble."

Indeed, a simple Google search for "Hillary Clinton" coupled with "Antichrist" for this book brought up over 663,000 references – ironically, a number very close to the biblical Number of the Beast: 666.

Clearly, many people do in fact believe that Hillary is the biblical Antichrist.

Is that possible, at least in theory?

The answer, calculated by several methods, is... yes.

What or Who Is the Antichrist?
What Is the Beast?

What or who exactly is the Antichrist? In popular terminology the word is often used to mean merely someone who opposes Christianity or the conventional morality of society. An example of this is the bestselling punk rock song "Anarchy in the UK" by the British band the Sex Pistols, an anthem for angry youth around the world in the 1970s, in which vocalist Johnny Rotten sings "I am an Antichrist / I am an anarchist."

However, the term Antichrist actually means something far more radical and supernatural. It is primarily, though not exclusively, a Christian term, and the word comes from the New Testament, where it appears five times in 1 John and 2 John.

It should be noted that the terms "Antichrist" and "Beast" are interpreted in many different ways by different biblical scholars and different Christian groups. Despite this disagreement, it can be generally said that many Christians view the Antichrist as an evil false messiah, a religious-political dictator who will emerge in the future to rule mankind, persecute God's people, and lead the human race to evil. This Antichrist will be totally evil. Some, but by no means all, Christians who believe in the Antichrist believe that Satan will possess and guide the Antichrist. Some believe the arrival of the Antichrist signals the beginning of the "End Times" of life as we have known it on earth, and that Jesus will appear in his Second Coming to battle this Antichrist. Some, citing I John 2:18, say there will be many Antichrists. Some say the Antichrist is also Satan; some say it is Satan's son.

Similarly, there are differing interpretations of the Beast. The term "the Beast" refers to the two beasts described in the Book of Revelation – one which is prophesied to arise from the sea, the other from the earth. Many believe the Beast will be a government or a powerful political and religious ruler who will rule earth and serve the Antichrist; others say the Beast itself, or one of them, are the Antichrist(s).

For the purpose of this book these centuries-old disagreements about the precise nature of the Antichrist and the Beast do not matter. It is enough for us to realize that almost all who believe in the Antichrist and the Beast agree they are evil, Satanic, and their arrival signals the beginning of a terrible time.

Which brings us to the key questions: Is Hillary indeed

the biblical Antichrist? How can we tell?

There are various widely accepted tests to see if Hillary indeed matches the descriptions of the Antichrist and/or Beast of the Book of Revelation. We will apply them in this chapter.

The Antichrist, the New World Order, and REAL ID

Many believe the Antichrist will be the head of, or even the embodiment of, the so-called "New World Order" – a vast all-powerful political and cultural controlling force that many feel is emerging in today's world. (See Chapter 13 for much more on this theory and on Hillary's current role in it.)

Some believe the Beast, aka New World Order, will demand the implanting of RFID chips in humans. These RFID chips, of course, will literally be the Mark of the Beast prophesied in Revelation 13:17: "And that no man might buy or sell, save he that had the mark, or the name of the beast, or the number of his name."

There are certainly many people seeking to implement a New World Order, and schemes for using technology to monitor and control the human race are actively being pursued by the government and ruling elites. Further, the technology needed to enforce the use of the Mark of the Beast – such as massive databases, point of sale data-capture, and powerful biometric ID and authentication systems – now exists and is being vigorously promoted by the world elites who are seeking to birth the New World Order.

End Times scholar Peter Lalonde notes in his book One World Under Antichrist: "the microchips currently used in 'smart cards' could easily fulfill the definition of 'the mark' which will be issued under the Antichrist regime."

In 2011 the Rutherford Institute, a nonprofit civil liberties organization, undertook the defense of Kaye Beach, a Christian who felt her religious liberty was jeopardized by such "smart card" drivers licenses, sometimes called REAL ID, which she believed indicated the beginnings of the biblical Mark of the Beast.

Like Kaye Beach, many Christians feel their religion explicitly commands them to resist the imposition of such government-mandated IDs:

"If any man worship the beast and his image, and receive his mark in his forehead, or in his hand, the same shall drink of the wine of the wrath of God, which is poured out without mixture [i.e., undiluted] into the cup of his indignation; and he shall be tormented with fire and brimstone in the presence of the holy angels, and in the presence of the Lamb." (Rev. 14:9-10).

Kaye Beach's case demonstrated not only the grounds for Christian objection to such intrusive cards, but the way that the mandating of such cards make it impossible to live without them – precisely as foretold in Revelation 13:17 quoted earlier.

"Whether a biometric ID card in the form of a driver's license or other government-issued form of identification is the mark of the Beast or merely the long arm of Big Brother, the outcome remains the same – ultimate control by the government," said John W. Whitehead, president of the Rutherford Institute. "As Kaye Beach's case makes clear, failing to have a biometric card can render you a non-person for all intents and purposes, with your ability to work, travel, buy, sell, access healthcare, and so on jeopardized."

In January 2008 the ACLU of Maryland also noted the Mark of the Beast nature of the REAL ID: "The law places no limits on potential required uses for REAL IDs. In time, REAL IDs could be required to vote, collect a Social Security check, access Medicaid, open a bank account, go to an Orioles game, or buy a gun. The private sector could begin mandating a REAL ID to perform countless commercial and financial activities, such as renting a DVD or buying car insurance. REAL ID cards would become a necessity, making them de facto national IDs. ... Information captured from each transaction could be used by the government and corporations to develop detailed profiles of people's daily activities."

A remarkably diverse coalition from across the political spectrum have joined together in rare unity to oppose the

REAL ID Act and similar national ID schemes. They include human rights and civil rights organizations such as the ACLU and the Rutherford Institute; the liberal People for the American Way; Christian advocacy groups such as the American Center for Law and Justice, formed by evangelical Pat Robinson; libertarian groups like the Cato Institute and the Libertarian Party; gun rights groups like Gun Owners of America; the editorial page of the Wall Street Journal; the AFL-CIO labor group; immigrant advocacy groups; numerous local and state elected officials; and many, many more.

Religious opposition to REAL ID is not just from out-of-mainstream religious groups. The ACLU noted that opposition to REAL ID included:

> American Friends Service Committee, National
> American Jewish Committee, National
> Catholic Charities, Hawaii
> Catholic Charities, West Virginia
> Catholic Charities Archdiocese of New Orleans
> Catholic Charities Immigration Clinic, Mississippi
> Catholic Conference of Kentucky
> Catholic Immigration Network, Massachusetts
> Catholic Legal Immigration Services, DC
> Catholic Social Services, Alaska
> First Presbyterian Church, North Carolina
> Florida Catholic Conference, Florida
> Interfaith Refugee and Immigration Ministries, IL
> Jesuit Refugee Service, Washington DC
> Jewish Community Action, Minnesota
> Jewish Labor Committee, National
> Jews for Racial and Economic Justice, New York
> Lutheran Social Ministries of New Jersey
> Mennonite Central Committee, Pennsylvania
> Navajo United Methodist Center, New Mexico
> Our Lady of Victory & Sacred Heart Churches, CA

Presbyterian Church (USA), Washington DC
Religious Action Center of Reform Judaism
Sikh Coalition, New York
Union for Reform Judaism, National
United Methodist Children's Home, Alabama
Washington Association of Churches, Washington

Yet, despite years of broad-based action against REAL ID and similar schemes, and some victories, the sinister New World Order agenda of national biometric IDs and internal passports for America citizens – something which, for many millions of people, is viewed as nothing less than the literal Satanic Mark of the Beast – continues to relentlessly re-emerge from Washington and move forward.

Hillary has long favored the REAL ID and other related technology.

As far back as 2003 she declared, while calling for close monitoring of immigrants in the U.S.: "[W]e might have to move towards an ID system even for citizens."

Hillary has also advocated a "no card, no care" National Patient Medical ID card, much like the REAL ID; no American would be able to get health care without it. Such a capability, of course, could also easily be folded into REAL ID-type national identity cards.

And while she was a U.S. senator Hillary voted for the REAL ID Act of 2005 – a bill to create the Mark of the Beast national ID monstrosity that so many Americans of diverse political and spiritual backgrounds fear and oppose.

Hillary = 666

Gematria is the ancient Hebrew method of analyzing numbers, which has roots in Assyro-Babylonian culture. Through the use of gematria we are able to give a numerical value to a word or phrase, and then seek meaning in the resulting number.

One of the most popular and widespread uses of gematria, especially in the West, is as a method to help identify the Antichrist and/or the Great Beast of the Book of Revelations, which, according to Revelation 13:18, "is Six hundred threescore and six" or 666.

And indeed, "To Mega Therion," Greek for "The Great Beast," itself adds up to 666 using the Greek form of gematria.

Of course, simply having a number that can be reduced to 666 is no sign, by itself, that a person is the Antichrist or the Beast. Indeed, many people's names can be expressed in those numbers by various ways.

However, this is important, according to many scholars and theologians, because after the Antichrist is revealed, one of the key proofs that he or she actually is the dreaded figure will be the fact that his or her name can be reduced to 666. This is one of the essential ways that the Beast can be identified.

Thus the Beast must have a name within which can be found 666, regardless of how many other names are also reducible to 666.

Does Hillary's name meet that test?

The New Testament (including Revelation 13:18) was written in Greek. Since Greek has its own personal numerical value, it makes sense to decode the number 666 in Greek.

Using the Greek alphabet, here is what we find:

Hillary = 248
(het=8, lamed=30, resh=200, yod=10)
Rodham = 249
(resh=200, dalet=4, hay=5, mem=40)
Clinton = 169
(koph=20, lamed=30, yod=10, nun=50, tet=9, nun=50)

William = 97
(vav=6, aleph=1, yod=10, lamed=30, yod=10, mem=40)
Jefferson = 400
(yod=10, peh=80, resh=200, samech=60, nun=50)

Clinton = 169

Thus:
Hillary=248 Rodham=249 Clinton=169 = 666
William=97 Jefferson=400 Clinton=169 = 666

So, yes: Hillary – and Bill – both meet that essential biblical requirement to be the Antichrist and/or the Beast.

(Thanks to the website Prophecy Flash for this analysis.)

Hillary: 666... at Birth

Now for another Hillary 666 shocker.

Hillary was born at Edgewater Hospital in Chicago, Illinois.

Zip code: 60660.

Note the three sixes: 666.

She lived until the age of three at 5735 N Winthrop Avenue, Chicago, Illinois.

Zip code: 60660.

Again, three sixes: 666.

Is this just another of the many extraordinary coincidences that seem to dot Hillary's life?

Or... is it something more?

Did Hillary Deliberately "Lose" to Barack Obama in 2008 – to Gain Occult Power?

It is important to note that one need not believe in numerology or the power or meaning of numbers to believe that Hillary herself – and those around her – may strongly believe in such things.

If she is a practicing occultist, as many claim, Hillary may well believe that numbers and symbols possess extraordinary power. Rev. David Bay, expert on the occult, argues that "the Satanist always places great power in numbers, especially the Black Magic Satanist."

Historically, he also argues, the number 33 has been one of the most powerful occult numbers.

Given that, consider the following:

Bill Clinton was the 42nd president of the United States. 4 plus 2 equals 6 – the first number in the 666 Number of the Beast. "6" also consists of two 3s... 33.

Following Clinton was George Bush, 43rd president. When Hillary ran in 2008 against Barack Obama, had she won she would have been U.S. president number 44.

However... if Hillary wins in 2016, she will be... president number 45. 4 plus 5 equals 9: upside down, the first number of the infamous 666.

Perhaps even more powerfully, that 6 is also 3 + 3... another 33, matching exactly Bill Clinton's 33!

Coincidence? Or could her desire to have her rule marked by such auspicious numbers have led Hillary – the most powerful woman in American politics, who seemed virtually destined for the White House in the early days of the 2008 primaries – to purposefully step aside for an unknown freshman senator from Chicago bearing the most unlikely name in the entire history of U.S. presidential politics – in order to later take command of the nation under a far more powerful number?

The Antichrist: Female or Male?

Some researchers claim Hillary cannot be the Antichrist – though she could be deeply involved with the Antichrist – because she is female and the Antichrist must be male.

However, if it turns out to be true – as discussed later – that Hillary is a reptilian shapeshifter, then she could in fact just as easily be male as female.

So she is not disqualified from the possibility of being the Antichrist merely by her gender.

Further, in this day of easy and inexpensive sex changes, it would not be medically difficult for Hillary to switch sexes. A few thousand dollars, some hormone therapy, a snip here and a reconstruction there – and voila! Hillary meets the biblical qualification for the Antichrist. It could even be done in total secret. Indeed, it could have already been done long ago.

From another angle, some observers have commented upon a perceived sexual ambiguity in Hillary. Acclaimed left-wing social critic Camille Paglia has described Hillary as "Hillary the man-woman and bitch goddess."

A "man-woman" – such as portrayed in the terrifying picture of Baphomet, often taken as a portrait of Satan – could indeed arguably fit the biblical requirement for the Antichrist.

Is Hillary the Beast Described in the Book of Revelation?

Perhaps the most famous biblical passage describing the Beast in the end days is Revelation 13:11–17. As we have noted, the two beasts in this passage, that together make up what is called the Beast, are interpreted in various ways. Some see the Beast as a government or union of governments that has embraced evil, like the New World Order, and are in service to Satan and is at war with Christianity; some see the Beast as a servant of the Antichrist or the Antichrists itself. The Beast's emergence is often seen as a sign of the End Times for those who believe in that theology. Whatever the interpretation, the Beast is wicked and of the devil.

It is possible, as we will show, to interpret the Beasts of Revelation 13:11–17 as matching Hillary to a remarkable and eerie degree:

Book of Revelation: "Then I saw another beast that rose out of the earth; it had two horns like a lamb and it spoke like a dragon."

Interpretation: "Two horns" is the classic sign for a victim of adultery, and Bill's sexual adventuring has of course made Hillary such a victim – she figuratively wears the two horns. "It spoke like a dragon" inevitably reminds us that Hillary is believed by millions of American to be, in fact, a giant reptilian being disguised as a human, as described in Chapter 8.

Book of Revelation: "It exercises all the authority of the first beast on its behalf, and it makes the earth and its inhabitants worship the first beast, whose mortal wound had been healed."

Interpretation: As we have seen, many believe the two beasts united form the Beast – just as Bill and Hillary have formed a remarkable and powerful political partnership, perhaps the most powerful such partnership in modern history. The "first beast" could of course be Bill, whose presidency almost received a "mortal wound" when he was impeached for lying to Congress about his sexual relationship with young White House intern Monica Lewinsky in 1995 and 1996, and who received another "mortal wound" with heart troubles beginning in 2004. Hillary, if she becomes president, will of course "exercise all the authority of the first beast" if the first beast is indeed former president Clinton.

Under this interpretation Bill and Hillary together are the beasts in the Book of Revelation, and their political partnership itself of these two "beasts" forms the Beast.

Book of Revelation: "It performs great signs, even making fire come down from heaven to earth in the sight of all…"

Interpretation: During his first campaign for president, Bill told voters that, if he were elected, the nation would "get two for the price of one," referring to the prominent role Hillary would play in the White House. And Hillary, as a close presidential adviser, sometimes described by critics as a "co-president," did indeed participate in making "fire come down from heaven" in numerous military engagements.

Hillary encouraged Bill to launch an attack on Serbian forces in Bosnia in 1994 and Serbia in 1999, forces that in no way threatened the U.S. "I urged him to bomb," she said.

As secretary of state, Clinton supported the disastrous and illegal U.S. bombing and other intervention in Libya, and cackled ghoulishly, almost spasmodically, when told of the death of that country's leader Mohmmar Khadaffi, laughing: "We came, we saw, he died."

As a U.S. senator, Hillary was a prominent advocate of the disastrous Iraq War, which has gutted much of the Middle East and, as of this writing, led to the death of hundreds of thousands of innocent people, a toll still increasing. She also voted on September 6, 2006 against an amendment to the Defense Appropriations Act that would have stopped the U.S. military from using cluster bombs in areas with concentrated civilian populations, a practice that has led to the death or maiming of thousands of utterly innocent children around the globe. To date, nearly 100 countries have banned this practice on humanitarian grounds – but not, in part thanks to Hillary, the U.S.

Award-winning progressive journalist Stephen Lendman noted of Hillary in August 2015: "She endorses using cluster bombs, toxic agents and nuclear weapons in U.S. war theaters. ... She was one of only six Democrat senators opposed to blocking deployment of untested missile defense systems – first-strike weapons entirely for offense."

Liberal icon Ralph Nader has said that "her militarism is absolutely shocking."

Truly, more than most political figures in history, Hillary can accurately be described as one who has literally made "fire come down from heaven" and rain death and dismemberment down upon millions of innocent men, women and children – and she has publicly pledged to do so as she feels necessary, should she become president.

Book of Revelation: "...and by the signs that it is allowed to perform on behalf of the beast, it deceives the inhabitants of earth, telling them to make an image for the beast that had been wounded by the sword and yet lived;"

Interpretation: These "signs" could be interpreted as the activities Hillary and Bill – again, "the beast that had been wounded ... and yet lived" by impeachment, heart ailments, credible accusations of rape and sexual abuse, and so on – perform together in the name of the Clinton Foundation, along with similar joint activities. The Clinton Foundation is the centerpiece of the Clintons' worldwide outreach, certainly a means "to make an image for the beast" if that beast is Bill (and/or Hillary). Furthermore, many of the Clinton Foundation's activities have been criticized in words that almost literally match the biblical description "it deceives the inhabitants of earth." (See Chapters 13 and 16.)

Book of Revelation: "...and it was allowed to give breath to the image of the beast so that the image of the beast could even speak and cause those who would not worship the image of the beast to be killed."

Interpretation: If the beast described here is Bill, it is again obvious that Hillary's political action is giving, and will continue to give, Bill and the statist political ideology he has served all his life, a prominent "voice" in world affairs.

The second part, the disturbing warning that the beast will "cause those who would not worship the image of the beast to be killed" of course brings to mind the controversial claims many have made (see Chapter 16) that there is a long series of unexplained or questionable deaths surrounding the Clintons, and that the Clintons have, and use when needed, a secret private police and espionage operation to harass, threaten and harm their opposition.

Also, of course, we are reminded of wars and conflicts around the globe, where those resisting U.S. control and domination have been harmed or killed by U.S. military and covert actions during the Clinton administration and with Hillary's approval as a U.S. senator and as secretary of state.

Book of Revelation: "Also it causes all, both small and great, both rich and poor, both free and slave, to be marked on the right hand or the forehead, so that no one can buy or sell who does not have the mark, that is, the name of the beast or the number of its name."

Interpretation: As we discussed earlier in this chapter, Hillary has supported a national identification system for U.S. citizens, along with the massive local, state and federal surveillance apparatus to support it. Certainly this would fulfill this verse. If Hillary has her way as president, no one would be able to buy or sell without the "mark of the Beast," that is, without the permission of the authoritarian State – without the permission of President Hillary Clinton.

So we see that, shockingly, a 2000-year-old verse from the Book of Revelation *could almost be a description of Hillary taken directly from a contemporary newspaper.*

CHAPTER EIGHT

Is Hillary a Giant Shapeshifting Reptilian Overlord?

"On its world, the people are people. The leaders are lizards. The people hate the lizards and the lizards rule the people."

"Odd," said Arthur, "I thought you said it was a democracy."

"I did," said Ford. "It is."

"So," said Arthur, hoping he wasn't sounding ridiculously obtuse, "why don't the people get rid of the lizards?"

"It honestly doesn't occur to them," said Ford. "They've all got the vote, so they all pretty much assume that the government they've voted in more or less approximates to the government they want."

"You mean they actually vote for the lizards?"

"Oh yes," said Ford with a shrug, "of course."

"But," said Arthur, going for the big one again, "why?"

"Because if they didn't vote for a lizard," said Ford, "the wrong lizard might get in."

– from So Long and Thanks for All the Fish
by Douglas Adams

"Hillary is a strange little person. ... She's like a lizard sliding off a rock." – feminist and author Germaine Greer
(The UK Telegraph, Dec. 16th 2000)

Prime Minister Assures Public He's Not a Shapeshifting Reptilian Alien, Honest

In mid-February 2014, New Zealand's Prime Minister John Key held what must surely be one of the strangest press conferences in history.

He assured a gathering of print and broadcast journalists that he was not a shapeshifting reptilian being conspiring to conquer the planet.

Key made the declaration after a citizen filed an Open Information Act (OIA) request that Key prove he wasn't a "shapeshifting reptilian alien ushering humanity towards enslavement."

However, Key admitted he couldn't offer concrete proof that he was not such a creature. Voters, he said, would have to rely on his... word. (Something growing numbers of voters are increasingly reluctant to do when it comes to politicians.)

Many, in fact, found Key's "disavowal" to be suspiciously equivocal.

"To the best of my knowledge, no," was his murky response to whether he was a shapeshifting reptilian being.

"I've taken the unusual step of not only seeing a doctor but a vet, and both have confirmed I'm not a reptile," he added.

(This part of his statement seems dubious; this author has found no reports in public records of such a doctor or veterinarian exam; the latter seems especially unlikely.)

"So I'm certainly not a reptile. I've never been in a spaceship, never been in outer space, and my tongue's not overly long either."

(Which is, of course, "exactly what lizard people would say," noted the snarky news commentary site Wonkette.)

In the same way, the government's official letter of reply to the OIA request didn't actually refute the charge, either. It merely stated that "the document alleged to contain the information requested does not exist or cannot be found."

Which sounds like a classic "non-denial denial," a political tool nicely defined by the London Sunday Times as "an on-the-record statement, usually made by a politician, repudiating a journalist's story, but in such a way as to leave open the possibility that it is actually true."

While Key clumsily tried to pass the question off as a joke, for increasing numbers of people around the world – including millions of Americans – it is no joking matter.

And Key is not the first prominent politician to be asked this.

In February 2011, on the "Opie and Anthony" radio show, the brilliant and incisive comedian Louis C.K. bluntly asked former U.S. Secretary of Defense Donald Rumsfeld – several times – a question that millions of Americans were also wondering about:

Was it true that Rumsfeld and U.S. Vice President Dick Cheney were actually lizard people, reptilian beings who delighted in the taste of human flesh?

Remarkably, Rumsfeld did not deny it; he simply refused to answer.

Louis C.K. interpreted Rumsfeld's refusal to answer as... an admission that the charges were true.

Obviously, it is unlikely that a politician who actually was a shapeshifting blood-drinking reptilian, part of a vast cabal of similar creatures exploiting the human race for centuries, would simply admit this offhandedly on a late-night radio or TV show.

Yet, as the reptilian hypothesis gains more and more millions of followers around the world, politicians and other elites can expect to be faced with more such questioning in the future.

And perhaps... shocking revelations are ahead.

Facebook Founder: "I Am Not a Lizard"

Facebook CEO Mark Zuckerberg is one of the wealthiest and most influential people on the planet. He has a net worth of over $50 billion and controls the most powerful social media platform on earth – one which he says will grow until "The Internet will be Facebook."

If Facebook were a country it would have the world's largest population after China and India.

Indeed, Peter Rojas, renowned tech journalist and entrepreneur, said this in June 2016 concerning Facebook's incredible political power:

"Facebook is a...platform through which an enormous percentage of the world's media now flows, whether you like it or not. ...the truth is that if Mark Zuckerberg wanted to tilt this election to Donald Trump or Hillary Clinton, he could do that. ...

"Obviously it's in their interest not to expose or be very up front about the power they have, but I don't think the rest of us should stick our heads in the sand and pretend that they don't."

Zuckerberg's extraordinary wealth and power have brought him the close attention of politicians and ruling elites around the world.

On Jun. 14, 2016, at the start of his first-ever live Q&A on Facebook, Zuckerberg was prepared to answer a host of questions about the Internet, Facebook, futurism, and other high tech topics.

But startlingly, one of the first questions he was asked was: "Mark, are the allegations true that you are secretly a lizard?"

"I'm going to have to go with 'No' on that," he said. "I am not a lizard."

Then, noted the Washington Post: "The Facebook founder paused to lick his lips."

Many found Zuckerberg's denial unconvincing. "That's exactly what a lizard person would say," one person tweeted.

The rumors that he is a shapeshifting reptilian have dogged Zuckerberg for many years. His photo on the cover of TIME magazine in 2010, when he was named TIME's Man of the Year, was described by many as looking distinctly reptilian. People called attention in particular to what seemed to be glowing green reptilian eyes and olive-tinted skin.

"Mark Zuckerberg looks like lizard in human skin," critic Luis Prada wrote of the cover. "If he wanted to, he could rip the feeble human meat off his skull and reveal his true self..."

Billionaire Facebook co-founder and former Zuckerberg roommate Dustin Moskovitz was one of the biggest donors of the 2016 Hillary campaign, giving as of early October 2016 a whopping $28 million.

Reptilians: Millions of Americans Believe

Why are such seemingly outlandish questions being asked? And why would politicians and other elites bother to respond, even if just to dismiss it as a joke?

In 2010 Jan Frel, editor-at-large and associate publisher at the left-wing news source Alternet, noted that "perhaps millions ... of people ... adhere to an overlapping series of modern-day conspiracy theories sharing a central thesis: Lizard-like aliens from outer space inhabit human bodies and control the human race."

A remarkable March 2013 poll conducted by the highly respected Public Policy Polling (PPP) asked 1,247 registered American voters this question:

> "Do you believe that shapeshifting reptilian people control our world by taking on human form and gaining political power to manipulate our societies, or not?"

The results:

4%   Do
....
88%   Do not
....
7%   Not sure
....

According to calculations by the Atlantic magazine, that's a whopping 12,556,562 potential American voters who believe in the reptilian conspiracy – and another 22 million or so more who are "not sure" whether or not it is true.

Somewhat more Republicans and independents are inclined to support the theory than Democrats, but one suspects, given the enormous stakes, that the issue crosses party lines – that few Democrats who believe in the reptilian theory would support a Democratic candidate they believed was a shapeshifting reptile.

The Hillary camp must surely be aware of this huge number of potential voters – and they also must know that it is far more than enough to decide an election.

Since 1824, when the popular vote for the presidency was first recorded, fully 14 of the 47 presidential elections in American history have been won by margins of 4 percent or less. That's almost one in three elections.

Now assume that just half of the 7 percent of voters who are undecided on the reptilian issue also decide to vote against Hillary out of fear she might be a reptilian. That would make 7.5 percent of the electorate. A whopping 22 of the 47 presidential elections since 1824 have been won by that margin. That's nearly HALF.

Plus, that poll was taken in 2013. Awareness of the reptilian conspiracy has grown enormously since then. No doubt the number of believers would be significantly higher – perhaps by many millions – if another survey was taken today.

Clearly, then, the growing belief in the reptilian conspiracy has the potential to cost Hillary millions of votes – more than enough to keep her out of the White House.

With her vast resources, she and her staff surely know this. Why, then, is Hillary not confronting it head-on? Why is she keeping silent about charges that would amount to the biggest political scandal in world history, charges that make the familiar allegations of wrongdoing in Benghazi or email skullduggery seem meaningless in comparison – charges that could well cost her the election?

After all, a blood test and a physical exam, conducted by unbiased doctors and scientists, with full transparency, could dismiss these charges.

The reptilian theory could in fact be the deciding factor in the 2016 presidential election.

Hillary and the "Penis of the Dragon"

On July 7, 1999 Hillary formally announced her intention of running for the U.S. Senate from New York.

Her announcement was made at a place called Pindars Corners in Delaware County in upstate New York, often described as a "rural hamlet."

Pindars Corners was the site of a farm owned by the retiring senator, the popular Daniel Patrick Moynihan.

So that obviously explains the choice of tiny Pindars Corner as the launching site for her U.S. senate campaign, doesn't it?

Maybe.

Or maybe not.

Consider this. "Pindar" is, according to some reptilian researchers, the code name of the highest-ranking reptilian shapeshifter on Earth – a hideous and utterly ruthless blood-gorged creature whose mere name strikes terror amongst all other reptilians and conspiracy operatives.

Coincidence? If so it would be an extraordinary one.

The use of the name Pindar at the start of her campaign might have been a signal from Hillary – if she herself is a high-ranking member of the secret ruling world elite.

What would that signal mean? Perhaps it was intended as a tribute, an acknowledgment of the great power of this terrible creature. Or perhaps it was a sign to other conspiracy members that Pindar himself had blessed her campaign and political aspirations.

We do not know. But many researchers of the occult and conspiracies believe that members of the conspiratorial power elite love to play games on the unsuspecting, and to reveal themselves to those who are in the know, via cryptic symbols and phrases whose meaning they understand but the rest of us do not.

Hillary's use of "Pindar" in her campaign may well have been one of those signals.

According to reptoid researcher and author **Dee Finney (who draws in part on the work of David Icke)**: "The leader of the Earth's Illuminati is called the 'Pindar.' ... The title, Pindar, is an abbreviated term for 'Pinnacle of the Draco,' also known as the 'Penis of the Dragon.' Symbolically, this represents the top of power, control, creation, penetration, expansion, invasion, and fear. The holder of this rank reports to the purebred reptilian leader in the inner Earth."

David Icke, today's best-known advocate of the millennia-old reptilian theory, writes of Pindar in his controversial book The Biggest Secret:

"Pindar attends the major Satanic ceremonies in Europe and then flies to California for the rituals there. ... Pindar, the 'Marquis de Libeaux' travels in a white limousine (a 'code-white' is a code understood by judges, police, the military etc. and it means: look the other way, or do not prosecute this person).

" ...the Queen [of England] makes cruel remarks about lesser initiates, but is afraid of the man code-named 'Pindar.'.. who is higher than her in Satanic rank. Pindar, apparently, bears a resemblance to Prince Charles."

Icke even speculates that Pindar may be the real father of Prince Charles – and further, that Princess Diana's death may in fact have been a murder, not an accident, and that Diana may have been pregnant – with Pindar's child.

If so, the deaths of Princess Diana and her child was actually a reptoid ceremonial sacrifice with great occult significance.

TIME Magazine on the Reptilian Conspiracy

No less than TIME magazine describes the reptilian theory as one of "the world's 10 most enduring conspiracy theories." Their summary of it begins this way:

"The Reptilian Elite: They are among us. Blood-drinking, flesh-eating, shapeshifting extraterrestrial reptilian humanoids with only one objective in their cold-blooded little heads: to enslave the human race.

"They are our leaders, our corporate executives, our beloved Oscar-winning actors and Grammy-winning singers, and they're responsible for the Holocaust, the Oklahoma City bombings and the 9/11 attacks...

"[A]ccording to former BBC sports reporter David Icke, who became the poster human for the theory in 1998 after publishing his first book, The Biggest Secret...they count among their number Queen Elizabeth, George W. Bush, Henry Kissinger, Bill and Hillary Clinton and Bob Hope. ...

"Icke even claims that the lizards are behind secret societies like the Freemasons and the Illuminati."

Similarly, academicians Tyson Lewis and Richard Kahn in their paper "The Reptoid Hypothesis: Utopian and Dystopian Representational Motifs in David Icke's Alien Conspiracy Theory" note that the reptilian hypothesis is "a major counter-cultural trend that is indeed global in proportions."

The Secret History of Reptilians and Humans

Strange as it may seem at first encounter, the concept that we are secretly ruled by reptilian beings is one that is found worldwide and throughout human history. Cultures that existed thousands of years BC have left us strange tales and images of humanoid reptilians.

Mesopotamia, in what is today known as Iraq, is often called "the cradle of civilization" because it is one of the oldest known places where cities and agrarian societies existed. In the early twentieth century archaeologists digging there, exploring sites of the Ubaidian culture (4000-5500 BC), were stunned to find 7,000 year-old statues of what are unquestionably *reptilian beings* engaged in ordinary activities. One, for example, is a humanoid reptilian suckling reptilian young. Other statues show reptilian beings holding scepters or staffs, indicating rulership. These astonishing statues were found alongside images of humans in similar mundane activities – leading some researchers bold enough to step out of the bounds of conventional thinking to ponder the inevitable question: Could two races – reptilian and human – have lived side-by-side?

Virtually every section of the world has ancient tales of reptilians, often ruling humans as gods, often from other worlds or dimensions, often demanding human sacrifices and human mates, often living in complex underground dwellings and tunnels that connect the globe.

The literature is vast, and can only be touched on here. Religious examples include:

- Satan is described as a cunning reptile from the very first book of the Bible to the last. In the Genesis story of Adam and Eve the serpent is a being part reptile and part human, sometimes depicted with legs, who speaks and interacts with the first humans, corrupting and manipulating them. Later in the Bible, and throughout popular Christian belief, Satan the serpent-being attempts to dominate human culture telepathically and physically from his underground kingdom.

- In Revelation 12:7-9 the New Testament describes Satan as reptilian: "the great dragon... that old serpent, called the devil, and Satan, which deceiveth the whole world..."

- Reptilian beings working with demons and the Antichrist are also predicted in the Book of Revelation 16:12-21:

"Then I saw three evil spirits that looked like frogs; they came out of the mouth of the dragon, out of the mouth of the beast and out of the mouth of the false prophet. They are spirits of demons performing miraculous signs, and they go out to the kings of the whole world, to gather them for the battle on the great day of God Almighty... Then they gathered the kings together to the place that in Hebrew is called Armageddon." (Elsewhere in this book we explore claims that Hillary is possessed by demons and/or is the Antichrist.)

- The Nephilimin in the Old Testament are believed by some theologians to be fallen angels who descended to earth and mated with humans. (Being fallen angels one might well be viewed as reptilians, just as the serpent in the Garden of Eden, and one might further speculate that they share the underground kingdom of Satan.) They subsequently preyed upon humans and lured them into sin. The Jerusalem Bible, a widely used and respected 20th-century translation of the Bible, suggests the Nephilim story is an "anecdote of a superhuman race." (We should note that there is considerable disagreement among theologians as to what the Nephilimin are.)

- The controversial doctrine known as the "Serpent Seed," a part of non-mainstream Christianity for centuries, and still adhered to today by some small sects, though considered heresy by the Catholic and Eastern Orthodox churches and most Protestants, takes this story further, maintaining that the serpent in the Garden of Eden mated with Eve, creating an alternative race with reptilian traits intermixed with human ones.

  The Anunnaki were deities in ancient Mesopotamian (Sumerian, Akkadian, Assyrian, and Babylonian) cultures. They were believed to have come from the sky to live on earth and in vast tunnels underground. Some researchers say they were reptoid beings – the same beings called Nephilimin in the Bible.

- The Mesoamerican god Quetzalcoatl was a feathered lizard.

- Tlaloc, a major deity in Aztec religion, had a mixture of human and reptilian features and lived underground.

- Hindu mythology features the Nāga, reptilians who

live underground, emerging to interact with humans.

- Japanese mythology and folklore feature reptilian humanoids the Kappa.

- Chinese legends are filled with stories of dragons who traveled from earth to the sky. The Four Dragon Kings, believed to rule the ocean and weather, could shapeshift from human to reptile. Fu Xi, part human, part serpent, was believed to have brought tools and culture to primitive man.

- Egyptian and Greek legends feature many reptilian beings and refer to serpent/reptilian gods who lived underground.

- The ancient British told of a reptilian god named Hu, known as "The Dragon-Ruler of the World."

- Hopi Indians worshiped a plumed serpent god known as Baholinkonga and shared legends and tales of shapeshifting reptilian beings, underground cities and vast tunnels.

- The serpent spirit Damballa, "The Great Master," is one of the most important of all voodoo loa (gods). Damballa is known as "the Sky Father" (a reference to extraterrestrial origin?) and is credited as being the creator of all life.

Over and over again certain themes appear in these myths, legends and beliefs that are found in cultures around the world spanning thousands of years. The reptilian beings are described as having come from the stars or the heavens. They are depicted as possessors of extraordinary power and knowledge. Sometimes they demand human sacrifice. Sometimes they kidnap humans and interbreed with them. They are often credited with imparting wisdom. Sometimes they are described as creators of the human race.

Another constant theme is the existence of vast underground realms and tunnels, occupied and used by various entities, including reptilians. A few of the names we may be familiar with: Hades, Hell, Tartarus, Xibalba, Agharta, Duat, and Patala. The great philosopher Plato, founding father of Western philosophy, believed the earth contained vast populated hollow regions connected via "tunnels both broad and narrow in the interior."

The astounding consistency in these ancient stories that span centuries and continents make many researchers wonder if they are not based on some underlying collective truth about the origins and early days of man.

But what about more recent times? We find that the same beliefs still exist today. A few examples:

- The American occultist and prolific author Dr. Maurice Doreal, founder in 1929 of the Brotherhood of the White Temple, claimed to have visited Tibet astrally after World War I, where he spent eight years studying with the Dalai Lama and other adepts and mystics. Interviewed by such respected media as United Press and Time and Life magazines, Dr. Doreal claimed to have traveled in vast tunnels criss-crossing the earth, accompanied by various spiritual entities and humans, and to be in touch with the Great White Lodge of Masters and other occult teachers and leaders who named him their "Supreme Voice." Dr. Doreal was heavily influenced by the teachings of Blavatsky student Annie Besant, still a very influential figure in occultism and world politics to this day. (More on Besant can be found in Chapter 13)

    Like so many others, Dr. Doreal wrote of an ancient war between humans and a "Serpent Race" ... with "bodies like man, but... heads... like a great snake and... bodies faintly scaled." These reptilians had hypnotic powers, could shapeshift into human form, and, he warns, "gradually, they and the men who called them took over the control of the nations." These reptilians, he warned, are still among us today.

- In 1933 mining engineer G. Warren Shufelt was surveying the Los Angeles area for valuable mineral deposits, using a radio-based x-ray scanner he had devised. To his amazement his device indicated a series of tunnels underneath Los Angeles, threading through the city and leading outwards. Further, the underground city was laid out in the shape of... a lizard.

On February 21, 1933, the County Board of Supervisors approved a contract with Shufelt to dig for the tunnels and the large gold deposits, relics and other treasures Shufelt believed were buried there.

The front page of the January 29, 1934 Los Angeles Times featured this explosive headline: "LIZARD PEOPLE'S CATACOMB CITY HUNTED: Engineer Sinks Shaft Under Fort Moore Hill to Find Maze of Tunnels and Priceless Treasures of Legendary Inhabitants."

The article began: "Busy Los Angeles, although little realizing it in the hustle and bustle of modern existence, stands above a lost city of catacombs filled with incalculable treasure and imperishable records of a race of humans further advanced intellectually than the highest type of present day peoples, in the belief of G. Warren Shufelt, geophysicist mining engineer now engaged in an attempt to wrest from the lost city deep in the earth below Fort Moore Hill the secrets of the Lizard People of legendary fame in the medicine lodges of the American Indian."

But in 1934 the project was abruptly halted by the city, for unclear reasons. (Safety concerns were cited by some, but there was a lot of similar construction digging in the same area that went on without concern.) The shaft were filled in. G. Warren Shufelt apparently disappeared; this author could find no further mention of him. Stories of strange incidents in the area persist to this day.

- Beginning in the early 1950s the American Buddhist monk and ufologist Dr. Robert Ernst Dickhoff, described in his bio as "Ph.D., D.D., Mystic, Adept, Mason of High Degree" and founder of the American Buddhist Society and Fellowship as well as the Buddhist UFO Research Center, wrote about hordes of malevolent alien man-eating reptilians infesting Earth, who can shapeshift into human form, who interact with humans, who practice "black magic and hypnotism" to control humans, and who travel throughout the earth in underground tunnels – all now-familiar themes in the reptilian conspiracy theory.

In his prescient and bleak early ufology classics Agharta: The Subterranean World (1951) and Behold ... The Venus Garuda (1968) Dr. Dickhoff writes of an ancient race of alien "serpents masquerading in convenient human bodies" who manipulated earthly politicians and religious leaders via violence and mind control. Dr. Dickhoff examined relics, statues, paintings and other artifacts from across centuries, continents, and civilizations, along with myths and religious origin stories, and concluded that, from the earliest days of the human race, humans have been essentially cattle for malevolent depraved alien winged reptilian beings.

He identifies them as "Garuda ... monstrous cannibalistic predators ... humanoid creatures resembling serpents and crocodiles, having human hands and feet ... of a higher order of intelligence than earthlings..." To the hideous Garuda, humans are mere "food supply ... meat machines ... herds of cattle." Human flesh is "the supreme ingredient in gourmet Garuda stew." Humans are captured and killed on earth to feed the Garuda; some are even kidnapped and taken into other worlds, where they are penned and raised like cattle, awaiting "stewpots and skillets of an unearthly sort." Grim stuff indeed.

Dickhoff further argues that Garuda agents have shapeshifted to take the form of humans, assuming leadership roles in religious and social affairs and intervening violently in human affairs throughout history. He outlines various ways the Garuda have influenced and corrupted human philosophies and religion to further manipulate humans.

On April 21, 1974 Dr. Dickhoff's views reached a startled mass American audience when he was the subject of the lead front page story in the national weekly newspaper The National News Extra. The headline, in large bold end-of-the-world capital letters, dramatically summarized Dickhoff's dark views in classic tabloid style:

HUMANS ARE BEING CANNED AND EATEN BY CREATURES FROM OUTER SPACE
A Top Scientist's Blood-Curdling Theory

- Bestselling writer and pioneer ufologist and Fortean John Keel in his 1968 classic Our Haunted World wrote:

  "...The parahuman Serpent People of the past are still among us. They were probably worshiped by the builders of Stonehenge and the forgotten ridge-making cultures of South America. ...

  "In some parts of the world the Serpent People successfully posed as gods... Whole civilizations based upon the worship of these false gods rose and fell in Asia, Africa, and South America. ... The human race would supply the pawns. ... Once an individual had committed himself, he opened a door so that an indefinable something could actually enter his body and exercise some control over his subconscious mind."

- Ufology (the science of the study of UFOs) is filled with reports of encounters with reptilian beings. In his book Extraordinary Encounters, UFO expert and former Fate Magazine editor Jerome Clark writes that reptilian beings "figure in a number of [UFO] abduction and contact reports." Indeed, anyone who digs into the vast and growing UFO witness and contactee literature will find copious reports of reptilian beings.

- The MUFON UFO Journal is published by the Mutual UFO Network, one of the oldest, largest and most respected civilian UFO-investigative organizations in the world. In its April 1993 issue respected UFO investigator John Carpenter summarized years of studying tales of human encounters with reptilians:

"Typically, these reptilian creatures are reported to be about six to seven feet tall, upright, with lizard-like scales, greenish to brownish in color with claw-like, four-fingered webbed hands.... Their faces are said to be a cross between a human and a snake, with a central ridge coming down from the top of the head to the snout. Adding to their serpent-like appearance are their eyes which have vertical slits in their pupils and golden irises. *Perhaps the most frightening and most controversial part of these stories are claims that the creatures occasionally are reported to have sex with abductees.*" (Emphasis added.)

- Other leading UFO researchers – including world-renowned veterans like Budd Hopkins, Linda Moulton Howe, Yvonne Smith, and more – report similar accounts, including terrifying stories of reptilians using advanced technology, mind control, and performing horrific and terrifying medical procedures. (See Chapter 9 for more on government mind control, which remarkably parallels and reinforces such stories as these.)

Mainstream Science Offers Evidence Backing the Reptilian Theory

Scientists estimate dinosaurs walked the earth for 165 million years – far longer than modern humans, believed by scientists to have appeared a mere 200,000 years ago, and whose civilizations have existed for only a fleeting 6,000 years. The dinosaurs adapted remarkably to changing circumstances. Many scientists now think that dinosaurs, rather than going extinct, evolved into birds.

The idea that dinosaurs could have evolved into birds – creatures of flight, covered with feathers, far smaller than most dinosaurs – is arguably far less likely than the theory that they could have evolved into a humanoid form and interacted with human beings. The many millions of years that dinosaurs trod the globe certainly gave them a lot of time for adaptive evolution – perhaps even time to evolve shapeshifting abilities in reaction to changing conditions.

- Evolutionary scientists generally believe that man evolved from reptiles. It is theorized that roughly 250 million years ago, after the appearance of the first reptiles, reptile evolution continued along two separate paths. From one branch, the Sauropsids, came today's reptiles and birds. From the other branch, Synapsida, came mammals – including humans. We have reptilian traces in our very genes. It takes no great leap of imagination to conceive of this process also leading to the evolution of the kinds of reptilian beings found in all the beliefs and religions of past cultures worldwide.

- In the development of the human fetus it runs through stages that are startlingly like fish, reptiles and non-primate mammals before it becomes fully human in appearance.

- In his 1990 book The Triune Brain in Evolution, award-winning physician and neuroscientist Paul D. MacLean of the Yale Medical School and the National Institute of Mental Health proposed a model of the brain that dubbed the basal ganglia "the reptilian complex," or the "R-complex" or "reptilian brain." The reptile brain – which includes the same structures found in the brains of reptiles, the brain stem and the cerebellum – controls such fundamental functions as heart rate, breathing, body temperature and the "fight or flight" survival instincts. MacLean argued this reptilian brain is responsible for instinctive behaviors involved in aggression, dominance, mating and territoriality. MacLean's argument received enormous publicity via Carl Sagan's Pulitzer Prize-winning 1977 book The Dragons of Eden, and, though controversial in part, is believed by many scientists today.

- "Could 'advanced' dinosaurs rule other planets?" was the startling title of a press release announcing a 2012 research paper by the eminent National Medal of Science-winning Columbia University chemist Ronald Breslow. The paper was accepted by the peer-reviewed Journal of the American Chemical Society. Dr. Breslow's primary subject was the evolution of amino acids on earth. But he also noted the possibility that advanced reptilian civilizations, evolving from different amino acids, might exist on other planets:

"An implication from this work is that elsewhere in the universe there could be life forms based on D amino acids and L sugars... Such life forms could well be advanced versions of dinosaurs," Dr. Breslow noted, while warning that "we would be better off not meeting them." The paper received funding from the National Science Foundation.

After being accepted by the Journal of the American Chemical Society and receiving enormous pre-publication publicity, the paper was abruptly withdrawn, on allegations that Dr. Breslow had "plagiarized" his own earlier work in the article. Some wondered if this was merely a cover for suppression of evidence supporting the reptilian hypothesis.

The UK Daily Mail headlined: "Study suggests alien worlds could be full of super-intelligent dinosaurs."

Of course, it does not take much extrapolation to see the additional possibility that such advanced ancient reptilian extraterrestrial races may have migrated to earth eons ago to mingle with, and rule, the primitive humans they encountered.

In 1982 renowned Canadian geologist/paleontologist Dale A. Russell, then curator of vertebrate fossils at the National Museum of Canada in Ottawa, ignited a scientific controversy when he argued that a species of smaller bird-like dinosaur called Troodon, believed to have perished about 65 million years ago in the Cretaceous–Paleogene extinction event – long before the emergence of humans – could have, if it had survived that extinction, evolved into "Dinosauroids," intelligent beings with bodies surprisingly similar to humans. Dr. Russell noted that the brain weight of Troodon had already evolved several times that of other dinosaurs, and – had Troodon evolution continued – brain size could have evolved to that of a human. Drawings and models of an evolved Troodon based upon Dr. Russell's descriptions were disturbingly humanoid, essentially matching the reptoid beings seen in UFOs, folklore, and religion, cited above. Arguments over Dr. Russell's controversial theory still rage today. A model of the evolved Troodon is on display at the acclaimed Dinosaur Museum of Dorchester, Dorset, England.

World-famous and acclaimed mainstream scientists who have speculated on aspects of the argument that dinosaurs might have evolved into intelligent humanoid beings had they not been (allegedly) wiped out 65 million years ago include:

- the above-mentioned Dale A. Russell;

- R. Séguin of the National Museums of Canada, who worked closely with Russell;

- award-winning paleontologist and author Simon Conway Morris of Cambridge University, who has argued that without the extinction of dinosaurs, bipedal intelligent humanoid dinosaurs would have been a sort of evolutionary inevitability, and might well have evolved alongside humans and interacted with them;

- renowned evolutionary biologist and author Richard Dawkins, who says Simon Conway Morris's argument for the theoretical possibility of a serpent race "is not to be dismissed";

- American psychologist Harry Jerison who, in 1978, gave a speech before the American Psychological Association entitled "Smart dinosaurs and comparative psychology," in which he argued that Dromiceiomimus theoretically could have evolved into a species with human intelligence.

- David Bruce Norman is a British paleontologist and Director of Cambridge University's Sedgwick Museum. A startling illustration of a walking reptilian appears in his acclaimed 1985 Illustrated Encyclopedia of Dinosaurs. A caption notes the evolutionary changes that might produce such a reptilian and observes that "given the right conditions, such changes would be quite feasible."

- the renowned Carl Sagan, who in his 1977 bestselling book The Dragons of Eden: Speculations on the Evolution of Human Intelligence, mused about the possibility, absent extinction, of the agile, fast-moving Saurornithoides dinosaurs evolving into more intelligent forms.

Sagan also noted *the reptilian nature of much of the political activity of those who rule us today*, and one can extrapolate from this why reptilian rule is so dangerous and antithetical to human freedom. Wrote Sagan:

"MacLean [see paragraph on Paul D. MacLean just above] has shown that the R-complex plays an important role in aggressive behavior, territoriality, ritual and the establishment of social hierarchies. Despite occasional welcome exceptions, this seems to me to characterize a great deal of modern human bureaucratic and political behavior. I do not mean that the neocortex is not functioning at all in an American political convention or a meeting of the Supreme Soviet; after all, a great deal of the communication at such rituals is verbal and therefore neocortical. But it is striking how much of our actual behavior – as distinguished from what we say and think about it – can be described in reptilian terms. We speak commonly of a 'cold-blooded' killer. Machiavelli's advice to his Prince was 'knowingly to adopt the beast.' ...

"I want to be very clear about the social implications of the contention that reptilian brains influence human actions. If bureaucratic behavior is controlled at its core by the R-complex, does this mean there is no hope for the human future? ... Neuro-anatomy, political history, and introspection all offer evidence that human beings are quite capable of resisting the urge to surrender to every impulse of the reptilian brain. There is no way, for example, in which the Bill of Rights of the U.S. Constitution could have been recorded, much less conceived, by the R-complex. ... But if the triune brain is an accurate model of how human beings function, it does no good whatever to ignore the reptilian component of human nature, particularly our ritualistic and hierarchical behavior. On the contrary, the model may help us to understand what human beings are about."

Especially, one might add, our political rulers – including presidential candidates.

Including Hillary Clinton.

This list of scientists and great thinkers who have wrestled with subjects related to the reptilian controversy could no doubt be expanded.

Of course, this is not to say that these distinguished mainstream scientists endorse the increasingly popular reptilian overlord conspiracy theories. Rather, it illustrates that, in recent years, the notion of intelligent humanoid reptilians has been found worthy of, at the least, serious speculation by some of the world's premiere scientists.

Thus, it hardly requires a leap of imagination to speculate that some such evolution actually occurred and that, as the innumerable ancient myths and tales found worldwide indicate, reptilian overlords existed and indeed still walk among us today, largely unseen yet exerting tremendous control over us, their far younger, far less evolved, bipedal mammalian latecomers to Earth.

It remains a theory, yes – but perhaps far more compelling and intriguing than it might seem upon first encounter.

Science Proves Shapeshifting Is Real

Stores of shapeshifting – the ability of humans to transform into other animals, insects, even plants and inanimate objects, as well as into creatures which share human and nonhuman animal traits – can be found in the stories, myths, and legends of virtually all lands and all times.

Books could be filled with examples. Indeed, we find it in the Iliad, among the very oldest known works of Western literature (approx. 8th-century BC), and far earlier than that in the Epic of Gilgamesh, the great Mesopotamia poem (circa 2100 BC) widely regarded as the earliest surviving literary masterpiece. Even the ancient cave drawings of Les Trois Frères, in France, dated approximately 13,000 BC, include depictions of what experts believe may be shapeshifting.

Shapeshifting has long been viewed as more than just fiction, however. In all lands at one time or another it has been believed that some people had the ability to change into animals and other creatures. This is found in many beliefs of totemism, shamanism, paganism and other religious and spiritual traditions and practices, and the belief still persists to this day.

Indeed, until a few centuries ago it was widely believed in Europe and America that, for example, witches were believed to be able to turn into cats; human lycanthropes into wolves; those cursed by the vampire into bats and snakes; and so on.

It is only in our supposedly enlightened modern age that such beliefs have been largely abandoned. The stories, however, persist, in literature and folk wisdom (often derided as "superstition"), and the more one explores the vast literature of the unexplained, the more one cannot help but wonder if, in our great and admirable desire to understand the world around us in terms of carefully defined scientific laws, we moderns may have dismissed some matters of extraordinary importance merely because they did not fit into our admittedly incomplete mental map of how the world and universe work.

Even modern science admits that shapeshifting of a sort is real and rooted in some way in the human psyche. We observed earlier that the human fetus runs through stages of development that resemble fish, reptiles and non-primate mammals.

An unknown number of people experience what psychologists call "species dysphoria," basically the feeling that one's body belongs to a different species than the species they were assigned at birth. Some report they feel the presence of phantom wings or claws; some react by dressing as animals or walking on all fours or speaking with growls and other animal sounds. Is it possible that such feelings are genuine urgings, understood by earlier human societies but now deemed illogical and pathological by modern psychiatry, much as homosexuality and gender dysphoria were treated as diseases by the psychiatric profession until recently?

Then there is the so-called "furry community," a fast-growing subculture of thousands of men and women who strongly identify with anthropomorphic animals – such as those found in cartoons, comics, and fantasy films – that show human personalities, intelligence, characteristics, and are sometimes able to speak or otherwise communicate, walk on two legs, and wear clothes. Examples of such anthropomorphic creatures in popular culture might include Bugs Bunny, Mickey Mouse and Scooby Doo. Many furries create their own anthropomorphic alter-egos that uniquely reflect their idealized furry selves. There is even furry porn, including photos, drawings and thousands of films, both animated and live-action.

Furries wear costumes that allow them to become their representative animals, and meet one another at conventions around the world. Many of them fervently hope that genetic engineering or other advances in science will in the very near future allow them to fully become the half-human, half-beast creatures their costumes picture and that their brains tell them are their true selves.

A 2008 survey found that fully 46 percent of furries surveyed answered "yes" to the question "Do you consider yourself to be less than 100 percent human?" Forty-one percent answered "yes" to the question "If you could become 0 percent human, would you?" Fully 29 percent said they felt they were "non-human species trapped in a human body." Is the longing of the furries another manifestation of a strong animal-human shapeshifting link that modern science refuses to acknowledge?

Even more importantly, science tells us that shapeshifting is found throughout the natural world. The ability of an organism to change its phenotype in response to changes in the environment is known as "phenotypic plasticity."

The recently discovered mutable rainfrog, a species of frog in Ecuador, can actually change its skin texture from spiny to smooth – a shapeshifting vertebrate.

The mimic octopus shows the remarkable ability to imitate sea snakes, jellyfish, stingrays, giant crabs, seashells, lion fish, and flatfish, and to make further shapes that seem to have no earthly correlation.

Cuttlefish are known as the "chameleons of the sea" because of their amazing shapeshifting abilities. They can instantly alter their skin color, pattern, and skin shape and texture. They can even disguise themselves as floating vegetation or the rocks, sand, and algae at the ocean floor. They use this power to capture prey, communicate with other cuttlefish, and frighten off predators. They can even rapidly change colors in a rippling pattern in order to hypnotize prey into immobility.

Still other creatures use various means to transform themselves dramatically when threatened. When threatened, a cat will instantly dramatically fluff out its tail, turn sideways and arch its back to seem far larger, and hop forward in a menacing and un-catlike manner, all to make itself appear to be a different and more formidable creature. Other animals dramatically change appearance by abruptly swelling in size when threatened, such as the puff adder, apes, howler monkeys and the porcupine fish. The adder, various eye-moths, and other creatures when threatened reveal what appear to be huge eyes patterned on their backs.

And then there are the strange, yet compelling eyewitness stories of werewolves and other shapeshifters – not from centuries past, but in modern America.

Author, cryptozoologist and newspaper reporter Linda S. Godfrey has been tracking such tales since the early 1990s. In her remarkable book Real Wolfmen she presents a catalog of bizarre yet compelling first-person accounts of unexpected and often terrifying encounters with strange dog- or wolf-like creatures – "anomalous, upright canids" – who sometime leave paw prints, and who resemble nothing less than the traditional werewolves that medieval Europeans and early Native Americans alike believed in and feared. It turns out that all across America there are tales of these creatures who can walk upright, interact with humans – and suddenly disappear.

There is a little-known but vast literature of similar strange and anomalous eye-witness reports that, while unproven, make, when considered together, a surprisingly powerful argument that there may well be much that is weird and unknown in our world today – that, as the Bard said, "There are more things in heaven and earth, Horatio, than are dreamt of in your philosophy."

Is it really so hard, then, to imagine the possibility of a race of shapeshifting reptilian humanoids? It would be difficult to imagine a more advantageous evolutionary trait – especially for a ruthless predator race whose favored prey is… humans.

Enter Icke

"In a remarkable period of 15 days as I traveled around the United States in 1998, I met more than a dozen separate people who told me of how they had seen humans transform into reptiles and go back again in front of their eyes. Two television presenters had just such an experience while interviewing a man who was in favor of the global centralization of power known as the New World Order. … I know other people who have seen [President George H.W.] Bush shapeshift into a reptilian." – David Icke,
The Biggest Secret (1999)

Today's greatest popularizer of the reptilian theory is David Icke, former British soccer star, celebrity BBC sportscaster and former British Green Party leader and spokesman.

Dr. Tyson Lewis and Dr. Richard Kahn, university professors and authors of the scholarly paper "The Reptoid Hypothesis: Utopian and dystopian representational motifs in David Icke's alien conspiracy theory" write of Icke's "international fame" and note that "Icke has an expansive popular appeal that cuts across political, economic, and religious divides, uniting a wide spectrum of left and right groups and individuals under his prolific and all-embracing meta-conspiracy theory."

Bestselling author Jon Ronson notes of Icke: "his career is now a global sensation... he lectures to packed houses all over the world, riveting his audiences for six hours at a time with extraordinary revelations..."

Icke's books and speeches have reached millions around the world. Indeed, tickets for Icke's sellout lectures sometimes go for as much as rock superstars the Rolling Stones, U2 and Madonna – pretty impressive for a man whose performance has no guitars, singers, dancers, light shows, or stage pyrotechnics, but consists simply of hours-long talks accompanied by a simple slide display.

What does Icke say that is so compelling?

His teachings are in fact complex and far reaching, and only some highlights can be described here. At their core is the belief that a secret group of reptilian humanoids called the "Babylonian Brotherhood" controls humanity and runs the world for their own benefit. These reptilians walk among us largely unknown, having the ability to shapeshift into human form.

Lewis and Kahn summarize key elements of Icke's encompassing theory: "Alien reptilian invasions, blood-sucking, pedophilic Illuminati agents acting as totalitarian world leaders, trans-dimensional alien-humans interbreeding to support a program of cosmic imperialism on an unimaginable scale..."

According to Icke many of the most prominent politicians and cultural leaders in the world are shapeshifting reptilians. Political leaders include – to name just a few – presidents George H.W. Bush and George W. Bush, Queen Elizabeth II, Al Gore, Mikail Gorbachev, William F. Buckley... and some of the most famous dynasties in the world: the Rothschilds, Habsburgs, Rockefellers, Astors, DuPonts, Mellons, and many other British and European royal families, as well as many renowned ruling elite Establishment families of the United States.

And of course... Hillary Clinton.

Prominent members of the entertainment industry Icke has identified as reptilians include Bob Hope, Boxcar Willie, and Kris Kristofferson.

Icke introduced his version of the reptilian hypothesis in his book The Biggest Secret (1999). There he explained that human beings were the result of a breeding program on earth run by an ancient extraterrestrial race of reptilians called Anunnaki from the constellation Draco.

These reptilians have interbred with humans to create a hybrid reptile-human race capable of shapeshifting from reptilian to human. Some live in tunnels and caverns inside the earth. Others move among us, in human society, in their human guise. From the beginning to today they have ruled humanity, and they maintain and solidify their political power through powerful secret societies. Icke calls these reptilians the "Babylonian Brotherhood" because their bloodlines originate in the Middle and Far East.

Modern secret societies controlled by the reptilians and used to maintain their rule over the world, according to Icke, include many of those associated with Hillary Clinton (as described in Chapter 13), among them the Council on Foreign Relations, the Trilateral Commission, the Bilderberg Group, and the United Nations. The Reptilian Brotherhood further runs the CIA, the Mossad, the major media, mainstream religion, and other controlling organizations of the world's elite.

The goal of the Reptilian Brotherhood is nothing less than

the total domination and control of the human race, whom the reptilians view as mere slaves and cattle. Ominous steps towards the completion of this plan are easy to see: unprecedented spying and surveillance, REAL ID, militarism, gun control, the steady move toward world government, the consolidation of world resources into the hands of a tiny government-corporate elite, and so on.

These reptilians engage in savage rites, including pedophilia, human sacrifice and the devouring of humans. Human blood is not just a tasty repast for the reptilians, Icke says, it is vital to their existence, for "without human blood the reptilians cannot hold human form in this dimension."

"The aim of the [Reptilian] Brotherhood and its interdimensional controllers has been to centralize power in the hands of the few," Ickes says in his 1995 book And the Truth Shall Set You Free.

"This process is now very advanced and it is happening on a global scale today thanks to modern technology. The game-plan is known as the Great Work of Ages or the New World Order, and it presently seeks to introduce a world government to which all nations would be colonies; a world central bank and currency; a world army; and a micro-chipped population connected to a global computer.

"What is happening today is the culmination of the manipulation which has been unfolding for thousands of years."

John Rhodes: Reptilian "Sleeper Cells" and U.S. Politics

American ufologist and cryptozoologist John Rhodes describes himself as "the world's foremost authority on Reptilian-Humanoids, or Reptilian Aliens." Rhodes has long been involved in exploration of the unexplained. He has lectured in the U.S. and internationally and has appeared on TV shows including MonsterQuest, The Conspiracy Zone, BBC Conspiracies, Animal-X, Unsolved Mysteries, and the History Channel's UFO Hunters. He says he has worked with law enforcement officials in cattle mutilation cases.

Rhodes runs the Reptoid Research Center (RRC), an organization whose mission statement is to:

- INVESTIGATE the accounts of individuals or groups claiming to have sighted or encountered any animal species described as bipedal, reptilian-humanoid ("Reptoid") or other reptilian cryptids, of various descriptions.
- ENCOURAGE members of the scientific community to undertake an expansive search for other-than-human, intelligent life forms in Earth's surface environment.
- ACQUIRE, REVIEW and SHARE information pertaining to the search for reptoids (aka reptilians) and the various observable phenomena related to their activities.
- REDIRECT the public's search for intelligent "alien" life from outer space towards Earth's more accessible, cavern-filled underworld, by offering consultant services to various electronic media, television, literature and film projects.

The Reptoid Research Center notes that it has "absolutely no financial ties to any religious, government or educational institutions. This financial independence permits the Center the rare freedom to study subjects without restraint or coercion from outside sources."

Rhodes' decades of research has convinced him that reptilian beings are real and interacting with top government and political leaders.

"There is more than enough evidence to indicate that a highly evolved reptilian life form is interacting with human beings. Their presence has been witnessed in every corner of the Earth by people from all walks of life."

According to Rhodes, "Theories as to the origin of reptilian 'alien' life forms appear to be threefold. From the accumulative evidence provided thus far, it has been determined that they are either:

a) Extra-Terrestrials (ETs): Beings from another planet or star system.
b) Inner-Terrestrials (ITs): Beings that are naturally evolved terrestrial (earth) life forms that reside in inner earth caverns, sub-cities, and underwater bases.
c) Inner-Dimensionals (IDs): other alien entities existing in vibrational levels (time/space travelers etc.).

"It is important to realize that, even though each theorized origin appears to be distinct in its own right, all three theories could be, and are probably, correct."

Rhodes warns of the terrifying possibility that many human beings – especially those in places of political power – may be the results of reptilian breeding experiments, and may be as unknowing sleeper agents awaiting the call of reptilian masters to join in revolt and conquer the human race.

By this theory, the reptilian overlords are setting the stage for their ultimate victory "by establishing a network of human-reptilian crossbred infiltrates within various levels of the surface culture's military industrial complexes, government bodies, UFO/paranormal groups, religious, and fraternal (priest) orders, etc. These crossbreeds, some unaware of their reptilian genetic 'mind-control' instructions, act out their subversive roles as 'reptilian agents,' setting the stage for an reptilian led ET invasion."

If Hillary is indeed a reptilian she could well be a key agent in the plan for a sudden reptilian takeover and enslavement of the human race. Should Hillary become president of the United States – the most powerful person on the planet – this would, of course, enormously facilitate this terrifying plan.

"We have been warned by the Hebrew, American Indian, Aztec and Hindu prophets that, at the 'End of Days,' we will encounter Dragons, Leviathans and serpent-gods," writes Rhodes.

"They shall, we are told, arrive as the harbingers of terror, death, redemption and salvation. From where they will come is a question that has eluded the finest of scholarly minds that study the prophesies. One thing we do know, however, and that is that they are here, on and in EARTH."

Is Hillary part of that plan – either knowingly or as another sleeper cell agent?

Is she a reptilian – one of... them?

Many say yes.

And some, as we shall now see, even claim to have proof – captured on camera.

Thousands of Videos Claim to Show Hillary and Others Shapeshifting into Reptilians

Today virtually everyone has easy access to cameras, and photographs and videos can be shared instantly with the world.

One result of this has been the capturing and circulation of thousands of videos that claim to show Hillary and other prominent ruling elite figures caught shapeshifting or transforming into reptilian humanoids.

Here is just a small sampling of the endless titles that come up on YouTube:

> "Reptilian Shapeshifters Hillary Clinton & Ukraine president Viktor Yushchenko"
>
> "Snake Lizard Hillary Clinton Reptilian"
>
> "Hillary Clinton Reptilian Eye – On Her Official Photo!"
>
> "Hillary Clinton Shapeshifting While Crying"
>
> "Hillary Clinton Loses Control on National TV and Reveals Her True Reptilian Form."
>
> "Hillary Clinton 100% Reptilian Hybrid"
>
> "Hillary Clinton Confirmed Reptilian Humanoid Kenite Shapeshifter"
>
> (HILARY R. CLINTON) "100% PROOF * REPTILIAN EYES"
>
> "Reptilian Aliens Bill & Hillary Clinton"

"Reptilian Shapeshifter – Hillary Clinton Private Party"

"Hillary Clinton with Reptilian Eyes"

"Hillary Clinton: Reptilian Sociopath"

"THEY LIVE AMONG U.S.: HILLARY CLINTON REPTILIAN SHAPE SHIFTER 2013 EXPOSED!"

... and on and on, page after page after page.

Many of the videos show Hillary's eyes becoming lidded in lizard-like fashion, or revealing pronounced reptilian slitted pupils. Some show a thin lizard-like tongue darting out from her mouth. In one video her hands suddenly and briefly morph into lizard-like claws.

Many are slowed down, to capture and reveal Hillary's alleged reptilian qualities and mannerisms.

Writing for the popular left-wing news site AlterNet, journalist Jan Frel notes: "In [one] interrupted transmission video, for example, Clinton's face turns gray, her eyeballs pixelate, and it briefly appears that she's literally melting on screen. This is gold for the reptilian researchers..."

(Frel, a skeptic, attributes such things to "mundane tech errors" or moments when "a reception snafu briefly distorts the broadcast" or even sometimes deliberate alterations – explanations some may find reminiscent of the unconvincing 1960s-era attempts to explain away all UFO sightings as either hoaxes or "swamp gas" or some similarly benign and banal phenomena.)

Of course, some skepticism is called for. There is no way to confirm if any of the countless videos flooding the Internet actually show Hillary exhibiting reptilian traits. Indeed, in an age where digital manipulation is easy, one must be wary of hoaxes as well as well-intentioned but erroneous interpretations.

Still, the sheer quantity of them is astounding. And watching some of them can be a deeply disturbing experience. A few example (titles and punctuation are unaltered):

"Hillary Clinton shapeshifting in bar" purports to show a lizard-like tongue darting briefly from her mouth. Alcohol, it is theorized, may loosen the control that reptilians maintain over their human shape. In slow motion the alleged tongue is easy to see, and may well send chills up the spines of viewers who surfed in merely to scoff.

"HILLARY CLINTON CAMP REPTILIAN TO THE CORE" claims to show four "Dracos" – reptilian shapeshifters from the fourth dimension in the constellation Draco – in Hillary's campaign disguised as humans, including a bodyguard caught in the midst of shapeshifting. The footage is indeed startling.

"Hillary Clinton reptilian eye on plasma TV" freezes a CNN appearance by Hillary, then closes in on her eyes, which do seem to have a distinctly reptilian slant to them. The charge that Clinton's eyes are reptilian, that her stare is piercing and nonhuman, is a common theme on many of the Hillary reptilian videos.

There is no doubting the sincerity of many of those who post.

Whether or not one believes such videos prove anything about Hillary's reptilian nature, they unquestionably do prove one very important thing:

Tens of millions of Americans today are fearful that Hillary is not human but rather is a diabolical shapeshifting blood-drinking reptilian being intent upon gaining total control of the world for monstrous purposes.

Hillary, Exorcisms... and Reptilian Shapeshifting

We noted in Chapter 4 that Hillary clearly exhibits some of the signs of demon possession. Further, we have documented her decades-long obsession with the occult and dark powers in many forms.

Given the seemingly endless stream of videos, described above, that claim to show Hillary caught in the middle of shapeshifting into a reptilian being, the following comments by prominent exorcist Fr. Gary Thomas are especially provocative.

Fr. Thomas is the mandated exorcist for the Diocese of San Jose, California, and was an apprentice of Fr. Carmine De Filippis, the renowned veteran Italian exorcist. Fr. Thomas's training was the subject of the 2010 book The Rite: The Making of a Modern Exorcist by Matt Baglio and the 2011 Hollywood movie based on the book, starring the great Anthony Hopkins.

In late 2012 Fr. Thomas made the following startling statement in an interview for Catholic Answers magazine:

"The [possessed] person can have very extreme facial contortions and a change in the voice. Sometimes their whole body language, including their face, *can take on the look of a reptile or a snake* [emphasis added], and I've had that happen a number of times."

Reptilian Continuity? Obama Administration Evades Reptilian Question

Incidentally, the charges of reptilian infiltration have followed President Barack Obama as well. In 2012 Obama made an appearance at the American Israel Public Affairs Committee conference. A video of a member of his Secret Service detail quickly went viral when it showed the agent looking shockingly like an alien shapeshifter and/or reptilian humanoid.

The video was so startling, and the reaction by thousands of shocked viewers so strong, that the White House felt it necessary to respond.

They did so with a carefully mocking tone, just as the New Zealand minister quoted earlier in this chapter did, just as people use words like "conspiracy theory" to dismiss serious allegations of government wrong-doing – allegations that sometimes prove to be correct.

Still, the very fact that the White House felt compelled to answer at all is evidence of the growing popularity of the reptilian theory.

Said Caitlin Hayden, chief spokeswoman for the National Security Council, to Wired magazine:

"I can't confirm the claims made in this video, but any alleged program to guard the president with aliens or robots would likely have to be scaled back or eliminated in the sequester. I'd refer you to the Secret Service or Area 51 for more details."

Wired magazine, one of the most respected technology news sources in the world, said they felt "journalistically obligated to observe that this isn't a flat denial."

A joke? Or possibly – an evasion? Another "non-denying denial" on what appears to be an increasingly sensitive subject?

Reptilian Rule in Mass Media

In recent years we've seen the idea of reptilian rulers of humanity become a popular theme in mass media. A few examples:

- In 1983, the television miniseries "V" featured alien reptiles plotting to take over the world.

- The 1985 hit movie "Enemy Mine" had an American fighter pilot fighting, and then learning to love, an alien reptilian from – shades of Icke! – the constellation Draco.

- "They Live," a 1988 high-paranoia trash-classic movie, features downtrodden earthlings who discover sunglasses that enable them to abruptly see the shapeshifting reptilian aliens who are secretly dominating and exploiting the unsuspecting human race.

   Years later, the star of the film, "Rowdy" Roddy Piper, startled many when he tweeted on September 27, 2013: "They Live is a Documentary!!"

   Roddy Piper died of a sudden heart attack just 22 months after that tweet, at the relatively young age of 61, leading some to wonder if he had revealed too much...

- The television sci-fi series BABYLON 5 has humans

warrior and reptilian "Narns" working together.
- The Star Wars movie universe includes the Trandoshan, large, carnivorous, reptilian humanoid slave-masters from the planet Trandosha.

- A key premise of the TV series "Stargate SG-1" – the longest-running North American science fiction television series in history – is that, in prehistoric times, parasitic reptilian aliens, the Goa'uld, possessed the ability to take over human bodies and use them as hosts. The Goa'uld posed as gods and thus seduced and enslaved mankind.

- The wildly popular kids' show "Barney" featured a friendly, loving father-mother figure reptilian, while the Teenage Mutant Ninja Turtles franchise shows reptiles as heroic, unstoppable law enforcers.

There are countless other examples. Indeed, sometimes it seems as if reptilians have taken over the entertainment world!

Which of course leads to this key question: Is all this simply a natural, normal entertainment theme? Or are the mass media in some way being used to repeatedly deliver the message that we should learn to fear, love and – above all – obey our reptilian rulers?

Outlandish as that might sound, consider the following. If, as David Ickes and many others claim, many of the political, entertainment, media and economic elites of the world are in fact secretly reptoids, the idea that they would use the mass media to indoctrinate humans is not at all unlikely. Governments and others have done that for centuries – and continue to do so today.

Incredible though it sounds, during the Cold War the CIA secretly funded and promoted the newly emerging U.S. abstract art movement, including the work of such highly controversial but now renowned artists as Jackson Pollock, Robert Motherwell, Willem de Kooning and Mark Rothko. This was part of a larger project to destabilize the Soviet Union by secretly promoting modern avant-garde art; the idea was to make the more traditional mainstream art favored by Soviet bloc countries seem stodgy in comparison to dynamic American art, thus almost subliminally associating the U.S. with progress, intellectual freedom and modernism. And that in turn was just a small part of similar CIA involvement in the arts, described by the Independent UK newspaper as "a vast jamboree of intellectuals, writers, historians, poets, and artists which was set up with CIA funds in 1950 and run by a CIA agent."

If governments will do something so unexpected and as extraordinary as that, while successfully keeping it secret for decades – imagine what shapeshifting reptilian overlords might be doing right now to subtly and subliminally encourage Americans to embrace their scaly rule.

As we noted in Chapter 10, some sources claim that the government has plans to exploit the UFO phenomena in a massive, worldwide propaganda false-flag operation – to use the terror of a fake UFO invasion to unite the planet into accepting rule by the world's elite in a New World Order. The reptilian story lends itself well to that scenario.

If Hillary is indeed a reptile, as so many claim, then she poses a danger not only to Americans but to all of humanity. As Reptile-In-Chief, what horrors might she impose upon us, her hapless human subjects?

Conclusion: "If it is anyone, it is Hillary"

The reptilian theory remains one of the most mysterious and controversial charges against Hillary. One of the strengths of the theory – one of the reasons it is so compelling and winning increasing interest and acceptance – is that it explains so much.

Our political, financial and cultural elites often seem so bloodthirsty, so unconcerned about human suffering and death, so detached, so lacking in empathy, so, yes... *cold-blooded*. The reptilian hypothesis explains this in a clear and unambiguous way. As odd as it seems upon first encounter, the theory has a powerful logical as well as emotional appeal to it. And millions of Americans have embraced it.

Still, though the unsubstantiated evidence for it may be compelling, it simply seems too far out to many otherwise open-minded researchers. And as this book goes to press, though there are some tantalizing leads, some remarkable claims, there is still no direct evidence proving that the reptilian hypothesis is true – or that Hillary is a reptilian.

After completing a draft of this chapter I consulted with an acquaintance who is an expert in many of the matters covered here (and other parts of this book as well). Fearing possible retaliation, he spoke under condition of strict anonymity. I asked him outright what he thought of the accusation that Hillary is a shapeshifting reptile, possibly possessing occult powers.

He thought a moment, then said there was as yet no solid proof of the reptilian theory, intriguing though it is.

"However, if it is true that there are reptilian shape-shifters," he said, "there is, without any doubt, no one on earth more likely to be one than Hillary."

And that is where we shall leave it – for now.

CHAPTER NINE

Project MONARCH: Mind-Controlled Sex Slaves, Ritual Child Abuse, and Murder

Do Mind-Controlled Sex Slaves Serve Bill and Hillary?

It is one of the most horrific, explosive and mind-boggling charges raised against Hillary Clinton.

Several women have written books claiming they were deliberately severely abused as children by the U.S. government as part of a secret mind-control program. The object of the program was to shatter their minds and turn them into zombie-like mind-controlled slaves, to be used for the sexual pleasure of the world's ruling elite and for various Top Secret espionage duties, including blackmail and murder.

Some of them have specifically named Hillary and Bill as having abused and raped them while they were in this state.

They further claim they were part of a world-wide network of such mind-controlled slaves.

Victims frequently give the name "Project MONARCH" to the government program they say has victimized them. Often the name MONARCH is used loosely as a generic description or catch-all term for victims to label what they say happened to them.

Unquestionably, these charges sound incredible, and they are unsubstantiated by any direct proof.

And yet… as we shall see, there is a well-documented and utterly shocking history of U.S. government mind-control experiments stretching over decades – a secret history that, incredibly, seems to parallel many of the charges of the alleged MONARCH victims.

Let's briefly examine some of the claims of these women, particularly as they concern the Clintons.

Cathy O'Brien: In her books Trance Formation of America (1995) and Access Denied: For Reasons of National Security (2004), O'Brien claims she was forced into child pornography by her father at a very young age. She claims she was made to attend ritual child sacrifices and witnessed blood-drinking and sexual abuse of children by, among others: Hillary and Bill Clinton, David Rockefeller, Henry Kissinger, Sen. Robert Byrd (her alleged controller), Sen. Arlen Specter, Al Gore, the Queen of England, Prince Charles, Prince Philip, Secretary of State Madeleine Albright, , Mexican president Miguel de la Madrid Hurtado, Prime Minister Tony Blair – and many more. She claims to have been abused by international pedophile rings, Satanists, and drug dealers, all working in partnership with various governments.

O'Brien says she was savagely raped by both Dick Cheney and George H.W. Bush after being chased through woods in a human hunting sport called "The Most Dangerous Game." And she remembers the horror of seeing George H.W. Bush transform into his true form: a reptilian.

O'Brien devotes a page or so in her book to describing, in grotesque, near-pornographic detail, her rape by Hillary Clinton. She claims Hillary was especially sexually excited by a strange face-like design that O'Brien's controllers had deliberately cut and scarred into her vagina.

"Apparently aroused by the carving in my vagina," writes O'Brien, "Hillary stood up and quickly peeled out of her matronly nylon panties and pantyhose. Uninhibited despite a long day in the hot sun, she gasped, 'Eat me, oh God, eat me now.'

"I had no choice but to comply with her orders..."

(Incidentally, the makers of a documentary film called "The Most Dangerous Game" had O'Brien examined on camera by a gynecologist, who in fact did find the type of vaginal scarring she describes. The film – which at the time of this writing is on YouTube – includes a photo of the scarring, which does appear to resemble her description.)

"Hillary knew I was a mind-controlled slave, and, like Bill Clinton, just took it in stride as a 'normal' part of life in politics," O'Brien says.

"It was Hillary Clinton that accessed my sex programming. It was Hillary that I was sexually exposed to," O'Brien said in a speech in Texas in 1996.

Like some other alleged MONARCH victims, she says the MONARCH treatment buried these memories deep within her, and she was able to access them through hypnosis.

She also claims that MONARCH used similar trauma-based mind-control programming on her daughter.

Brice Taylor is the pseudonym of **Susan Ford.** In her 400-plus-page 1999 book Thanks for the Memories, based on what she says are erased memories recalled after nearly 13 years of therapy, she claims she was born into a family of multi-generational Satanists, who subjected her to sickening mind control and ritual abuse in order to shatter her personality and make her a Project MONARCH sex slave.

Of her book Ted Gunderson, former Los Angeles FBI senior special agent in charge, said: "Thanks for the Memories confirms facts furnished by many other witnesses. [Brice Taylor] is credible, knowledgeable and truthful."

Taylor says that from the age of ten years she was a sex-slave for every U.S. president from JFK to Bill Clinton, with the exception of Jimmy Carter.

She says she was raped by Bill and Hillary several times. She further claims that she AND her underage daughter were forced to have sex with Bill just before his inauguration.

Taylor also says she sexually serviced Hillary alone. She further reports, as others have claimed, that Bill and Hillary used cocaine.

As other alleged mind-controlled victims have reported, she says she was sexually abused by political and entertainment elites as well as political figures like Hillary and Bill. Indeed, like others, she names an astonishing array of alleged abusers, including: Frank Sinatra, Bob Hope, Lee

Iacocca, Sylvester Stallone, Ed McMahon, Johnny Carson, Sammy Davis Jr., Dean Martin, Gene Kelley, Mickey Rooney, Hugh Hefner, Don Ho, Henry Kissinger, Ted Kennedy, Al Gore and more – as well as federal agents, military figures and Mafia bosses.

In another commonly reported MONARCH detail, she says she was also used as an agent to deliver secret messages between members of the ruling elite.

Laurel Aston claims she became a victim of Satanic ritual abuse and government mind control at age two. She writes:

"The Clintons both abused me sexually even as an underage child. As well as later in life. Bill... is a bisexual who prefers men. ... I was provided to both Clintons beginning in childhood. While enslaved by the CIA U.S. military in the home of a Nazi–CIA goat (cover) family...

"I was taken to Washington and the White House. I was even raped in the Oval office which was Bill's thing. Barry Gordon was a disappeared CIA head who had to fake his own death to avoid prosecution. Gordon provided me to Hillary Clinton in my early 20s. Hillary wanted me as her exclusive property. Gordon prepped me by drugging me then having me raped, tortured and sodomized by many men. Barry Gordon then made the offer to me to become Hillary's private sex toy and to receive protection from rape by no one but her."

Arizona Wilder says she is a Project MONARCH mind-control ritual abuse victim, programmed to be a sex slave and occult high priestess. She says she has conducted human sacrifice rituals ceremonies with Bill and Hillary and many others of the ruling elite, including members of the Rockefeller and Rothschild families, Henry Kissinger, George W. Bush, George H.W. Bush, Jeb Bush, Ronald and Nancy Reagan, Gerald Ford, LBJ, the Queen of England and other members of the Royal Family, Tony Blair, and many more of the most famous people in the world.

Still other women have publicly made similar claims of mind control and use by the government as sex slaves and/or covert agents, but without specifically mentioning the Clintons. Among them:

Carol Rutz says her abuse by the CIA began at age four. In her book A Nation Betrayed she describes how, as an adult, she recovered memories of her abuse in the CIA programs Bluebird/Artichoke and MK-ULTRA. (These programs are described later in this chapter).

"Through a series of FOIA requests to various departments of the government, I have amassed an incredible amount of material that validates my personal experiences. The CIA bought my services from my grandfather. Over the next twelve years, I was tested, trained, and used in various ways. Electroshock, drugs, hypnosis, sensory deprivation, and other types of trauma were used to make me compliant and split my personality. The 'Manchurian Candidate,' where a programmed alter or personality is created to respond to a post-hypnotic trigger then perform an act and not remember it later, was just one of the operational uses of the mind-control scenario by the CIA."

She estimates there are thousands of victims like her. "There have to be thousands. I have heard from hundreds. So if I have heard from hundreds, there have to be thousands."

Kathleen Sullivan holds degrees from Baylor University and Arizona State University and has taught at two universities. In her 2003 book Unshackled: A Survivor's Story of Mind Control, she says she was a victim of mind control from childhood until well into adulthood, when flashbacks and nightmares led her to recover shocking memories of her abuse as a Project MONARCH Manchurian Candidate–type victim. She recalls serving as an assassin, prostitute, and participant in Satanic rituals and horrible medical experiments. She also recalls taking part in the blackmailing of national political leaders.

She accuses her father of terrorizing her for years and forcing her to kill her own child. Taking part in her victimization, she claims, were intelligence personnel, military personnel, doctors and mental health professionals, cult leaders, pedophiles, pornographers, drug dealers and Nazis,

Cisco Wheeler claims she was born into a multi-generational Satanic family and traumatized beginning in the womb. In a radio interview Wheeler says "I entertained governors, mayors, ministers. I was trained in sexual activity there, and I was part of the Illuminati function within the British Royal Family during elite meetings."

Claudia Mullen addressed the 1995 Senate Advisory Committee on Human Radiation Experiments: "Between the years 1957 and 1984 I became a pawn in the government's game. Its ultimate goal was mind control and to create the perfect spy, all through the use of chemicals, radiation, drugs, hypnosis, electric shock, isolation in tubs of water, sleep deprivation, brainwashing, verbal, physical, emotional and sexual abuse.

"I was exploited unwittingly for nearly three decades of my life and the only explanations given to me were that 'the end justifies the means' and 'I was serving my country in their bold effort to fight communism.' I can only summarize my circumstances by saying they took an already abused seven-year-old child and compounded my suffering beyond belief.

"The saddest part is, I know for a fact I was not alone. There were countless other children in my same situation and there was no one to help us..."

Christine DeNicola also addressed the 1995 Senate Advisory Committee on Human Radiation Experiments: "I was a subject in radiation, as well as mind-control and drug experiments performed by a man I knew as Dr. Green. ...

"All these experiments were performed on me in conjunction with mind-control techniques and drugs, in Tucson, Arizona. Dr. Green was using me mostly as a mind-control subject from 1966 to 1973. His objective was to gain control of my mind and train me to be a spy assassin.

"...Dr. Green ruthlessly used electric shock, drugs, spun me on a table, put shots in my stomach and my back, dislocated my joints, and [used] hypnotic techniques to make me feel crazy and suicidal. ...

"These horrible experiments have profoundly affected my life. I developed multiple personality disorder because Dr. Green's goal was to split my mind into as many parts as possible so he could control me totally."

(The final report on the 1995 Senate Advisory Committee on Human Radiation Experiments – which documented extraordinary abuse by the government, including illegal, secret non-consenting testing on numerous unknowing children and adults – was issued on October 3, 1995 – the same day as the verdict in the O.J. Simpson case. This of course led to it being virtually ignored by the media – a time-tested government technique to bury controversial news.)

Evaluating the MONARCH Charges

Such charges as these (and there are others making similar claims) strain the imagination.

And yet...

As incredible as they sound, there is intriguing, horrifying evidence that the U.S. government has aggressively pursued exactly the kind of research and activities these women describe.

So how do we evaluate the charges of these alleged MONARCH victims? Especially when there is not even any record of any such government program with that name?

If these seemingly outrageous charges against Hillary and others are worthy of being considered, several things that, at first glance may also seem beyond belief, must be proven.

Specifically, **the following must be shown to be true:**

1. The federal government had programs to create mind-controlled agents and slaves.
2. The CIA and other participating government and private sector agencies knew that such experiments and activities were illegal, and continued doing them anyway.
3. Such experiments were successful in creating mind-controlled assassins and mind-controlled sex slaves, as well as "sleeper agents" (so-called "Manchurian Candidates") who carried within their minds hidden multiple personalities that could be awakened by the government when desired.
4. Such experiments must necessarily have involved a vast number of players, including experts in such

fields as psychology, hypnosis, drug abuse and other areas related to mind control; such experiments must also have involved the participation of some of the country's leading institutions.
5. The U.S. government performed such dangerous, painful, invasive and criminal experiments on innocent unsuspecting American citizens illegally, without their consent or knowledge.
6. The U.S. government forced children to participate in such dangerous, painful, invasive and criminal experiments.
7. Some alleged MONARCH victims claim to have experienced torture by Nazis, Satanists, and pedophiles, For this to be true there would need to be examples of collaboration between U.S. government agencies and such people.
8. Because some of these claims are recent, we would need reason to believe that such experiments and programs are going on today (or at least were active in the very recent past).
9. To even begin to give credence to the charges that Bill and/or Hillary are involved in such activity, as some victims claim, we would need at the very least some indication that the Clintons and/or other ruling elite figures could be involved in pedophile rings, sexual abuse and related matters.

Impossible? Absurd?

Let us look closer at each of these accusations.

1. The federal government had programs to create mind-controlled agents and slaves

That the federal government, particularly the CIA, aggressively pursued the creation of mind-controlled agents for decades is not speculation. It is well-documented fact.

The efforts began prior to World War II, but were not exposed until the 1970s, and even then, only a tiny amount of what these projects did were made public. The story is one of the darkest, most obscene chapters in American history. And some experts believe this still goes on secretly today.

Through a series of programs falling broadly under the name Operation MK-ULTRA, the federal government used drugs, hypnosis, electronic brain implants and other means to try to gain control over the minds of unsuspecting subjects. Though it sounds like science fiction, or perhaps horror fiction, the CIA's efforts to use little-known mind-control techniques to create mind-controlled agents, including assassins and sex slaves, is a well-documented matter of historical record.

MK-ULTRA was approved on April 13, 1953 by CIA Director Allen Dulles. Recent research has revealed Dulles to be among the most sinister figures in American history. His biographer David Talbot, author of the massive and heavily footnoted The Devil's Chessboard, describes Dulles as "a psychopath" and says his decades-long career in American deep secret politics was "a reign of treason." Millions of people around the globe have died because of the policies and activities Dulles instituted. Indeed, Dulles' interventions around the world created enormous hostility against the U.S. And the deaths and horrors continue to this day. As Talbot notes: "Dead for nearly half a century, Dulles's shadow still darkens the land."

Dulles was one of the key architects of the post-World War II national security state strategy that still operates as U.S. policy today, and still engages in massive crimes against the American people and others around the globe. MK-ULTRA is just one of the many horrific and lawless programs and policies enacted by Dulles and his colleagues and underlings that transformed post-World War II America in a tragic and horrific manner.

MK-ULTRA was the umbrella label for hundreds or perhaps even thousands of super-secret efforts by the CIA to create mind-controlled sleeper agents and slaves. The projects included testing on thousands, perhaps tens of thousands, of unwilling and unknowing subjects, among them children, prisoners, mental patients and others. These victims were subjected to unethical mind-control experiments directly in violation of U.S. and international law, the Nuremberg Code, and all decency and morality. Drugs, hypnosis, sensory deprivation, isolation, psychosurgery, verbal abuse, sexual abuse, radiation, electroshock and outright torture were used in outrageously unethical experiments on unsuspecting and non-consenting subjects. The CIA also explored the use of electronic brain implants, sometimes placed into unwilling subjects.

These monstrous operations on American soil constituted nothing less than a secret war against American citizens. Indeed, the CIA's own charter prohibited it from carrying out operations in the United States. Yet MK-ULTRA continued despite being completely illegal and unethical. MK-ULTRA experiments also were conducted at secret sites in Europe, Asia, and elsewhere.

MK-ULTRA was vast in scope. Even today, we have no idea of just how widespread MK-ULTRA was. In some experiments, the criminality was so obvious that the CIA kept no records (as documented in recovered CIA memos). Of thousands of documents that were kept, most were deliberately destroyed in 1973 by order of CIA Director Richard Helms, who feared that a congressional investigation into MK-ULTRA crimes was eminent.

By accident, a fraction of documents related to MK-ULTRA escaped this destruction and were discovered a few years after the attempt to erase all traces of MK-ULTRA's existence. More were declassified in 2001. Together these give us just a glimpse at the years of horror and the startlingly wide scope of MK-ULTRA. The fact that they reveal so much, yet constitute only a small percentage of what was done, makes them all the more frightening. They leave us no doubt that this parade of horrors extended deep into American life.

Nor was this a mere side interest of the CIA. According to a secret memorandum later uncovered, MK-ULTRA was granted up to six percent of the CIA research budget in 1953, free of oversight or accounting.

In the 1977 Congressional hearings on MK-ULTRA, CIA head Admiral Stansfield Turner noted there were "149 [known] MK-ULTRA subprojects, many of which appear to have some connection with research into behavioral modification, drug acquisition and testing or administering drugs surreptitiously."

As noted, MK-ULTRA was a continuation of federal mind-control experiments begun prior to World War II. The work really got underway immediately after World War II and the creation of the CIA.

Preceding MK-ULTRA was BLUEBIRD, approved by the first director of the CIA, Roscoe Hillenkoetter, on April 20, 1950. The object of BLUEBIRD was to discover and perfect methods of forcing an unwitting subject "to do our bidding against his will and even against such fundamental laws of nature as self-preservation."

A January 1952 CIA memo outlined some research areas for BLUEBIRD. Among them (wording is from the memo):

- Can we create by post-H [hypnotic] control an action contrary to an individual's basic moral principles?
- Can we in a matter of an hour, two hours, one day, etc., induce an H condition in an unwilling subject to such an extent that he will perform an act for our benefit?
- Could we seize a subject and in the space of an hour or two by post-H control have him crash an airplane, wreck a train, etc.?
- Can we by H and SI [sleep inducing] techniques force a subject to travel long distances, commit specified acts and return to us or bring documents or materials?
- Can we guarantee total amnesia under any and all conditions?
- Can we "alter" a person's personality?
- Can we devise a system for making unwilling subjects into willing agents and then transfer that control to untrained agency agents in the field by use of codes or identifying signs?
- How can sodium A or P or any other sleep inducing agent be best concealed in a normal item, such as candy, cigarettes, coffee, tea, beer, medicines?

In August 1951, Project ARTICHOKE (also known as Operation ARTICHOKE) arose from BLUEBIRD. ARTICHOKE became MK-ULTRA in 1953.

MK-ULTRA, in turn, eventually morphed into MK-SEARCH, according to the 1977 House Committee, who wrote that MKSEARCH "was the name given to the continuation of the MK-ULTRA program. Its purpose was to develop, test, and evaluate capabilities in the covert use of biological, chemical, and radioactive material systems and techniques for producing predictable human behavioral and/or physiological changes in support of highly sensitive operational requirements." Funding commenced in FY 1966, and supposedly ended in FY 1972.

Of course, we now know (and shall further see below) that the CIA had declared in Top Secret memos that they were keeping no records on many of their more controversial projects. So any public CIA statement that any of these programs were discontinued is simply not believable – especially since, as we shall show below, MK-ULTRA and other programs early on achieved some astonishing successes.

In an April 3, 1953 internal CIA memo then-Deputy Director Richard Helms, later to be CIA head, said of MK-ULTRA: "We intend to investigate the development of a chemical material which causes a reversible, nontoxic aberrant mental state, the specific nature of which can be reasonably well predicted for each individual. This material could potentially aid in discrediting individuals, eliciting information, and implanting suggestions and other forms of mental control."

MK-ULTRA Subproject 119, according to a surviving CIA memo dated August 17th, 1960, proposed to review the literature and scientific developments on the electronic control of human behavior, including "Techniques of activation of the human organism by remote electronic means."

A 1955 MK-ULTRA document says that the program was seeking, among other things, "Materials which will cause temporary/permanent brain damage and loss of memory… Materials and physical methods which will produce amnesia for events preceding and during their use… Substances which alter personality structure in such a way that the tendency of the recipient to become dependent upon another person is enhanced."

Such methods would of course create exactly the kinds of sexual slaves that the alleged MONARCH victims describe. It would also give the government a powerful tool for discrediting critics of this program, or any government program. By using such techniques to inject false memories, even absurd ones, into the real memories of victims, their stories could be made to seem ludicrous.

Clearly this decades-long research, with dozens of known subprojects (and perhaps hundreds or even thousands that were covered up or never recorded), indicates that mind control – including experiments on human beings with the aim of creating secret agents and surreptitiously controlling the behavior of others – was a longtime and major interest of the CIA and other elements of the federal government.

2. The CIA and other participating government and private sector agencies knew that such experiments and activities were illegal, and continued doing them anyway

There is absolutely no doubt that those running MK-ULTRA knew the program was illegal and unethical yet pursued it anyway, and that they worked hard to keep knowledge of it suppressed precisely because of its criminal nature.

As we mentioned earlier, the CIA's own charter prohibited it from carrying out operations in the United States.

In 1957 the CIA's inspector general wrote the following in a secret memo about MK-ULTRA to CIA Director Allen Dulles:

"Precautions must be taken not only to protect operations from exposure to enemy forces but also to conceal these activities from the American public in general. The knowledge that *the Agency is engaging in unethical and illicit activities* would have serious repercussions in political and diplomatic circles." (Emphasis added.)

An April 3, 1953 CIA memo entitled "Two Extremely Sensitive Research Programs" warns: "Even internally in CIA, as few individuals as possible should be aware of our interest in these fields and of the identity of those who are working for us. At present, this results in ridiculous contracts, with cut-outs [trusted individuals or organizations working as intermediaries, without full information on the program], which do not spell out the scope or intent of the work."

In a July 26, 1963 memorandum the CIA's Inspector General wrote the following about MK-ULTRA to CIA Director Allen Dulles's successor John Alexander McCone (the sentence order is altered for clarity, but sentences are unaltered):

"TSD [Technical Services Division of the CIA] initiated a program for covert testing of materials on unwitting U.S. citizens in 1955. TSD has pursued a philosophy of *minimum documentation in keeping with the high sensitivity of some of the projects*. Some files contained little or no data at all. There are just two individuals in TSD who have full knowledge of the MK-ULTRA program, and most of that knowledge is unrecorded... (Emphasis added.)

"Over the ten-year life of the program, many additional avenues to the control of human behavior have been designated under the MK-ULTRA charter, including radiation, electro-shock, harassment substances, and paramilitary devices.

"The concepts involved in manipulating behavior are found by many people both within and outside the Agency [CIA] to be distasteful and . ...unethical.

"Some MK-ULTRA activities *raise questions of legality implicit in the original charter*. (Emphasis added.)

"*A final phase of the testing of MK-ULTRA products places the rights and interests of U.S. citizens in jeopardy.* (Emphasis added.)

"Public disclosure of some aspects of MK-ULTRA activity could induce serious adverse reaction in U.S. public opinion.

"*Present practice is to maintain no records* of the planning and approval of test programs." (Emphasis added.)

As we shall see, the U.S. government committed blatantly illegal radiation experiments on unknowing American citizens. A 1947 Atomic Energy Commission memo makes it clear that the government knew these were illegal and wanted to keep them secret while continuing to perform them:

"It is desired that no documents be released which refers to experiments with humans and might have adverse effect on public opinion or result in legal suits. Documents covering such work field should be classified 'secret.'"

As an example of the kinds of ethical boundaries that were crossed, veteran journalists Alexander Cockburn and Jeffrey St. Clair describe hideous and blatantly criminal experimentation during the Vietnam War, conducted on captured prisoners in July of 1968 as part of the CIA's monstrous Phoenix Program:

"A team of CIA psychologists set up shop at BienHoa Prison outside Saigon, where NLF suspects [note: *suspects*, not even proven to be enemies of the U.S.] were being held after Phoenix Program roundups. The psychologists performed a variety of experiments on the prisoners. In one, three prisoners were anesthetized; their skulls were opened and electrodes implanted by CIA doctors into different parts of their brains. The prisoners were revived, placed in a room with knives and the electrodes in the brains activated by the psychiatrists, who were covertly observing them. The hope was that they could be prompted in this manner to attack each other. The experiments failed. The electrodes were removed, the patients were shot and their bodies burned."

Prior to the horrors above, these prisoners were tortured, then dosed with massive amounts of LSD.

3. Such experiments were successful in creating mind-controlled assassins and mind-controlled sex slaves, as well as "sleeper agents" (so-called "Manchurian Candidates") who carried within their minds hidden multiple personalities that could be awakened by the government when desired

MK-ULTRA reported startling success in all of these things.

Renowned psychologist **George Hoben Estabrooks** was a Harvard University graduate, a Rhodes Scholar, chairman of the Department of Psychology at Colgate University, and one of the world's leading authorities on hypnosis. Estabrooks worked with the U.S. government before World War II on hypnosis and mind control, and was involved in MK/ULTRA.

Over the years Estabrooks made it plain that the CIA could – and did – use hypnotism, drugs and other nefarious means to shatter personalities and create Manchurian candidate-style multiple personality mind-controlled slave agents:

"I can hypnotize a man – without his knowledge or consent – into committing treason against the United States."

"The key to creating an effective spy or assassin rests in splitting a man's personality, or creating multiple personalities, with the aid of hypnotism.... This is not science fiction. ...I have done it."

"It is child's play now to develop a multiple personality through hypnotism."

"Perhaps you have read The Three Faces of Eve. The book was based on a case reported in 1905 by Dr. Morton Prince of Massachusetts General Hospital and Harvard. ... Clinical hypnotists throughout the world jumped on the multiple personality bandwagon as a fascinating frontier. By the 1920s, not only had they learned to apply post-hypnotic suggestion to deal with this weird problem, but also had learned how to split certain complex individuals into multiple personalities like Jekyll-Hydes.

"During World War II, I worked this technique with a vulnerable Marine lieutenant I'll call Jones. Under the watchful eye of Marine intelligence I split his personality into Jones A and Jones B. Jones A, once a 'normal' working Marine, became entirely different. He talked communist doctrine and meant it. He was welcomed enthusiastically by communist cells, and was deliberately given a dishonorable discharge by the Corps (which was in on the plot) and became a card-carrying party member. All I had to do was hypnotize the whole man, get in touch with Jones B, the loyal American, and I had a pipeline straight into the communist camp. ...

"Trained in auto-suggestion, or self-hypnosis, such a subject can pass every test used to spot a hypnotized person. Using it, he can control the rate of his heartbeat, anesthetize himself to a degree against pain of electric shock or torture. ...

"I would be surprised if many secret services are not now actually employing hypnotic methods for some of their underground activities...

"...two hundred trained operators, trained in the United States, could develop a unique, dangerous army of hypnotically controlled agents..."

And finally this disturbing end-justifies-the-means statement from Estabrooks:

"War is the end of all law. When we speak of keeping within the rules of the game we are childish, because it is not a game and true rules never hold. In the last analysis any device is justifiable which enables us to protect ourselves from defeat."

Dr. Jose Delgado, Director of Neuropsychiatry at Yale University Medical School, invented the stimoceiver or transdermal stimulator, a device implanted in the brain to transmit electrical impulses that modify basic behaviors such as aggression or sensations of pleasure. Delgado was able to control to a significant degree animal and human subjects' behaviors using electronic stimulation.

In his book Physical Control of the Mind he declared: "the feasibility of remote control of activities in several species of animals has been demonstrated [...] The ultimate objective of this research is to provide an understanding of the mechanisms involved in the directional control of animals and to provide practical systems suitable for human application."

Delgado also wrote that in his he experiments had "used electrodes implanted for days or months to block thought, speech, and movement, or to trigger joy, laughter, friendliness, verbal activity, generosity, fear, hallucinations, and memory."

Delgado also said that "brain transmitters can remain in a person's head for life. The energy to activate the brain transmitter is transmitted by way of radio frequencies."

In a 1966 speech Delgado said his work supported "the distasteful conclusion that motion, emotion, and behavior can be directed by electrical forces and that humans can be controlled like robots by push buttons."

Some suspect that, knowingly or unknowingly, Delgado was involved with MK-ULTRA research. Much of his was funded by the Office of Naval Intelligence, which clandestinely distributed CIA funding.

Today research on implants and other electronic means to control human behavior, based on Delgado's pioneering research, is vigorously pursued by the U.S. government and funded by many millions, perhaps billions, of tax dollars. In 2013 the Defense Advanced Research Projects Agency (Darpa) announced tentative success in an experiment to telepathically transmit messages between the brains of two rats connected by 21st century versions of Delgado's brain implants. On Darpa's drawing board: the use of brain implants to control drones and other weapons.

An ARTICHOKE document dated January 7, 1953 explicitly describes the successful creation of multiple personalities for espionage and other purposes in two 19-year-old women volunteer subjects, in a manner that clearly parallels the claims of the alleged MONARCH victims quoted at the beginning of this chapter:

"These subjects have clearly demonstrated that they can pass from a fully awake state to a deep H [hypnotic] controlled state via the telephone, via some very subtle signal that cannot be detected by other persons in the room, and without the other individuals being able to note the change.

"It has been shown clearly that physically individuals can be induced into H [hypnotic state] by telephone, by receiving written matter, or by the use of code, signals, or words.

"It has also been shown by experimentation with these girls that they can act as unwilling couriers for information purposes, and that they can be conditioned to a point where they believe a change in identity on their part even on the polygraph." (Exact language; paragraph broken into smaller sections for easier reading.)

From another ARTICHOKE document: "A CIA Security Office employee was hypnotized and given a false identity. She defended it hotly, denying her true name and rationalizing with conviction the possession of identity cards made out to her real self. Later, having had the false identity erased by suggestion, she was asked if she had ever heard of the name she had been defending as her own five minutes before. She thought, shook her head, and said, 'That's a pseudo if I ever heard one.' Apparently she had true amnesia for the entire episode."

A 1954 experiment successfully hypnotizing a woman with a terror of guns into firing a gun at another woman upon command, with no memory of doing so afterwards – the very definition of a mind-controlled "Manchurian Candidate" assassin.

A September 25, 1951 report tells of successfully hypnotized two women into transporting and setting off a (test) bomb.

As far as sexual control and abuse of innocent unwitting civilians, a 1951 CIA document reports:

"On 2 July 1951 approximately 1:00 p.m. the instruction began with [deleted name, presumably an instructor in hypnosis working for the CIA] relating to the student some of his sexual experiences. [Deleted] stated that he had *constantly used hypnotism as a means of inducing young girls to engage in sexual intercourse with him.* [Deleted], a performer in [deleted] orchestra, was *forced to engage in sexual intercourse* with [deleted] while under the influence of hypnotism. [Deleted] stated that he first put her into a hypnotic trance and then suggested to her that he was her husband and that she desired sexual intercourse with him." (Emphasis added.)

Here is evidence *from the CIA itself* of the existence of such sexual abuses, and their interest in it, dating back to the very early 1950s.

Which begs the question: How many more women were put under mind control and raped by CIA agents and operatives? How much more advanced are the techniques being used today, well over half a century later?

4. Such experiments must necessarily have involved a vast number of players, including experts in such fields as psychology, hypnosis, drug abuse and other areas related to mind control; such experiments must also have involved the participation of some of the country's leading institutions

Congressional hearings in 1977 were able to document, despite CIA destruction of most MK-ULTRA files, some 80 institutions, including colleges, universities, hospitals, prisons, and more, that were used by the CIA in MK-ULTRA experiments. Some were used unwittingly, some participated with knowledge of what they were doing.

Among them: University of California at Berkeley, City College of New York, Boston Psychopathic Hospital, Mt Sinai Hospital New York, Columbia University, University of Illinois Medical School, National Institute of Mental Health (NIMH)-sponsored Addiction Research Center Lexington KY, University of Rochester NY, Missouri Institute of Psychiatry, Harvard University, Massachusetts General Hospital, University of Maryland Medical School, Emory University, New York State Psychiatric Institute, Baylor University, University of Wisconsin, University of Delaware, Veterans Administration Hospital Palo Alto CA, Rockefeller Foundation, California Prison Medical Facility at Vacaville...

In his book BLUEBIRD: Deliberate Creation of Multiple Personality by Psychiatrists, Dr. Colin A. Ross provides proof, based on 15,000 pages of documents obtained from the CIA under the Freedom of Information Act, "that there was extensive political abuse of psychiatry in North America throughout the second half of the twentieth century, perpetrated not by a few renegade doctors, but by leading psychiatrists, psychologists, pharmacologists, neurosurgeons and medical schools." This includes MK-ULTRA as well as other criminal U.S. government projects.

Following are a few prominent people who were also key MK-ULTRA figures:

World-renowned psychiatrist **Donald Ewen Cameron** (1901-1967) had impeccable credentials. He was the first chairman of the World Psychiatric Association and president of the Canadian and American Psychiatric Associations, the American Psychopathological Association and the Society of Biological Psychiatry. Cameron had also been a member of the Nuremberg Trials medical tribunal, 1946–47.

Yet in the 1950s and 1960s, working under contract for a CIA front organization entitled the Human Ecology Foundation, Cameron conducted a series of monstrous experiments on hundreds of patients without their knowledge or consent. These patients were in no way volunteers; they had no idea they were being experimented upon. They had simply entered a highly regarded psychiatric institution seeking help with personal problems.

Cameron's experiments were straight out of a torture-porn horror movie. They included the administration of electroshock therapy dozens of times over recommended limits, keeping patients in drug-induced comas for weeks or months at a time, dosing them with experimental drugs including LSD, sensory deprivation in so-called "sleep rooms," and exposing patients to RF and electromagnetic signals. Cameron invented and used a hideous process called "psychic driving," in which tapes of repetitive spoken messages were played through headphones or speakers up to sixteen hours a day, for as long as hundreds of hours, to helpless drugged and electroshocked patients, in the belief that their minds were wiped clean and the tapes would install new personalities.

These ghastly experiments – described simply as "torture" by award-winning journalist Naomi Klein – caused great damage to unsuspecting victims; some patients were left permanently comatose.

"The frequent screams of patients that echoed through the hospital did not deter Cameron or most of his associates in their attempts to 'depattern' their subjects completely," writes John Marks in his essential book on the topic, The

Search for the Manchurian Candidate.

These crimes took place between 1957 and 1964 at the Allan Memorial Institute of McGill University in Montreal, Quebec, which Cameron founded with funding from, among other sources, the Rockefeller Foundation. Many documents of Cameron's work were destroyed; others were classified for over half a century.

"We hanged Nazis for doing the sort of things Cameron did," said Jonathan Rauh, an attorney for the families of some of the abused patients, in 1985.

The U.S. government apparently made use of Cameron's work, and allegedly still does so to this day. A 2012 article in the McGill University newspaper noted: "Even today, remnants of Cameron's experiments at the Allan Memorial appear in torture methods at places like Guantanamo Bay."

Cameron believed that government, under the guidance of enlightened psychiatrists like himself, should exercise total control over virtually every aspect of the lives of its citizens/subjects. To achieve this total control, government should use tools including, but not limited to, police, hospitals, schools, psychiatry and mind control. Experts should decide who was fit to have children or hold various political and economic positions in society. Cameron was a confirmed enemy of competing ideologies such as the belief that individuals have inalienable rights. Cameron was an associate of Allen Dulles, the ruthless, treasonous, Nazi-connected CIA director, who he first met in the 1940s; Cameron even treated Dulles' depressed wife.

At the end of World War II Cameron urged that all Germans over the age of twelve be given electroshock treatment to literally burn Nazism from their minds. (An example of a leading MK-ULTRA figure willing to do unethical experiments on children.) He also argued that Germans should not be allowed to have children or work in positions of authority because of what he believed was a genetic tendency to submit to authoritarianism.

Louis Jolyon "Jolly" West (1924-1999) was a highly regarded American psychiatrist who led UCLA's department of psychiatry and the Neuropsychiatric Institute for 20 years. West's MK-ULTRA work included "Psychophysiological Studies of Hypnosis and Suggestibility" and "Studies of Dissociative States."

Rather startlingly, given his work in these areas, and given the accusations that MK-ULTRA created mind-controlled assassins, West performed the court-ordered pre-trial psychiatric evaluations of both Jack Ruby and Patty Hearst – who were both often described by observers as seemingly mind-controlled or brainwashed; years later, West assumed care of Oklahoma City bomber Timothy McVeigh following his arrest.

(Considering McVeigh, one cannot help but think of the Top Secret 1951 MK-ULTRA precursor experiments several decades earlier, in which subjects were hypnotized into performing mock assassinations or planting mock bombs.)

West prescribed psychiatric drugs for Jack Ruby that Ruby denounced as "poison"; Ruby died of cancer in prison two years later. The CIA is alleged to have experimented with drugs that could be surreptitiously given to victims to cause cancer.

West also explored how the War on Drugs – ratcheted up by President Richard Nixon in 1971 as a way of attacking blacks and the antiwar left – could be used for political manipulation and control of the public. In their 1975 book Hallucinations: Behavior, Experience, and Theory, West and co-author Ronald K. Siegel wrote

"The role of drugs in the exercise of political control is also coming under increasing discussion. Control can be through prohibition or supply. The total or even partial prohibition of drugs gives the government considerable leverage for other types of control. An example would be the selective application of drug laws…against selected components of the population such as members of certain minority groups or political organizations."

One could not find a more accurate description of how the War on Drugs has operated in practice.

In the early 1970s, West proposed the creation of the Center for the Study and Reduction of Violence, to be the "world's first and only center for the study of interpersonal violence." Its goal was to engage in human experimentation – including psychosurgery, drugs, electric shock, electrodes in the brain and chemical castration – to explore ways to alter behavior. "Pre-delinquent" children would be identified, in coordination with law enforcement officials, so they could be treated to prevent their future crimes. The facility would be, West noted, "securely fenced." Despite strong support from then-governor of California Ronald Reagan, and offers of federal funding, the proposal generated such outrage that it was abandoned – at least, publicly.

In Operation Mind Control Walter Bowart described West as "perhaps the chief advocate of mind control in America today. From his participation in the development of brainwashing techniques for the U.S. Air Force to his involvement in the CIA's famous MK-Ultra projects, West has figured so prominently in the research and development of the invisible war that his public career appears like a carefully constructed espionage 'cover.'"

Sidney Gottlieb (1918–1999) received a Ph.D. in chemistry from the California Institute of Technology. He joined the CIA in 1951 and was appointed head of MK-ULTRA by the treasonous CIA director Allen Dulles in 1953. Gottlieb became known as the "Black Sorcerer" and the "Dirty Trickster." Gottlieb, who from reports called himself a "Dr. Strangelove" (after the deranged scientist in Stanley Kubrick's masterpiece) was not just interested in chemical mind control. He became fascinated by the occult and the supernatural, consulting with exorcists, psychics, witches, studying black magic and so forth. Gottlieb said he personally had taken LSD more than 200 times.

Harris Isbell, M.D. (1910-1994) was the director of research for the NIMH Addiction Research Center at the Public Health Service Hospital in Lexington, Kentucky from 1945 to 1963. He used drug-addicted prisoners from the Lexington Public Health Service Hospital – a federal facility whose mission was to treat drug abusers – for his experiments, including MK-ULTRA experiments. Some of the prisoners were sentenced drug offenders, others had voluntarily entered the hospital to receive treatment for their addictions. Dr. Isbell bribed these addicts with heroin and morphine into "volunteering." (This use of such bribery was omitted from his published research.) They were administered various drugs to test their effects, including LSD, psilocybin, and DMT. Sometimes the doses were huge. In one experiment, subjects were given progressively higher doses of LSD daily – for 77 straight days.

Dr. Paul Hoch (1902-1964) was born in Hungary and educated in Germany. The psychiatrist and eugenicist was appointed New York's Commissioner of Mental Hygiene in 1955 by New York governor and major Skull and Bones donor (and husband of key Bill Clinton donor Patricia Harriman) Averell Harriman. He was reappointed by Governor Nelson Rockefeller.

Described as a "wonderfully warm, understanding human being" by Governor Rockefeller, Dr. Hoch did secret and illegal experiments on unsuspecting patients for the CIA and the U.S. Army in the 1950s involving such things as psychosurgery, spinal injections of LSD and mescaline, brainwashing, and electroconvulsive therapy. Martin A. Lee and Bruce Shlain, authors of the acclaimed history Acid Dreams: The Complete Social History of LSD: The CIA, the Sixties and Beyond, call Hoch "a mad scientist" and describe one Hoch experiment: "a hallucinogen was administered along with a local anesthetic and the subject was told to describe his visual experiences as surgeons removed chunks of his cerebral cortex."

We have earlier mentioned **George Hoben Estabrooks,** one of the world's leading authorities on hypnosis; and psychosurgeon **Richard Delgado,** pioneer in electronic brain control.

This list of MK-ULTRA monsters could be expanded. And it must always be remembered that the vast majority of MK-ULTRA files were deliberately destroyed by the CIA to keep them secret. What we know is only the tip of the iceberg.

Sums up Colin A. Ross: "The CIA doctors violated all medical codes of ethics dating back to Hippocrates, including the Nuremberg Code. ... Most of these experiments were conducted by psychiatrists with Top Secret clearance. These included Louis Jolyon West, chairman of the department of psychiatry at the University of Oklahoma and later at UCLA; Dr. Robert Hyde in Boston; Dr. Carl Rogers at the University of Wisconsin; Dr. Martin Orne at Harvard; Dr. Charles Osgood at the University of Illinois; Dr. James Hamilton at Stanford; Dr. Charles Geschichter at the University of Richmond, and Dr. Harold Abramson and Dr. Harold Wolff at Cornell. Other Top Secret-cleared MK-ULTRA contractors included Dr. Maitland Baldwin, a neurosurgeon at the National Institutes of Health and Dr. Carl Pfeiffer, a pharmacologist at Emory. ...

"The mind-control experiments and operational programs violate basic human rights and all codes of medical ethics."

5. U.S. government agents and contractors performed such dangerous, painful, invasive and criminal experiments on innocent unsuspecting American citizens illegally, without their consent or knowledge

As we have already touched on earlier, it is well documented beyond question that the U.S. government did this under the programs linked with MK-ULTRA and elsewhere.

Colin A. Ross, M.D. says of the MK-ULTRA and related mind-control experiments, in his book BLUEBIRD: Deliberate Creation of Multiple Personality by Psychiatrists:

"Throughout the 20th century, academic psychiatry provided no public commentary, ethical guidance, or moral oversight of any kind concerning mind-control experimentation, despite the fact that the leading psychiatrists and medical schools were well funded by the CIA and military for mind-control research. Mental patients, cancer patients, prisoners, and [other] unwitting citizens were experimented on by mind-control doctors at Yale, Harvard, McGill, Stanford, UCLA, and other major universities. These human guinea pigs were never told that they were subjects in military and CIA mind-control experiments, and they never gave informed consent. They received no systematic follow-up to document the harm done to them. The welfare of the 'human subjects' was not a relevant variable in the academic equation."

Journalist Eileen Welsome won a Pulitzer Prize for her decade of research in her book The Plutonium Files: America's Secret Medical Experiments in the Cold War (1999). It documents that the U.S. government conducted literally thousands of secret radiation experiments on many thousands of unsuspecting American citizens, including children, pregnant women, prisoners, hospitalized elderly patients, and the mentally challenged between the 1930s to the 1990s, injecting or otherwise exposing them to radioactive plutonium, often with horrific and fatal results.

Jonathan D. Moreno is an American philosopher and historian who specializes in bioethics, science, and national security. He has published seminal works on the history, sociology and politics of biology and medicine and has served as a senior staff member for two presidential advisory commissions and testified before both the U.S. House and Senate.

His 2000 book Undue Risk: Secret State Experiments on Humans exposes numerous secret and horrific U.S. government experiments on innocent and unknowing Americans. It covers some of the same ground as Welsome's book, but is broader in scope. Among the subjects he covers:

- the over 200 biological warfare "field tests" conducted between 1949 and 1969 in which the U.S. Army released infectious bacterial agents in cities across America without telling residents; Army and Air Force mind-control experiments (1950-1975) that administered LSD and other dangerous chemicals to thousands of subjects, often without consent;
- the post-World War II U.S. protection of the monstrous Japanese "mad scientist" General/Dr. Shiro Ishii, whose ghastly Unit 731 conducted medical experiments on helpless captives, killing thousands in

agonizing torture; Ishii was spared prosecution for his war crimes in exchange for his germ warfare data based on human experimentation, and some researchers speculate he may have been smuggled into the U.S. to work on further bioweapons experiments;
- secret government contracts with hospitals to test dangerous research drugs on utterly unsuspecting patients...

...and on and on, a parade of horrors that were Top Secret until recently and today remain unknown to the vast majority of Americans, who go about their daily lives certain that the government that constantly claims to defend and protect them would never do anything like this to them or their loved ones.

Operation Midnight Climax was an MK-ULTRA sub-project created by "Dr. Strangelove" Sidney Godlier. It is known to have operated at least from 1953 to 1964 (some sources say the late 1960s) in San Francisco, Marin, and New York. The CIA hired prostitutes to hang out in bars and lure unsuspecting men to CIA safe houses disguised as brothels. There these prostitutes would secretly slip LSD and other drugs into their customers' drinks, then have sex with them. Hidden CIA agents would watch the sex acts and film the responses of the bewildered, drugged American citizens (who were never told of their drugging). Agents would also sometimes visit local bars and restaurants, striking up conversations with patrons, slipping LSD into their drinks, and watching the results. (Note that this project not only tested drugs but also, by its nature, field-tested methods of sexual blackmail.)

The shocking murder of professional tennis player Harold Blauer shows what the government was capable of doing in these criminal experiments. Blauer died in 1952 when he was injected with a fatal dose of a mescaline derivative at the New York State Psychiatric Institute of Columbia University. The injection had no role in his treatment; it was part of secret research on unsuspecting patients funded by the Department of Defense. Indeed, the doctor who gave the injection said he had no idea what the substance the Army had given him even was: "We didn't know whether it was dog piss or what we were giving him." The Department of Defense colluded with the Department of Justice and the New York State Attorney General to conceal evidence of this for 23 years.

Finally, some quotes from MK-ULTRA operatives to ponder:

> "[T]he hand of the military must not be tied by any silly prejudices in the minds of the general public. ...In the last analysis any device is justifiable which enables us to protect ourselves from defeat." – top CIA mind-control figure George Estabrooks.

> "I never gave a thought to legality or morality. Frankly, I did what worked." – unnamed CIA mind-control agent quoted in The Search for the Manchurian Candidate: The CIA and Mind Control: The Secret History of the Behavioral Sciences by John D. Marks.

> "...it was fun, fun, fun. Where else could a red-blooded American boy lie, kill, cheat, steal, rape and pillage with the sanction and bidding of the All-highest?" – Federal Bureau of Narcotics officer George Hunter White, who oversaw Operation Midnight Climax drug experiments on unsuspecting civilians for the CIA, in a letter to MK-ULTRA leader Dr. Sidney Gottlieb, aka "Dr. Strangelove/The Black Sorcerer."

For Project MONARCH purposes, note White's use of the word "rape."

The history of MK-ULTRA shows large numbers of credentialed persons and institutions willing to perform secret, illegal mind-control experiments on U.S. citizens and keep this secret – exactly as the alleged Project MONARCH victims at the beginning of this chapter have claimed.

6. The U.S. government forced children to participate in such dangerous, painful, invasive and criminal experiments

There is no doubt that children were used in some MK-ULTRA experiments as well as many of the non-MK-ULTRA experiments mentioned above, and there is good reason to speculate that more experiments may have been performed upon children and left unrecorded or lost when the CIA destroyed its MK-ULTRA records.

A surviving MK-ULTRA document concerning proposed research in ESP specifically mention (separately) *both the creating of dissociative states and the use of children*: "that in working with individual subjects, special attention will be given to dissociative states which tend to accompany spontaneous ESP experiences. Such states can be induced and controlled to some extent with hypnosis and drugs. ... The data used in the study will be obtained from group ESP experiments which have yielded significant results, high scoring subjects (including control series and records taken after they 'lost' their ability, from special groups such as psychotics, *children* [emphasis added] and mediums, and from psychological and educational tests in which answers are of the multiple [unreadable]...

"The experimenters will be particularly interested in dissociative states, from the abasement de neveau mental to multiple personality in so-called mediums, and attempts will be made to induce a number of states of this kind using hypnosis."

(Note that this wording does not say that dissociative states were to be created in children in this experiment. But it does show MK-ULTRA interest in both subjects.)

In his book BLUEBIRD: Deliberate Creation of Multiple Personality by Psychiatrists, Dr. Colin A. Ross, M.D. notes: "The documented [non-MK-ULTRA] mind-control research includes putting brain electrodes in *children* as young as 11 years old and controlling their behavior from remote transmitters; giving 150 mcg of LSD per day to children age 7-11 for weeks and months at a time..."

Dr. Ross concludes chillingly: "Dr. [George] Estabrooks did experiments on *children*. He corresponded with FBI Director J. Edgar Hoover about using hypnosis to interrogate juvenile delinquents. *His experimentation on children raises the possibility that investigators have attempted to create*

Manchurian Candidates in children. Such a possibility might seem far-fetched until one considers the [numerous non-MK/ULTRA] LSD, biological and radiation experiments conducted on children, the fact that four MK-ULTRA Subprojects were on children, and that hypnotic subjects described in the CIA documents include girls 19 years of age. ...

The U.S. government has conducted dangerous, secret, illegal and non-consensual experiments on children outside MK-ULTRA which further proves the willingness to do such things and keep them secret. A few examples:

- In 1961, researchers at Harvard Medical School, Massachusetts General Hospital, and Boston University School of Medicine gave radioactive iodine to seventy mentally disabled children at Wrentham State School.

- MIT gave radioactive substances to children at Fernald School in their food. Parents were told on the consent form that the experiments were aimed at "helping to improve the nutrition of our children." Radioactive material was not mentioned.

- Doctors funded by the Army Medical Research and Development Command injected severely mentally disabled children with the hepatitis virus at Willowbrook State School in the 1950s and 1960s.

- In Guatemala from 1946 to 1948 – even as the Nuremberg trials were going on and Nazi doctors were being tried for unethical experiments on non-consenting subjects – U.S. doctors, funded by the U.S. National Institutes of Health, secretly infected Guatemalan soldiers, prostitutes, prisoners, mental patients *and orphan children* with syphilis and other sexually transmitted diseases, without informed consent. The diseases were treated only with antibiotics. About 1300 people were infected, but only about 700 received treatment; at least 83 were dead a few years later (though incomplete records make it impossible to know how many, if any, died as a result of the infections). U.S. doctors and other persons involved realized what they were doing was illegal and unethical. The leader of the project, Dr. John Charles Cutler, went on to work with the infamous and similarly secret Tuskegee, Alabama syphilis experiments.

Again, this is just a sampling. The well-documented and harrowing book Against Their Will: The Secret History of Medical Experimentation on Children in Cold War America, by Allen M. Hornblum, Judith L. Newman, and Gregory J. Dober tells the horrific story of how thousands of American children warehoused in orphanages, children's homes and hospitals – "cheaper than lab animals and less problematic to deal with than adults," and totally incapable of giving informed consent – were the victims of horrific government and non-government experiments. Helpless children were given electric shock, poisoned, injected with radioactive material, infected with diseases and not treated so as to track the progress of the disease, given LSD and other drugs, placed into psychological experiments that left permanent mental damage, and faced further horrors as well. Sometimes, in another echo of the Project MONARCH stories, the little-valued children in these institutions were also abused and raped by the staff of the institutions in which they were placed. The book also links this ruthless use of children with earlier theories of eugenics, another well-documented ruling-elite obsession.

So, to answer the question in this section: Yes. Clearly there have been, in the recent past, powerful well-funded elements in the U.S. government, as well as private sector organizations, willing to do horrific secret and illegal mass experiments on children – exactly as the alleged MONARCH victims claim.

7. Some alleged MONARCH victims claim to have experienced torture and abuse by Nazis, Satanists, and occultists. For this to be true there would need to be examples of collaboration between U.S.

government agencies and such persons

Again, this sounds outrageous. But it is now well documented that the U.S. government brought Nazi scientists to America after World War II – including notorious concentration camp torture-doctors – to conduct horrible experiments on American citizens, including children. These experiments went on for years.

Furthermore, top Nazi scientists and doctors, again including concentration camp torture-doctors, worked alongside U.S. scientists, doctors, and secret agents on the CIA mind-control program MK-ULTRA and its offshoots, from the earliest days of those programs. As one examines the MK-ULTRA-related projects, correlations between them and Nazi concentration camp experiments are apparent.

As for Satanists and occultists, the evidence is less direct, but what is known is provocative and disturbing.

According to his biographer David Talbot, CIA director Allen Dulles, who was very active in Germany before and during World War II, "was more in step with many Nazi leaders than he was with President Roosevelt." An anti-Semite, according to Talbot, Dulles met with both Hitler and Goebbels in the 1930s. Talbot writes that Dulles "clung to a sympathetic view of the Fuhrer" until past the mid-1930s. Prior to the outbreak of war, Sullivan and Cromwell, the law firm of Allen and brother John Foster Dulles, "was at the center of an intricate network of banks, investment firms, and industrial conglomerates that rebuilt Germany after World War I." Some of those relationships remained strong during and after the war.

Supreme Court justice Arthur Goldberg, who served in U.S. intelligence during World War II, declared bluntly that "the Dulles brothers were traitors." Indeed, Talbot's opening chapter is entitled "The Double Agent," a reference to Dulles' wartime activities that favored Nazis in direct defiance of the policies of President Roosevelt. Such actions, Talbot says, constituted treason. Talbot writes that during World War II Dulles, then a top OSS agent, illegally hid U.S. assets of German corporations, shredded documents to protect such businesses, and kept information about the horrors of Nazi prison camps from reaching President Roosevelt.

Had Roosevelt survived the war, Talbot says, Allen and John Foster Dulles "would likely have faced serious criminal charges for their wartime activities."

Immediately after the war, Dulles rescued Hitler's chief of intelligence Reinhard Gehlen and hundreds of his fellow Nazis and spies, and turned Gehlen's Nazi spy ring into... the core of the CIA's new European branch. In 1999 the National Security Archives noted that "at least five associates of the notorious Nazi Adolf Eichmann worked for the CIA, 23 other Nazis were approached by the CIA for recruitment, and at least 100 officers within the Gehlen organization were former SD or Gestapo officers..." Nazis in Gehlen's Nazi/CIA spy ring included SS officers, intelligence officials, police, and non-German Nazi collaborators. And far from being reformed, some were what the U.S. government itself described as "ardent Nazis." Among those rescued by Dulles and other U.S. agents were Nazis who had performed monstrous human experiments in concentration camps.

For example, Kurt Blome was a high-ranking Nazi scientist in charge of all research into biological warfare for the SS and the Wehrmacht. Blome oversaw and participated in gruesome chemical and biological weapons testing on concentration camp inmates. Among his World War II goals was the development of new chemical and biological weapons from plague, cholera, anthrax, typhoid, cancer-causing viruses, nerve gas and the like, intended to be used against the civilian populations of the United States, Britain and the Soviet Union, among other targets. The U.S. government saved Blome from likely execution at the Nuremberg Trials, instead hiring him to work on chemical warfare experiments and MK-ULTRA-type mind control.

Blome worked as part of the CIA's Project BLUEBIRD, which would become MK-ULTRA. Among his responsibilities was serving as chief medical officer at a Top Secret CIA/Department of Defense black site called Camp King in the American zone of occupied Germany. Here Blome and other Nazi doctors, working alongside CIA scientists and agents, administered dangerous combinations of powerful mind-bending drugs and performed other criminal and inhumane experimental interrogation methods on captured Soviet spies, defectors, and others. "Disposal of the body is not a problem," they were told.

And Camp King was no rogue operation. CIA head Allen Dulles approved the project and was kept appraised. Here is an excerpt from one of the few surviving documents, a secret memo from Dulles outlining the kinds of interrogation techniques to be tried:

"In our conversation of 9 February 1951, I outlined to you the possibilities of augmenting the usual interrogation methods by the use of drugs, hypnosis, shock, etc., and emphasized the defensive aspects as well as the offensive opportunities in this field of applied medical science." Such research was best conducted overseas, Dulles explained, since foreign governments "permitted certain activities which were not permitted by the United States government (i.e., anthrax etc.)."

Operation Paperclip author Annie Jacobsen notes that Camp King activities have never been fully revealed by either the CIA or Department of Defense.

So here we have it: confirmation of Nazis working with the CIA on top secret MK-ULTRA-type (and perhaps simply MK-ULTRA) mind-control experiments in the very earliest days of those experiments. We cannot know what other such collaborations were hidden in the thousands of MK-ULTRA files the CIA destroyed, or in the mind control experiments the CIA has admitted it conducted but kept no records of.

Dulles and other U.S. operatives saved many other Nazi war criminals, part of secret and sometimes illegal efforts that brought thousands of Nazis into the United States and Latin America and returned others to places of power in post-war West Germany.

It is a horrific irony that far more Nazis were slipped into the U.S. after World War II than were Holocaust survivors seeking to immigrate.

Operation Paperclip (sometimes called Project Paperclip) was a Top Secret program conducted during and after the final days of World War II. Operation Paperclip secretly brought over 1500 German scientists, engineers and technicians to America. Especially prized were scientists specializing in rocketry, chemical weapons, chemical reaction technology, and medicine.

President Harry Truman officially started Operation Paperclip in August 1945. His order expressly excluded anyone found "to have been a member of the Nazi Party, and more than a nominal participant in its activities, or an active supporter of Nazi militarism."

However, those involved in the recruiting of German scientists knew that would have prohibited most of them. So Dulles and others simply ignored President Truman's orders, as well as similar policies agreed upon by the leaders of the Allied nations.

These 1500-plus German and Nazi scientists, including devout Nazis, war criminals, and Nazis complicit in mass murderer, were brought to the U.S. clandestinely and illegally, without proper State Department review and approval or other legal review process. False biographies were created and evidence of war crimes deleted from their records so they could be given security clearances to work for the U.S. government. *Much information surrounding Operation Paperclip is still classified.*

In turn, these Nazi scientists laid the foundation of NASA and the U.S. ICBM program, among other things. (For more on the Nazi influence on NASA, see Chapter 10.)

In the previous section we pointed out that it is well documented that, beginning in the 1940s and running at least into the 1970s, the U.S. government conducted monstrous and illegal radioactive experiments upon U.S. citizens.

Some of the scientists involved in those criminal radiation experiments were... Nazis smuggled into the U.S. by Operation Paperclip. Incredibly, Nazi scientists who had conducted monstrous experiments on prisoners in Nazi concentration camps were secretly imported into the U.S. to conduct horrific illegal experiments on American citizens – with the blessings of, and funding by, the U.S. government. They worked alongside U.S. doctors and scientists in what, again, amounts to a secret war against American citizens.

Thus the claims by alleged Project MONARCH victims that they were tormented and tortured by Nazis arguably deserves perhaps a bit more consideration than it might seem upon first encounter.

As for the use of torture itself, there is no doubt that the CIA has used, promoted and taught torture since its earliest days. Historian Alfred McCoy's 2006 book, A Question of Torture: CIA Interrogation from the Cold War to the War on Terror, details this depraved history. Indeed, from 1970 to 1988 Congress held four major hearings to expose the CIA's illegal use of torture.

The CIA even printed torture how-to manuals and distributed them to foreign allies. The notorious 1963 "KUBARK Counterintelligence Interrogation" (KUBARK was a CIA codename for itself), used and updated for years, taught torture interrogation techniques. Among its suggestions: in choosing an interrogation site "the electric current should be known in advance, so that transformers and other modifying devices will be on hand if needed"; "An environment still more subject to control, such as water-tank or iron lung, is even more effective."

The criminality of this, and the CIA leadership's willingness to break the law, was expressed in a 1980s CIA interrogation manual, which at one point declares "Illegal detention always requires prior HQS [headquarters] approval." Similarly, the CIA "Human Resource Exploitation Training Manual" from the 1980s notes that "The use of force, mental torture, threats, insults or exposure to inhumane treatment of any kind as an aid to interrogation is prohibited by law, both international and domestic; it is neither authorized nor condoned," though the manual itself teaches such things.

Such CIA coercion techniques appear in manuals used by the U.S. military in training courses between 1987 and 1991. The manuals were used at the notorious U.S. Army School of the Americas, and manuals were distributed by the hundreds to U.S. military allies in at least eleven South and Central American countries where atrocities were reported. They were used in the Vietnam War and other international conflicts. Though such techniques were allegedly abandoned after they became publicly known and denounced, the same techniques were used to abuse prisoners at the Abu Ghraib prison in Iraq and in Afghanistan and Guantanamo.

Interestingly, from the MONARCH perspective, the CIA interrogation manuals discuss the use of hypnotism and drugs, key areas of MK-ULTRA research. Some critics contend that MK-ULTRA experiments laid the groundwork for subsequent CIA torture methods.

The Mengele Connection?

As if charges of Nazi participation in MK-ULTRA and the alleged Project MONARCH were not enough, almost as if deliberately designed to further strain our credulity there is the even wilder, even more hard to believe charge by several alleged MONARCH victims that they were abused and programmed specifically by the infamous Nazi torture doctor Josef Mengele – known as the "Angel of Death" because of his monstrous human experiments, including experiments on children, at the Auschwitz death camp.

Some examples:

- An alleged MONARCH victim known as "*Sara in Minnesota*" who has testified before Congress on mind control, told conspiracy researcher Dr. Henry Makow that she "spent the better part of my first three or four years" tortured by, among others, Mengele.

 "Mengele et al tortured me many times in many locations I have heard mentioned by other MK-ULTRA survivors, including several hospitals here in the U.S. and on military bases. The tortures included but were not limited to rapes, disjointing, killing animals and other children in front of me or being forced to watch as adults were tortured, electric shock, injections with LSD and anectidine and many other substances, cattle prod up the vagina or rectum, witnessed murders, occultic rituals, many bizarre sex acts. It was very calculated and continues to the present. ... Mengele was alive and well and living in the U.S. as an honored guest of the United States government as late as 1987."

- *Arizona Wilder* also says she was abused and programmed by Mengele.

- *Cisco Wheeler* says "My primary programmer was Dr. Green, who was Dr. Josef Mengele. ...my father was trained by Mengele, he was his #2 man. ... [Mengele also] went by [the names] Dr. Fairchild, Dr. Green. ...I am sure that he infiltrated every state, and I know he has worked up in Canada."

- *Carol Rutz* also claims that one of her programmers and torturers, "Dr. Black," was actually Mengele. In an interview with the Rutherford Foundation, she says "I believe that [CIA head and MK-ULTRA founder] Allen Dulles knew. I know there were a number of doctors that worked with Dr. Black who knew that he was Josef Mengele. Mengele was brought to the United States covertly. ... [W]hen I saw Josef Mengele's face in a photograph, I recognized him as Dr. Black. He had an accent. He wore shiny black shoes. But more than once I was told not to look at his face. However, there came a point in time where he actually identified himself to me. I probably was around 16 years old when that happened. He referred to me as one of the 'Mengele kids.' That was the time I heard his name mentioned or he himself spoke his name. Other than that, it was always Dr. Black in front of me."

Rutz further claims that *many other mind-control survivors remember Mengele*. He "also worked in Canada because there are *many Canadian survivors* who also remember him. Some of these survivors were in orphanages. ... Moreover, as time went on and I spoke with more and more survivors, other people remembered the same face as that of Josef Mengele when they saw a picture of him."

If even the documented tales of criminal government experiments on civilians, and postwar CIA collaboration with Nazis are hard for many to believe – though, as we have shown, they are true and more horrific than most Americans know or would believe possible – these tales of a postwar Mengele working with the CIA on secret criminal mind-control programs surely seems to stretch belief past the breaking point.

And yet...

It is documented that Mengele escaped Germany after World War II. It is further documented that he traveled the world after that. Indeed, Mengele was reported around the globe, often far from South America – even in the United States.

According to People magazine (June 24, 1985) Mengele "was reportedly seen in Paraguay, Brazil, Chile, Bolivia, Peru, West Germany, Austria, Portugal, Miami and Westchester County, New York." The famed Nazi hunter Simon Wiesenthal said Mengele had been seen on the Greek island of Kythnos in 1960, in Cairo in 1961, in Spain in 1971, and in Paraguay in 1978. Award-winning journalist Gerald Posner, in his book, Mengele: The Complete Story, says that in March 1956 Mengele flew from Argentina to Switzerland, with a stopover in New York City.

Mengele supposedly died while swimming in Brazil in 1979 and was buried under a false name, and a 1985 forensic examination of his remains identified him. However, prior to the 1985 identification, there were post-1979 Mengele sightings. Simon Wiesenthal declared in 1985 – six years after Mengele supposedly died, but before the forensic evidence allegedly identified his remains – that he was found alive. In 1985 a mock trial for Mengele – still thought to be alive –was held in Israel.

An Auschwitz survivor has quoted Mengele as saying "The more we do to you, the less you seem to believe we are doing it." If MK-ULTRA exists in some form today, that quote could be its motto.

We have seen that other Nazi torture-doctors and war criminals were secretly and illegally admitted to the U.S. or otherwise worked with U.S. forces in illegal programs including some at least similar to, if not part of, MK-ULTRA. There is no reason to think that the same U.S. forces who sought out and rescued other Nazi war criminal scientists would have hesitated to also rescue and employ Mengele if he was thought to be of sufficient use or value.

Finally, whether or not Mengele was actually involved, if there were Nazis and/or German nationals involved in MONARCH experiments, as the alleged MONARCH victims claim, it would be natural enough for one or more to adopt the name Mengele as a macabre, ironic cover name, perhaps to strike fear into the hearts of victims.

Nazi UFO Aliens?

And then there is an even more mind-blowing Nazi-weirdness association: the bizarre phenomena of the so-called "Nazi Aliens."

As we touch on in Chapter 9, many UFO researchers have speculated – outlandish though it may seem at first – that the UFO abduction phenomena is closely connected with MK-ULTRA-type programs today, and that either (1) aliens are cooperating with the U.S. government in such programs or (2) "aliens" don't exist at all and are simply a government ruse to disguise various super-secret government projects, ranging from experimental aircraft testing to MK-ULTRA-type mind-control, genetic, or other experiments on humans.

Since 2005 former Canadian Defense Minister Paul Hellyer – a highly accomplished man and respected figure in Canadian politics for over half a century – has strongly and very publicly insisted that UFOs are very real and are active in the world. Further, he says the major governments of the world know this.

In 2015 Hellyer told the UK Daily Mail that one species or type of alien entities are called "Nordic Blondes." (As we have noted, these same reported aliens are also called "Nazi Aliens.") Hellyer said if you saw one you'd probably ask yourself, "I wonder if she's from Denmark or somewhere."

Indeed, from the earliest days of UFO encounters in the 1950s up to the present day, such entities have repeatedly been reported by witnesses.

Exactly as Defense Minister Hellyer notes, they are typically described as tall (six to seven feet), completely human in appearance, strongly resembling Nordic-Scandinavians, often with blond hair and blue eyes. They are usually friendly, smiling, and are sometimes called "Space Brothers."

The less flattering nickname "Nazi Aliens" evolved based on how the striking features of these aliens seemed to match Nazi racial purity archetypes – and, more interestingly, how they sometimes have been reported *speaking German, or English with a German accent.*

Given the strange history of Nazi occult practices; the monstrous breeding and eugenics experiments conducted by the Nazis; documented secret Nazi weapons including craft strongly resembling flying saucers; the postwar influence of Nazis on the U.S. space program; and the postwar Nazi involvement in the CIA and in secret illegal U.S. military and science activities – the sudden appearance of these blonde German-speaking "Nazi Aliens" just after the end of World War II – at about the same time MK-ULTRA was kicked off – inevitably raises all sorts of disturbing speculations.

Add to this the fact that Kenneth Arnold, whose June 24, 1947 sighting of a string of UFOs flying past Mount Ranier is generally regarded as the first UFO sighting of the modern era, made a drawing of the type of craft he saw – and many have observed that it has a distinct resemblance to a specific experimental Nazi fighter plane, the radical and futuristic Horten Ho 229.

Even today, the all-wing and jet-propelled Horten Ho 229 looks downright otherworldly. In February 2016 the BBC said it was "decades ahead of its time ... more spaceship than aircraft ... looks more like a flying saucer than a fighter plane ... Only now are we realizing how inspired it was." Further, it was equipped with never-before-seen stealth anti-radar technology.

This stunning craft was part of the near-war's-end Nazi

Jäger-Notprogramm (Emergency Fighter Program) aimed at quickly producing what were described as "wonder weapons" that would enable the Nazis to turn looming defeat into a devastating victory. Some writers say that the Nazi's wonder craft could have done exactly that if it had been produced in time.

Near the end of the war the U.S. military, under Operation Paperclip, seized a partially assembled model of the Horten Ho 229 V3 and secretly transported it to the U.S.

Is it really too outrageous to wonder if what Arnold saw was actually a test flight of reconstructed Nazi UFO-like crafts? *The United States Air Force didn't think that idea was too farfetched.* In the late 1940s, Project Sign, the Air Force's first known investigation of flying saucers, which evolved into the more famous Project Blue Book, seriously explored the possibility that UFOs might be a secret Soviet aircraft – based on the Horten Ho 229 and related Nazi technology.

Similarly, in 2010 the UK Telegraph summarized an article from the respected German news magazine PM: "Eyewitnesses captured by the Allies after WW2 claimed to have seen [a Nazi prototype] saucer produced in Prague fly on several occasions in early 1945."

With all this in mind, let us look at the first and perhaps most famous case of alien abduction, that of Barney and Betty Hill, which they said occurred on the night of September 19-20, 1961. Under hypnosis Barney Hill described what he saw as a group of "strangely not human" figures moving with "the precision of German officers." Describing one, Hill said "He looks like a German Nazi. He's a Nazi." They were dressed in shiny black uniforms with peaked caps – a description matching SS uniforms – and spoke what sounded like… German.

An early recorded encounter with the "Nazi Aliens" type was reported by Nebraska grain buyer and salesman Reinhold Schmidt. Schmidt said that on November 5, 1957 he came across a large cigar-shaped object in a field. A ray shot out from it and paralyzed him. Two men carried him into the ship, where he encountered a crew of human-looking space aliens, four male, two female. They claimed to be from Saturn. And they spoke… German.

Wrote Schmidt: "When these people spoke among themselves they used high German, which I happen to understand, as I graduated from a school in which both German and English were taught. I could speak, read, and write German at the time, and I still speak and understand it fairly well. But these people all spoke to me in English with a German accent."

Elsewhere Schmidt wrote that "the crew spoke German and acted like German soldiers."

Schmidt was eventually told to leave the ship, and he watched it soar away. He went to local police, who told him there had already been another report of a strange craft in the air. Schmidt adds: "A county official told me later that the craft had stalled a tractor, two cars, and a large truck... all of which had been beneath the path of the ship during its takeoff."

The deputy sheriff accompanied Schmidt to the landing site, and they reported seeing deep imprints and an oily residue.

One of the many interesting things about Schmidt's encounter is that he didn't think the occupants were extraterrestrial beings, and he was surprised when news stories wrote of his encounter as one with "aliens." After all, inside the ship he had noticed common Roman and Arabic numbers on their instruments, and the occupants were human in appearance and spoke German. His first inclination was to think it was a Russian craft gathering data on Sputnik, manned by German scientists.

After his encounter Smith was constantly harassed by government agents, seeking to change or distort his story – a quite common theme in UFO literature.

The day after Schmidt's encounter, which was reported across America, 12 year-old Everett Clark of Dante, Tennessee, a suburb of Knoxville, reported seeing a landed craft with two human figures outside. They spoke, he said, with a German accent.

George Adamski, perhaps the most famous contactee of the 1950s, wrote that the blond-haired blue-eyed "Venusian" aliens he encountered sometimes spoke in German.

Similar stories abound in UFO contactee reports. Most of the "Nordics" reported don't speak German or wear SS-type uniforms, it should be noted. But the Nazi Aliens/Nordics/Space Brothers are one of the most reported alien "types" in UFO contacts, particularly in the reports from the 1950s and early 1960s in the U.S., Europe and other parts of the world.

There are also persistent claims of covert U.S. government cooperation with Nordic/Nazi Aliens (and other alien types). One of the most astonishing comes from respected scholar and U.S. Congress and Pentagon consultant Timothy Good, who claims that President Dwight D. Eisenhower had secret meetings in 1954 with the Nordics and, later, with Crowleyan LAM-type Greys – meetings initiated by telepathy.

As reported in the UK Daily Mail, February 28th 2016: "Former American President Dwight D. Eisenhower had three secret meetings with aliens, a former U.S. government consultant has claimed... Eisenhower and other FBI officials are said to have organized the showdown with the space creatures by sending out 'telepathic messages' ...the claims from Mr. Good, a former U.S. Congress and Pentagon consultant, are the first to be made publicly by a prominent academic... The initial meeting is supposed to have taken place with aliens who were 'Nordic' in appearance, but the agreement was eventually 'signed' with a race called 'Alien Greys,'"

Good has impressive credentials. Lord Hill-Norton, former chairman of the NATO Military Committee, says: "I have the highest regard for Good's absolute integrity, his determination and skill as a researcher, and his wide and detailed knowledge of the UFO experience."

Good has lectured at universities and prominent organizations including the Institute of Medical Laboratory Sciences, the Royal Canadian Military Institute, the Royal Geographical Society, the Royal Naval Air Reserve Branch, the French Air Force, the British House of Lords All-Party UFO Study Group, and the Oxford and Cambridge Union societies. In addition to consulting with Congress and the Pentagon, he is a bestselling author of several acclaimed books on the UFO question.

Further, Good's incredible Eisenhower story is backed up in various degrees by witnesses. One witness is Bill Kirklin, who was a medic at Holloman Air Force Base in 1955 where he says he saw President Eisenhower arrive for a secret meeting. Kirlin says he overheard officers talking about alien crafts, alien autopsies, the Roswell crash, and related matters. Kirklin's commanding officer told Kirlin he and his wife had seen a hovering alien craft, and it was all classified beyond Top Secret.

Dr. Michael E. Salla also has an impressive resume. Salla has held academic appointments in the School of International Service, American University, Washington DC, and Australian National University, Canberra, Australia. He was researcher in residence in the Center for Global Peace (2001-2004) and conducted research and fieldwork in the ethnic conflicts in East Timor, Kosovo, Macedonia, and Sri Lanka. He has a PhD in Government from the University of Queensland, Australia, and an MA in Philosophy from the University of Melbourne, Australia. He has written or edited several books and over 70 papers and other publications.

His 2004 paper "Eisenhower's 1954 Meeting with Extraterrestrials: The Fiftieth Anniversary of First Contact?" explores the evidence for the Eisenhower incident.

Excerpts:

"There is circumstantial and testimonial evidence supporting Eisenhower's meeting with extraterrestrials... A meeting with extraterrestrials may well have been the true purpose of his visit [to what is now Edwards Air Force base]...There are a number of other sources alleging an extraterrestrial meeting at Edwards Air force base that corresponded to a formal First Contact event. These sources are based on testimonies of 'whistleblowers' that witnessed documents or learned from their 'insider contacts' of such a meeting. ... Col. Phillip Corso, a highly decorated officer that served in Eisenhower's National Security Council alluded to a treaty signed by the Eisenhower administration with extraterrestrials in his memoirs. ..."

It is commonly asked: If such things are true, why don't more witnesses step forward to corroborate? Dr. Stella has a persuasive answer:

"Penalties for disclosing classified information concerning extraterrestrials are quite severe. In December 1953, the Joint Chiefs of Staff issued Army-Navy-Air Force publication 146 that made the unauthorized release of information concerning UFOs a crime under the Espionage Act, punishable by up to 10 years in prison and a $10,000 fine."

We should also remember that there is a disturbing record of severe government harassment and punishment of whistleblowers and witnesses who have dared to step forward, both on the UFO issue and other matters.

Further, Steve Bassett, named "Researcher of the Year" at the 2014 International UFO Conference, has warned that there seems to be a pattern of *unusual deaths* among UFO investigators: "There are a number of death clusters relating to various [UFO] issues over the past 20 years."

UFO researcher Nigel Watson agrees: "As long ago as 1971, researcher Otto Binder claimed that at least 137 UFO investigators had died under mysterious circumstances during the 1960s. A 30-year-long study by UFO researcher Timothy Hood [a former U.S. government adviser] has also revealed that since the 1970s there are numerous cases of UFO researchers and investigators who have been murdered, suffered a sudden death or been the victims of suspicious 'suicides' or inconclusive natural causes."

Author Nick Redfern has devoted an entire book to this grim topic: Close Encounters of the Fatal Kind.

Concerning government abuse of non-UFO whistleblowers, one need only consider Chelsea Elizabeth Manning, sentenced to 35 years in prison, or Edward Snowden, forced to flee the U.S. and live in exile after revealing evidence of a secret government war against the privacy and liberty of Americans.

No wonder, then, that many people might refuse to come forward with what they know.

Adding to the creepiness of the "Nazi Aliens" controversy, in the UFO encounter literature there are unsettling reports of Aryan "Nazi Aliens" seen working side-by-side with reptilians and Crowleyan LAM-like "Greys"; claims that the Nazi Aliens and reptilians can shapeshift; sightings of UFOs decorated with swastikas and iron crosses; and, again, reports of German-speaking or German-accented beings in UFOs.

In many ways the UFO abduction phenomena seems to parallel MK-ULTRA: the hypnotizing of victims, the erasure or alteration of memories, medical and psychological experiments conducted on kidnapped victims, mind control, eugenics, an interest in children, multi-generational family abuse by aliens, government misdirection and secrecy and apparent suppression of evidence, and so on.

Remember too that the U.S. covertly and illegally imported Nazi torture doctors to the U.S. at the end of World War II, and used them to secretly conduct illegal experiments upon American citizens – including MK-ULTRA projects.

Putting the history of MK-ULTRA, the history of post-war Nazi and CIA connections, the fact that the Project Paperclip importation of Nazi scientists into the U.S. closely times with the enactment of MK-ULTRA (and related projects), and the voluminous UFO literature alongside the unproven but provocative claims of alleged MONARCH victims makes for disturbing speculations. Is there some awful connection here? We do not at present know. But these parallels are eerie and provocative.

We are forced to ask: Did the U.S. government secretly capture Nazi UFO technology and integrate it into MK-ULTRA? Did the CIA or some other shadowy and ruthless secret agency assign some of the German scientists smuggled into the U.S. by Project Paperclip – perhaps even the infamous Mengele himself – to fly about the country and the world, conducting MONARCH-like mind-control experiments and genetic testing and experimenting, in the disguise of alien encounters? Or, to speculate even further, could all this be taking place with the assistance of monstrous beings from other worlds or other dimensions?

As author and California State University Long Beach professor and conspiracy researcher Robert Guffey asks:

"Think about it: Are we being invaded from outer space or from Langley, Virginia [location of CIA headquarters]?"

Such suggestions of Nazi connections have led many to speculate that the "K" in MK-ULTRA stands for "Kontrolle," German for "Control." (Officially, the "MK" is said to be a CIA code indicating that the project was sponsored by the agency's Technical Services Staff, which designed technology and gadgetry for CIA clandestine operations; the word "Ultra" had earlier been used to indicate the most secret classification of World War II intelligence.)

Satanism, the Occult, and the U.S. Government

Regarding Satanism, exorcism, demon possession, black magic, psychic powers and related matters, the CIA's and military's long and deep interest in, and exploration of, these subjects, though not known widely to the public, is well documented.

The wide-ranging history Acid Dreams: The Complete Social History of LSD: The CIA, The Sixties, and Beyond, by Martin A. Lee and Bruce Sharline notes that the CIA, which was created on September 18, 1947, was interested in the psychic and the occult from its earliest days:

"The CIA's interest in parapsychology dates back to the late 1940s. ...

"In 1952 the CIA initiated an extensive program involving 'the search for and development of exceptionally gifted individuals who can approximate perfect success in ESP performance.' The Office of Security, which ran the ARTICHOKE project, was urged to follow 'all leads on individuals reported to have true clairvoyant powers' so as to be able to subject their claims to 'rigorous scientific investigation.'

"Along this line the CIA began infiltrating séances and occult gatherings. A memo dated April 9, 1953, refers to a domestic – and therefore illegal – operation that required the 'planting of a very specialized observer' at a séance in order to obtain 'a broad surveillance of all individuals attending the meetings.'"

A subset of MK-ULTRA was the covert CIA/Department of Defense Project MK-OFTEN, also referred to as Operation Often. MK-OFTEN was headed by the chief of the CIA's Technical Services Branch, the notorious Dr. Sidney Gottlieb – MK-ULTRA head and long obsessed with the supernatural, nicknamed by his peers the "Black Sorcerer." MK-OFTEN's mission statement was to "explore the world of black magic" and "harness the forces of darkness and challenge the concept that the inner reaches of the mind are beyond reach. The project will aim to create a new kind of psycho-civilized human being."

To this monstrous end, Dr. Gottlieb and other CIA agents consulted and recruited Satanists, demonologists, witches, warlocks, mediums, psychics, clairvoyants, astrologers, and other practitioners of the darkest realms of the occult; activities allegedly explored included attempting to raise the dead. In 1972, according to author Gordon Thomas in his book Secrets & Lies: A History of CIA Mind Control and Germ Warfare, they sought the assistance of the monsignor in charge of exorcisms for the Catholic archdiocese of New York, who, Thomas writes, "flatly refused to cooperate."

Among those they did work with was Sybil Leek. Leek is popularly considered a bland innocuous astrologer. But she had a far more interesting history than one might think: she says she knew the infamous Beast 666 Aleister Crowley as a child, and he was a friend of her father; she also knew HG Wells, one of the leading architects and publicists of the New World Order/Round Table/Fabian Socialist world takeover schemes that resulted in the Council on Foreign Relations and the streams of ruling elite organizations that followed. Note again the long and intimate connections between spy agencies, political movements, and the occult: Crowley was a secret agent for the British in World War I and, some argue, World War II as well; he certainly associated with prominent British intelligence agents during World War II.

The Stargate Project is yet another example of the government's deep and long-term interest in psychic powers, magic, the occult and related matters. (It is further discussed in Chapter 10.) This top-secret government project involved the CIA and other agencies and spent millions of dollars exploring and field-testing such psychic phenomena as remote viewing, astral projection/out-of-body experiences, clairvoyance, ESP, psychokinesis and more. Begun in 1978, it was officially ended in 1995, but many believe it still goes on secretly today.

Michael A. Aquino and the Temple of Set: Then there is the strange story of Michael A. Aquino and the Temple of Set. Aquino joined the Church of Satan in 1969 and rose quickly to become its #2-ranking official and the right-hand man of founder Anton LaVey. In 1975 Aquino and several other members left because of disagreements with LaVey. Aquino believed Satan had guided him to do this.

Unlike LaVey, Aquino and his followers believed Satan was a real entity, and Aquino also believed in the reality of Crowleyan black magic. In 1976 Aquino performed a ritual to invoke Satan; according to Aquino, Satan himself then dictated a manuscript to Aquino, The Book of Coming Forth by Night, to be the founding document of the new Temple of Set, to be headed by Aquino. According to Aquino, Satan also told Aquino that his (Satan's) name was Set, which had been used by his followers in ancient Egypt. Set was also called the Prince of Darkness in Egypt. The Book of Coming Forth by Night also linked Aquino's Temple of Set with the teachings of Aleister Crowley.

What makes this all the more interesting is Aquino's background during this time. While leader of the Temple of Set he described himself as "a lieutenant colonel, Military Intelligence, U.S. Army... qualified as a Special-Forces officer, Civil Affairs officer, and Defense Attaché ...a graduate of the Command and General Staff College, the National Defense University, the Defense Intelligence College, and the State Department's Foreign Service Institute."

In 1989 he listed 16 separate military schools that he had attended, including the JFK Special Warfare Center at Fort Bragg, North Carolina, and "Strategic Intelligence" at the Defense Intelligence College, at Bolling Air Force Base in Washington, DC.

In 2013 Aquino further elaborated on his military intelligence background: "1969-70 saw me in southeast Asia as a **PSYOP** Command & Control Team Leader and Air

Operations Officer ... I became more deeply involved in Special Operations, qualifying first in Civil Affairs and then Military Intelligence Branches. In 1976 I was selected for the Foreign Area Officer career program, cross-trained at the State Department's Foreign Service Institute and the Central and Defense Intelligence Agencies, finally being designated one of the Army's extremely rare Political-Military Affairs Officers. As a Defense Attaché, my assigned area was NATO/West Europe, and I also worked closely with the U.S. Information Agency. In 1987 I attended the National Defense University, then in 1990 was selected as one of the Army's first Space Intelligence Officers. After completing Joint SIO qualification with the Air Force, I spent my final four years of active duty at Cheyenne Mountain with J2X/MJ of HQ U.S. Space Command/NORAD. Appropriately for ATS, my security clearance until my retirement was TS/Special Intelligence Access in compartments *some of whose own names are themselves classified.* [Emphasis added.] ... At various times I worked with DIA, CIA, NRO, DOS, USIA [before it was DOS-absorbed], and of course the other DOD services. ... I didn't have much to do with NSA, because it's SIGINT (signals intelligence) while I was HUMINT (human intelligence) [and later SPACEINT]."

"Satanist accused of molesting girl; Soldier calls probe a witch hunt" was the title of a November 8, 1987, San Jose Mercury News story on Aquino, which included this: "In 1982, Aquino performed a Satanic ritual in the Westphalian castle used as an occult sanctuary by Heinrich Himmler's SS Elite in Nazi Germany. Aquino, in a Temple of Set newsletter, told of performing the ritual in the castle's Hall of the Dead while on a tour of NATO military installations in Europe."

(Regarding the accusation of child molestation in the headline above, after an investigation Aquino was not charged; the case involved accusations of ritual child abuse in 1986 at the U.S. Army's Presidio Child Development Center in San Francisco. No arrests were made, but the case remains controversial among some researchers. In 1987 there were roughly two dozen reports of child abuse at U.S. military day care centers and elementary schools, without convictions. Some describe these as part of a so-called "Satanic Panic" of false and hysterical child abuse accusations in the 1980s; others say they indicate MK-ULTRA/MONARCH-type secret government activity.)

In 1980, while serving with the U.S. Army Reserve 7th Psychological Operations Group, Aquino co-authored a controversial article entitled "From PSYOP to MindWar: The Psychology of Victory," in which he introduced and endorsed the concept of "MindWar," a more radical kind of psy-ops directed against the people of the U.S. as well as foreign enemies and allies.

Wrote Aquino: "MindWar must reach out to friends, enemies and neutrals alike across the globe ... through the media possessed by the United States which have the capabilities to reach virtually all people on the face of the Earth. These media are, of course, the electronic media – television and radio. State of the art developments in satellite communication, video recording techniques, and laser and optical transmission of broadcasts make possible a penetration of the minds of the world such as would have been inconceivable just a few years ago. ... You seize control of all of the means by which his government and populace process information to make up their minds, and you adjust it so that those minds are made up as you desire."

Aquino notes that U.S. law forbids the use of propaganda against the American people, but says that MindWar would be exempt from that, because it would tell the "truth" – as the government perceives it – rather than lies, which he says are a defining characteristic of propaganda. The more cynical reader might wonder if the government, military, and secret government agencies can be trusted, or even expected, to hew strictly to beaming the truth (whatever it may determine that to be) into the minds of all, citizen, friend, and foe alike.

Near the end of the article Aquino says that, to help the universal acceptance of whatever "truth" the government will be trying to implant, other methods may be useful: "There are some purely natural conditions under which minds may become more or less receptive to ideas, and MindWar should take full advantage of such phenomena as atmospheric electromagnetic activity, air ionization, and extremely low frequency waves. ... Infrasound vibration (up to 20 Hz) can subliminally influence brain activity to align itself to delta, theta, alpha, or beta wave patterns, inclining an audience toward everything from alertness to passivity. Infrasound could be used tactically, as ELF-waves endure for great distances; and it could be used in conjunction with media broadcasts as well."

Such mechanical means of inducing suggestible and subliminal-receptive states of minds upon unsuspecting populations are, of course, the very essence of MK-ULTRA. (Though this of course does not indicate Aquino was involved with MK-ULTRA.)

Indeed, the American people may already be victims of MindWar-type control. Cass Sunstein, head of President Obama's White House Office of Information and Regulatory Affairs, wrote favorably of initiating secret propaganda and surveillance campaigns – currently illegal – against the American public to combat "conspiracy theories." He also called for restricting First Amendment protections of free speech. (This is further covered in Chapter 13.) And researcher Matthew Alford, after examining documents obtained under the Freedom of Information Act together with information received through personal interviews, suspects that over 10,000 recent movies, TV shows and video games may have been clandestinely affected by the CIA and other government organization, as described in Chapter 9.

In a 2003 edition of his MindWar article, the Satanist Aquino notes that "The rumor mill soon had it [his original MindWars article] transformed into an Orwellian blueprint for Manchurian Candidate mind control and world domination. My own image as an occult personality added fuel to the wildfire: MindWar was now touted by the lunatic fringe as conclusive proof that the Pentagon was awash in Black Magic and Devil-worship."

Imagine that.

* * *

In this section we have explored the charge by alleged MONARCH victims that the U.S. government has cooperated with such figures as Nazis, Satanists, and occultists, and aided some of them in committing and/or covering up crimes of torture and abuse they committed against innocent Americans.

We have shown that, in fact, this nightmarish charge is true.

8. Because some of these claims are recent, we would need reason to believe that such experiments and programs are going on today (or at least were active in the very recent past)

As one would expect, the CIA assures us that MK-ULTRA-type experiments are no longer conducted. But we must remember that the CIA itself said many MK-ULTRA programs were conducted without records being kept, and that the CIA set out to destroy all records of MK-ULTRA when word came out that the program might be exposed in the early 1970s. The CIA mostly succeeded in this; the vast majority of such records were destroyed. What little we know about this parade of horrors was discovered in records accidentally overlooked by the CIA, a small percentage of the whole.

Dr. Sidney Gottlieb, the MK-ULTRA "Black Sorcerer" himself, said of MK-ULTRA in 1977: "The bottom line on this whole business has not yet been written."

There is certainly no reason to believe an agency that covered up and lied about such programs for decades, destroyed records, kept some projects off-record altogether, continued to engage in highly questionable, violent, illegal activities worldwide after MK-ULTRA was exposed, and still keeps information on such projects secret, could possibly be credible on this.

Certainly it strains credulity to believe that, if the government learned how to create mind-controlled agents, it would not do so today, and would not continue to pursue innovation and refinement in this. And, as we have seen over and over again, the government is quite capable of keeping even such large, mass-scale projects secret for years, even decades – perhaps forever.

Further, there are indications that MK-ULTRA continued, in one guise or another, despite CIA statements to the contrary. A few:

- Author and 14-year CIA veteran Victor Marchetti has said that the CIA claim that MK-ULTRA was halted is just a "cover story" and that CIA mind-control research continued.

- On May 29, 2014 the MIT Technology Review carried an article entitled "Military Funds Brain-Computer Interfaces to Control Feelings: A $70 million program will try to develop brain implants able to regulate emotions in the mentally ill." The article described experiments that sounded like a continuation of the research (if not the means) of MK-ULTRA: "...part of a sweeping $70 million program funded by the U.S. military... to use brain implants to read, and then control, the emotions of mentally ill people. ... Researchers say they are making rapid improvements in electronics, including small, implantable computers. Under its program, Mass General will work with Draper Laboratories in Cambridge, Massachusetts, to develop new types of stimulators. The UCSF team is being supported by microelectronics and wireless researchers at UC Berkeley, who have created several prototypes of miniaturized brain implants. Michel Maharbiz, a professor in Berkeley's electrical engineering department, says the Obama brain initiative, and now the DARPA money, has created a 'feeding frenzy' around new technology. 'It's a great time to do tech for the brain,' he says."

- Scientific American magazine in October 2005 noted that DARPA, the Defense Advanced Research Projects Agency, is "a major funder of brain-implant research."

- A bit of time researching the subject online brings up many more articles and public statements indicating major government ongoing interest in mind-control research roughly along the same lines of MK-ULTRA.

- According to researchers Jeffrey Kaye and H.P. Albarelli Jr: "A November 2006 instruction from the Secretary of the Navy (3900.39D) informs that the undersecretary for the Navy would heretofore be the 'Approval Authority for research involving: (a) Severe or unusual intrusions, either physical or psychological, on human subjects (such as consciousness-altering drugs or mind-control techniques).'"

- The Washington Post, based on information from whistleblower Edward Snowden, calculated that the U.S. government in fiscal year 2013 allocated $52.6 billion for a "black budget" of secret spy programs. This is in addition to a separate $23 billion devoted to intelligence programs supporting the U.S. military. The Post said the CIA, post-9/11, had been "transformed from a spy service struggling to emerge from the Cold War into a paramilitary force."

So, yes, the names have changed... but the spirit of MK-ULTRA and its related programs undoubtedly marches on today in some form or other. Which lends at the very least some credence to the claims of alleged Project MONARCH victims that they are victims of secret government programs, since tens of billions of dollars flow into such secret programs every year.

The reports we have examined of government success in creating mind-controlled agents read like science fiction. Yet remember – they are *well over fifty years old*. Some date back to the early 1950s, with references to pre-1950s efforts as well.

It boggles the mind to imagine what technologies could have been developed since then, in secret labs, with bottomless secret funding, with all the resources of the most powerful government and advanced spyocracy in all human history.

9. We would need evidence that the Clintons and/or

other ruling elite figures could be connected to pedophile rings, sexual abuse and related matters

Some of the most extreme charges made against Hillary and Bill by the alleged MONARCH victims is that they are part of a worldwide ring of ruling elite pedophiles, who sexually abuse young children who have been made into mind-control slaves by the government.

This seems so outrageous that one is inclined to dismiss it out of hand. And indeed, let us acknowledge at the start that there is no hard evidence connecting participation in such activity to the Clintons.

Looking closer, these charges have four primary components.

1) The government, and/or some other group, engages in the mind-control creation of sex slaves, including young children.
2) Some leading government officials are pedophiles.
3) These officials are supplied with sex slaves.
4) Bill or Hillary, or both, have participated in some way in this.

Regarding Point 1, we have already seen in this chapter that, as far back as the 1950s if not earlier, the government explored techniques involving hypnosis, drugs, surgery and other means that could be used to create creation of mind-controlled agents, sex slaves and Manchurian Candidates – with at least some apparent success.

Now let us examine the other points.

Bill Clinton and the Billionaire Pedophile of "Orgy Island"

The charge that Bill Clinton – along with countless other prominent politicians, world-famous businessmen and celebrities – was a participant in a worldwide pedophilia network sounds too incredible to believe.

Yet recently startling evidence emerged of exactly such a network – and of Bill's years-long involvement with the leading organizer of this network. And there are accusations that their relationship went further than publicly revealed.

In 2008 Florida billionaire money manager Jeffrey Epstein pleaded guilty in Florida to one count of soliciting underage girls for sex (and one count of adult solicitation). He served just over a year in county jail for this.

However, this was just the tiny tip of a huge iceberg of child abuse. As the news site Gawker reports:

"[S]prawling local, state, and federal investigations into the eccentric investor's habit of paying teen girls for 'massages' – sessions during which he would allegedly penetrate girls with sex toys, demand to be masturbated, and have intercourse – turned up a massive network of victims, including 35 female minors whom federal prosecutors believed he'd sexually abused. He has reportedly settled lawsuits from more than 30 'Jane Doe' victims since 2008; the youngest alleged victim was 12 years old at the time of her abuse."

Some of these settlements were reportedly for amounts up to one million dollars – pocket change for billionaire Epstein, but plenty to buy the silence of victims.

As The Florida Sun-Sentinel reported, police began what became an 11-month long investigation in March 2005 "when a woman contacted the Palm Beach police fearing that Epstein had molested her 14-year-old daughter. The girl told detectives she'd been invited to Epstein's mansion, where she was paid $300 after stripping to her underwear and massaging Epstein as he masturbated. Police then located a community college student who gave a sworn statement that she had taken six girls, all between the ages of 14 and 16, to Epstein.

"Police referred the case to the FBI. In September 2007, [lawyer Alan Dershowitz of OJ Simpson case fame] helped Epstein negotiate a then-secret non-prosecution agreement with the U.S. Attorney's Office, which deferred to the Palm Beach County State Attorney's Office for criminal charges, court records show."

The victims were not told of the plea bargain until after it was done. Epstein's deal barred and shelved more than 13,000 documents from the lengthy near-year-long police investigation into Epstein's criminal activities, as well as 500 pages of documents telling how the deal itself was negotiated.

The Sun-Sentinel continues: "In 2008, Epstein pleaded guilty to a [single] state charge of soliciting prostitution with a minor and served 13 months of an 18-month sentence."

Epstein served the "jail" time of his sentence in a private wing of the Palm Beach prison, secluded from contact with other prisoners, and according to the Palm Beach Daily News he was "let out on work release six days a week for up to 16 hours a day." During the year-long "house arrest" portion of his sentence, the newspaper reports, Epstein "flew around the country on his private jets to conduct business, with approval from the court and his probation officer. He also went to Home Depot and Sports Authority for large periods of time, all approved by his probation officer." Some "house arrest."

To many the deal seemed unreal, outrageous. FOX News described it as "a deal shrouded in secrecy." Paul Cassell – a lawyer for one of the victims as well as a former federal judge and a law professor – was quoted in TIME: "How does a guy who sexually abused 40 girls end up doing basically one year in a halfway house... This stinks to high heaven."

Spencer Kuvin, a lawyer who represented some of Epstein's alleged victims, told the UK Daily Mail Online that "Forty potential victims were identified in this case and he served a little over a year in a county lock-up. Other criminals who have done this to just one girl receive far harsher sentences, often of five to ten years. ...

"I have often thought he traded information with the federal government. Either that or he used his extensive list of contacts in both the financial and political world to garner favor."

Billionaire Epstein's team of lawyers reflected his enormous wealth and influence. It included such world-famous legal heavy hitters as Dershowitz, Kenneth Starr, Gerald Left, Roy Black, Guy Lewis, and Martin Weinberg, among others.

Some legal experts say the charges Epstein could have faced could have put him behind bars for up to 15 years. Epstein's underage victims allege Epstein had them travel out of state and abroad on his private jets to have sex with his associates. If true, this would constitute sex trafficking – a federal crime far more serious than the state crimes he was convicted of.

But that is just the start. Alleged victims claim that, in addition to Florida girls, Epstein molested underage girls brought to him from South America, Europe, and the former Soviet republics. One civil suit by alleged victim Virginia Roberts claims that Epstein was once given a "birthday gift" of three 12-year-old girls imported from France, who were molested for a day then flown back to Europe.

Along with other estates and homes around the world (including a 45,000 square foot, eight story, forty room mansion in New York City that is reportedly the largest private residence in Manhattan), Epstein owns a 78-acre private island in the U.S. Virgin Islands nicknamed "The Island of Sin" and "Orgy Island," where, according to the UK Daily News, "teenage 'sex slaves' were allegedly abused by the banker and some of the world's most powerful men."

The billionaire pedophile allegedly flew underage teenage girls to the "Island of Sin" in a private jet, which locals called "the Lolita Express." The jet was rumored to have a bed for in-flight sex. Says the UK Daily News: "It is claimed they [underage girls] were made to take part in depraved orgies."

In 2015 court filings, alleged Epstein victim Virginia Roberts claimed that Epstein "loaned her out" to "many other powerful men, including numerous prominent American politicians, powerful business executives, foreign presidents, a well-known Prime Minister, and other world leaders ..." and that Epstein had required her to be sexually available to his "adult male peers, including royalty, politicians, academicians, businessmen" and others.

Her filing alleges that "Epstein's purpose in 'lending' [he and other young girls] to such powerful people [was] to ingratiate himself with them for business, personal, political and financial gain, *as well as to obtain blackmail information.*" (Emphasis added.)

Says Roberts: "Based on my knowledge of Epstein and his organization, as well as discussions with the FBI, it is my belief that federal prosecutors likely possess videotapes and photographic images of me as an underage girl having sex with Epstein and some of his powerful friends."

Roberts claims she was flown around the world as a sex slave to be victimized by the wealthy and powerful.

All of this, of course, is extraordinarily reminiscent of the charges of alleged MONARCH victims, who claim they were taken from place to place to serve the ruling elite as mind-controlled sex slaves or espionage agents, sometimes for blackmail reasons.

Among those Virginia Roberts and other alleged victims named as having traveled to Epstein's "Orgy Island": Bill Clinton and Prince Andrew. Roberts said she did not have sex with Bill, but had sex with Andrew three times, including once in an eleven person orgy. Both Bill and Prince Andrew vigorously denied any wrongdoing. Bill denies ever being on the island. Allegations against Prince Andrew, who was also defended by Dershowitz, were dropped at the same time.

There is a photograph of Virginia Roberts with Prince Andrew, who has his arm around her, taken in early 2001 when she was 17 years old. Also in that same photo is British socialite Ghislaine Maxwell, daughter of disgraced British media tycoon Robert Maxwell and a close friend of Bill Clinton, who has been accused of procuring underage girls for Epstein and in other ways participating in his pedophilia enterprise, charges Maxwell strongly denies.

Prince Andrew was photographed in New York's Central Park with Epstein after the billionaire convicted pedophile was released from prison.

According to Roberts: "[Bill] Clinton was friends with Ghislaine Maxwell who was Epstein's longtime companion and helped to run Epstein's companies, kept images of naked underage children on her computer, helped to recruit underage children for Epstein, engaged in lesbian sex with underage females that she procured for Epstein, and photographed underage females in sexually explicit poses and kept child pornography on her computer..."

A 2011 Vanity Fair article on Ghislaine Maxwell's and Epstein's relationship noted that Maxwell "is passionate about Bill Clinton, with whom she is close friends." Maxwell attended Chelsea Clinton's wedding in 2010.

Maxwell is one of several people accused of being a procurer for Epstein. She has strongly denied charges that she procured underage girls for Epstein.

Virginia Roberts says she was so afraid of retaliation that she omitted names and details from her accusations.

"I have listed a few of the powerful people that Epstein forced me to have sex with in my earlier declaration," Roberts said in court documents. "There were others, though, who I continue to refrain from naming publicly, out of fear for physical repercussions."

Roberts describes "physical abuse that I suffered when Epstein forced me to have sex with other people... Without going into the details of the sexual activities I was forced to endure, there were times when I was physically abused to the point that I remember fearfully thinking that I didn't know whether I was going to survive."

Bill Clinton, according to flight logs obtained by FoxNews.com, was, as the New York Post put it, a "frequent flier" on Epstein's "Lolita Express" private passenger jet. According to Gawker: "The logs also show that Clinton shared more than a dozen flights with a woman who federal prosecutors believe procured underage girls to sexually service Epstein and his friends and acted as a 'potential co-conspirator' in his crimes." That would be, of course, Ghislaine Maxwell.

Regarding the number of flights, Fox News reported that "Flight logs obtained exclusively by FoxNews.com show the former president taking at least 26 trips around the world aboard the 'Lolita Express' – even apparently ditching his Secret Service detail for at least five of the flights."

The Inquisitor website reported in 2016 that "trips taken between 2001 and 2003...indicate Bill enjoyed 'extended junkets' worldwide with the pedophile..."

While Bill was never deposed, court documents note that police seized and examined "Epstein's personal phone directory from his computer" which "contains e-mail addresses for Clinton along with 21 phone numbers for him,

including those for his assistant (Doug Band), his schedulers, and what appear to be Clinton's personal numbers."

Further, according to the UK Daily Mail newspaper: "During plea negotiations, [Epstein's] lawyers had emphasized his close relationship with Bill Clinton."

Says the UK Daily Mail: "A July 2007 letter to the South Florida State U.S. Attorney's office, written by lawyers Alan Dershowitz and Gerald Lefcourt, claimed that Epstein had been part of the original group that set up the [Clinton] Foundation's Clinton Global Initiative."

The letter reads in part: "Mr. Epstein was part of the original group that conceived the Clinton Global Initiative, which is described as a project 'bringing together a community of global leaders to devise and implement innovative solutions to some of the world's most pressing challenges."

Fox News reported in August 2016 that the Clinton Foundation did not respond to their questions about Epstein's role, if any, in the Foundation's founding. But Epstein's name is not mentioned in any founding documents.

The letter by Epstein's lawyers further said: "In a feature article about Mr. Epstein in New Yorker magazine, former president Clinton aptly described Mr. Epstein as a 'committed philanthropist with a keen sense of global markets and an in-depth knowledge of 21st century science.' President Clinton reached this conclusion during a month-long trip to Africa with Mr. Epstein, which Mr. Epstein hosted."

Bill apparently ended his association with Epstein in 2005, after Epstein was arrested and his illegal activities with minors made public.

"The documents clearly show that Bill flew with Epstein and then suddenly stopped, raising the suspicion that the friendship abruptly ended, perhaps because of events related to Epstein's sexual abuse of children," the court documents state.

However, according to secret HSBC Switzerland bank records leaked in 2014 by a whistleblower to the International Consortium of Investigative Journalists, Epstein sent $25,000 to the Clinton Foundation from his secret Swiss account in 2006.

As stated earlier, Virginia Roberts says she did not have sex with Bill Clinton. "I only ever met Bill twice but Jeffrey had told me that they were good friends." She says she saw Clinton on Epstein's Orgy Island with "two young girls that I could identify. I never really knew them well anyways. It was just two girls from New York." She says she did not see Clinton having sex with these two girls. Clinton was in one of "four or five different villas on the island separate from the main house."

Roberts further says: "I remember asking Jeffrey, 'What's Bill Clinton doing here?' kind of thing and he laughed it off and said 'Well, he owes me a favor.'" Roberts says Epstein "never told me what favors they were. He told me a long time ago that everyone owes him favors. They're all in each other's pockets."

Despite Roberts' testimony, there is no proof that Bill visited Epstein's infamous "Island of Sin."

Clinton was far from the only powerful politician associated with Epstein. The UK Guardian said that "Epstein's contacts book... reads like a directory of the world's global elite."

A court-obtained list of Epstein contacts included such names as Henry Kissinger, former Israeli prime ministers Ehud Olmert and Ehud Barak, and at least three Kennedys. Epstein associated with dozens of leading U.S. politicians and world celebrities. (This is not to imply that any of them were involved in Epstein's illegal conduct.)

This, of course, ties in remarkably with the claims of alleged MONARCH victims who say they were sent to sexually service a wide variety of celebrities from many fields and nations.

Conservative pundit Ann Coulter noted: "This is the elites circling the wagon and protecting a pederast. ...This is a really important story. ... This is not just a Clinton sex scandal; this is the elites getting cozy and covering up and protecting one another."

In March 2016 New York Post Page Six journalist Richard Johnson reported that Epstein "has a house full of young beauties at his East 71st Street mansion" who "appeared to be at least 17, the age of consent in New York State." Johnson's source told him that "Half of them are from the former Soviet Union and the other half are a mix of Americans and Europeans," and that the Russians are flown in to the mansion and to Orgy Island by Russian "matchmakers" working for Epstein.

Conchita Sarnoff, executive director of Alliance to Rescue Victims of Trafficking and author of Trafficking, a book on the Epstein case, noted in the Daily Beast that "many of [Epstein's] high-powered acquaintances availed themselves of Epstein's private jets, for which the pilot logs, obtained by discovery in the civil suits, sometimes showed that bold-face [well-known] names were on the same flights as underage girls."

"Bill Clinton ... associated with a man like Jeffrey Epstein, who everyone in New York, certainly within his inner circles, knew was a pedophile," said Sarnoff. "Why would a former president associate with a man like that?"

Sarnoff said 12 American publishers had turned down her explosive and well-researched book because of the Bill Clinton material. She eventually signed a contract with the Mexican subsidiary of Random House. Later, however, she said the publisher told her "They will not publish the book unless I take out the Clinton stuff." Rather than do so, she self-published it in 2016.

Human rights activist Heather Marsh argues that the Epstein story is important not because of the celebrity connections, but rather because it is indicative of an "*interconnected global network of influence* and potential blackmail..." (Emphasis added.)

Court documents contain further allegations that Epstein used hidden cameras to film sex acts of some of his prominent friends and visitors.

According to Virginia Roberts' filing: "Some of the photographs in the defendant's possession were taken with hidden cameras set up in [Epstein's] home in Palm Beach. On the day of his arrest, police found two hidden cameras…"

The blackmail potential for such photos and videos is, of course, incredible – and it also matches yet another recurring theme in some of the stories told by alleged MONARCH victims: that they were forced into participating in precisely such blackmail.

Bill's Disturbing "Animalistic" Sexuality

In September 2015, Hillary said during a speech that every person who makes claims of sexual assault should be believed immediately upon making the claim, listened to carefully, and then a process of careful investigation should take place.

"[E]very survivor of sexual assault" should "have the right to be heard," Hillary said. "You have the right to be believed and we're with you."

It is in that spirit that we have examined the claims of the women quoted at the beginning of this chapter, the women who say they are MONARCH victims who were raped and abused by Bill and Hillary Clinton.

For these terrible charges to be true, we must believe among other things that Bill and/or Hillary are sexual predators on a vast scale.

Concerning Bill, there are some disturbing, if inconclusive, facts and accusations.

We noted earlier the startling story of his friendship and travels with the pedophile and child sex peddler billionaire Jeffrey Epstein.

Bill has also been accused many times of being a sexual predator, a sex addict, and a violent rapist.

Indeed, so voluminous is the literature about allegations of Bill's sexual abuse, and of Hillary's enabling that abuse, that an entire book of nearly 500 pages has been written about it: The Clintons' War on Women by Roger Stone and

Robert Morrow.

According to author Stone, there are "many, many ways in which the Clintons have been tied to sexual abuse, cover-ups, strong-arm tactics, drugs, lies, and the intimidation of victims."

The most famous example is Bill's abuse of the 22-year-old White House intern Monica Lewinsky. While the relationship was not sexual harassment by legal definitions, it was extraordinarily and disturbingly inappropriate: the most powerful man in the world having sex with a young woman who was under his protective care.

Lewinsky herself noted this in a 1999 TIME interview, where she described Bill's creepily aggressive and "animalistic" sexuality: "It was definitely inappropriate. And the way he was flirting with me was inappropriate. So I think was the eye contact. And the way he looks at women he's attracted to. He undresses you with his eyes. And it is slow, from the bottom of your toes to the top of your head back down to your toes again. And it's an intense look. He loses his smile. His sexual energy kind of comes over his eyes, and it's very animalistic."

Washington Post columnist Kathleen Parker wrote that Bill's relationship with Lewinsky "was a clear case of sexual harassment by the very definition promoted by feminists – that is, a person in a superior workplace position making (or responding to) sexual overtures toward an employee, regardless of consent."

It should also be remembered that, as the story became public, Bill lied constantly about the relationship, presumably thus indicating his willingness to lie about other such matters.

Is Bill a Sex Addict?

Former Dallas lawyer Dolly Kyle was a childhood friend of Bill. She met Bill when she was 11 and he was 12, was his girlfriend in high school, and claims to have had a sexual affair with him from the mid-1970s until roughly 1991.

She is author of the 2016 book Hillary: The Other Woman.

According to Kyle, Bill confessed to her in 1987 that he was a "sex addict" – someone for whom sex was a self-destructive obsessive problem like drug addiction, compulsive gambling, or alcoholism. Yet he refused to get treatment or other help.

Speaking on the Breitbart News Daily radio show, Kyle said: "We [she and Bill] went through the 25 questions that you ask yourself if you're a sex addict. He absolutely was. Is. He admitted it. This is like an Alcoholics Anonymous or drug-addict thing. You don't have to go to a counselor to know you're an alcoholic. You go to an AA meeting, you hear the questions, you know that's who you are. And then you do something about it. But he's done nothing about it."

In her book Kyle writes that in 1987, Clinton told her that he had had sex with approximately 2,000 women.

The 2,000 number parallels claims by Linda Tripp, a pivotal figure in the Monica Lewinsky scandal with a rare insider's view. Tripp served in the West Wing of the White House during the Bill Clinton administration. She was first posted just outside the Oval Office and then later given an office directly adjacent to Hillary's second floor West Wing office.

In a 2016 radio interview with journalist and author Aaron Klein, Tripp said:

"Everyone knew within the West Wing, particularly those who spent years with him, of the thousands of women. ... This is a pattern of behavior that has gone on for years. And the abuse of women for years."

"...remember I worked closely with the closest aides to the president. ...it was common knowledge...within the West Wing that he had this problem. It was further common knowledge that Hillary was aware of it."

Is Bill a Rapist?

Women have been charging Bill Clinton with sexual assault for most of his adult life. There are more than a dozen public accusations, and the threats and harassment most of the women report receiving make one wonder if other women have remained silent out of fear.

It should be emphasized, however, that none of the rape or sexual assault charges have been proven true, and that investigators have found inconsistencies in some of the claims.

In 1969, while Bill was in Britain on his Rhodes scholarship, nineteen-year-old Eileen Wellstone claimed that he raped her. Bill said he'd had sex with her, but said it was consensual.

A State Department employee who investigated the accusation told the Capitol Hill Blue news site he believed the victim's story.

"There was no doubt in my mind that this young woman had suffered severe emotional trauma," he said. "But we were under tremendous pressure to avoid the embarrassment of having a Rhodes Scholar charged with rape. I filed a report with my superiors and that was the last I heard of it."

Wellstone re-confirmed the incident to the Washington Times in 1999. She did not speak further, asking the media to leave her alone.

In his book Unlimited Access, former FBI agent Gary Aldrich reported that Bill left Oxford University for a "European tour" in 1969 and was told by University officials that he was no longer welcome there. Bill later accepted a scholarship to Yale Law School and did not complete his studies at Oxford.

Lip-Biting Rape

Clinton critic Roger Stone, author of The Clintons' War on Women, has noted Bill's "proclivity to bite the upper lip of his rape victims as both a signature disabling move and a bid to keep their mouth shut."

This dates back to the earliest rape accusation. Eileen Wellstone, the young British woman who accused Bill of raping her in 1969, also said he bit her on the lip.

Why is this significant? First, because this signature move

features in several rape and assault accusations against Bill.

Second, according to an anonymous source who claimed to be a former rape investigator with the New Orleans Police Department, quoted by the conservative NewsMax.com on February 23, 1999 and widely repeated, lip biting is a common M.O. for rapists.

"The reason rapists bite is because, even with the full weight of her attacker on top of her, the woman is often able to resist the parting of her legs by locking her ankles. The rapist's arms are busy keeping her pinned down. The only weapon the rapist has left is his teeth, which he uses to bite while demanding she open her legs.

"The lips are very sensitive. Biting them is so painful it distracts the victim, allowing a rapist to overcome her resistance. The victim can only hold out for so long as the blood flows into her mouth. Some women are stronger than others and I've seen their lips half-torn from their faces before they give up."

Thus the use of this technique, if true, might strongly suggest that Bill is an experienced serial rapist. (We should again note, in fairness, that the source for this claim is anonymous.)

Juanita Broaddrick is a former Arkansas nursing home administrator and Clinton gubernatorial campaign volunteer. She says Bill raped her in April, 1978. She graphically described it on Dateline NBC, February 24, 1999:

"...Then he tries to kiss me again. And the second time he tries to kiss me he starts biting my lip ... He starts to, um, bite on my top lip and I tried to pull away from him. And then he forces me down on the bed. And I just was very frightened, and I tried to get away from him and I told him 'No,' that I didn't want this to happen but he wouldn't listen to me. ...

"It was a real panicky, panicky situation. I was even to the point where I was getting very noisy, you know, yelling to 'Please stop.' And that's when he pressed down on my right shoulder and he would bite my lip. ...

"When everything was over with, he got up and straightened himself, and I was crying at the moment and he walks to the door, and calmly puts on his sunglasses. And before he goes out the door he says 'You better get some ice on that.' And he turned and went out the door."

A friend and employee corroborated the story, saying that she found Broaddrick on a hotel bed "in a state of shock," her pantyhose torn in the crotch and her lip badly swollen.

In 2016 Broaddrick was still haunted, saying on Twitter: "I was 35 years old when Bill Clinton, Arkansas attorney general, raped me and Hillary tried to silence me. I am now 73....it never goes away." And: "BC raped me-HC [Hillary] threatened me!"

Broaddrick's story of cold-blooded assault by Bill sounds eerily like the treatment described by the alleged MONARCH victims at the beginning of this chapter.

In his 1996 book Partners in Power: The Clintons and Their America, Roger Morris – former National Security Council staff member, historian and author – described another alleged biting attack, this time during Bill's term as Arkansas attorney general:

"A young woman lawyer in Little Rock claimed that she was accosted by Clinton while he was attorney general and that when she recoiled he forced himself on her, biting and bruising her. Deeply affected by the assault, the woman decided to keep it all quiet for the sake of her own hard-won career and that of her husband.

"When the husband later saw Clinton at the 1980 Democratic Convention, he delivered a warning. 'If you ever approach her,' he told the governor, 'I'll kill you.' Not even seeing fit to deny the incident, Bill Clinton sheepishly apologized and duly promised never to bother her again."

The left wing author and journalist Christopher Hitchens took the rape, sexual assault and harassment charges made against Bill very seriously. In his 1999 book No One Left to Lie To: The Triangulations of Bill Clinton, he called Broaddrick an "extremely principled and credible lady."

"In my opinion, Gennifer Flowers was telling the truth; so was Monica Lewinsky, and so was Kathleen Willey, and so, lest we forget, was Juanita Broaddrick, the woman who says she was raped by Bill Clinton," Hitchens wrote at Slate.com in 2008.

Is Hillary a Terrorist and Sexual Abuse Enabler?

On a 2016 radio show Dolly Kyle elaborated on a claim discussed earlier in this chapter: "If [Bill] had sex with 2,000 women or even 200 women, but probably 2,000 is closer, and Hillary was married to him… if she didn't know what he was doing than what's wrong with her brain?

"Certainly she's an enabler, but worse than that. She's a co-conspirator. … Hillary had to know what was going on and she latched on to his coattails to get herself to the White House, which is the plan that they are following."

In her role as "enabler," Kyle says, Hillary not only covers up accusations of rape and other abuse by Bill, but actually uses force and the threat of force – "terrorism" in Kyle's word – to cover up and protect Bill.

"…if Billy Clinton has had sex with 2,000 women and we know about a dozen of us, where are the rest? Well I'll tell you where they are. They are cowering in fear because of [Hillary's] terrorism."

In her 2016 book Hillary: The Other Woman, Kyle describes the Clintons: "Billy and Hillary Clinton continue to be lying, cheating, manipulative, scratching, clawing, ruthlessly aggressive, insatiably ambitious politicians… nothing about them has changed in the past forty-plus years, except that they have deluded more and more people.

"The Clintons and their misled supporters have rewritten history to suit their political agenda, which is to get votes to get power to get money to get more power to get more money.

"The Clintons' vicious cycle of intertwining greed and power addictions will have no limit, unless someone stands up and announces, 'The emperor has no clothes!'"

Linda Tripp, who worked in the White House near both Clintons, backs this up: "I watched a lying president and a lying first lady present falsehoods to the American people. … [Hillary] made it her personal mission to disseminate information and destroy the women with whom he dallied. ... [Hillary claims to be] a champion of women's rights worldwide in a global fashion, and yet all of the women she has destroyed over the years to ensure her political viability continues is sickening to me."

Bill and Hillary have long been accused of threatening and terrorizing alleged victims of Bill's sexual abuse.

Gennifer Flowers, who claims she was Bill's mistress for 14 years, backs up the allegations of other women with similar details and observations.

She, too, describes Hillary as an "enabler" who "never accepted her responsibility at being an enabler."

And she, too, says that she fears that her life is in danger.

She says she has damaging evidence against Bill in a safety deposit box, and the Clintons know this. She credits this with keeping her alive.

"It's something that he [Bill] is aware that I have and *it's probably the reason that I'm still around*,' she said during a 2015 radio interview. (Emphasis added.)

Kathleen Willey is a former White House volunteer aide who claims that Bill sexually assaulted her during a November 29, 1993 private meeting in the Oval Office. She says he embraced her tightly, kissed her on the mouth, grabbed her breast, and pushed her hand onto his genitals. She escaped his clutches – and that same day her husband was found dead from a gunshot wound in rural Virginia. His death was determined to be a suicide by investigators. She made public her suspicions that the Clintons were involved in her husband's death, pointing to similarities with White House aide Vince Foster's famously controversial death, which investigators also said was a suicide.

Tripp, who at the time of Willey's alleged assault worked just outside the Oval Office, told Newsweek reporter Michael Isikoff In 1997 that she had encountered Willey coming out of the Oval Office "disheveled," with "her face red and her lipstick was off."

In 2016, after watching CNN reporter Chris Cuomo make remarks indicating his ignorance of the decades of sexual abuse stories involving Bill and Hillary, Willey wrote an Open

Letter to Cuomo, telling him about the "multiple assaults and rapes involving numerous women who never knew one another, telling the same [or] similar stories.

"This is NOT about infidelities, indiscretions, adultery, girlfriends or consensual sex. This is about Bill Clinton's multiple sexual assaults and rapes for over 40 years and Hillary Clinton's threatening, bullying, intimidating and terrorizing all of the women who have suffered at his hands. It's as simple as that. ...

"I was viciously assaulted after that event in the Oval Office [Bill's alleged sexual assault] by Clinton allies in the media and by goons who actually threatened the lives of my children to try to silence me two days before I was to be deposed, under oath, in Paula Jones' sexual harassment case, 4 years later ...

"... The threatening acts of terror continued for months. My pets went missing or died mysteriously way before their time. My car was vandalized, I discovered a stranger at my basement door at 3 a.m. one morning. Strange and threatening phone calls never seemed to stop. Someone broke into my house in the middle of the night while I was asleep upstairs.

"And I am not the only one [Hillary Clinton] attacked. There are many others, Juanita Broaddrick, Paula Jones, Dolly Kyle, Gennifer Flowers, to name only a few. I have heard from many other women, who have told me similar stories of what Bill Clinton did to them, but [are] still too afraid to go public with them. I don't blame them in the slightest."

Linda Tripp, who revealed the Monica Lewinsky scandal, backs this up, saying in 2016 she feared she and Lewinsky faced the danger of murder from the Clintons:

"I say today and I will continue to say that I believe Monica Lewinsky is alive today because of choices I made and action I took. That may sound melodramatic to your listeners. I can only say that from my perspective I believe that she and I at the time were in danger, because nothing stands in the way of these people achieving their political ends.

"I think that had it not become public when it did, particularly in light of the Paula Jones lawsuit, which was coming to a head with President Clinton's deposition, that we may well have met with an accident. It's a situation where unless you lived it as I did you would have no real framework of reference for this sort of situation."

Capitol Hill Blue notes that its 1999 story on Bill's numerous alleged rape and sexual assault victims was "confirmed with more than 30 interviews with retired Arkansas state employees, former state troopers and former Yale and University of Arkansas students. *Like others, they refused to go public because of fears of retaliation from the Clinton White House.*" (Emphasis added.)

Over and over again, the same stories about sexual abuse followed by harassment, threats and sometimes violence is told.

Former Miss Arkansas Sally Miller (formerly Sally Perdue) alleges she had an affair with Bill for three months in 1983. She kept the affair secret, but when state troopers spoke of the affair during Bill's 1992 presidential campaign, the harassment began. After her Jeep window was shot out – from the inside – she says: "I went to the local police and filed a report, and they told me to go to the FBI in St. Charles, Missouri, where I also filed a report. On the way out of the FBI, a car almost ran me over. The agent I was standing with said, 'Lady, you need to get protection. They're all after you.'" Miller eventually fled to China, where she took a job with Coca Cola – until, she says, the Clinton harassment started again, and she was dismissed. Since she announced plans in 2016 to write a book on the subject, the harassment has resumed, she says. As a result she carries a gun with her and has issued a public statement that should she be found dead of apparent suicide no one should believe it.

If such harassment – even to the point of death threats and possibly beyond – is true, how have the Clintons managed to survive politically?

Because of the brutality and efficiency of the Clinton private army (discussed further in Chapter 16), says Candice E. Jackson, author of Their Lives: The Women Targeted by The Clinton Machine.

"For a long time, the Clintons were successful by developing a group of loyalists from their early Arkansas days.

The team used a predictable pattern of a combination of bribery, threats, and harassment. ... The Clintons, when you're talking about their methods of harassment and intimidation, are brilliant at using intermediaries and third parties to threaten women. Their hands stay so clean, it's impressive. And the media looks the other way entirely."

Dick Morris, close friend of Bill and political adviser in Clinton's Arkansas years and 1996 reelection campaign, said that the 1992 Bill Clinton campaign team had a $100,000 unit, partially funded by taxpayer dollars via federal matching funds, to "hire private detectives to go into the personal lives of women" alleged to have had sex with Clinton, "to develop compromising material – blackmailing information, essentially – to coerce them into signing affidavits saying they did not have sex with Bill Clinton."

Christopher Hitchens notes that the Clintons maintained a "quasi-governmental or para-state division devoted exclusively to the bullying and defamation of women" and further notes that "The hiring of private detectives for the investigation and defamation of inconvenient women was [Hillary's] idea."

Also highly disturbing – and fully confirmed – is the sexist derogatory language that Hillary and/or Clinton associates have used to mock and discredit Bill's accusers, including misogynist hate speech terms like "floozy," "bimbo," "trash," "whore" and "stalker." James Carville, a longtime strategist for Bill, infamously said of Gennifer Flowers (and implicitly other accusers): "If you drag a hundred-dollar bill through a trailer park, you never know what you'll find."

It should be remembered that in 1992 Bill went on "60 Minutes" with Hillary at his side to earnestly deny having an affair with Gennifer Flowers. Flowers then produced audio tapes to back up her claim. Under oath in 1998 Bill admitted to a sexual encounter with her.

MONARCH Implications of Bill's Sexual Abuse

Bill's alleged rapes, abuse and inappropriate sexual behavior, his allegedly self-confessed sex addiction, and casual sex with perhaps thousands of women, is the very portrait of a man used to treating women as sexual objects to be brutally used and discarded.

Returning to the women who claim to be mind-controlled MONARCH sex slaves, is it possible that Bill learned to treat women this way precisely because he has been for decades supplied with an endless supply of mind-controlled sex slaves at his command?

Is it possible that some of the sexual abuse reported by his victims was the result of mistakes or carelessness on his part – that he thought they were mind-controlled MONARCH sex slaves?

Is it likely that a man almost constantly in the public eye could have sex with many thousands of women – unless they were supplied to him constantly through a top-secret MONARCH-like program?

Is it possible that Hillary's cover-ups of Bill's abuse, and her allegedly terroristic use of violence to do so, is more than just a cover-up for political reasons – that she is covering up a project far more vast and horrific – perhaps like the alleged MONARCH program and its tentacles?

For now, we can only speculate – and explore still more related material for clues.

MONARCH Claims of World-Wide Pedophile Rings

The alleged MONARCH victims insist, again and again, that there are world-wide pedophile rings that supply underage sex slaves to the wealthy and powerful.

The Jeffrey Epstein pedophilia scandal gave us one look at the alleged existence of such a ring, with considerable documentation – one that matches the MONARCH descriptions in many ways.

Appallingly, many other reports give us further reason to suspect the existence of such rings. Here are a few examples from around the world.

Belgium: Signs of a Child Kidnapping Ring Cover-Up

Belgian serial killer and child molester Marc Dutroux was convicted in 2004 of having kidnapped, tortured and sexually abused six girls from 1995 to 1996, ranging in age from 8 to 19, four of whom he murdered.

Dutroux stated he was part of a Europe-wide pedophile ring protected by police officers, businessmen, doctors and high-ranking politicians.

Prior to this arrest he had been convicted in 1989 of multiple child rapes, but was released from prison in 1991 after serving just three and a half years of his 13-year sentence.

In the investigations leading to his 1996 arrest for murder, there was an astounding amount of police errors and oversights. Dutroux's own mother had earlier written to police that she feared her son was keeping girls imprisoned in his house. Yet early progress in the investigation occurred only when family members, upset at the repeated failures of the police, hired a private investigator, who quickly homed in on Dutroux.

It was seven and a half years after his 1996 arrest before Dutroux went to trial. During this time there were multiple suspicious deaths of witnesses. All this added to speculation of a cover-up at the highest levels of government.

A dungeon and cell, where Dutroux kept and tortured kidnapped children, was indeed discovered in one of his several homes. A videotape was found during the investigations showing Dutroux raping a Slovakian child, further raising suspicions of an international child sex ring.

An outraged Belgian public became convinced that there was a massive cover-up and Dutroux was being protected. In an October 1996 event now known as the "White March," an incredible 300,000 Belgians marched on the capital in protest.

A 2004 poll found that two out of three Belgians believed that Dutroux was being protected by "very highly placed people."

The UK Observer noted that "far from being investigated, leads pointing to a [pedophile] network seem rather to have been ignored or buried."

Belgium is, of course, a European power center; both the European Union and NATO are headquartered there.

Britain: "Jim'll Fix It" – The Horrific and Well-Connected Life of Jimmy Savile

Jimmy Savile, who died in 2011 at the age of 84, was not just one of Britain's most famous celebrities, he was festooned with awards and honors from the ruling elite:

- In 1972 Savile was appointed Officer of the Most Excellent Order of the British Empire, entitled to append "OBE" to his signature.
- In the 1990 Queen's Birthday Honours he was made a Knight Bachelor "for charitable services," entitled to use the honorific prefix "Sir."
- Savile was honored with a Papal knighthood in 1990 when Pope John Paul II made him a Knight Commander of the Pontifical Equestrian Order of Saint Gregory the Great (KCSG).
- He was awarded an honorary doctorate of law (LLD) by the University of Leeds and an honorary doctorate from the University of Bedfordshire.
- He had the Cross of Merit of the Order pro merito Melitensi, awarded to those who have brought honor to the Sovereign Military Order of Malta (a highly prominent lay religious order of the Catholic Church since 1113) by promoting Christian values and charity as defined by the Roman Catholic Church.
- British streets were named after him.

From 1975 until 1994, Savile starred in "Jim'll Fix It," a hit television show. The show's premise (which would eventually be seen as the blackest irony): Savile would make the wishes of children who wrote to the show come true.

Savile was a very familiar face among the power elite, and constantly in the public eye. Indeed, in the late 1980s Savile acted as an informal marriage counselor between Prince Charles and Princess Diana. He was a years-long friend of Margaret Thatcher, meeting with her many times including celebrating eleven consecutive New Year's Eves with her (and later telling Esquire magazine, "I knew the real woman and the real woman was something else.") He met Prince Charles, who reportedly sent gifts on his 80th birthday with a note reading (creepily, in retrospect): "Nobody will ever know what you have done for this country, Jimmy. This is to go some way in thanking you for that."

Yet for decades, it was widely suspected and whispered that Savile was a serial pedophile. Allegations dated back nearly 50 years – to 1964. But nothing was done.

There are indications of a massive cover-up of his half-century of child abuse; both the government and media largely ignored repeated claims of child abuse, molestation and rape. And the cover-up seemed to continue somewhat after his death in 2011. BBC journalist Tony Gosling notes that "many of those who eventually told us about the Savile scandal have now lost their jobs."

After Seville's death, the allegations of child abuse that had gone strangely unexplored suddenly became public and widely discussed.

By December 2012 nearly 600 alleged sexual abuse victims of Savile and some of his associates had come forward, and a police investigation was underway. Even some of the child guests on "Jim'll Fix It" accused him of molesting them.

As the investigations proceeded it was charged that he abused children at least 28 separate hospitals. The number of his victims may top 1,000.

There is testimony that he had entry to at least one mortuary, in order to sexually abuse corpses.

On June 26, 2014, UK secretary of state for Health Jeremy Hunt denounced Savile in the House of Commons. Hunt confirmed that complaints had been raised before 2012 but that the British government had ignored them. Said Hunt:

"Savile was a callous, opportunistic, wicked predator who abused and raped individuals, many of them patients and young people, who expected and had a right to expect to be safe. His actions span five decades – from the 1960s to 2010. ... As a nation at that time we held Savile in our affection as a somewhat eccentric national treasure with a strong commitment to charitable causes. Today's reports show that in reality he was a sickening and prolific sexual abuser who repeatedly exploited the trust of a nation for his own vile purposes."

In addition to being a child molester and necrophiliac, there are allegations that Savile was a participant in violent Satanic rituals.

BBC journalist Tony Gosling: "Psychotherapist Valerie Sinason... personally interviewed two of his victims in her London-based 'Clinic for Dissociative Studies' who told her at Stoke Mandeville Hospital in Buckinghamshire that they had been repeatedly sexually abused in horrific rituals they described as 'Satanic.'

"Wearing robes and masks in the hospital basement and to Latin chants of 'Hail Satanus,' the idea, it seems, was two-fold: for Savile to 'share' his victims with other abusers and also to so deeply traumatize the children with supernatural threats of demons and devil masks that, through fear, they would never dare breathe a word to anyone. ...

"Sinason has not been the only one to talk of Satanic ritual abuse in connection with Savile. Britain's most popular TV journalist ever, Roger Cook, also exposed what he believed was a Satanic ritual abuse ring in Savile's home town of Leeds, Yorkshire."

According to UK investigators, Savile boasted that he had police contacts who suppressed letters and reports alleging abuse. Each week he met with a group of police at his penthouse in what they called the "Friday Morning Club."

Savile's case thus shows a direct connection between ruling elites in government and media, and child abuse, government cover-ups, mind control, violence and perhaps even Satanism – matching in remarkable ways the horrific, seemingly implausible stories told by the alleged Project MONARCH victims at the start of this chapter.

The Savile horror has not proved that any of these elites knew of, and supported, Savile's abuse, though investigations continue as this book goes to press. But it does add heft to the MONARCH victims' claims of big-name sexual abusers moving freely among the elite.

Britain: Operation Hydrant and More

In 2014 British police launched "Operation Hydrant" to oversee an explosion of child sexual abuse allegations that could no longer be ignored. The news source Vice said that pedophilia scandals "swallowed Britain whole" in 2014.

Operation Hydrant collects information on "non-recent" cases of child sexual abuse from police investigations in England, Wales, Scotland and Northern Ireland. In December 2015 the BBC reported that Operation Hydrant had 2,228 suspects under investigation. Of these, 302 were classified as people of "public prominence" (including 99 politicians and 147 media celebrities). 1,217 alleged offenders operated within institutions (including 86 religious institutions, 39 medical establishments, 25 prisons or young offenders institutes, 22 sports venues, and 10 community institutions such as youth centers). Of the suspects, 286 had died, and 554 were classified as unknown or unidentified.

Yet many feared the Operation Hydrant findings would ultimately become just another in an allegedly long string of police cover-ups of sex abuse by the rich and powerful.

In a May 2015 report entitled "Revelations of British Pedophile Ring Spur Flood of Abuse Reports" U.S. National Public Radio (NPR) reporter Vicki Barker said of Operation Hydrant:

"The police haven't always been part of the solution. There are allegations that senior officers helped quash previous investigations. ... Dolphin Square, a...vast 1930s apartment complex, has long been a bolt-hole for the British establishment, but Dolphin Square is also one of several addresses across London where one pedophile ring, comprising some of Britain's most powerful men, allegedly abused underage boys in the 1960s, '70s and '80s, boys as young as 6 bused in from care homes or the slums. There are tales of orgies and even one allegation of murder. ...

"In March [2015], the BBC reported that an undercover police team investigating the ring in the early 1980s was ordered to hand over all of its evidence and the officers threatened with prosecution under the Official Secrets Act. ...

"Jon Bird helps run the National Association for People Abused in Childhood, or NAPAC. For decades, he says, its hotline has been hearing from men who say they were abused as children at Dolphin Square and elsewhere. The few who went to the police at the time got nowhere."

Investigations in the past had identified possible UK pedophile rings, some allegedly involving the rich and powerful, but they were hushed up or subverted or otherwise left unexplored and unpursued. Leads vanished, files disappeared, interests shifted...

Indeed, the UK Daily Mail reported allegations that over 100 investigations into child sex abuse, some involving prominent and powerful elites, had vanished: "Home Office permanent secretary Mark Sedwill reveals that 114 files relating to historic allegations of child sex abuse, from between 1979 and 1999, have disappeared from the Home Office."

Peter McKelvie, former child protection officer, was reported in the UK Daily Mail as saying that senior politicians, military figures and even people linked to the royal family were among the alleged abusers and that reports indicate abuse may have been going on for well over half a century, but – yet again – cover-ups prevented investigations.

On July 9, 2014 the UK Independent noted that "new claims continued to emerge of links to pedophile networks at the highest levels of politics, public bodies and the clergy."

Summarizes Mark Watts, editor of the investigative news site Exaro, which has reported extensively on the scandal: "I think we have come across the biggest political scandal in Britain's postwar history. It goes way beyond Jimmy Savile. We're talking about people in positions of real power in Britain and the ensuing cover-up."

The Catholic Church Pedophile Cover-Ups

Thousands of cases of child sexual abuse committed by Catholic priests have been uncovered and publicized in recent decades in the United States, Canada, Ireland, the United Kingdom, Mexico, Belgium, France, Germany and Australia and in other nations throughout the world.

According to BishopAccountability.com, a respected online archive established by lay Catholics to battle the problem:

"Thousands of Catholic clergy and religious [leaders] have raped and sodomized tens of thousands of children – perhaps more than 100,000 children – since 1950. These crimes were committed in secret, and bishops nurtured that secrecy. Over 17,000 survivors have broken through the silence, and their accounts have created an in-depth picture of the crisis, both in their own writings and in the work of journalists and law enforcement officials. Attorneys have obtained diocesan documents that reveal additional survivor witnesses and also document parts of a huge cover-up. But for every account that is known, hundreds are not yet public. ...

"It is a matter of public record that U.S. bishops have knowingly transferred thousands of abusive priests into unsuspecting parishes and dioceses, placing fear of 'scandal' ahead of the welfare of children."

According to BishopAccountability.com, between 1950 and 2011 U.S. bishops received complaints of sexual abuse by more than 6,000 priests – 5.6 percent of U.S. priests. The highly praised book Sex, Priests, and Secret Codes: The Catholic Church's 2,000 Year Paper Trail of Sexual Abuse – written by three distinguished critics of priest child abuse – two former priests, one a current priest and counselor – argues that this is a problem that begun in the earliest days of the church and spans the church's history right up to the present. Their book notes, among many other revelations, that "The histories of many priest abusers record that they were abused in their childhood by an adult, and a large number of those adults were priests or religious brothers. A significant number of priests introduce candidates for the priesthood to sex. In fact, 10 percent of priests report that they had some sexual contact with a priest or fellow seminarian in the course of their studies."

These scandals were widely known among church figures, who covered them up and who enlisted powerful political, legal, and economic figures to help with the cover-up – yet another example that parallels the claims of alleged MONARCH victims that the rich and powerful and famous assisted in their victimhood.

Hollywood: Pedophile Networks and Mind Control; "MK-ULTRA mind-control rules in Hollywood"

Corey Feldman, perhaps the biggest child star of the 1980s, has said in public statements and in his biography Coreyography that pedophilia is rampant in Hollywood.

"I can tell you that the No. 1 problem in Hollywood was and is and always will be pedophilia. That's the biggest problem for children in this industry," Feldman told ABC in 2011.

"I was surrounded by [pedophiles] when I was 14 years old. ... They were everywhere. ...There was a circle of older men ... around this group of kids. And they all had either their own power or connections to great power in the entertainment industry."

Feldman says he was repeatedly abused by powerful Hollywood figures, and that similar sexual abuse led to the suicide of his close friend and fellow child star Corey Haimes.

Today, some experts say, the problem is worse than in the 1980s. Anne Henry, co-founder of BizParentz Foundation, an organization that supports families of children working in the entertainment industry, told FOX News in 2013:

"Pedophiles and predators in Hollywood are just as rampant today, if not more so. The entertainment industry is much larger than it was in their day."

In 2016 she told the UK Daily Mail: "This problem has been endemic in Hollywood for a long time... Very bad people are still working here, protected by their friends."

Documentarian Amy Berg, who exposed massive sex abuse in the Catholic Church in her Oscar-nominated 2006 documentary "Deliver Us From Evil," addresses the subject of Hollywood child abuse in her 2015 documentary "An Open Secret." As happens over and over again to those investigating child abuse rings, powerful forces have attempted to silence the film. Despite her reputation, Berg struggled for months to find a company willing to distribute the film, and even small film festivals refused to show it.

And then there is the stunning accusation made by renowned actress, comedian, writer, television producer, director and political activist Rosanne Barr during a 2013 interview on the current affairs TV program "Breaking The Set":

"Hollywood is the one that keeps all this power structure, and all this culture of racism and sexism and classism and genderism in place. ... And they do it at the behest of their masters who run everything.

"[Hollywood] is a culture of mind control, too. *MK-ULTRA mind-control rules in Hollywood.* If you don't know [about MK-ULTRA], Google that and look into it." (Emphasis added.)

If pedophilia is rampant in Hollywood today, so is a powerful connection with the CIA – the organization that brought Nazi spies and scientists to the U.S. and gave us MK-ULTRA mind-control programs. The organization that alleged Project MONARCH victims say is behind the MONARCH program of mind-controlled sex slaves and pedophile rings.

The 2012 book The CIA in Hollywood: How the Agency Shapes Film and Television by film scholar Tricia Jenkins details how the CIA has helped mold major American films and television shows that paint the CIA in a positive image. As she notes, this arguably constitutes propaganda directed against the American people – a violation of U.S. law since the 1950s; further, she notes that the selective nature of this assistance arguably violates the First Amendment: "the CIA's refusal to support all filmmakers seeking its assistance constitutes a violation of the First Amendment's right to free speech."

For decades this highly questionable relationship between the CIA and Hollywood was secret. Now it is somewhat known, but remains shadowy. The CIA now has an entire department called the Entertainment Industry Liaison, whose first head was longtime CIA officer – and first cousin of Academy Award-winning actor Tommy Lee Jones – Chase Brandon. According to film scholar Jenkins, the CIA actually pitches film and TV ideas to Hollywood writers and directors and regularly meets with Hollywood elites and power brokers, offering filmmakers valuable cooperation and assistance for projects that present the CIA in a favorable light or otherwise advance the CIA's agenda. But many of the CIA-Hollywood relationships remain sub rosa, off the record, she notes.

Ex-CIA agent Bob Baer, whose own memoirs were the basis for the Academy Award-winning film Syriana, told the UK Guardian in 2008: "All these people that run studios – they go to Washington, they hang around with senators, they hang around with CIA directors, and everybody's on board."

Among the more controversial CIA-influenced films of recent years was "Zero Dark Thirty," widely denounced by critics and journalists as endorsing the use of torture. Internationally renowned investigative journalist Glenn Greenwald, writing in the UK Guardian, echoed many others when he denounced the film as "pernicious propaganda" presenting the "glorification of torture" and noting that it "presents torture as its CIA proponents and administrators see it: as a dirty, ugly business that is necessary to protect America. ... Indeed, from start to finish, this is the CIA's film: its perspective, its morality, its side of the story, The Agency as the supreme heroes. ... This film has only one perspective of the world – the CIA's – and it uncritically presents it for its entire 2-1/2-hour duration."

The subhead of an article on Zero Dark Thirty by award-winning journalist Peter Maass in The Atlantic declared that the film "represents a troubling new frontier of government-embedded film making."

Documents of CIA-Hollywood discussions about the film, obtained under the Freedom of Information Act by the conservative organization Judicial Watch, were significantly redacted – blacked out – by CIA censors.

The CIA's desire to justify and legitimize torture should not be surprising, coming from an organization that has researched, used and taught torture since its founding days shortly after World War II. But the surreptitious propagandizing for torture via Hollywood constitutes a kind of Michael Aquino "MindWar" directed against the American people that is disturbing in the extreme.

CIA influence over U.S. movies and TV programming is nothing new, and as noted it predates by decades the establishment of the CIA's Entertainment Industry Liaison in 1996. As journalists Matthew Alford and Robbie Graham noted in the UK Guardian in 2008:

"Luigi Luraschi was the head of foreign and domestic censorship for Paramount in the early 1950s. And, it was recently discovered, he was also working for the CIA, sending in reports about how film censorship was being employed to boost the image of the U.S. in movies that would be seen abroad. ... In 1950, the agency bought the rights to George Orwell's Animal Farm, and then funded the 1954 British animated version of the film."

Surely that is the height of irony: the Orwellian CIA funding their own version of Orwell's anti-authoritarian novel!

Graham Greene angrily disowned the 1958 adaptation of his Vietnam-set novel The Quiet American, describing the film as having been turned into a "propaganda film for America"; the script, in fact, had been totally rewritten by the director under the influence of the CIA.

Given the astonishing influence the CIA secretly cultivated over U.S. and foreign media and popular culture revealed in Chapter 13, its secret involvement in shaping American movies should not be surprising.

A few other recent films the CIA has been shown to have been involved in:

- "Argo," which shows the CIA in a positive light while ignoring sensitive questions about the film's key subject, the 1980 Iranian hostage crisis;
- "The Sum of All Fears," a wildly pro-CIA thriller which, critic Matthew Alford notes, "celebrates and makes light of the enormous covert powers of a

globally operating U.S. national security state and its allies."
- "The Good Shepherd" (2006), a story about CIA head of counter-espionage James Jesus Angleton which neglects to mention his paranoia or involvement in MK-ULTRA.
- "Charlie Wilson's War," which glorifies the story of 1980s U.S. covert supplying the Afghan mujahideen with weaponry, but neglects to mention how these weapons would later be used against the U.S.

The list could be greatly expanded.

The Pentagon, too, offers copious assistance – with similar strings attached. According to the publishers of Operation Hollywood: How the Pentagon Shapes and Censors the Movies, by veteran Hollywood journalist David L. Robb, Hollywood gets "access to billions of dollars' worth of military equipment and personnel for little or no cost" but "the cost in terms of intellectual freedom can be quite steep. In exchange for access to sophisticated military hardware and expertise, filmmakers must agree to censorship from the Pentagon."

The result: "the final product that moviegoers see at the theater is often not just what the director intends but also what the powers-that-be in the military want to project about America's armed forces. Sometimes the [Pentagon] censor demands removal of just a few words; other times whole scenes must be scrapped or completely revised" at the Pentagon's request.

In his book Reel Power: Hollywood Cinema and American Supremacy, journalist and professor Matthew Alford examines dozens of major studio big-budget films and concludes that "the film industry routinely promotes the dubious notion that the United States is a benevolent force in world affairs and that unleashing its military strength overseas has positive results for humanity."

U.S. government involvement with the shaping and production of these films is one of the reasons why.

In his 2016 book The Writer With No Hands, Alford takes this thesis further. After examining thousands of pages of documents obtained under the Freedom of Information Act (FOI), along with private testimony, he concludes, shockingly:

"...as many as 10,000 films, TV shows and video games had been affected quietly or secretly by the national security state."

Alford further suspects that "several major Hollywood films are ghost written, covertly, by CIA operatives."

His fellow researcher, Tom Secker of SpyCulture.com, after examining over 1500 FOI documents, agrees:

"The sheer scale of the Army and the Air Force's involvement in TV shows, particularly reality TV shows, is the most remarkable thing about these files. 'American Idol,' 'The X-Factor,' 'MasterChef,' 'Cupcake Wars,' numerous Oprah Winfrey shows, 'Ice Road Truckers, ' 'Battlefield Priests,' 'America's Got Talent, ' 'Hawaii Five-O,' lots of BBC, History Channel and National Geographic documentaries, 'War Dogs,' 'Big Kitchens' – the list is almost endless. And this is alongside blockbuster movies like Godzilla , Transformers, Aloha and Superman: Man of Steel."

And speaking of The Writer With No Hands...

Hollywood: The Screenwriter Who Lost His Hands

Some also claim there is an even darker side to the CIA involvement with Hollywood. In 1997 screenwriter Gary DeVore (Dogs of War, Raw Deal, Time Cop) was working on a script set during the 1989 U.S. invasion of Panama. It was to be his directorial debut.

DeVore heavily researched the script. He said it would reveal "the real reason" for that invasion, including "disturbing details."

His wife Wendy later told CNN: "He had been very disturbed over some of the things that he had been finding in his research."

DeVore spent a great deal of time with CIA agents, including traveling with them to Panama and elsewhere, apparently discussing the film. On the night of June 28, 1997 Wendy received a disturbing phone call from Gary; he sounded frightened and there seemed to be someone in the car with him. It was the last she would hear from him. He simply disappeared. Within days, Wendy was visited by agents from the FBI, CIA, NSA and DOD. One asked for access to Gary's computer; later it was discovered that earlier drafts of the script on the computer, along with research material, had disappeared.

Fully a year later, his dead body was suddenly found – in his SUV beneath just 12 feet of water under a busy highway. There was much that seemed suspicious. Journalist and professor Matthew Alford details many of the anomalies in his book The Writer With No Hands.

Perhaps most eerily, Devore's hands were missing – replaced with hand bones estimated to be 200 years old. A message? The coroner said the cause of death was unknown. Devore's laptop, containing the final finished draft of the script, was gone.

Some of those familiar with Devore's plans for the movie believe the script might have been based on the idea that the Panama invasion was simply a diversion: a way for U.S. intelligence agents to retrieve from Panama dictator Manuel Noriega a stash of tapes of U.S. officials and others involved in sexual and/or criminal activities that left them vulnerable to blackmail.

This idea was not merely a movie plot invention. According to the UK Daily Mail, Devore's remaining research materials included an article clipped from London's now defunct Sunday Correspondent newspaper "alleging dictator General Manuel Noriega had compiled a stash of sex tapes featuring top-ranking U.S. officials... Noriega, the article explains, ran a well-known 'honey trap': inviting diplomats to his home filled with alcohol, drugs, beautiful women, and beautiful men – and covertly filming their antics."

This should sound familiar by now. Blackmail has been mentioned by alleged MONARCH mind-control victims as one of the reasons for their exploitation; several claim they were used as bait in government blackmail schemes. Sexual blackmail was also suspected by some to be part of Jeffrey Epstein's pedophile operation – remember the cameras allegedly hidden throughout his Florida mansion, and the suspicions by victim Virginia Roberts that she was used by Epstein in producing blackmail material – and some have speculated this was one reason Epstein got off with so remarkably light a sentence for his crimes.

As Jay Stanley, Senior Policy Analyst, ACLU Speech, Privacy, Technology Project, wrote in 2013: "Sometimes when I hear public officials speaking out in defense of NSA spying, I can't help thinking, even if just for a moment, 'What if the NSA has something on that person and that's why he or she is saying this?' ...The breadth of the NSA's newly revealed capabilities makes the emergence of such suspicions in our society inevitable."

To sum up: We have earlier seen how the CIA has been involved in mind control via MK-ULTRA and numerous other programs. (Indeed, the CIA's secret influence over the spoken, written and broadcast media is arguably just another form of mind control.) We have heard the claims of alleged MONARCH victims that they were used in massive government pedophile rings. We have briefly explored arguments that there is significant pedophilia in Hollywood.

Now we see that there is a solid CIA-Hollywood-media connection. We further know that the CIA has never shirked from working with criminals, including the Mafia, gangland hit men, and drug traffickers. And we know that the CIA has secretly and illegally conducted mind-control and propaganda experiments on unsuspecting American citizens.

Finally, we know that Hollywood, speaking broadly, has consistently championed the Clintons – publicly, at least – throughout their political careers.

None of this proves the various Project MONARCH accusations in this chapter. But these links cannot help but add at least some credibility to such accusations, as well as raise further questions.

Satanism, Child Exploitation, the CIA and the Finders (Florida, Washington DC)

And then there is the bizarre, disturbing mystery of the Finders.

In February 1987 police discovered six small children living in a foul-smelling white Dodge van with two adults, described in the subsequent police report as "well-dressed white men." The dirty, disheveled, insect-bitten children seemed malnourished, were behaving strangely and, according to the police report, showed signs of "sexual abuse" and "apparent Satanism."

"The children were unaware of the functions of telephones, television and toilets," the report continued, "and stated that they were not allowed to live indoors and were only given food as a reward..."

This was the beginning of the strange and haunting story of the Finders cult, which has been documented in the Washington Post, the New York Times, US News and World Report and other respected mainstream media.

According to Special Agent Ramon J. Martinez, United States Customs Service, the two men said "they both were the children's teachers and that all were en route to Mexico to establish a school for brilliant children ..."

The notion of kidnapped children taken to secret schools for abusive training by shadowy operatives is of course straight out of the stories of those who claim to be victims of MK-ULTRA/MONARCH type sex-slave training.

Based on this, police raided a Washington DC warehouse and apartment building used by the Finders, where they found what appeared to be a massive child kidnapping and child abuse ring. There were files about local babysitters, local child care centers, and apparent instructions for kidnapping children. There were photos of nude children and what appeared to be a video studio. Human urine and feces were stored in jars.

Special Agent Ramon J. Martinez in his official memo says the raid uncovered "a room equipped with several computers, printers, and numerous documents. Cursory examination of the documents revealed detailed instructions for obtaining children for unspecified purposes. The instructions included the impregnation of female members of the community known as the Finders, purchasing children, trading, and kidnapping.

"There were telex messages using MCI account numbers between a computer terminal believed to be located in the same room, and others located across the country and in foreign locations. One such telex specifically ordered the purchase of two children in Hong Kong to be arranged through a contact in the Chinese Embassy there. Another telex expressed interest in 'bank secrecy' situations. Other documents identified interests in high-tech transfers to the United Kingdom, numerous properties under the control of the Finders, a keen interest in terrorism, explosives, and the evasion of law enforcement.

"Also found in the 'computer room' was a detailed summary of the events surrounding the arrest and taking into custody of the two adults and six children in Tallahassee the previous night. There were also a set of instructions which appeared to be broadcast via a computer network which advised the participants to move 'the children' and keep them moving through different jurisdictions, and instructions on how to avoid police attention…"

Police also found "numerous files relating to activities of the organization in different parts of the world. Locations I observed are as follows: London, Germany, the Bahamas, Japan, Hong Kong, Malaysia, Africa, Costa Rica, and 'Europe.'"

Agent Martinez also reported that the seized Finders evidence included "numerous photos of children, some nude, at least one of which was a photo of a child 'on display' and appearing to accent the child's genitals … a series of photos of adults and children dressed in white sheets participating in a 'blood ritual.' The ritual centered around the execution, disembowelment, skinning and dismemberment of the goats at the hands of the children, this included the removal of the testes of a male goat, the discovery of a female goat's 'womb' and the 'baby goats' inside the womb and the presentation of a goat's head to one of the children."

It seems almost beside the point to point out that the goat's head is a classic Satanic symbol.

The entire set-up eerily parallels the numerous

descriptions by alleged MONARCH victims of the child-abuse and child-trauma-based mind-control techniques allegedly used by MONARCH programmers. Indeed, all of the above would have fit perfectly into any of the accounts of child abuse told by alleged MONARCH victims.

Agent Martinez also reported that "numerous documents were discovered which appeared to be concerned with international trafficking in children, high tech transfer to the United Kingdom, and international transfer of currency."

Then this astonishing investigation was... abruptly called off. By the Justice Department, who said it was "a matter of national security."

Agent Martinez says he was told off the record that "the investigation into the activity of the Finders had become a CIA internal matter."

The mystery has never been solved or fully explained. US News and World Report (Dec. 27, 1993/Jan. 3, 1994 issue) in a story entitled "Through a Glass, Very Darkly: Cops, Spies and a Very Odd Investigation" said that Finders leader Marion Pettie said that his late wife had worked for the CIA and his son worked for Air America, a CIA-controlled company.

A memo by an anonymous source printed in the conspiracy research magazine Steamshovel Press says that Finders leader Pettie himself was involved with the pre-CIA OSS, the CIA, and other intelligence agencies for decades, in an informal way, including running a safe house for members of intelligence agencies. According to the memo, Pettie's "mentor and role model" was wealthy newspaper publisher and political leader "Charles E. Marsh ... an intimate of FDR, Henry Wallace and later Lyndon Johnson."

(Interestingly, Charles E. Marsh's own mentor and role model was the enigmatic Colonel Edward M. House, power-behind-the-throne to President Wilson and a key figure in laying the groundwork for the Council on Foreign Relations and similar ruling elite organizations. We note in Chapter 13 the charges that Colonel House was involved in conspiratorial and occult organizations and even charges that he had occult powers. The occult interests and activities of Marsh's close associate U.S. Vice President Henry Wallace are explored in Chapter 13.)

Pettie died in 2003.

In the bizarre and still-mysterious Finders case we see once again many of the elements found in the accusations of alleged Project MONARCH victims: secret and/or secretive government agencies, government cover-ups, connections to past years of political intrigue, seemingly occult ritualistic violence, worldwide networks of pedophiles and abusers, organized child abuse, kidnapped children, and so on.

Conclusion: The Shocking Truths Behind the Claims of Alleged MONARCH Victims Against Hillary

At the start of this chapter we noted the mind-boggling charges of several women who say that, as children, they were seized by agents of the U.S. government and, through trauma-based mind-control techniques, turned into mind-controlled sex slaves and "Manchurian Candidate"-type agents – and were subsequently employed and abused by Hillary and Bill Clinton and many other members of the global ruling elite.

We noted, then examined, nine key things that would have to be true in order to take the charges of MONARCH victims – including their charges against Bill and Hillary – seriously.

In this chapter we have shown:

1. The federal government has had, since before World War II – and continuing to this day – a strong interest in creating mind-controlled agents. MK-ULTRA, the CIA umbrella program for numerous government mind-control projects, was specifically designed to explore this – and did, for many years.
2. The CIA and other participating government agencies knew that many of their experiments and activities were illegal, and continued doing them anyway.
3. Such experiments were successful in creating mind-controlled assassins and mind-controlled sex slaves, as well as "sleeper agents" hidden within multiple personalities (so-called "Manchurian Candidates") that could be awakened and activated by the government when desired.

4. These experiments involved a vast number of players, including renowned experts in such fields as psychology, hypnosis, drug abuse and other areas related to mind control; and the experiments involved the participation (sometimes knowingly, sometimes not) of some of the country's most distinguished leading institutions.
5. The U.S. government performed many such dangerous, painful, invasive and criminal experiments related to mind control and related topics on innocent unsuspecting American citizens, illegally, without their consent or knowledge.
6. As the alleged MONARCH victims claim, children were illegally used in some of these horrific illegal experiments.
7. Some alleged MONARCH mind-control victims claim to have experienced torture by Nazis, Satanists, and occultists. There is proof that Nazi scientists were, in fact, involved in the CIA's mind-control MK-ULTRA program from the very start, and there are examples of the government working with Nazis, Satanists and occultists.
8. There is testimony indicating that secret illegal mind-control experiments did not end in the 1970s, as the CIA and others claimed. The government itself acknowledges that mind-control research is going on today and is a top government priority.
9. As alleged MONARCH victims claim, there is evidence indicating the possibility of world-wide pedophile rings catering to the depraved wealthy and powerful, with blackmail as a component. Though it must again be emphasized that there is no evidence connecting Bill Clinton with this kind of illicit activity, there are eyebrow-raising personal connections between Bill and convicted billionaire pedophile Jeffrey Epstein of the notorious "Island of Sin" and "Lolita Express." There are also decades of claims that Bill has engaged in abusive sexual behavior (involving adult women), and that Hillary has used harassment, threats, and possibly violence to shield Bill (and herself) from the

consequences of his alleged sexual misbehavior and crimes.

All of these shocking facts at the very least add credibility to the incredible claims of the alleged Project MONARCH victims at the beginning of this chapter: that the U.S. government has created, used, and may still be using, mind-controlled "Manchurian Candidate" sleeper agents and sex slaves.

We cannot prove their claims. But we can look at them with newly opened eyes and see these charges have far more of a basis in history and science than one might ever have imagined.

There may be more shocking revelations in the future.

CHAPTER TEN

UFOS: The Clinton Connection

"It is possible that UFOs really do contain aliens, and the government is hushing it up." – world-renowned physicist Stephen Hawking, in a 1998 interview

"It was known among the high CIA people, and the people who had contact with these people, that the Clintons were on the prowl for UFOs..." – UFO researcher William LaParl

Numerous polls show that a strong majority of Americans believe in the existence of UFOs – and also believe aliens have visited Earth.

For example, a 2012 survey by National Geographic found that fully 77 percent – more than three out of four – of Americans believe that aliens have visited our planet.

The same poll found that fully 30 percent of Americans believe that "extra-terrestrial intelligent life has already contacted us *but the government has covered it up.*" (Emphasis added.)

It's not just the general public who wonder about such things, either. Many of the most powerful people in the world are also very, very interested.

The annual World Economic Forum meeting in Davos, Switzerland – better known by its nickname Davos – is attended by many of the world's political and economic elites, prominent among them Bill and Hillary Clinton.

At Davos the elites mix, mingle, make deals and, many say, set the agenda for the future of the world. (For more on this see Chapter 13.)

In 2004 Davos attendees met for a secret behind-closed-doors discussion with some of the world's leading UFO experts. The topic: "Have Extraterrestrials Made Contact with Government Leaders?"

"The [UFO] panelists are the best in their domain; they all have expertise in specific fields," Philippe Bourguignon, the forum's co-chief executive officer, told reporter A. Craig Copetas of Bloomberg News. "The themes and sessions at Davos reflect the global agenda."

Davos officials, said Copetas, "maintain their five-day program on Partnering for Security and Prosperity *requires an unambiguous examination of extraterrestrial presence on Earth.*" (Emphasis added.)

At the 2010 Davos, Dr. Jill Tarter of SETI – the nonprofit research organization that searches for signals in outer space indicating the presence of intelligent life – spoke to the assembled ruling elite on the possibility of life on other planets.

In 2013 Davos hosted a debate and discussion which explored the implications of the "discovery of alien life," noting: "Proof of life elsewhere in the universe could have profound psychological implications for human belief systems."

It is known that Bill and Hillary are deeply interested in UFOs and related phenomena. Indeed, the breadth and depth of their interest may surprise you.

Less known is… why.

The Long Clinton Interest in UFOs

On August 21, 1995 Hillary met privately with billionaire Laurance S. Rockefeller – one of the five children of John D. Rockefeller – to discuss UFOs and paranormal/occult matters. A photograph of her taken at the time shows her carrying the book Are We Alone? Philosophical Implications of the Life of Discovery of Extraterrestrial Life, by internationally acclaimed physicist, cosmologist, and astrobiologist Paul Davies.

The book is intriguing, given later statements by Hillary. Here's how the publisher describes it: "The authentic discovery of extraterrestrial life would usher in a scientific revolution on par with Copernicus or Darwin, says Paul Davies. Just as these ideas sparked religious and philosophical controversy when they were first offered, so would proof of life arising away from Earth."

The Rockefeller meeting came about when President Bill Clinton's Science Adviser, Dr. Jack Gibbons, sent Hillary an August 4, 1956 briefing memo, writing: "Mr. Rockefeller ... will want to talk with you about his interest in extrasensory perception, paranormal phenomenon, and UFOs." Gibbons also noted Rockefeller's interest in "precognition, super-human strength, endurance in life saving roles, telepathy, and others." (To that list one might add Rockefeller's funding of research into psychokinesis, remote viewing, psychedelics, cults and other areas of the paranormal and the strange.)

Novelist and UFO researcher/abductee Whitley Strieber says that Laurance Rockefeller personally told him that Bill Clinton also secretly attended that meeting.

After their meeting, Rockefeller wrote to Bill in a now-declassified letter, urging him to release secret U.S. government information about UFOs and other paranormal matters. Hillary herself was involved in the drafting of this letter to the president.

Rockefeller also made sure Hillary and the president received a Rockefeller-funded 148-page document entitled "UNIDENTIFIED FLYING OBJECTS BRIEFING DOCUMENT: THE BEST AVAILABLE EVIDENCE."

This Rockefeller-funded UFO briefing – originally distributed only to political leaders and other highly influential individuals – expresses deep concern about "the intensive efforts by the governments of the world to withhold information about" UFOs, including "the apparent crash in 1947 of a strange craft on a sheep ranch in New Mexico: the so-called 'Roswell Incident.'" It quotes numerous leading military, government and science leaders and astronauts asserting the seriousness of the subject and the possibility of UFOs being of extraterrestrial origin. These statements strongly contradict the official Air Force denials of alien craft. For example, the first director of the CIA, Admiral Roscoe Hillenkoetter: "Unknown objects are operating under intelligent control... It is imperative that we learn where UFOs come from and what their purpose is." The Rockefeller document contained descriptions of some of the most persuasive UFO cases, including photographs and diagrams.

Laurance Rockefeller's interests in the occult, the paranormal, and the unexplained were deep and wide. For decades he used his unlimited wealth and influence to fund extensive and sometimes highly controversial research in this strange area.

Some examples:

- Laurance Rockefeller funded the Green Earth Foundation headed by Terence McKenna. McKenna was a popular and highly influential psychedelic researcher who theorized, among other things, that psychoactive plants could induce not just psychedelic delusions, or "trips," but actual "trans-dimensional travel" to "parallel dimension[s]" where a drug user could encounter literal beings, including "higher dimensional entities" from alien civilizations, and perhaps human ancestors and Earth spirits. McKenna said that while using DMT he met intelligent basketball-shaped entities he described as "self-transforming machine elves." McKenna argued that the monotheistic religions of the past few millennia – including Christianity, Judaism and Islam – had failed, and he urged a return to psychedelic shamanism. (Once again we note the recurring New World Order themes of communication with otherworldly beings and the replacement of Christianity with other belief systems.) He further speculated that psychedelic mushrooms might actually be a species of high intelligence, arriving on earth after traveling through space, and that the mushrooms are actively attempting to form a relationship with humans.

- Laurance Rockefeller was chief funder of the Human Potential Foundation (HPF) which in 1995 produced the first "disclosure" conference, "When Cosmic Cultures Meet," to pressure the White House to disclose information about UFO phenomena. Speaking at the event was a who's who of UFO researchers.

The president of the Human Potential Foundation was retired naval intelligence officer Commander C.B. "Scott" Jones, Ph.D. Jones had a remarkable background. He was involved in Navy, Defense Intelligence Agency, and interagency intelligence activities for many years, travelling the globe, briefing the President's Scientific Advisory Committee, testifying before House and Senate committees, and so on. He also had a deep interest in UFOs and related unexplained phenomena. Remarkably, from 1985 to 1991 he was on the staff of U.S. Senator Claiborne Pell of Rhode Island for the sole and explicit purpose of researching UFOs, ESP and other paranormal subjects.

In 2007 Dr. Jones told President Bill Clinton's science adviser Dr. John Gibbons that he had come to believe a friend and writer had been targeted by government mind-control technology. "There are reasons to believe that some government group has interwoven research about this [mind-control] technology with alleged UFO phenomena," he wrote. "If that is correct, you can expect to run into early resistance when inquiring about UFOs, not because of the UFO subject, but because that [UFO activity] has been used to cloak research and applications of mind-control activity." (For much more on the government's long history of mind-control projects see Chapter 9.)

Journalist Richard Farley, who worked for the Human Potential Foundation, said that Rockefeller's interests seemed to be promoting "alternative religious and psychiatric/psychological paradigms, including so-called 'UFOs' and 'abductions,' having 'Global Mind Change' potentials."

- Laurance Rockefeller funded the highly controversial Princeton Engineering Anomalies Research (PEAR) program at Princeton University that studied among other things "anomalous human/machine interactions, which addresses the effects of consciousness on random physical systems and processes" and found "clear evidence that human thought and emotion can produce measurable influences on physical reality."

- Laurance Rockefeller funded research into remote viewing and the crop circles phenomena.

- Laurance Rockefeller funded the controversial alien abduction research of Dr. John E. Mack, the Pulitzer Prize-winning biographer and Harvard Medical School psychiatrist. In Mack's work, many of Laurance Rockefeller's interests came together: the shamanistic notions of Terence McKenna; UFO abductions; crop circles; the familiar message, funded and pushed by Rockefeller institutions for decades, that population growth and human activity may be threatening the planet and must be halted; and the eugenics/genetic/breeding research that was funded by Rockefeller institutions prior to the rise of the Nazis in Germany.

According to Dr. Mack, the UFO experience is "both literally, physically happening to a degree; and it's also some kind of psychological, spiritual experience occurring and originating perhaps in another dimension. And so the phenomenon stretches us, or it asks us to stretch to open to realities that are not simply the literal physical world, but to extend to the possibility that there are other unseen realities from which our consciousness, our, if you will, learning processes over the past several hundred years have closed us off."

"...the [UFO] abduction phenomenon is in some central way involved in a breeding program that results in the creation of alien/human hybrid offspring."

Dr. Mack writes in Passport to the Cosmos: Human Transformation and Alien Encounters: "I was astonished to discover that in case after case powerful messages about the human threat to the Earth's ecology were being conveyed by the beings to the experiencers in vivid, unmistakable words and images... Indeed, it seems to me quite possible that the protection of the Earth's life is at the heart of the abduction phenomenon. Perhaps no one has been more surprised than I have that the damage we have been inflicting upon the Earth's life forms appears not to have gone 'unnoticed' by whatever intelligence or creative principle dwells in the cosmos, and it is providing some sort of feedback to us, however strange the form this has taken appears to be."

During an interview on NBC's "The Today Show" Dr. Mack explained further: "The purpose of doing this work is to open us to the idea that the universe may be vastly more interesting, containing entities, energies, beings that we did not know existed. When we open that consciousness, we open to a larger reality. We're not simply Earth-bound in our consciousness as if we were the top intelligence in the cosmos. We come more modestly to realize we are in connection with energies, beings, whatever it may be that is beyond ourselves. And that would be a very healthy development for this species, it seems to me."

We will see these themes repeated in different ways throughout this chapter.

In addition to this parapsychological stew he was funding, Laurance Rockefeller was also involved in the political machinations more commonly associated with the Rockefeller elite.

Along with the other Rockefeller brothers he was part of the mysterious and highly influential Rockefeller-funded "Special Studies Project" which ran between 1956 and 1960. The stated goal of the study was to "define the major problems and opportunities facing the U.S. and clarify national purposes and objectives, and to develop principles which could serve as the basis of future national policy." It was led by Rockefeller protégé and future war criminal Henry Kissinger; Kissinger's contribution was later published as "International Security – The Military Aspect," which called for massive increases in defense spending to counter alleged Soviet military superiority, and which became U.S. policy via President Eisenhower. The findings of the Rockefeller "Special Studies Project" were published as a book entitled "Prospect for America: The Rockefeller Panel Reports" and the book speaks enthusiastically of "the opportunity before America to create a *new world order*..." [emphasis added] as well as the importance of ceding U.S. sovereignty to the United Nations. In essence, the book is a guide to using the U.S. to create the now-infamous global New World Order. Indeed, the book reads like a preview of U.S. foreign policy, trade policy, and monetary policy that would be seen in decades to come. Remarkably, parts of the "Special Studies Project" papers remain restricted even today, well over half a century later.

Laurance Rockefeller was also associated with Reader's Digest, long a tool of the CIA and the ruling elite; in 1973 he was named a director of that publication. As the book Theirs Was The Kingdom: Lila and DeWitt Wallace and The Story of the Reader's Digest by John Heidenry notes, Reader's Digest "enjoyed an intimate relationship with the agency [CIA] perhaps unmatched by any other major American communications giant, with the exception of Time-Life ... the Digest was to become...a highly valuable propaganda outlet for both the CIA and, to a lesser extent, the Federal Bureau of Investigation..." and had "been serving as a primary conduit for CIA and FBI propaganda, self-promotion, and disinformation since the days of Allen Dulles and J. Edgar Hoover..."

Bill and Hillary and UFOs

In early 1993, just before the start of his first term, president-elect Bill Clinton appointed his trusted political operative Webster Hubbell as White House liaison to the United States Department of Justice.

Upon doing so he gave Hubbell a remarkable assignment:

"If I put you over there in Justice I want you to find the answer to two questions for me: One, who killed JFK. And two, are there UFOs?"

In his 1997 autobiography, *Friends in High Places*, Hubbell says "Clinton was dead serious" in this request.

It seems astounding that Bill would go to the trouble of assigning this particular mission to such a close associate unless it was a matter of great importance to him.

Hubbell was someone Bill could trust to keep secrets, someone from Bill's earliest days in Arkansas, someone he trusted – and, perhaps very importantly, a Washington outsider, not part of the Establishment/Insiders/ruling elite.

It is quite possible that Bill was deeply concerned about two factors that potentially threatened his presidency:

(1) the idea of assassination by the CIA or other shadowy extra-legal groups;
(2) the possibility that the government and president were in fact controlled by alien beings.

What did Bill and Hillary know that prompted this investigation? And what, if anything, did they discover?

The CIA, and other shadowy groups, were well aware of the Clintons' interest in UFOs, says one UFO researcher.

"It was known among the high CIA people, and the people who had contact with these people, that the Clintons were on the prowl for UFOs..." William LaParl, a UFO researcher and friend of top CIA scientist Ronald Pandolfi, told UFO author Grant Cameron.

"She (Hillary) was almost an equal mover with him on this," Laparl said. "...If anything she may have slightly been pushing it more than he was. ... Hillary even kind of tried to indirectly get me involved, as kind of like an outside researcher. ...She was putting out feelers that she needed help and stuff like that. They were open to any kind of input along these lines."

Ex-CIA agent Darrel Simms – who says he was first abducted by aliens in 1952 when he was four years old – also reports that Hillary and Bill were deeply interested in UFOs, requesting books and documents and offering to fund his research in this area. (Simms declined.)

Further, Hillary, like Bill, assigned a top campaign confederate to explore the UFO question: John Podesta.

John Podesta: Clinton UFO Point Man

John David Podesta was chairman of the 2016 Hillary Clinton presidential campaign and is a leading figure in the spider web of connected organizations working to bring to birth what many call the New World Order.

Podesta, a former chief of staff to President Bill Clinton, and a senior adviser to Barack Obama, is founder of the enormously influential Center for American Progress, a progressive think tank. As a member of the Joint Ocean Commission Initiative, he works to advance the New World Order agenda by eroding U.S. sovereignty on ocean matters. The Joint Ocean Commission Initiative is a partner of Citizens for Global Solutions (CGS) which in turn is a member organization of the World Federalist Movement, whose declared goal is a one-world government.

According to the CGS website (May 2015): "The World Federalist Institute (WFI) aims to advance education about a federal government for the world and steps towards it. Such a world government would deal with global problems while national governments handle national concerns, much as in the U.S. the federal government undertakes national solutions while the states resolve state problems."

Podesta has had a longtime and widely known fascination with UFOs. Podesta wrote the foreword to Leslie Kean's respected 2010 book, UFOs: Generals, Pilots, and Government Officials Go on the Record.

At a 2002 press conference organized by the Coalition for Freedom of Information, Podesta spoke on the importance of disclosing government UFO investigations to the public.

"It's time to find out what the truth really is that's out there," he said. "We ought to do it, really, because it's right. We ought to do it, quite frankly, because the American people can handle the truth. And we ought to do it because it's the law."

When he left the Obama administration, Podesta stated that "my biggest failure of 2014 [was]...not securing the disclosure of the UFO files."

Will he have another chance if Hillary is elected? Or – did he in fact discover something, something so huge and/or terrifying that he cannot share with the public?

Or – as we shall consider below – is this all a front for a long-planned false-flag operation for global conquest?

Hillary: "We May Have Already Been Visited by UFOs"

On December 30, 2015 Hillary answered a New Hampshire reporter's question about UFOs: "Yes, I'm going to get to the bottom of it."

She followed with this startling statement: "I think we may have been [visited already]. We don't know for sure."

She further told the reporter she might create a task force to investigate Area 51, the mysterious and infamous top-secret CIA-created Nevada base whose very existence was not admitted by the CIA until 2013, believed by some investigators to be a site where crashed alien bodies and recovered technology are explored and alien-based technology is researched.

"Maybe we could have, like, a task force to go to Area 51," Hillary said.

But is a task force necessary – and can Hillary be trusted to lead it?

After all, Bill has already closely examined Area 51 – and issued a Presidential Determination to keep its secrets hidden, even at the cost of American lives.

President Bill Clinton Hides Area 51 from Investigation – While Poisoning Americans with Top-Secret Substances

Both Bill and Hillary have repeatedly stated their interest in UFOs and Area 51 and their desire to share all such information to the public.

But when Bill was given a golden opportunity to do so, he instead used his presidential powers to bury Area 51's secrets even deeper.

In 1994, several civilian contractors and the widows of contractors sued the USAF, claiming they were exposed to poisons when large amounts of unknown chemicals were burned in open pits and trenches. Such burnings are illegal under federal law, punishable by up to 15 years in prison. Workers suffered respiratory ailments, strange skin conditions including the growth of hard membranes on their skin they dubbed "fish scales," cancer, lung problems and more. One must assume that these terrible substances, burned in such a manner, may well have spread outside Area 51 as well.

However, the federal government demanded that this suit be dismissed because it would expose classified information and threaten national security. When the court rejected this argument, Bill overrode the court's ruling by issuing a Presidential Determination, exempting "The Air Force's Operating Location Near Groom Lake, Nevada," i.e., Area 51, from environmental disclosure laws. The suit was then dismissed, and the Supreme Court refused to hear an appeal.

Each year since, presidents have issued Presidential Determinations continuing this extraordinary exemption.

As a result, Area 51 workers, suffering from dreadful ailments, face ten years in prison if they disclose anything about their jobs.

And for all we know, the burnings are still going on, poisoning countless innocent and unaware civilians.

Thus Bill chose to let utterly innocent American citizens suffer and die from severe poisoning rather than risk Area 51 giving up even a few of its secrets.

So perhaps one should view with skepticism promises by Bill or Hillary to reveal the mysteries of Area 51.

Is Hillary's Public UFO Interest Part of a False-Flag Conspiracy to Trick the World into Accepting a New World Order?

"In our obsession with antagonisms of the moment, we often forget how much unites all the members of humanity. Perhaps we need some outside, universal threat to make us realize this common bond. I occasionally think how quickly our differences would vanish if we were facing an alien threat from outside this world." – President Ronald Reagan, in a speech to the 42nd General Assembly of the United Nations, Sept. 21, 1987

"If we were visited someday, I wouldn't be surprised, I just hope it's not like Independence Day, the movie, that it's a conflict. May be the only way to unite this increasingly divided world of ours. If they're out there, think of how all the differences among people on earth would seem small if we felt threatened by a space invader..." – Bill Clinton, Jimmy Kimmel show, April 2014

"Today Americans would be outraged if UN troops entered Los Angeles to restore order [referring to the 1991 LA Riot]; tomorrow they will be grateful. This is especially true if they were told there was an outside threat from beyond [i.e., a UFO invasion], whether real or promulgated, that threatened our very existence. It is then that all peoples of the world will plead with world leaders to deliver them from this evil. The one thing every man fears is the unknown. When presented with this scenario, individual rights will be willingly relinquished for the guarantee of their well-being granted to them by the World Government." – attributed to Henry Kissinger at the Bilderberg Conference, Evian, France, May 21, 1992. (This widely cited quote is not confirmed, and has been challenged as to accuracy; it was supposedly, unbeknownst to Kissinger, was taped by a Swiss delegate.)

"The aliens won't let it happen. You'd reveal all their secrets. They exercise strict control over us." – President Barack Obama on the Jimmy Kimmel show on March 12, 2015, responding to whether he had learned government secrets about UFOs.

When Kimmel remarked that Bill Clinton said he'd looked into the matter and found nothing, Obama responded: "That's what we're instructed to say."

As the quotes above indicate, we must also consider another scenario. "False flags" are covert acts – often including acts of violence, threats, and/or terrorism – designed to look like another party has committed them. The name "false flag" comes from naval warfare incidents where one side would fly a flag other than its own, thus tricking their opponent.

Could a phony alien invasion be the ultimate "false flag" – a faked invasion?

Could the Clintons' interest in UFOs be simply a trick – a set-up for an incredibly sophisticated staged alien landing, to manipulate the human race into accepting a New World Order and draconian restrictions on liberty in order to fight a fake enemy?

Before dismissing the idea outright, consider a few similar false flags and hoaxes the government is known to have planned or carried out:

- **Operation Northwoods:** This was a mind-boggling 1960s proposal by the U.S. Joint Chiefs of Staff to stage a fake Cuban invasion of America in order to justify a U.S. invasion of Cuba. Only President Kennedy's rejection of this plan kept this lunatic and criminal plan from being carried out. Under Operation Northwoods the CIA would have conducted terrorist acts in the U.S., including sinking a warship in Cuban territorial waters (shades of "Remember the Maine"), staging terrorist campaigns in the U.S. blamed on Cuba, violating U.S. airspace with U.S. planes disguised as Cuban, and – yes – blowing up a U.S. airliner and holding mock funerals for the alleged victims. Anyone familiar with "9/11 was an inside job" arguments will find this plan from nearly a half-century earlier to be... disturbing.

- **Gulf of Tonkin Incident (1964):** In August 1964,

President Lyndon Johnson told Congress and the American public that North Vietnam had attacked U.S. vessels on the "high seas." This led Congress to pass the Tonkin Gulf Resolution, the historic legislation that justified a massive escalation in the war in Vietnam. This alleged incident never happened as described, and Johnson later admitted, "For all I know, our Navy was shooting at whales out there."

- **Project TP-Ajax (1953):** As part of the criminal CIA overthrow of the democratically elected government of Iran, the CIA planned bombings on mosques and on key Iranian public figures, to be blamed on Iranian Communist Party members. At least one bombing is known to have occurred; more is not known because the CIA destroyed almost all records pertaining to TP-Ajax.

- **COINTELPRO (1956-1971...?):** was a horrific series of covert and sometimes blatantly illegal FBI projects that infiltrated domestic political organizations to disrupt, discredit and smear these organizations and other Vietnam War critics, civil rights leaders, prominent cultural leaders, feminists, journalists and others engaged in legal and constitutionally protected political activities. COINTELPRO was nothing less than a secret FBI war against America and the Bill of Rights. In the 1970s a Senate investigation would denounce it as a "sophisticated vigilante operation aimed squarely at preventing the exercise of First Amendment rights of speech and association."

    FBI Director J. Edgar Hoover ordered COINTELPRO agents to "expose, disrupt, misdirect, discredit, neutralize or otherwise eliminate" these activists and organizations. False-flag COINTELPRO tactics including anonymous phone calls, IRS audits, the circulation of phony forged documents, false media reports, wrongful imprisonment, and the spread of information obtained by illegal wiretapping and bugging. Some have charged the FBI went even further, using violence, intimidation, and even assassination. An example of the latter: COINTELPRO tried to torment Martin Luther King Jr. into committing suicide.

COINTELPRO was blatantly criminal. Like MK-ULTRA, many researchers say COINTELPRO was never actually shut down but merely renamed and hidden, and still goes on today, internationally as well as domestically.

- **False-Flag Space Satellite Attack to Start War with Cuba:** In the early 1960s the U.S. Department of Defense's Operation Mongoose included numerous proposals to fake a Cuban attack on the U.S. as a cause for war. Among them: a plot to blame Castro if the 1962 Mercury manned space flight crashed: "The objective is to provide irrevocable proof that, should the MERCURY manned orbit flight fail, the fault lies with the communists, et al. Cuba ... This to be accomplished by manufacturing various pieces of evidence which would prove electronic interference on the part of the Cubans"; paying a Cuban commander to attack U.S. forces: "bribe one of Castro's subordinate commanders to initiate an attack on [the U.S. Navy base at] Guantanamo."

Given all this – and this is but a sampling – it is difficult to conceive of any false-flag plot, however strange, complex or violent – that some elements in the U.S. government would not, under some circumstances, try on its own people and the people of other lands.

And in fact, there is already a long and horrifying known history of *UFO false flags and cruel disinformation campaigns against U.S. citizens who investigate UFOs*: Recent research proves that the CIA, the military, and other parts of the U.S. government have been engaged for decades in dirty tricks, false flags, and disinformation campaigns against UFO researchers. In some cases these actions have led to the torment and even death of utterly innocent U.S. citizen UFO researchers. These are detailed in Mark Pilkington's book Mirage Men and the documentary film based on that book. Pinkerton interviewed intelligence agents, government disinformation specialists, and non-government UFO investigators, and lays out the case that, for over half a century, U.S. intelligence agencies have spread various UFO stories as misinformation to hide other government programs and as aspects of Cold War psychological warfare and various counterintelligence programs. The story of government agents deliberately manipulating – even wrecking the lives of – innocent U.S. citizens is quite terrifying. And of course it just hints at what other manipulations and false-flag events we may not be aware of.

Some prominent figures have predicted UFO false-flag operations for many years. Some even claim to have knowledge of such plans.

Dr. Carol Rosin presents an impressive resume: first woman corporate manager of an aerospace company, Fairchild Industries; a space and missile defense consultant who has consulted to companies, organizations, government departments, and even U.S. intelligence agencies; she has testified before Congress, the Senate, and the President's Commission on Space; was a consultant to TRW working on the MX missile; founder of the Institute for Security and Cooperation in Outer Space think tank; and spokesperson for world-renowned rocket scientist Wernher von Braun in the last years of his life. NASA called von Braun "without doubt, the greatest rocket scientist in history." In 1975, he received the National Medal of Science.

In December 2000 Dr. Rosin said that von Braun had repeatedly warned her that the U.S. military-industrial complex was planning to earn great wealth and gain unprecedented control over the civilian population by a series of carefully planned and staged phony wars. Von Braun told her he had learned that this would begin with a trumped-up phony Cold War, go on to phony threats from so-called rogue nations, and morph into a worldwide war on terrorism.

That's a concise summary of U.S. foreign policy for the past few decades – and Dr. Rosin said all this before the events of 9/11 that launched a surveillance state in America and a zillion-dollar global war on terrorism.

Dr. Rosin says von Braun told her the culmination of all this would be the ultimate trump card: a phony alien "false flag" attack to convince Americans and the rest of the world to mobilize and spend immense sums of money to put weapons into space.

"Wernher von Braun actually told me that the spin was a lie – that the premise for space-based weaponry, the reasons that were going to be given, the enemies that we were going to identify – were all based on a lie. ...

"Who would benefit from these space-based weapons? They are the people who work in that arena, people in the military, in industries, in universities and labs, in the intelligence community. ... This is what our economy has been based on in this country and spreading around the world – war."

Similarly, Col. L. Fletcher Prouty, former Chief of Special Operations for the Joint Chiefs of Staff under President John F. Kennedy and a vigorous critic of the CIA and the military-industrial complex, mused: "It will be interesting to see what 'enemy' develops in the years ahead. It appears that 'UFOs and aliens' are being primed to fulfill that role for the future."

Certainly the meme that a war with aliens would bring about the unity of mankind has been planted by prominent and powerful people for many years:

General Douglas MacArthur to West Point cadets, May 12, 1962:

"We deal now, not with things of this world alone, but with the illimitable distances and as yet unfathomed mysteries of the universe. ... We speak in strange terms of harnessing the cosmic energy... of ultimate conflict between a united human race and the sinister forces of some other planetary galaxy..."

General Douglas MacArthur again, October 8, 1955:

"Because of the developments of science, all the countries on earth will have to unite to survive and to make a common front against attack by people from other planets. The politics of the future will be cosmic, or interplanetary."

NASA in 1959 commissioned The Brookings Institution to prepare a report for NASA entitled "Proposed Studies on the Implications of Peaceful Space Activities for Human Affairs," which noted:

"The knowledge that life existed in other parts of the universe might lead to a greater unity of men on earth, based on the oneness of man or on the age-old assumption that any stranger is threatening."

Ronald Reagan made several other references to alien invasions as a way of uniting humanity, similar to his quote at the start of this section. Like this one from December 4, 1985:

"I couldn't help but say to him [Soviet Premiere Gorbachev] just how easy his task and mine might be if suddenly there was a threat to this world from some other species from another planet outside in the universe. We'd forget all the little local differences that we have between our countries and we would find out once and for all that we really are all human beings here on this Earth together."

Filmmaker Steven Spielberg reports that, after a White House special screening of his classic film "E.T.," **President Reagan** clapped him on the shoulder and said, "You know, there aren't six people in this room who know how true this really is." (Spielberg subsequently attended the 1999 Bilderberg meeting at Sintra, Portugal.)

Michael Michaud, a diplomat in the Nixon State Department, wrote an article explaining the Nixon administration's concern about alien invasions:

"Aliens from other solar systems are a potential threat to us, and we are a potential threat to them. … Our basic interest will be to protect ourselves from any possible threat to Earth's security..."

Soviet Premiere Mikhail Gorbachev, in a February 16, 1987 speech to the International Forum at the Grand Kremlin Palace in Moscow stated:

"At our meeting in Geneva, the U.S. president said that if the earth faced an invasion by extraterrestrials, the United States and the Soviet Union would join forces to repel such an invasion. I shall not dispute the hypothesis, though I think it's early yet to worry about such an intrusion."

General Carlos Castro Cavero of the Spanish Air Force said in 1976: "I believe that UFOs are spaceships or extraterrestrial craft... The nations of the world are currently working together in the investigation of the UFO phenomenon. There is an international exchange of data."

And what of Hillary and Bill? The lesson clearly isn't lost on them.

"The good thing about [the alien invasion movie] Independence Day is there's an ultimate lesson for that – for the problems right here on Earth. We whipped that problem [in the movie] by working together with all these countries. And all of a sudden the differences we had with them seemed so small once we realized there were threats that went beyond our borders. ... That's the lesson I wish people would take away from Independence Day." – President Bill Clinton, 1996.

"You know, you see story after story after story about how the movie audiences leap up and cheer at the end of the movie ["Independence Day"] when we vanquish the alien invaders, right? I mean, what happened? The country was flat on its back, the rest of the world was threatened, and you see all over the world all these people have all of a sudden put aside the differences that seem so trivial once their existence was threatened, and they're working together all over the world to defeat a common adversary." – President Bill Clinton speaking again in 1996 on the movie "Independence Day."

And still talking about it three years later:

"If we were being attacked by space aliens, like in that movie, 'Independence Day,' we'd all be looking for a foxhole to get in together and a gun to pick up together. The absence of a threat sometimes causes us to lose our sense of focus, our center, our concentration... you know, if we were being attacked by space aliens, we wouldn't be playing these kind of games [political conflicts over issues of race, religion and sex]. These kinds of games are only possible because the economy is strong and the American people are self-confident..." – President Bill Clinton, October 28, 1999.

And: "If we were being attacked by space aliens, we wouldn't be playing these kinds of games." – President Bill Clinton, November 7, 1999, frustrated by Republican legislation. Remarkably, upon hearing that, conservative broadcaster Rush Limbaugh responded by saying, *"What's he going to do? Arrange one?"*

"[In] the theater in which I saw it [Independence Day], there were great cheers as people of all different races and backgrounds and societies around the globe came together as human beings to save ourselves." – Hillary, October 13, 1998, at Spanish Hall, Prague Castle.

"When you look at popular culture today, positive images of the future are often hard to come by. You look at the movies that have tried to predict what will happen in the future, and we often see a lot of death and destruction and environmental degradation. It's not just that people might live under domes on Mars, but they would have to live under domes here on this planet because of what we will have done to our environment. Or whether we will have to join together as human beings to stave off attacks from aliens in outer space, and then we'll have to put aside our really petty differences – differences in our own country and differences among people around the world – to stand up for our common humanity..." – Hillary, speaking at the Mars Millennium Project Kick-off, January 14, 1999.

Remember, too, that when Hillary privately met with Laurance S. Rockefeller in 1995 to discuss UFOs and the paranormal, she was photographed carrying under her arms the book Are We Alone? Philosophical Implications of the Life of Discovery of Extraterrestrial Life. That book deals with the profound social upset and philosophical chaos that the discovery of alien life could have upon the world.

There are other examples of political figures speaking on this theme. Indeed, it seems on its way to becoming a political meme.

Scientist and renowned ufologist Jacques Vallee – the real-life model for French researcher Lacombe in Steven Spielberg's "Close Encounters of the Third Kind" – explored this hypothesis in his pioneering 1979 UFO classic Messengers of Deception – UFO Contacts and Cults:

"UFOs are real. They are physical devices used to affect human consciousness. They may not be from outer space. Their purpose may be to achieve social changes on this planet, through a belief system that uses systematic manipulation of witnesses and contactees; covert use of various sects and cults; control of the channels through which the alleged 'space messages' can make an impact on the public. ...

"Visitors from outer space... would offer the space effort – and all its attendant industry – a new purpose in life. They would rescue Western civilization from its acute spiritual malaise. They would help transcend political emotions and pave the way for a unification of that enormous economic marketplace: Planet Earth.

"Take these possibilities into consideration, and you will begin to understand why the idea of life in space is no longer a simple scientific speculation but a social and political issue as well. ..."

Vallee is one of many researchers who have noted that the messages received by contactees from alleged space aliens often include exhortations to reject democracy and unite the world under a single massive government – perhaps not coincidentally, a primary goal of many of the world's ruling elites.

Writes veteran UFO investigator Brad Steiger in his book The Fellowship: Spiritual Contact Between Humans And Outer Space Beings: "[T]he Space Beings appear definitely concerned with seeing that all humankind is 'united as one' on this planet. ... Contactees have been told that the Space Beings hope to guide Earth to a period of great unification... The Space Beings also seek to bring about a single, solidified government..."

"A great many of the contactees purvey philosophies which are tinged, if not tainted, with totalitarian overtones," wrote Paris Flammonde in The Age of Flying Saucers.

And Vallee (Messengers of Deception) notes that messages given from aliens to contactees include "fantastic economic theories, including the belief that a 'world economy' can be created overnight, and that democracy should be abolished in favor of Utopian systems, usually dictatorial in their outlook."

Numerous researchers and investigators note that top-secret technological advances by the U.S. government make such a massive modern-day "War of the Worlds" or "End-

Times Rapture" hoax ever more possible. Canadian journalist Serge Monast first speculated in 1994 on the existence of a government program called "Project Blue Beam" allegedly designed to accomplish this greatest hoax of all time. In his book of the same title he warns that the U.S. government is preparing to use highly advanced technology, including spectacular holographs and auditory transmissions, to create a false-flag alien invasion and/or a worldwide religious movement or "rapture" as an excuse to bring the nations of the world together in a tyrannical one-world government – exactly in the way President Reagan mused about, as quoted above.

Similarly, Jerry E. Smith, author of HAARP: The Ultimate Weapon of the Conspiracy, describes technology that would allow ruling elites to secretly "take over the world by projecting holographic images into the sky while beaming thoughts directly into our heads, telling us to accept the new 'god' of their design." (HAARP stands for "High-frequency Active Auroral Research Project.")

Congressional lobbyist Stephen Bassett of the Paradigm Research Group, who lobbies for the release of classified UFO material, issued a similar warning during a lengthy 2016 interview in Pacific Standard magazine:

"We have to be extremely wary that some element of the government – doesn't have to be the entire government – or intelligence branches may foolishly decide that selling an alien threat as part of the disclosure process will serve their interests. Because, you know, every nation in the world has got its certain share of war mongers running the show. And trying to sell, falsely, an alien threat would be a colossal blunder on the part of government, which is not unfamiliar with colossal blunders."

Dr. Steven Greer – founder of the worldwide (and at one time Laurance S. Rockefeller-funded) Disclosure Project movement, who has spoken on this topic with some of the most influential political and media figures in the world – concurs:

"Since 1992 I have seen this script unveiled to me by at least a dozen well-placed insiders. ...after 60 years, trillions of dollars and the best scientific minds in the world pressed into action, a secretive, shadowy group – a government within the government and at once fully outside the government as we know it – has mastered the technologies, the art of deception, and the capability to launch an attack on Earth and make it look like ETs did it.

"In 1997, I brought a man to Washington to brief members of Congress and others about this plan. Our entire team at the time met this man. He had been present at planning sessions when ARVs [Alien Reproduction Vehicles, aircraft back-engineered from recovered crashed alien discs] – things built by Lockheed, Northrup, et al, and housed in secretive locations around the world – would be used to simulate an attack on certain assets, making leaders and citizens alike believe that there was a threat from space, when there is none.

"Before he could testify, his handlers spirited him away to a secret location in Virginia until the briefing was over...

"Sound familiar? Wernher von Braun warned of such a hoax, as a pretext for putting war in space. And many others have warned of the same.

"...I know this all sounds like science fiction. Absurd. Impossible. Just like 9/11 would have sounded before 9/11. But the unthinkable happened and may happen again, unless we are vigilant."

The similarities between these schemes and documented false-flag operations of the past, such as those described above, are obvious.

Such a scheme would at one fell swoop forcibly pull together the all-powerful elite-controlled one-world government promoted by the numerous organizations that Hillary Clinton is affiliated with – as described in Chapter 13. It would quickly move the world population to embrace the New World Order schemes of those shadowy organizations, as outlined in the Rockefeller "Special Studies Project" findings published in the book Prospect for America: The Rockefeller Panel Reports, described at the beginning of this chapter. One must also remember that Hillary associate Laurance Rockefeller spent large sums on alien and paranormal research – much of which has focused on the theme that aliens may be interacting with the human race in order to prepare us for a transformation that will solve human problems of war, overpopulation, and so on.

Outrageous? Nick Pope, a former acting Deputy Director in the Directorate of Defense Security at the British Ministry of Defense, outlined the entire scenario in a remarkable interview in the UK Daily Mail, June 7, 2012:

"It has been a widely held belief in Ministry of Defense circles that 'aliens' have been able to detect us for decades via TV and radio broadcasts. What once seemed like science fiction is steadily being realized by central governing bodies as distinctly real.

"If aliens have studied our psychology, they may choose to appear in our skies on a significant date... On their arrival it is difficult to say what they would do: explore, help or destroy. Our resources make us quite a special threat.

"The government must – and has planned – for the worst-case scenario: alien attack and alien invasion. Space shuttles, lasers and directed-energy weapons are all committed via the Alien Invasion War Plan to defense against any alien ships in orbit. If UFOs came into our atmosphere, RAF jets such as the Eurofighter Typhoons, and missiles... would be well equipped to enter the fray.

"And if the aliens landed ... The TA [British Territorial Army volunteer reserves] and the Reserves would be called out and conscription potentially introduced. ...

"Aliens may possess weapons or advanced technology we've no idea of. Aliens may have invisibility, a death ray, teleportation, force fields and other things we can't even guess at.

"Beyond this, unity is key, but as history dictates, this is not so easy.

"The logical course is to unite the world against the alien threat, combining our military strength and fighting under the United Nations. ...

"The final and perhaps biggest flaw is preparation. ...we must... cast our eyes further afield and be prepared for even the most seemingly unfathomable."

Pope worked at the UK Ministry of Defense for 21 years. His postings included being assigned to the Joint Operations Center during the Persian Gulf War, where he was a briefer in the Air Force Operations Room. His work between 1991 and 1994 with the UK equivalent of America's Project Bluebook UFO investigation team earned him the nickname of "the real Fox Mulder."

Canadian Defense Minister: "UFOs Are Real... and the U.S. Is Preparing to Launch an Intergalactic War Against Them"

Paul Hellyer served as Canada's defense minister from 1963 to 1967. He has said that "UFOs are as real as the airplanes flying overhead" and says that governments around the world are hiding aliens. He further says aliens are deeply concerned about global politics.

In 2015 during a speech at the University of Calgary, Hellyer declared that aliens have "been visiting our planet for thousands of years" and dislike the way our society functions.

He sounded the by-now familiar note: The aliens feel "we spend too much time fighting each other, we spend too much money on military expenditures and not enough on feeding the poor and looking after the homeless and sick."

"They are very much afraid that we might be stupid enough to start using atomic weapons again... They are very concerned about that ... because the whole cosmos is a unity, and it affects not just us but other people in the cosmos.

"Decades ago, visitors from other planets warned us about where we were headed and offered to help. But instead, we, or at least some of us, interpreted their visits as a threat, and decided to shoot first and ask questions after...

"Trillions, and I mean thousands of billions of dollars have been spent on projects about which both the Congress and the commander-in-chief have been kept deliberately in the dark."

In November 2005, Hellyer bluntly accused President George W. Bush of plotting an "Intergalactic War":

"The United States military are preparing weapons which could be used against the aliens, and they could get us into an intergalactic war without us ever having any warning... The Bush Administration has finally agreed to let the military build a forward base on the moon, which will put them in a better position to keep track of the goings and comings of the visitors from space, and to shoot at them, if they so decide."

Is Hellyer right? Or is this yet another effort, at the highest levels of government, to set the stage for a false-flag alien invasion hoax?

Hellyer's startling remarks are echoed by other prominent political figures.

In December 2012 Russian Prime Minister Dmitry Medvedev, said that "the president of Russia is given a special Top Secret folder [that] in its entirety contains information about aliens who have visited our planet. Along with this, the president is given a report of the Special Service that exercises control over aliens in our country. I will not tell you how many of them are among us because it may cause panic."

Lord Admiral Hill-Norton, Five Star Admiral of the Royal Navy, former head of the British Ministry of Defense, former chairman of the NATO Military Committee, said in an interview for the 2002 film "Out of the Blue: The Definitive Investigation of the UFO Phenomena":

"[T]here are objects in our atmosphere which are technically miles in advance of anything that we can deploy, that we have no means of stopping them coming here, and that we have no defense against them should they be hostile ... There is a serious possibility that we are being visited and have been visited for many years by people from outer space, from other civilizations. ...it behooves us, in case some of these people in the future or now should turn hostile, to find out who they are, where they come from, and what they want. This should be the subject of rigorous scientific investigation..."

One could fill pages with similar statements.

The Voice of Vrillion: Prank, Encounter... or False-Flag Rehearsal?

In fact, an event rather along the lines described above, though on a far smaller scale, actually occurred.

At 5:10 pm on November 26, 1977 thousands of British TV viewers were stunned when a news bulletin was suddenly interrupted by a deep, slow-speaking voice that identified itself as "Vrillon from the Intergalactic Mission."

(Reports vary as to the name. Strangely, the name some heard as "Vrillon," others heard and reported as "Asteron" or "Gillon.")

In calm, even, deep tones, the voice spoke in perfect English for an estimated five-and-a-half minutes. This is believed to be a transcript:

"This is the voice of Vrillon, a representative of the Ashtar Galactic Command, speaking to you. For many years you have seen us as lights in the skies. We speak to you now in peace and wisdom as we have done to your brothers and sisters all over this, your planet Earth. We come to warn you of the destiny of your race and your world so that you may communicate to your fellow beings the course you must take to avoid the disaster which threatens your world, and the beings on our worlds around you. This is in order that you may share in the great awakening, as the planet passes into the New Age of Aquarius. The New Age can be a time of great peace and evolution for your race, but only if your rulers are made aware of the evil forces that can overshadow their judgments. Be still now and listen, for your chance may not come again. All your weapons of evil must be removed. The time for conflict is now past and the race of which you are a part may proceed to the higher stages of its evolution if you show yourselves worthy to do this. You have but a short time to learn to live together in peace and goodwill. Small groups all over the planet are learning this, and exist to pass on the light of the dawning New Age to you all. You are free to accept or reject their teachings, but only those who learn to live in peace will pass to the higher realms of spiritual evolution. Hear now the voice of Vrillon, a representative of the Ashtar Galactic Command, speaking to you. Be aware also that there are many false prophets and guides operating in your world. They will suck your energy from you –- the energy you call money – and will put it to evil ends and give you worthless dross in return. Your inner divine self will protect you from this. You must learn to be sensitive to the voice within that can tell you what is truth, and what is confusion, chaos and untruth. Learn to listen to the voice of truth which is within you and you will lead yourselves onto the path of evolution. This is our message to our dear friends. We have watched you growing for many years as you too have watched our lights in your skies. You know now that we are here, and that there are more beings on and around your Earth than your scientists admit. We are deeply concerned about you and your path towards the light and will do all we can to help you. Have no fear, seek only to know yourselves, and live in harmony with the ways of your planet Earth. We of the Ashtar Galactic Command thank you for your attention. We are now leaving the plane of your existence. May you be blessed by the supreme love and truth of the cosmos."

A prank? Perhaps. But as police and technology experts investigated, a station spokesman said "We have no idea how it was done" and noted any such hoax would take "fairly expensive and sophisticated equipment." To this day the event remains unexplained.

Was this perhaps a rehearsal for the kind of "alien invasion" false-flag scenario discussed above? It certainly fits the model. It has all the themes: the uniting of the human race, the abandonment of weapons, the kind of political and spiritual ideas and philosophy that Laurance Rockefeller funded.

Or – was an editorial that appeared in the Eugene, Oregon Register-Guard onto something when it noted: "Funny thing – no one seems to have considered that 'Asteron' might have been for real. Or that what he said made a great deal of sense."

Incidentally, the date of the Vrillon message was also the same month that Spielberg's "Close Encounters of the Third Kind" – discussed above – was released.

As a side note, the name "Vrillon" is an intriguing and provocative one, given all the links we have seen. and will shortly further see, between UFOs, occultism, Nazis, subterranean cities, transmitted manuscripts, and secret societies.

Vril, The Power of the Coming Race – yes, that's Vril, as in... Vrillon – is an 1871 occult novel by the renowned author Edward Bulwer-Lytton. The novel describes a race of superior beings called "Vril-ya" – a word in pronunciation almost identical to Vrillon – who live underground in huge caverns connected by tunnels under the earth. Their highly advanced society is made possible by their control of an extraordinarily powerful energy called Vril.

Many occultists over the years have believed that the novel is more than fiction – that it based on fact and contains key occult truths, high among them the concept of Vril power. Among those who believed that Vril power was real were Theosophy founder Helena Blavatsky and her early disciple William Scott-Elliot, who spread the idea among their followers around the world. The mystic Rudolf Steiner, founder of the esoteric spiritual movement Anthroposophy, and the Fabian socialist playwright George Bernard Shaw were also intrigued by the idea of Vril.

Some researchers further say that there was a secret Vril Society in pre-Nazi Berlin, devoted to exploring Vril power and other esoteric and occult knowledge. German rocket engineer Willy Ley, who immigrated to the U.S. in 1937, wrote of the existence of such a Vril Society in Berlin. In their landmark book on the influence of the occult, The Morning of the Magicians (1960), Jacques Bergier and Louis Pauwels write that the secret occult Vril Society existed in pre-Nazi Berlin and was connected with the Thule Society as well as the British occult group the Hermetic Order of the Golden Dawn.

Both of those last two organizations are highly interesting in the light of the themes explored in this book. The Thule Society, established in 1918, was an occult secret society that was the origin of what would become the Nazi Party; the distinguished Hitler biographer Ian Kershaw notes that the Thule Society's "membership list... reads like a who's who of early Nazi sympathizers and leading figures in Munich."

The Hermetic Order of the Golden Dawn was a highly influential international occult group supposedly founded upon, and led by, psychic transmissions from otherworldly beings, the "Secret Chiefs." Among the key members of the

Hermetic Order of the Golden Dawn was the ubiquitous Aleister Crowley.

There is no doubt that the Thule Society and the Hermetic Order of the Golden Dawn existed. The arguments for the existence of a Vril Society in Germany are intriguing, but there is no definitive proof for this at the present time.

Some researchers, among them Bergier and Pauwels in The Morning of the Magicians, claim that the occult beliefs of the Vril Society fed directly into the Nazi Party, leading to Nazi efforts to build space ships, interdimensional craft, and other partly occult-inspired technology. If true, it is genuinely eerie to imagine that, even as American rocket scientist Jack Parsons was writing down transmitted messages from alien beings and invoking Satan's blessings for rockets being launched in the U.S. (as described just below), Nazi scientists were exploring rocketry and esoteric craft under the inspiration of occult ideas transmitted by alien beings speaking through mediums.

Could it be that someone – or something – was (and perhaps still is) deeply interested in inspiring occultists to help the human race get into outer space...?

And of course, some of these Nazi rocket scientists were brought to the U.S. to aid America's space program – which, as we shall see, has deep occult – and Crowleyan – roots as well.

NASA and the Occult

NASA, seemingly a benign, rational, squeaky-clean enterprise, in fact has long and deep connections to black magic, occultism, conspiracy, Satanism and Nazism dating back to its very origin. As documented elsewhere in this book, after World War II, Operation Paperclip secretly – and in treasonous defiance of the stated wishes of presidents Roosevelt and Truman – smuggled some 1500 Nazi scientists into the United States, among them SS members and war criminals who would have otherwise faced trial and execution for their crimes. These formed a major part of the U.S. rocketry and space program, and when NASA was created in

1958 as the civilian branch of the space program, ex-Nazis were folded right in.

Also at the end of World War II, the Nazi's European spy ring was brought directly into the newly formed CIA, becoming the foundation of the post-World War II European branch of the CIA. The CIA, in turn, can be linked to horrific secret experiments upon the American people and to crimes and conspiracies domestically and abroad.

These two Nazified U.S. agencies – the CIA and NASA – complemented and strengthened one another. The CIA Nazis inflated reports of Soviet missile success, thus leading the U.S. government to give more funding to its own efforts and to NASA. At the same time, of course, all of this greatly increased the power and influence of the postwar U.S. military-industrial complex, run by America's ruling elite.

Far less known are NASA's links to black occultism, even to the most infamous and influential occult figure of the 20th century: the man who called himself "the Beast 666," known internationally as "the wickedest man in the world": Aleister Crowley.

To explore the NASA/Crowley/occult link, we begin with John "Jack" Whiteside Parsons. Jack Parsons was one of the most brilliant and innovative rocket scientists in history, the father of modern rocketry. A university drop-out, largely self-educated, he invented a radically new type of rocket fuel that made space exploration possible.

Parsons was co-founder of the Rocket Research Group, the first U.S. government-sanctioned rocket research group. He was co-founder of the Jet Propulsion Laboratory (JPL) at Caltech in Pasadena, California, which NASA gained control of in 1958 and which formed a major part of what we know as NASA; today JPL is the world's leading institution for the exploration of outer space. (Some today say JPL really stands for "Jack Parsons' Laboratory"; whether truth or witticism, this indicates his monumental influence.) Parsons also co-founded Aerojet Engineering, today a billion-dollar-plus giant company employing thousands of scientists and working on massive government contract projects.

Parsons' revolutionary work with rocket fuels and design

made NASA – indeed, the entire modern space age – possible. Wernher von Braun – the Nazi rocket pioneer and SS member (and alleged war criminal) smuggled to the U.S. after World War II via Operation Paperclip and nicknamed "The Father of Rocket Science" – reportedly said that Parsons deserved that title more than he did. Parsons biographer John Carter claims Parsons accomplished more in rocket science than renowned rocket pioneer Robert H. Goddard. A crater on (appropriately enough) the dark side of the moon, Crater Parsons, is named in his honor.

Now the surprise: Parsons was also a deeply committed practitioner of black magic. As British journalist Russell Miller notes, Parsons "was, perhaps, the last man anyone would have suspected of worshiping the devil ... He believed, passionately, in the power of black magic, the existence of Satan, demons and evil spirits, and the efficacy of spells to deal with his enemies."

In a parallel to his success as rocket pioneer, Parsons was also one of the most successful and influential occultists of the century. Indeed, he inspired, among others, a young Anton Szandor LaVey, who corresponded with him in the 1940s. LaVey would go on to found the Church of Satan in 1966.

Parsons claimed to have first invoked Satan at the age of 13. Parsons believed that magic was a real force in the universe, explainable through quantum physics. He joined the Ordo Templi Orientis (OTO) – the secret black-magic cult of the notorious Aleister Crowley – in 1941, and was soon appointed by Crowley to lead the Southern California OTO lodge. Crowley declared that Parsons was not a man, but was instead a black-magic god in human form; Parsons eventually believed he had become an incarnation of the Antichrist.

Parsons addressed Crowley as "Most Beloved Father" and signed his letters "Thy son, John." The admiration was mutual. Crowley wrote that Parsons "is the most valued member of the whole Order, with no exception!"

Parsons was also a close associate of underground filmmaker Kenneth Anger, himself a black magician and Crowley follower and a good friend of Church of Satan founder Anton LaVey; indeed, Anger lived for a while with LaVey, and LaVey chose Anger as godfather (Satanfather?) to his daughter. Anger had "Lucifer" tattooed on his chest, and his films, such as "Invocation of My Demon Brother" (1969) and "Lucifer Rising" (1972), often featured occult and Crowleyan themes; one film is dedicated to Lucifer. Charles Manson associate Bobby Beausoleil, a friend of Anger and a Church of Satan member, acted in both of those films and later composed and recorded the soundtrack for "Lucifer Rising" using largely handmade instruments while serving a life sentence for participating in a Manson Family murder; helping Beausoleil perform the music was fellow prisoner, Manson Family member and murderer Clem Grogan. In prison, Beausoleil, too, tattooed "Lucifer" across his chest. (LaVey's grandson, Stanton LaVey, also has "Lucifer" tattooed across his chest.)

So, Jack Parsons: rocket scientist by day, black magician by night. And the two seemingly divergent paths often crossed; during rocket tests, Parsons was frequently overheard reciting Crowley's poem "Hymn to Pan" to invoke success. The creature Pan, half-human, half-goat, has been interpreted in many ways; some consider Pan to be Satan. The goat-like Baphomet is seen by many as a version of Pan and thus Satan. Baphomet is the official symbol of the Church of Satan. Aleister Crowley chose the name Baphomet for himself when he became the Outer Head of the Order for the OTO.

Crowley's "Hymn to Pan" concludes:

> And I rave; and I rape and I rip and I rend
> Everlasting, world without end.
> Mannikin, maiden, maenad, man,
> In the might of Pan.
> Io Pan! Io Pan Pan! Pan! Io Pan!

Thus the early launchings of what would become the U.S. space program were "blessed" by a violent ode to Satan, recited fervently by one of the world's leading black magicians, who would come to consider himself to be nothing less than the Antichrist.

Parsons lived in a large rooming house he owned that included an OTO temple, where blasphemous black magic sexual rites were regularly performed and where Parsons claimed to invoke supernatural effects and contacts. Like his mentor Crowley, Parsons was a polydrug user, habitually consuming alcohol, marijuana, cocaine, amphetamines, peyote, mescaline and opiates. Among those Parsons brought into the Lodge: a young pulp writer named L. Ron Hubbard, who would later become famous as the founder of Scientology, which has been accused of being a mind-control cult. Hubbard became Parsons' intimate partner in ceremonial magic.

Crowley and Parsons both engaged in black magic rituals designed to open a portal (sometimes called a "stargate" or "wormhole" or "interdimensional doorway") to allow alien entities to enter this world. (See below for the U.S. government's separate Stargate program.) Crowley claimed to be in contact with otherworldly beings, perhaps from other dimensions or other planets. His 1904 book The Book of the Law, one of his most important works, was, he claimed, dictated to him telepathically by an entity named Aiwass – yet another of the many curious examples of books dictated via telepathic contact with otherworld entities that are found throughout this book. Aiwass told Crowley: "I am a god of war and vengeance" (which sounds surprisingly like "Ogou" – the voodoo god of war and politics summoned in the Haitian voodoo ceremony attended by Hillary and Bill in 1975, just prior to the launching of their political career).

In 1918 Crowley, in a series of rituals called the Amalantrah Working, established contact via a medium with a type of entity he said was named LAM. Crowley produced a detailed drawing of the LAM entity, and it is astonishing similar – indeed, virtually identical – to the thousands of drawings of aliens today commonly called "Greys" – triangular face, large dark eyes, etc. Half a century later, Greys began to be reported by witnesses all over the world. Millions would see the classic Grey facial features on the cover of Whitley Strieber's Communion, a 1987 bestselling nonfiction book in which Strieber recounts the terrifying story of his repeated abductions and torments by strange, seemingly unearthly beings.

Jack Parsons shared Crowley's great desire to contact and work with alien entities and serve as a conduit for their communications. Eventually this wish would be fulfilled and Parsons would produce his own otherworldly transmitted works. At one point Parsons felt he was possessed by an entity calling itself "Belarion Armillus Al Dajjal, the Antichrist," who spoke through him at times and dictated manuscripts (yet again, we see automatic/transmitted writings, a recurring theme in the events described in this book). In the 1949 work entitled "The Manifesto of the Antichrist," dictated to Parsons by the entity Belarion, Belarion states his purpose: "I shall bring all men to the law of the BEAST 666, and in His law I shall conquer the world."

In January 1946 Parsons and Hubbard began one of the strangest and riskiest – and perhaps most influential – occult experiments of the twentieth century: a now-legendary series of sex magic rituals entitled The Babalon Working. The Babalon Working was an effort to open a portal to this world to allow alien beings to enter; to invoke the Scarlet Woman/Great Whore of Babylon described in the Book of Revelation, and deliver her to Parsons so they could engage in ritual sex magic together to birth a "moon child" or demon-child; and in doing so ultimately destroy Christianity and begin a new era of mankind, the Aeon of Horus, dominated by Crowleyan-type magic and philosophy.

According to Parsons, there were extraordinary manifestations during and after the ritual. He mentions wind storms, electrical power disruptions, and the sudden appearance of a "brownish yellow light about seven feet high" witnessed by several people, which Parsons banished using a magical sword and occult rites.

The question must be asked: Did the brilliant rocket scientist and leading black magician Parsons have any success? Did his Babalon Working ceremony actually open a portal to another world – inviting demonic entities to enter this one?

The English occultist Kenneth Grant, an associate of Crowley and one of the most prominent occultists of the 20th century, thought so. "*Parsons opened a door and something flew in,*" he declared.

Certainly strange and extraordinary things followed that bizarre, blasphemous ceremony; indeed, some argue it marked the beginning of a new era in human history.

Award-winning filmmaker and Ufologist Jim Nichols notes of the Babalon Rising ceremony that "the modern UFO era began exactly a year and a half later on June 24th, 1947, with Kenneth Arnold's [UFO] sighting over the Cascade Mountains in Washington State as well as the UFO crash at Roswell, New Mexico."

Kenneth Arnold's historic sighting of nine unidentified flying objects speeding past Mount Rainier was followed immediately by the astounding phenomenon today known as the "Great Flying Saucer Flap of 1947." In the month immediately after the Arnold sighting, nearly one thousand UFO sightings – in every state in America – were reported in the press and to the U.S. military – at least a fourth of which were made by pilots, scientists, multiple eyewitnesses, or backed by photos. That figure comes from researcher Ted Bloecher, who combed newspapers across the U.S. to compile it. Bloecher emphasizes that he was not able to examine many U.S. newspapers, and so he roughly estimates there were probably at least twice that many UFO sightings in that brief period of just a few weeks.

Also in 1947: the renowned Roswell, New Mexico UFO crash incident, which remains highly controversial to this day. On July 8, 1947, the Roswell Army Air Field (RAAF) issued a press release declaring that Air Force personnel had recovered a "flying disc," which had crashed on a ranch near Roswell. According to the press release: "The many rumors regarding the flying discs became a reality yesterday ... The flying object landed on a ranch near Roswell sometime last week." The Roswell Daily Record newspaper, on the same day, ran a dramatic front page headline announcing: "RAAF Captures Flying Saucer on Ranch Near Roswell." The Associated Press ran a national story on the incident, beginning: "The army air forces here today announced a flying disc has been found ... and is in possession of the army."

Some Roswell witnesses have reported they saw the U.S. military handling alien "Greys" bearing remarkable resemblance to the LAM entity Aleister Crowley claimed to have contacted and sketched out back in 1918. Among them was Lieutenant Walter Haut, author of the original 1947 Air Force press release on the subject. Haut downplayed the topic during his lifetime, but after his death a sealed affidavit was opened in which he confessed he had been part of a cover-up and had, in fact, seen dead aliens and a crashed space ship.

"I am convinced that what I personally observed was some kind of craft and its crew from outer space," Haut wrote in his death-bed testimony.

Dr. Edgar Mitchell, Apollo 14 astronaut and sixth man to walk on the moon, said he was told confidentially by reliable military and intelligence sources that alien beings were in fact found at Roswell and that the government has covered up Roswell and other truths about UFOs for decades. Of such government-employed informers, he said in 1998: "Many of these folks are under high-security clearances, they took oaths and they feel they cannot talk without some form of immunity."

1947 was also the year of the infamous Maury Island Incident, a UFO encounter in Puget Sound just three days before Kenneth Arnold's famous UFO sighting – and which featured the first recorded encounter with the sinister "Men In Black."

Also in 1947: What some claim is the very first "flying disc" UFO photo, taken July 4, 1947 by U.S. Coast Guardsman Frank Ryman in his front yard in Lake City, Washington and printed the next day in the Seattle Post-Intelligencer newspaper.

Still more: 1947 was the year of black magician Aleister Crowley's death. (Mission accomplished?) In a few years, Crowley's tenets would begin to flood the entertainment world, until one could argue convincingly that today we live in a noticeably Crowleyan age. (See Chapter 6 for more on this.)

1947 was also the year of the creation of the Nazi-infused secrecy-shrouded sinister CIA, which would soon launch horrific and illegal mind-control and occult experiments still not widely understood or made public to this day.

The CIA was created by the 1947 National Security Act, a radical restructuring of the U.S. government's military and intelligence agencies after World War II, which gave birth to the U.S. security state, the "Deep State" that arguably has secretly run America since, to disastrous effect.

Within a few years after the 1947 UFO sightings, aliens would be reported around the world and implicated in stories of abductions, mind control, human sexual abuse, animal mutilations, government conspiracy and more.

Two types of alien beings appear again and again in witness reports. One is the small Grey creatures whose appearance startlingly matched Aleister Crowley's 1918 drawing of the LAM entity – and who were first reported in that extraordinary year, 1947.

On August 14, 1947 artist R.L. Johannis encountered what may be the first reported encounter with LAM-like "Grey" aliens. Johannis said that while hiking and painting near Friuli, Italy he came across a large disc-shaped object. Nearby were two beings about three feet tall with green skin and large, bulging eyes with vertical pupils. One shot him with a ray gun that paralyzed him but left him conscious. Unable to move, he watched them get back in the saucer and fly away.

Also fascinating is the second type of aliens prominent in early UFO reports: tall (six to seven feet), human in appearance, strongly resembling Nordic-Scandinavians, often with blond hair and blue eyes. These were often friendly, smiling, and were sometimes nicknamed "Space Brothers." A less flattering nickname also evolved: "Nazi Aliens," based in part on how their striking features seemed to match Nazi racial purity archetypes.

As we saw in Chapter 9, these Nazi Aliens are believed by some to be playing a major role in UFO/political mysteries to this very day.

So, 1947: strange, portentous days indeed.

And, lest we forget, 1947 was also the birth year of... Hillary Clinton.

At, as we noted in Chapter 7, Edgewater Hospital in Chicago, Illinois. Zip code: 60606.

666. The number adopted as a name by Aleister Crowley. *The number of the Beast.*

Could the unusually strong interest in UFOs by Hillary and her confederates be connected in any way to the strange and terrible experiment conducted by Aleister Crowley a century ago?

"Then the angel carried me away in the Spirit into a wilderness. There I saw a woman sitting on a scarlet beast that was covered with blasphemous names and had seven heads and ten horns. The woman was dressed in purple and scarlet, and was glittering with gold, precious stones and pearls. She held a golden cup in her hand, filled with abominable things and the filth of her adulteries. The name written on her forehead was a mystery: Babylon the Great, The mother of prostitutes and of the abominations of the earth. ... When I saw her, I was greatly astonished." – Revelation 17: 3-7

The Stargate Project: UFOs, Remote Viewing and Psychic Spooks

The Stargate Project is perhaps the best-known of the top-secret government projects involving psychic powers. It was a U.S. Army project created in 1978 by the Defense Intelligence Agency and involving the CIA, the Defense Intelligence Agency (DIA), the U.S. Army, U.S. Air Force, U.S. Navy, and other government agencies.

The Stargate Project investigated a full array of psychic phenomena including remote viewing, astral projection/out-if-body experiences, ESP, psychokinesis and more, to explore their usefulness in military and espionage. Some of this was done at the CIA-connected Sanford Research Institute, which has been used for CIA behavior modification programs. Many of those programs remain Top Secret today (giving yet more credence to the idea that MK-ULTRA-type experimenting goes on today).

Among those deeply involved in the Stargate Project was psychic Ingo Swann, originator of the psychic espionage technique explored and practiced by the Army and the CIA known as "controlled remote viewing."

Swann, who had Top Secret clearance from the U.S. government, claimed he personally knew of government contact with UFOs and had himself encountered an alien being. In his 1998 book Penetration: The Question of Extraterrestrial and Human Telepathy, Swann tells of working with an unnamed secret government intelligence organization studying extraterrestrials. Swann claims to have used his remote viewing powers to see an alien base, roads and construction activity on the dark side of the moon. He believed that large numbers of aliens, some in contact with the government, were living on earth, disguised in human-like bodies – a theory very much in sync with stories of shapeshifting reptilians, we should note.

The Stargate Project was allegedly shut down in 1995, after a CIA report determined it had not been successful. But was it really ended? Many doubt that. One is reminded of the dubious claims that MK-ULTRA and similar mind-control programs were shut down years ago. It is rather hard to believe that the Army and CIA spent 25 years working steadily in these areas, spending millions of dollars, and then abruptly discovered it was a waste of time and shut it down.

In fact, some distinguished figures believe the Stargate Project achieved remarkable success. Among them was the distinguished statistician Jessica Utts, who would go on to serve as president of the American Statistical Association chair of the Department of Statistics at the University of California, Irvine, and to give presentations on statistical matters around the globe.

Utt's stunning report received extensive worldwide coverage. Among her conclusions:

"Using the standards applied to any other area of science, it is concluded that psychic functioning has been well established. The statistical results of the studies examined are far beyond what is expected by chance. Arguments that these results could be due to methodological flaws in the experiments are soundly refuted. Effects of similar magnitude of those found in government experiments have been replicated at a number of laboratories across the world. ...

"It is clear to this author that anomalous cognition is possible and has been demonstrated. This conclusion is not based on belief, but rather on commonly accepted scientific criteria. The phenomenon has been replicated in a number of forms across laboratories and cultures. ... Resources should be directed to the pertinent questions about how this ability works."

Former Secretary of Defense William Cohen told Newsweek in 2015: "I did support the Stargate program... There seemed to be a small segment of people who were able to key into a different level of consciousness. ...there were a number of remote-viewing tests conducted that I found impressive."

Brian Buzby, who in the 1980s was an Army lieutenant colonel in charge of the Pentagon's ESP program, wrote a report for the Army arguing that remote-viewing was effective. "I believed in it then, and I believe in it now," Buzby told Newsweek in 2015. "It was a real thing, and it worked."

The first psychic to work directly for the Pentagon was Army Chief Warrant Officer Joseph McMoneagle. He began remote viewing for the government in 1978. When he retired in 1984, McMoneagle was awarded the Legion of Merit, given for exceptionally meritorious conduct. Newsweek reported his award states he served in a "unique intelligence project that is revolutionizing the intelligence community" and produced "critical intelligence unavailable from any other source" for the Joint Chiefs of Staff, DIA, NSA, CIA and Secret Service. That is remarkably high praise for a program those same agencies would suddenly announce was so unfruitful it was to be immediately and permanently abandoned.

Further, there are strong indications that, contrary to denials, the government continues to this day to explore and use psychic espionage. Days before the 9/11 terror attacks, UK psychic Christopher Robinson provided U.S. and UK intelligence agencies with a prediction/warning that twin towers in a large city – perhaps, he specified, New York or London – would be hit by planes and many people would die. Following 9/11 Robinson says he met many senior U.S. intelligence agents, some of whom, he claims were "extremely knowledgeable" about psychic remote viewing. Robinson says the NSA has tested psychics against intelligence targets, including Iran's nuclear facility.

The NSA's interest in remote viewing and other psychic matters was first documented in 1975. Many believe it continues today.

Acclaimed filmmaker Vikram Jayanti, who has production credits for two Academy Award-winning documentaries, has explored this subject and spoken to senior CIA operatives and researchers. He was quoted in the UK Daily Mail: "A former U.S. Senate aide active in foreign intelligence told me that rather than being shut down, America's use of psychic spies merely went what he called 'deeper black' – or further into the shadows."

Top Secret America: U.S. Mystery Black Budget Programs

If there are indeed secret programs related to UFOs or UFO-related false-flag hoaxes, there is ample manpower and money to back them up.

More than a dozen Washington Post journalists spent two years exploring the mysterious world of U.S. government secret programs. They summarized their results in 2010 in an astounding report, available online, entitled Top Secret America.

"The top-secret world the government created in response to the terrorist attacks of Sept. 11, 2001, has become so large, so unwieldy and so secretive that no one knows how much money it costs, how many people it employs, how many programs exist within it or exactly how many agencies do the same work."

The investigation "discovered what amounts to an alternative geography of the United States, a Top Secret America hidden from public view…

"A hidden world, growing beyond control… a defense and intelligence structure that has become so large, so unwieldy, and so secretive that no one knows how much money it costs, how many people it employs, or whether it is making the United States safer."

The Washington Post discovered 1,271 government organizations and 1,931 private companies in 10,000 locations in the United States that are working on counterterrorism, homeland security, and intelligence. They found the intelligence community includes 854,000 people holding top-secret clearances. Many are private-sector contractors; the Post estimated over a quarter-million private contractors may work in this vast shadowy empire.

The United States Department of Defense has a secret "black budget" it uses to fund "black projects" – secret funding of secret projects it will not admit exists. The annual cost of the United States Department of Defense black budget was estimated at $30 billion in 2008 but was increased to an estimated $50 billion in 2009.

Information made public by whistle blower Edward Snowden allowed the Washington Post to estimate over $50 billion in 2012 black budget expenditures – about the size of the entire defense budgets of the UK, France or Japan.

And that figure may be just the tip of a massive iceberg.

Trillions of dollars are unreported, unaccounted for by the military. On July 16, 2001, Secretary of Defense Donald Rumsfeld told the House Appropriations Committee: "...the financial systems of the Department of Defense are so snarled up that we can't account for some $2.6 trillion in transactions that exist, if that's believable."

"Snarled up?" Or... deliberately made impenetrable so that vast amounts can be funneled to Beyond-Top-Secret black budget projects?

And since then things have gotten far worse. In June 2016 a report by the Pentagon's Office of Inspector General stated that the U.S. Army had *$6.5 trillion* in unaccountable expenditures.

As veteran journalist Dave Lindorff noted: "There are enough opportunities here for corruption, bribery, secret funding of 'black ops' and illegal activities, and of course for simple waste to march a very large army, navy and air force through."

Canada's former Minister of National Defense Paul Hellyer charged in 2008 that trillions, not just billions, had been spent on black projects. "It is ironic that the U.S. should be fighting monstrously expensive wars allegedly to bring democracy to those countries, when it itself can no longer claim to be called a democracy when trillions, and I mean thousands of billions of dollars have been spent on projects which both Congress and the commander-in-chief know nothing about."

Secret Agencies

The notion that there cannot be large secret organizations in government – or, if there were, they would never violate the law or threaten U.S. citizens or be able to keep secrets from the public – is absurd and thoroughly disproven by history. Here are a few examples:

- **The National Security Agency (NSA)** was established by President Truman in a secret memo in 1952. Its existence was hidden from the public until the mid-1960s. Because of this extreme secrecy those who did know of it joked that NSA stood for "No Such Agency."

    A 1975 investigation led by Sen. Frank Church found that the NSA had abused this secrecy, illegally spying on U.S. citizens engaged in constitutionally protected speech activities.

    The 2013 revelations of NSA whistle blower Edward Snowden showed, among other things, that the NSA operated under its own secret interpretation of the Patriot Act; that members of Congress were unaware of this secret interpretation or the existence of numerous controversial NSA programs and were denied access to basic information about them, and thus unable to engage in any meaningful oversight; the NSA violated its own rules thousands of times a year and spied on over a billion people around the world, mostly innocent, including U.S. citizens; collected without cause or warrant the contents of millions of emails from U.S. citizens and tracked nearly everything users did on the Web.

Thus the NSA, a secret U.S. government organization unknown to the public for nearly a quarter-century, was found to be secretly engaged in crimes, cover-ups and deceptions and to be essentially impossible to monitor or control – and yet allowed to continue on its merry way.

- **The National Reconnaissance Office (NRO)** was founded in secret in 1960 and operated that way until a 1973 Senate committee report accidentally exposed its existence. The organization remained largely unknown; a 1985 New York Times article gave some details about its operations. Its existence was not declassified until 1992.

- **"The Pond" or "the Lake"** were the names used by those few who knew of it for a U.S. espionage organization formed in 1942. The Pond existed for 13 years, operated in America and abroad, and was kept totally secret for over 50 years, until in 2001 a moving company stumbled across papers referring to it in a Virginia barn and turned them over to the CIA. The CIA, which had known of the Pond since its founding, finally released information about the Pond in 2010. This half century of secrecy was successfully maintained despite the fact that the Pond worked within prominent multinational corporations as cover, including American Express, Chase National Bank, Remington Rand, and Philips, and worked variously for Military Intelligence, the State Department, the CIA and the FBI. The Pond engaged in cryptography, espionage and covert actions. According to Associated Press the Pond had "40 chief agents and more than 600 sources in 32 countries." At one point the Pond reported on U.S. government workers to Senator Joe McCarthy. Thousands of pages relating to the organization remain classified.

As far as keeping criminal actions against the U.S. public secret, it is now well-documented that the CIA, FBI and U.S. military committed numerous crimes against U.S. citizens that remained secret for years. For example, details of the mind-boggling horrific MK-ULTRA CIA program, U.S. military atrocities, and government-sponsored secret experiments on American citizens can be found in Chapter 9.

Who says the government can't keep a secret?

CHAPTER ELEVEN

Indications of Occult or Alien Power Manifested by Hillary

Throughout this book we have explored evidence and arguments for the claim that Hillary is involved in the occult, the paranormal, the alien, the ungodly and the unholy. That she even may be something other than human.

The evidence is startling. Some find it persuasive.

If any of this is true, one would suspect that Hillary may well have acquired powers beyond those of most humans – and that she would be capable of feats not easily explained by conventional means.

Needless to say, any manifestations of such powers would be kept totally secret. Any revealing of such abilities would be accidental or disguised.

Still, Hillary has been in the public eye for over half a century. And during that time, some intriguing – if not downright strange – signs have in fact been recorded.

So let's examine some evidence – admittedly mostly tentative, but still provocative – from journalists, government agents, experts on the occult, and other prominent sources – that may indicate Hillary does in fact have – and use – such occult/supernatural/paranormal powers.

"Laser Beam" Eyes that "Pierce Skulls"

"A senior permanent employee, who I knew to be a strong supporter of the Clintons, had looked forward to meeting her [Hillary]. He held a position that ensured that someday he would.

"One day he saw Hillary Clinton walking in his direction down a corridor in the OEOB [the Eisenhower Executive Office Building]. She looked in no particular hurry, so he thought it might be a good time to say hello. She approached with Secret Service agents walking several paces behind her.

"Working up his best smile, he said, 'Good morning, Mrs. Clinton.' She stared right through him. He told me it was as if she had 'pierced his skull with laser beams.'"

– FBI agent Gary Aldrich, from his #1 New York Times bestseller Unlimited Access: An FBI Agent Inside the Clinton White House

Referring to this passage, Rev. David Bay, Bible prophecy scholar, occult expert and director of the controversial Cutting Edge Ministries notes: "This type of powerful stare is... very typical of the behavior of a practicing witch."

Indeed, for centuries witches and demon-possessed humans have been credited with such forceful, piercing, hypnotic stares. So have shapeshifting creatures in the guise of humans – think of the vampire's legendary hypnotic trance-inducing stare – as well as UFO aliens in stories of alien abduction. (All of these possibilities are discussed elsewhere in this book.)

As we discuss in Chapter 8, YouTube is filled with videos showing Hillary's eyes switching back and forth from a human to a seemingly non-human state.

"The eye is the lamp of the body. So, if your eye is healthy, your whole body will be full of light, but if your eye is bad, your whole body will be full of darkness. If then the light in you is darkness, how great is the darkness!" – Matthew 6:22-23

Invulnerability

Assassination is an ever-present threat to American presidents.

Four presidents have been the victims of assassinations. Two others were wounded in assassination attempts but survived.

Every president since Kennedy (with the exception of Johnson) has been the target of serious assassination attempts. Presidents commonly receive death threats.

While president, Bill Clinton himself faced at least four serious assassination attempts: a 1994 plot that resulted in one arrest; a small airplane crashing into the White House in 1994; at least 29 shots fired by an assassin into the White House with a semi-automatic rifle; and a 1996 bombing attempt in Manila.

Standing between the presidents and possible death are, first and foremost, America's storied Secret Service agents, dedicated, highly trained, and famously pledged to throw their bodies in front of their charges and take an assassin's bullet if necessary.

Given all this, it would seem extraordinarily reckless – indeed, downright insane – for a president's wife to want to travel without these Secret Service agents or to hinder them in any way in their job.

Yet that's exactly what Hillary did, according to FBI White House security agent Gary Aldrich.

Quoting again from Aldrich's bestseller Unlimited Access:

"She has told her Secret Service Protective Detail agents in public to 'Stay the f--k back, stay the f--k away from me! Don't come within ten yards of me, or else!'

"When the agents have tried to explain to the First Lady that they cannot effectively guard her if they must remain so far away, her reply is, 'Just f--king do as I say, okay?'

"The First Lady has even bragged publicly, in her newspaper column, about evading the Secret Service to go on a joy ride."

According to agent Aldrich, Hillary also sometimes simply threw the Secret Service out of the White House, thus making it impossible for them to protect her there. In fact, Bill and Hillary made it so difficult to guard them that many times the Secret Service was unable to protect them.

This happened so often, Aldrich says, that "Every time one of the members of the First Family countermands efforts to guard him or her, an agent prepares a memo noting the events. The memo goes into a Secret Service file so that the agents, and the agency, are covered."

Others confirm this. Ronald Kessler, award-winning

journalist, former Washington Post and Wall Street Journal reporter, and author of multiple New York Times bestsellers bluntly notes in his book The First Family Detail: Secret Service Agents Reveal the Hidden Lives of the Presidents:

"Because Hillary Clinton is so nasty to agents, being assigned to her protective detail is considered a form of punishment and the worst assignment in the Secret Service."

This behavior, it should be noted, started well before Bill Clinton's election. Journalist David Brock, writing in 1993 for the conservative American Spectator, found the same pattern:

"Hillary...kept her distance [from the troopers]. When she left the residence, she never informed them of her schedule. In fact, when she could Hillary avoided even speaking to them." She humiliated them in public and cursed at them."

Brock speculates this might be "possibly because she disdained their role in facilitating his [Bill's] philandering."

Perhaps. But of course it could be for other, more sinister reasons.

Some experts say it could indicate Hillary believes she possesses powers against attack – powers possibly gained from occult practices, demons, or alien technology.

Occult researcher and self-professed former witch Joseph "Doc" Marquis is the author of numerous books on the occult. He has been a guest on national television and radio shows and has, he says, trained "therapists, clinicians, psychiatrists, psychologists, local and state police, and former/present day members of the FBI" on occult matters.

Doc Marguis bluntly explains Hillary's disdain for Secret Service protection:

"Such disdain of authority is common among 3rd to 6th level witches in the Illuminati. They believe their personal demons will protect them at all times. They also do not want the Secret Service observing anything they may be doing that is of an occult nature. Occultic behavior is either illegal or terrifyingly immoral, and certainly considered disgusting by anyone not in the occult."

Pastor David Bay of Cutting Edge Ministries, who has written extensively on the intersection of the occult and politics, concurs:

"Once you look at the Clintons' behavior in disdaining or outright refusing Secret Service protection, through the prism that they are powerful practicing Illuminist witches, their attitude makes a lot of sense.

"A person advances through the various levels of Illuminist witchcraft primarily by receiving into their souls and bodies more demons, and more powerful demons.

"Thus, such a demon-possessed witch would have complete confidence in their powerful indwelling demons to protect them from any harm! ... Such a witch would believe that his or her personal demons would guarantee their safety!"

Indeed, a Secret Service agent who spent five years as a member of Hillary's protective detail bluntly said (as reported by Newsmax, March 20, 2001):

"Only one word adequately describes that woman: witch."

In fact, the charge that Hillary and some of her associates are in fact practicing witches is one that has followed her since her Arkansas days. As discussed in Chapter 4, former Clinton operative Larry Nichols claims Hillary regularly travelled from Arkansas to California to worship with other witches in an occult church. Nichols said Bill himself told him this.

Certainly many observers have noted that Hillary is constantly surrounded by a ring of carefully chosen intimates who protect her from random contact with ordinary people. As Vanity Fair editor Graydon Carter wrote in the Nov. 2015 issue of that magazine: "No other recent presidential candidate – not Obama, not Bush, not even Nixon – has been as inaccessible as Hillary has been from day one of her campaign."

Such striking seclusion by a world-famous celebrity certainly invites speculation.

Looking beyond witchcraft, there may be other, equally sinister, explanations for Hillary's isolation and constant rejection of Secret Service protection. If Hillary is in fact a shapeshifting reptilian – as millions of adherents to the reptilian hypothesis believe, as explored in Chapter 8 – there is a very good reason she would want to be away from human guards – except those on her side, working to protect her reptilian secret – at night. For, according to some researchers, reptilians cannot retain their human form without concentration. During sleep or periods of relaxation – exactly the same times that the Clintons barred Secret Service from their chambers – they revert to their hideous reptile form.

Certainly it cannot be denied that if Hillary is a shapeshifting human-flesh-eating reptile, she would not want the Secret Service seeing her transform into that. And she might feel especially vulnerable to human attack while sleeping in her true form of a seven-foot-tall ghastly reptilian being.

Hillary Does Not Sweat

In August 2012 the highly respected Conde Nast Traveler magazine featured a profile of Hillary, written by its deputy editor Kevin Doyle, entitled "Nine Days with the Most Traveled secretary of state in History."

The story was commented upon by mainstream media outlets around the world.

Doyle, who flew a whopping 19,000 miles with Hillary, reported that Hillary... does not sweat.

"Literally," he emphasizes.

In the opening paragraph of the article, he writes:

"But even after living under the klieg-light scorch of media scrutiny as first lady (eight years), senator (eight years), and now the sixty-seventh secretary of state (three years and counting), there's one very intimate detail that most people still don't know about Hillary Clinton, and which I shall divulge: She does not sweat. Literally. She does not even glow. No matter how high the heat, not a drop nor a drip nor a bead nor so much as the faintest glisten can be detected anywhere about her person."

Note that Doyle emphasizes that he is not speaking metaphorically or generally. He is clear: "She does not sweat. Literally."

This remarkable trait is noticed and remarked upon by those around her, Doyle continues.

"It's an improbable physical anomaly that was cited more than once... by longtime aides and members of the press corps..."

This raises some very serious questions.

Medically speaking, any human being who doesn't sweat faces grave health concerns. Of course, it is possible that Hillary suffers from hypohidrosis, a serious medical condition where the body produces inadequate sweating. Hypohidrosis can lead to hyperthermia, heat exhaustion, heat stroke and potentially death.

It is also possible, given the above descriptions, that she suffers from anhidrosis, an extreme case of hypohydrosis, the complete inability to produce sweat or sweat normally. This rare medical condition can lead to sickness, even fatal heat stroke.

These seem unlikely, however, since there is no record of Hillary ever exhibiting these signs, and there are no medical reports associating her with these conditions that this author has been able to find.

Thus, Occam's Razor compels us to consider a simpler – if far more disturbing – answer as the more likely one: Hillary Clinton does not sweat because... she is not human.

In particular, we are reminded of the accusations that *Hillary is a reptilian being disguised as a human. Because reptiles do not sweat.* It is possible that some of the possessed, or alien beings, may not sweat, either.

Even more remarkably, other trained professional observers have reported Bill Clinton as sometimes demonstrating the same inability to sweat, even after extreme exertion.

In his article "Living with the Clintons" (American Spectator, January 1994) journalist and Hillary biographer

David Brock writes:

"According to the troopers, Clinton often visited his regular Little Rock girlfriends in the early morning during what were ostensibly long jogs. 'He would jog out of the mansion grounds very early most mornings and then we would go pick up him at a McDonald's at 7th Street and Broadway,' Patterson said. 'When we picked him up, half the time he would be covered in sweat and the other half of the time there wouldn't be a drop of sweat on him, even in the middle of July in Little Rock. Sometimes I'd ask him; 'How far did you run today governor?' And he would say, 'Five miles.' I'd tell him there must be something wrong with his sweat glands because he didn't have a drop of sweat on him. He'd say, 'I can't fool you guys, can I?'"

Of course, trooper Patterson's assumption was that Bill's lack of sweat was because he had used the run as a ruse to cover a sordid adulterous rendezvous.

But... could his interpretation be wrong? Patterson probably never considered the possibility – little discussed at the time – that Bill might be a shapeshifting reptilian. But certainly that would serve equally well, perhaps even better, as an explanation for such incidents.

That makes Bill Clinton's remarks to the troopers – "I can't fool you guys, can I?" – downright eerie. Because, of course, if he was a reptilian, he was in fact *fooling them all the time* about his greatest and most horrible secret. What better way to hide a hideous secret like this than to disguise it as a mundane, squalid sexual vice?

The odds of both Bill and Hillary Clinton having some kind of rare sweat gland problem seem astronomically unlikely. We are compelled to look for more likely explanations. And that inevitably leads us to consider the possibility that both Bill and Hillary Clinton are in some profound way nonhuman, perhaps reptilians or perhaps deeply involved in occult or alien activities.

Superhuman Powers of Endurance and Strength

In the same article cited above, Conde Nast Traveler's

Doyle notes that "longtime aides and members of the press corps" have observed what he calls Hillary's "superhuman stamina... and a steel-trap mind."

Doyle also observes: "Those close to her say that she benefits from the ability to sleep on command – and to draw on reserves of energy lacking in most mortals."

Once again we see Hillary described as something different than human ("superhuman... reserves of energy lacking in most mortals.")

Occult Manipulation of the Stock Market?

In 1978 and 1979, while still First Lady of Arkansas, Hillary – who had no prior experience in investing – made an astounding series of trades of cattle futures contracts. Just ten months later, her $1,000 investment had generated nearly $100,000, the beginning of the Clinton's multi-million dollar fortune.

Good luck? Market savvy?

Not according to experts, who say the odds against such success are unbelievably, mind-bogglingly high.

In a Fall 1994 paper for the Journal of Economics and Finance, economists from the University of North Florida and Auburn University concluded that the odds of such an astounding return on an investment like this were – at best – 1 in 31 trillion.

Yes, 1 in 31 *trillion*. Remember that a trillion is a *thousand billion*.

For comparison, the chance of winning Powerball with a lottery ticket is 1 in 175 million – almost a sure thing compared to 1 in 31 trillion.

Your odds of being struck by lightning during your lifetime are a mere 1 in 12,000.

Your odds of being struck by lightning in a given year are 1 in 960,000.

What are the odds that an asteroid impact will kill you in a given year? According to the Economist magazine in 2013, the chances are 1 in 74,817,414 – again, far, far greater odds than Hillary overcame in her ten months of playing the stock market.

No wonder her accomplishment raised eyebrows among financial experts around the world.

The editor of the Journal of Futures Markets said in April 1994, "This is like buying ice skates one day and entering the Olympics a day later." And then winning a gold medal, we might add.

In 1998, Marshall Magazine, a publication of the distinguished Marshall School of Business, stated: "These results are quite remarkable. Two-thirds of her trades showed a profit by the end of the day she made them and 80 percent were ultimately profitable. Many of her trades took place at or near the best prices of the day."

And Newsday quoted an unnamed New York trader: "The chances of Hillary having legitimately made that money without some grandfather making sure [that] only winning trades were going into her account are lower than a meteor hitting you when you leave your office today."

Such astounding, almost unprecedented results, brought forth charges of fraud and criminality. Some critics sought to prove that she had benefited from favoritism, but nothing was proven.

If there was no favoritism, fraud or other criminal activity – and remember, intensive investigation by some of the best criminal investigators in America failed to reveal any evidence of criminal conduct – then arguably the most logical explanation for her beating beyond-astronomical odds of 1 in 31 trillion is... some kind of occultic power.

Mind Control / Hypnotism / Dream Control?

We have written earlier of the strange power of Hillary's gaze. Here is a another example, from a 2014 interview with Hillary in the bestselling UK magazine The Stylist, conducted by editor-in-chief Lisa Smosarski.

"Throughout my interview with Hillary, she is fiercely engaged; her eyes – sparkly, wide, alert – remain firmly focused on me," Smosarski writes. "She is warm, considered, talks slowly and thoughtfully and uses – consciously or not – tactics that put me at ease."

Smosarski further writes that Hillary's laugh is "utterly disarming" – and further notes: "That Sunday night, five days before we would meet, I had a dream that I was interviewing Hillary."

If Hillary has occult powers, entering into dreams and implanting suggestions for an upcoming encounter would fit right in, as observers of the occult have noted for centuries.

The idea that Clinton might have used occult powers to control journalist Smosarski is an interesting one, because the resulting interview was at the time widely lambasted as wildly uncritical, absurdly fawning; the Washington Free Beacon lambasted it as "undoubtedly one of the puffiest Hillary Clinton puff pieces of all time..." and notes, eerily, that "Hillary might as well have written the (un-bylined) piece herself."

Indeed...

Did in fact Hillary dictate the article telepathically to editor Smosarski in a dream, one wonders? Or... did Smosarski interview and write under the influence of Hillary mind control or hypnotism?

This may sound unlikely to those unfamiliar with such things. However, throughout this book we have that books whose authors say were dictated to them telepathically, by mysterious unknown otherworldly entities, have played a surprisingly large role in advancing the plans of America's ruling elite – of which Hillary is most certainly a leading member and operative.

We have also seen that the U.S. government, for decades, has been deeply interested in such methods of remote mind control – and has explored and used them secretly in sinister and horrific ways.

Could this widely ridiculed article in fact be an example of such mind-manipulation?

In her article "How Witches and Warlocks Manipulate Our Dreams," Pam Sheppard, a licensed therapist, an ordained minister and author of six Christian non-fiction books, writes that witches and warlocks can – and do – use demons to influence dreams.

"[D]emons used dreams to pursue and fight against the person to whom they are sent," she writes. "I know from personal experience what demons try to do to a person while they are asleep. ...For example, demons will come into your sleep for the sole intention of weakening your will to live, while you are in the altered state of sleep."

In Bill Clinton: The Inside Story by Robert E. Levin, Clinton's Yale friend Jeffrey Glickel describes the strange story of Bill and Hillary's first encounter in the Yale library:

"Little by little, though, I noticed Bill's concentration begin to slacken and his interest to wane. It was becoming clear to me that Bill's focus was somewhere other than the Law Journal. As I continued to talk, Bill's eyes seemed to wander; glancing over my shoulder with increasing frequency...

"I managed to sneak what I hoped was an inconspicuous glance to see what was attracting Bill's attention. There seated at a nearby desk with a stack of books and notepads was my classmate Hillary Rodham. After a while, Hillary walked over to us and said to Bill, 'Look, if you're going to keep staring at me and I'm going to keep staring back, we should at least introduce ourselves.'"

Continues Glickel: "At that moment, Bill Clinton was at a loss for words and *momentarily forgot his own name.*" (Emphasis added.)

Similarly, Bill himself has said when the two first met he was "dumbstruck. I couldn't think of my name."

That Hillary's stare should be so powerful as to induce him away from his studies, wipe his mind to the extent he couldn't even remember his own name, and put him totally under her control sounds less like a romantic encounter than some kind of eerie occultic mind control or hypnotic trance.

Indeed, the description of Hillary's mental control over Bill sounds eerily like the claims of alleged victims of sinister Top Secret U.S. government mind-control programs like MK-ULTRA.

Is it possible that Bill was groomed very early in his life, perhaps by some MK-ULTRA-type mind-control program – to be Hillary's slave, tool and mind-controlled conduit to power? Other alleged victims of MK-ULTRA mind control have reported similar incidents in their pasts. Certainly Bill's troubled childhood of emotional and physical abuse by his mother and stepfather is the kind some experts say makes a young child particularly susceptible to mind control.

Bill's documented involvement with voodoo (discussed in Chapter 2), his lifelong association with occult and conspiratorial organizations, his seemingly carefully greased path into power... all could have been part of a decades-long plan, perhaps even a plan launched well before he was born. It is possible that Bill could be a victim, targeted from the beginning, simply another mind-controlled slave of the dark secret occult societies who, some charge, rule the earth.

If so, the rise of Hillary to supreme power over the entire human race could well be the ultimate goal of such a sinister scheme.

CHAPTER TWELVE

Could It ALL Be True?

In this book we explore a number of extraordinary charges that have raised against Hillary Clinton – charges that millions of Americans believe.

- That she is a shapeshifting reptilian overlord who feeds on human flesh and blood.

- That she is a blood-drinking, Satan-worshiping, child-sacrificing Satanist, a high-ranking witch, a voodoo *mambo* or high priestess.

- That she is possessed by demons. That she talks with the dead, and communes with strange and perhaps hostile entities from other planets, other dimensions, and/or other non-Earth worlds.

- That she is an authoritarian, a statist, a terrorist conspirator working in tandem with numerous secret societies seeking to enslave the human race to serve a global ruling elite.

- That she possesses supernatural powers, has an army of mind-controlled sex slaves and secret spies, that she could be the Great Beast of the Book of Revelation or even the Antichrist.

And still more.

Does the presence of so many seemingly outrageous charges cancel each other out?

Must we pick one over the other?

No. For they could *all* be true – at the same time. Indeed, it is quite likely that, if any one of these charges are true, several are.

It does not take much imagination to see that someone could be a Satanist, a witch, a demon-possessed member of secret conspiracies, a shapeshifting reptilian, an alien being, a member of the ultra-powerful world ruling elite, and more... all at the same time.

For example, suppose Hillary is, as millions believe, a reptilian. Satan, often rendered as the Serpent, could well be connected to the reptilian conspiracy theories and the ancient tales of serpent overlords found in every culture on earth. Thus a reptilian might also be involved in worship of Satan. Satanism and witchcraft easily complement one another. Demon possession, some experts argue, can result from, and often accompanies, witchcraft and Satanism. To gain power over the human race, political conspiracy as well as various forms of occultism would seem a natural route. Many believe there is a reptilian-UFO connection, and reports of reptilians in UFOs are quite common in UFO reports; so the modern belief in UFOs is quite compatible with the ancient belief in a serpent master race. And many researchers believe there is a direct link between modern UFO phenomena and the occult. Such connections go on and on.

So there is no reason to think that, in theory at least, Hillary could not be a Satanist, witch, blood-drinking child enslaver and murderer, secret society conspirator, terrorist, totalitarian, demon-enslaved voodoo practitioner, shapeshifting reptilian overlord, alien agent, even the Antichrist and more... all at once.

Indeed, if anything, there is a remarkable consistency, unity, shared beliefs and shared history among these world views.

So we must further open our minds and consider that several – even ALL – of the charges against Hillary that are explored in this book could, in theory at least, be true. Yes, even each and every one!

And of course, if even one is true, then the consequences for America – for the human race – are staggering.

CHAPTER THIRTEEN

Hillary's Secret, Occult and Conspiratorial Societies

"There exists a shadowy government with its own Air Force, its own Navy, its own fundraising mechanism, and the ability to pursue its own ideas of national interest, free from all checks and balances, and free from the law itself." – Sen. Daniel Inouye (D-Hawaii), Senate Select Committee on Secret Military Assistance to Iran and the Nicaraguan Opposition (Iran-Contra hearings), 1987.

"We are ruled, though it may be difficult to imagine, by a small dynastic power structure, largely consisting of powerful banking families, such as the Rothschilds, Rockefellers, and others. They emerged in controlling the financial system, extended their influence over the political system, the educational system, and, through the major foundations, have become the dominant social powers of our world, creating think tanks and other institutions which shape and change the course of society and modern human history." – journalist Andrew Gavin Marshall.

"There is something behind the throne greater than the king himself." – Sir William Pitt, House of Lords, 1770.

"Tell me thy company, and I'll tell thee what thou art." – Miguel de Cervantes

"In the next century, nations as we know it will be obsolete; all states will recognize a single, global authority. National sovereignty wasn't such a great idea after all." – Council on Foreign Relations and Skull and Bones member Strobe Talbott, TIME magazine, July 20, 1992. Talbott was deputy secretary of state under Bill Clinton (1994 to 2001); he became friends with Clinton when both were Rhodes Scholars.

"How I Learned to Love the New World Order" – title of an April 1992 op-ed in the Wall Street Journal by U.S. Senator Joe Biden, who became U.S. vice president under President Obama.

"...most of the major events of world significance are masterfully planned and orchestrated by an elite coterie of enormously powerful people who are not of one nation, one ethnic grouping, or one overridingly important business group. They are a power unto themselves for whom those others work. Neither is this power elite of recent origin. Its roots go deep into the past." – Col. L. Fletcher Prouty, Chief of Special Operations for the Joint Chiefs of Staff under President John F. Kennedy.

"For more than a century ideological extremists at either end of the political spectrum have seized upon well-publicized incidents ... to attack the Rockefeller family for the inordinate influence they claim we wield over American political and economic institutions. Some even believe we are part of a secret cabal working against the best interests of the United States, characterizing my family and me as 'internationalists' and of conspiring with others around the world to build a more integrated global political and economic structure – one world, if you will. If that's the charge, I stand guilty, and I am proud of it." – David Rockefeller in his 2002 autobiography Memoirs.

"By the time you become the leader of a country, someone else makes all the decisions; you just sign your name." – Bill Clinton

How the CIA Uses the Term "Conspiracy" to Hide the Crimes of Ruling Elites

"We'll know our disinformation program is complete when everything the American public believes is false." – CIA Director William Casey, February 1981, as recorded and quoted by Barbara Honegger, a researcher and policy analyst for the Reagan administration.

"We live in a dirty and dangerous world. There are some things the general public does not need to know and shouldn't. I believe democracy flourishes when the government can take legitimate steps to keep its secrets and when the press can decide whether to print what it knows." – Katharine Graham, Washington Post publisher, in a speech at CIA headquarters, November 1988.

A warning and clarification. Any attempt to describe the various organizations described in this chapter as playing a significant role in world affairs is inevitably met with the charge that one is a "conspiracy theorist" in making them, or that such documentation amounts to a "conspiracy theory."

Few people realize, however, that today's use of the "conspiracy theory" label to instantly dismiss and discredit criticisms and those who make them was actually established as a tactic by... the CIA, a few years after the 1963 Warren Commission, as part of a CIA propaganda campaign to silence critics who found the Establishment-approved "lone gunman" theory of the Kennedy assassination unsatisfying.

CIA Document 1035-960, "Concerning Criticism of the Warren Report," was written in April 1967 and sent to overseas CIA bureaus and "assets." This secret document was not made public until 1976, when the New York Times obtained it via the Freedom of Information Act.

Written at a time when the CIA had hundreds of journalists secretly planted in major media throughout America and around the world, this document recommended that CIA "propaganda assets" including authors and journalists use the word "conspiracy" and related terms to discredit challenges of the Warren Commission.

The secret report also mentioned specific methods for discrediting such theories:

"To employ propaganda assets to answer and refute the attacks of the critics. Book reviews and feature articles are particularly appropriate for this purpose. ... Our ploy should point out, as applicable, that the critics are (I) wedded to theories adopted before the evidence was in, (II) politically interested, (III) financially interested, (IV) hasty and inaccurate in their research, or (V) infatuated with their own theories.

"Point out also that parts of the conspiracy talk appear to be deliberately generated by communist propagandists. ...

"Such vague accusations as that 'more than ten people have died mysteriously' can always be explained in some natural way..."

The New York Times (Dec. 26, 1977) said this document "provides a detailed account of at least one instance in which the agency mustered its propaganda machinery to support an issue... the conclusion of the Warren Commission..."

Ironically, then, the use of such terms as "conspiracy theory" to discredit responsible criticism of dubious government assertions is itself a conspiracy – generated by the CIA.

Dr. Lance DeHaven-Smith, Florida State University professor, former president of the Florida Political Science Association, and author of more than a dozen scholarly books, writes in his Conspiracy Theory in America:

"The CIA's campaign to popularize the term 'conspiracy theory' and make conspiracy belief a target of ridicule and hostility must be credited, unfortunately, with being one of the most successful propaganda initiatives of all time... the conspiracy-theory label has become a powerful smear that, in the name of reason, civility, and democracy, preempts public discourse, reinforces rather than dissolves disagreements, and undermines popular vigilance against abuses of power."

DeHaven-Smith makes this CIA connection – and its implications in discussions of American politics to this very day – clear:

"...the conspiracy-theory label was popularized as a pejorative put down by the CIA in a global propaganda program to attack critics of the Warren Commission's conclusion that President Kennedy was assassinated by a lone gunman with no government foreknowledge or assistance.

"The CIA campaign called on foreign media corporations and journalists to criticize 'conspiracy theorists' and raise questions about their motives and judgments. Any and all criticisms of the lone-gunman account of the assassination were lumped together as 'conspiracy theories,' declared groundless and pernicious, and attributed to ulterior motives and the influence of communist propagandists.

"Today, the conspiracy-theory label is widely used as a verbal defense mechanism by U.S. political elites to suppress mass suspicions that inevitably arise whenever shocking political crimes benefit top leaders or play into their agendas, especially when those same officials are in control of agencies responsible for preventing the events in question or for investigating them after they have occurred."

The fact that the 1967 CIA memo seems focused on foreign media corporations and journalists illustrates a CIA ruse to circumvent laws prohibiting the use of propaganda against the American people. Such rules were easily gotten around by feeding disinformation to CIA-controlled foreign media, which could then be picked up by CIA-controlled or influenced U.S. journalists and quoted and circulated in the U.S.

This was made clear by the heroic Democratic senator Frank Church of Idaho. Church chaired the Church Committee, which investigated and uncovered shocking and sometimes horrific examples of illegal practices by the NSA, CIA and FBI.

"I thought that it was a matter of real concern that planted stories intended to serve a national purpose abroad came home and were circulated here and believed here because this would mean that the CIA could manipulate the news in the United States by channeling it through some foreign country," Church said.

That the CIA continually duped and misinformed the public by manipulating the media is well documented.

In Katharine the Great, a biography of Washington Post publisher Katharine Graham, journalist Deborah Davis notes that Washington Post publisher Philip Graham was part of a CIA effort entitled Operation Mockingbird to infiltrate and utilize the media. She notes Graham hired a number of writers and editors who had "intelligence backgrounds." Davis also charged, controversially, that Washington Post editor Ben Bradlee of Watergate fame had CIA connections and wrote CIA propaganda.

The CIA's recruitment of the media was tremendously successful, Deborah Davis writes: "By the early 1950s [the CIA] 'owned' respected members of the New York Times, Newsweek, CBS, and other communications vehicles, plus stringers, four to six hundred in all, according to a former CIA analyst."

Carl Bernstein of Watergate fame wrote a lengthy article for Rolling Stone in 1977 detailing CIA infiltration and manipulation of the American mainstream media. He noted:

"Among the executives who lent their cooperation to the Agency were William Paley of the Columbia Broadcasting System [CBS], Henry Luce of Time Inc., Arthur Hays Sulzberger of the New York Times, Barry Bingham Sr. of the Louisville Courier-Journal, and James Copley of the Copley News Service. Other organizations which cooperated with the CIA include [ABC, NBC], the Associated Press, United Press International, Reuters, Hearst Newspapers, Scripps-Howard, Newsweek magazine, the Mutual Broadcasting System, the Miami Herald and the old Saturday Evening Post and New York Herald-Tribune.

"By far the most valuable of these associations, according to CIA officials, have been with the New York Times, CBS and Time Inc. ...

"The CIA even ran a formal training program in the 1950s to teach its agents to be journalists. Intelligence officers were ...placed in major news organizations with help from management."

Deborah Davis quotes a former CIA agent on the ease of recruiting and corrupting journalists: "You could get a journalist cheaper than a good call girl, for a couple hundred dollars a month."

In addition the CIA built and funded some student and cultural exchange organization fronts, sometimes prodding reluctant college students into becoming spies.

Readers are urged to view any "conspiracy theories" with the same careful consideration and skepticism they would give to any ideas encountered in print – including especially the often-controversial ideas explored in this book.

However... readers should also not fall for a blanket discrediting and dismissal of any and all such theories as "conspiracy theories" – especially when doing so is itself the result of a conspiracy instigated by the CIA and secretly passed into the American public through CIA-controlled newspapers, magazines, books, organizations, and so forth.

Conspiracy Theory – or Power Elite Analysis?

"There's a reason that education sucks, and it's the same reason it will never ever ever be fixed. It's never going to get any better, don't look for it. ... Because the owners of this country don't want that. I'm talking about the real owners now, the big, wealthy, business interests that control all things and make the big decisions.

"Forget the politicians, they're irrelevant.

"Politicians are put there to give you that idea that you have freedom of choice. You don't. You have no choice. You have owners. They own you. They own everything. They own all the important land, they own and control the corporations, and they've long since bought and paid for the Senate, the Congress, the state houses, and the city halls. They've got the judges in their back pockets. And they own all the big media companies so they control just about all the news and information you get to hear.

"They've got you by the balls.

"They spend billions of dollars every year lobbying to get what they want. Well, we know what they want; they want more for themselves and less for everybody else.

"But I'll tell you what they don't want – they don't want a population of citizens capable of critical thinking.

"They don't want well informed, well-educated people

capable of critical thinking. They're not interested in that. That doesn't help them. That's against their interest. ...they don't want people that are smart enough to sit around their kitchen table and figure out how badly they're getting fucked by a system that threw them overboard 30 fucking years ago. ...

"The table is tilted folks, the game is rigged.

"Nobody seems to notice, nobody seems to care. Good honest hard working people, white collar, blue collar, it doesn't matter what color shirt you have on. Good honest hard working people continue, these are people of modest means, continue to elect these rich cocksuckers who don't give a fuck about them. They don't give a fuck about you. They don't give a fuck about – give a fuck about you! They don't care about you at all, at all, at all.

"And nobody seems to notice, nobody seems to care. ...

"That's what the owners count on..."

– comedian George Carlin, "The Big Club"

Despite the ongoing efforts to smear the very idea of "conspiracy theories," millions of Americans believe that, at least some of the time, "conspiracy" explains some government actions better than anything else.

Indeed, even Cass Sunstein, head of President Obama's White House Office of Information and Regulatory Affairs – and someone who advocates the use of government force to suppress some conspiracy theories because "the existence of such theories raises significant challenges for policy and law" – was forced to acknowledge the truth of some conspiracy theories in his notorious 2008 paper "Conspiracy Theories":

"Of course some conspiracy theories, under our definition, have turned out to be true. The Watergate hotel room used by Democratic National Committee was, in fact, bugged by Republican officials, operating at the behest of the White House. In the 1950s, the Central Intelligence Agency did, in fact, administer LSD and related drugs under Project MK-ULTRA, in an effort to investigate the possibility of 'mind control.' Operation Northwoods, a rumored plan by the Department of Defense to simulate acts of terrorism and to blame them on Cuba, really was proposed by high-level officials (though the plan never went into effect)."

In the same paper Sunstein advocated fighting the spread of anti-government conspiracy theories by, among other things, having government agents secretly infiltrate and surveille groups that discuss such theories; directing government propaganda against the American public to dissuade belief in some theories; and in other ways using government force, sometimes in secret, to hinder or suppress conspiracy discussions. (Sunstein says he wants the government to direct such efforts against only "false" and "harmful" conspiracy theories; of course, it will be the government that will decide, in secret, which are true and which are false, and the government is hardly likely to be fair or accurate in determining this; indeed, the government is far more likely to feel threatened by conspiracy theories that are true. One can imagine, for example, what the Nixon administration's views on the legitimacy of a Watergate conspiracy theory would be. In essence, Sunstein is proposing the creation of nothing less than an Orwellian Ministry of Truth, right out of 1984.) Sunstein also advocates radical and authoritarian new restrictions on the First Amendment right of free speech.

All of the above, of course, sounds like... a huge government conspiracy against the American people.

We might suggest that it is precisely the elements of truth in some conspiracy theories that truly threaten America's elites and those who, like Sunstein, serve them.

The idea that government agents and other elites sometimes conspire is hardly strange or radical. As one considers the obvious interlocking connections between government, corporations, the wealthy, the mass media, the secret national security state epitomized by the CIA and NSA, it becomes clear that these forces often act together to advance political agendas favorable to them.

Indeed, over and over again, as we examine the organizations in this chapter, we will see the same names, the same individuals, the same shared backgrounds.

No wonder the CIA, and others in the power elite, denounce such thinking as "conspiracy theory." Such thinking opens minds to the possibility that much of what we think is political reality is in fact a sham and illusion – an orchestrated con game to trick us into accepting the depredations and rule of the power elite. Ultimately the power of the ruling elite rests not on guns and police and military. Rather, it rests on the ability of the elite to hoodwink us into believing their rule is legitimate and inevitable. An openness to considering the possibility of conspiracy, and other government plots and schemes, thus challenges the ability of the ruling elite to control society – making it arguably one of the most dangerous form of thinking and analysis from the perspective of the ruling class.

A more useful term, and model, than conspiracy theory is "power elite analysis," a term popularized by the libertarian economist Murray N. Rothbard. "Power elite analysis" is the attempt to study the actions of the privileged and powerful – the "power elite" – who, seemingly, play a wildly disproportionate role in world affairs.

The term "power elite" and its implications were explored in the 1956 classic The Power Elite by the distinguished sociologist C. Wright Mills.

Mills defined the "power elite" as: "those political, economic, and military circles, which as an intricate set of overlapping small but dominant groups share decisions having at least national consequences. Insofar as national events are decided, the power elite are those who decide them. ... They accept one another, understand one another, marry one another, tend to work and to think if not together at least alike."

Dictionary.com defines "power elite" this way: "A term used by the American sociologist C. Wright Mills to describe a relatively small, loosely knit group of people who tend to dominate American policymaking. This group includes bureaucratic, corporate, intellectual, military, and government elites who control the principal institutions in the United States and whose opinions and actions influence the decisions of the policymakers."

The idea is simple, clear and persuasive: the rich and the

powerful work together with the government to expand their wealth and power through the use of political power. The more we accurately understand this, says the theory, the better we understand the world around us.

Many of the elite know and acknowledge this. David Rothkopf has impeccable Establishment credentials, including serving in the Bill Clinton administration as Acting Under Secretary of Commerce for International Trade and (in the quasi-private sector) a stint as Managing Director of Kissinger Associates, Inc.

In his acclaimed 2008 book Superclass: The Global Power Elite and the World They Are Making, Rothkopf argues there is a global Elite (his capitalization), or superclass, of about 6,000 people on the planet who run the governments, largest corporations and international finance groups, media, religions and overt criminal organizations. These 6,000 shape world events. And "there are meetings where they get together and views are formed."

We will be examining some of those "meetings" in this chapter.

Government Conspiracy:
Millions of Americans Believe

Despite all the Establishment overt and covert efforts to discredit so-called conspiracy theories about ruling elites, millions of Americans continue to believe there is truth to such theories.

A March 2013 poll of 1,247 registered American voters conducted by Public Policy Polling (PPP) drew the following responses:

> "Do you believe that a secretive power elite with a globalist agenda is conspiring to eventually rule the world through an authoritarian world government, or New World Order, or not?"

28% Do
....

46% Do not

....

25% Not sure

....

The Clinton Conspiracy Network

Between them, the political partnership of Bill and Hillary that some have dubbed "Clinton Inc" has ties to almost every known organization associated with power elite political conspiracy and occult practices.

The ones we shall examine in this chapter are:

The Rhodes Conspiracy
Council on Foreign Relations (CFR)
The Trilateral Commission
The Atlantic Council
The Fellowship
Davos World Economic Forum
Clinton Global Initiative Annual Meeting
The Bilderbergers (Bilderberg Group)
Skull and Bones
Bohemian Grove

Please note: One could easily write a lengthy book about any one of these organizations; indeed, many such books have been written. Our goal is simply to briefly describe them and their agendas and explore their connections with the Clintons.

As we shall see, high among the obsessions of many of these interlocking groups, repeatedly encountered, is a desire for what is sometimes described as a "New World Order," a supranational political power that would transcend national authority and bend the world to the desires of the elites.

In its most extreme form this takes the form of an actual world government, complete with its own laws and police and army to enforce them. Such an arrangement would, of course, put the governing of every person on the planet under the direct control of a tiny, remote, unresponsive group of elites.

It is difficult to imagine a more terrifying concept. Yet some of the most powerful people on the planet are working hard to see it become reality.

"The affirmative task we have now is to actually create a new world order." – Vice President Joe Biden, April 5, 2013.

"Out of these troubled times, our fifth objective – a new world order – can emerge." – President George H. W. Bush, September 11, 1990. Bush used the phrase "a new world order" at least 42 times between the summer of 1990 and the end of March 1991.

"We are not going to achieve a new world order without paying for it in blood as well as in words and money." – Arthur Schlesinger, Jr., presidential historian and special assistant to President Kennedy.

"We believe we are creating the beginning of a new world order coming out of the collapse of the U.S.-Soviet antagonisms." – Brent Scowcroft, national security advisor to presidents Richard Nixon. Gerald Ford, George H. W. Bush and Barack Obama.

"I think that his [Obama's] task will be to develop an overall strategy for America in this period, when really a 'new world order' can be created. It's a great opportunity." – Henry Kissinger, January 5, 2009.

Perhaps leftist foreign policy critic Noam Chomsky defined the essence of the emerging "New World Order" most succinctly: "The New World gives the orders."

Bill, Hillary and the Rhodes Conspiracy to Take Over the World

"The government of the world was Rhodes' simple desire." – Sarah Gertrude Millin, biographer of Cecil Rhodes.

In 1968 Bill Clinton was honored with a Rhodes Scholarship – one of the world's most prestigious academic awards – upon graduating from Georgetown University.

Each year Rhodes Scholarships offer some of the world's most outstanding non-British students the opportunity to study at the University of Oxford in Britain. A Rhodes Scholarship is a ticket to lifelong success in one's chosen field.

However, there is a strange and dark history to these scholarships.

The Rhodes Scholarships were established by Cecil Rhodes (1853-1902), South African financier, British statesman and industrialist, and one of the wealthiest men in the world.

Rhodes was a man with a plan – a breathtaking one – and the resources to back it to the hilt. Put simply, Rhodes wanted Britain to take back the United States under its rule, restore and expand the British Empire, and empower a white elite to take over and rule the entire world.

And the Rhodes Scholarships were created as a key part of this secret, sinister, grotesque scheme.

In 1877, while studying at Oxford in-between running his African diamond empire, Rhodes wrote the first of seven wills; each of the seven became a separate and legally binding document. The first will created funding for:

"...the establishment, promotion and development of a Secret Society, the true aim and object whereof shall be for the extension of British rule throughout the world...

"...colonization by British subjects of all lands where the means of livelihood are attainable by energy, labor and enterprise, and especially the occupation by British settlers of the entire Continent of Africa, the Holy Land, the Valley of the Euphrates, the Islands of Cyprus and Candia, the whole of South America, the Islands of the Pacific not heretofore possessed by Great Britain, the whole of the Malay Archipelago, the seaboard of China and Japan...

"*the ultimate recovery of the United States of America as an integral part of the British Empire...*

"and, finally, the foundation of so great a Power as to render wars impossible, and promote the best interests of humanity."

In 1890 he added the goal that his secret society should work towards "gradually absorbing the wealth of the world."

One cannot help but note that the above eerily mirrors a good bit of American and British foreign policy since that time.

Rhodes' racism and imperialism are clear in many statements. In 1877 he said:

"It is our duty to seize every opportunity of acquiring more territory ... more territory simply means more of the Anglo-Saxon race, more of the best, the most human, most honorable race the world possesses ... the absorption of the greater portion of the world under our rule simply means the end of all wars."

Rhodes described the traits he was looking for in his Rhodes Scholars: "smugness, brutality, unctuous rectitude, and tact." Which actually sounds like a job description for the Clintons – and others seeking and holding political office or power in America today.

After Rhodes' death, his cause was continued by other wealthy members of the ruling elite. The Rhodes scheme was advanced by the creation of the so-called Round Table Movement of international secret societies mostly formed between 1910 and 1915. Round Table Groups were established in Britain, South Africa, Canada, New Zealand, Australia, India, and the United States. The British Round Table is the Royal Institute for International Affairs, forerunner of the U.S. Council on Foreign Relations (CFR). To this very day, these and similar groups, some discussed in this chapter, are the powerful engines driving the push for the creation of a New World Order committed to global government – again, very much along the lines laid out by Cecil Rhodes back in 1877.

But has it been successful?

In 1966 Carrol Quigley, a brilliant and highly respected historian and political scientist, published his astounding and revelatory book Tragedy and Hope: A History of the World in Our Time. This thousand-plus-page book details a secret worldwide conspiracy based upon Cecil Rhodes' original scheme – to control mankind by creating a cadre of elite leaders – "the Anglo-American Elite" – trained to quietly seize power.

Quigley (1910-1977) was no uneducated wild-eyed conspiracy theorist. He was a genius in several fields and a highly respected professor who taught at Princeton, Yale, and finally at the School of Foreign Service at Georgetown University. He was also a consultant to the U.S. Department of Defense, the House Committee on Astronautics and Space Exploration; and the U.S. Navy. His mainstream Establishment credentials are impeccable and unimpeachable. And he was intimately familiar with the conspiracy he wrote about.

In fact, Quigley *approved* of this conspiracy and its aims, and wrote his book partly in order to give them the credit he felt they deserved. As he said in Tragedy and Hope:

"I know of the operations of this network because I have studied it for twenty years and was permitted for two years, in the early 1960's, to examine its papers and secret records. I have no aversion to it or to most of its aims and have, for much of my life, been close to it and to many of its instruments. I have objected, both in the past and recently, to a few of its policies ... but in general my chief difference of opinion is that it wishes to remain unknown, and I believe its role in history is significant enough to be known."

Quigley outlined the conspiracy's origins, nature and goals.

"Rhodes... left his fortune to form a secret society, which was to devote itself to the preservation and expansion of the British Empire. And what does not seem to be known to anyone is that this secret society... continues to exist to this day...

"To be sure, [it] is not a childish thing like the Ku Klux Klan, and it does not have any secret robes, secret handclasps, or secret passwords. It does not need any of these, since its members know each other intimately. It probably has no oaths of secrecy nor a formal procedure of initiation. It does, however, exist and holds secret meetings.... This Group is, as I shall show, one of the most important historical facts of the twentieth century... an international Anglophile network which operates, to some extent, in the way the radical Right believes the communists act.

"In fact, this network, which we may identify as the Round Table Groups, has no aversion to cooperating with the communists, or any other groups and frequently does so" in its goal of fulfilling the Rhodes plan to "confederate the whole of it (the world), with the United Kingdom, into a single organization."

Quigley further notes: "The powers of financial capitalism had another far-reaching aim, nothing less than to create a world system of financial control in private hands able to dominate the political system of each country and the economy of the world as a whole. This system was to be controlled in a feudalistic fashion by the central banks of the world acting in concert, by secret agreements arrived at in frequent private meetings and conferences."

And what about the rest of us – the masses who Quigley describes as "the ordinary individual"? How will we fare in this "feudalistic" "secret" system run by these world elites?

"...[the ordinary individual's] freedom and choice will be controlled within very narrow alternatives by the fact that he will be numbered from birth and followed, as a number, through his educational training, his required military and other public service, his tax contributions, his health and medical requirements, and his final retirement and death benefits."

This Orwellian dystopia the elites have planned for us is all for our own good, of course.

But is it really possible that a small group of highly influential individuals, no matter how determined or brilliant or wealthy, can conspiratorially work together to change mass opinion?

Yes, and it goes on constantly, all around us. Quigley spells out how it commonly works:

"Thus, a statesman (a member of the Group) announces a policy. About the same time, the Royal Institute of International Affairs publishes a study on the subject, and an Oxford don, a Fellow of All Souls (and a member of the Group) also publishes a volume on the subject (probably through a publishing house, like G. Bell and Sons or Faber and Faber, allied to the Group).

"The statesman's policy is subjected to critical analysis and final approval in a 'leader' in The Times, while the two books are reviewed (in a single review) in The Times Literary

Supplement. Both the 'leader' and the review are anonymous but are written by members of the Group.

"And finally, at about the same time, an anonymous article in The Round Table strongly advocates the same policy.

"The cumulative effect of such tactics as this, even if each tactical move influences only a small number of important people, is bound to be great.

"If necessary, the strategy can be carried further, by arranging for the secretary to the Rhodes Trustees to go to America for a series of 'informal discussions' with former Rhodes Scholars, while a prominent retired statesman (possibly a former Viceroy of India) is persuaded to say a few words at the unveiling of a plaque in All Souls or New College in honor of some deceased Warden. By a curious coincidence, both the 'informal discussions' in America and the unveiling speech at Oxford touch on the same topical subject. ...

"By the interaction of these various branches on one another, under the pretense that each branch was an autonomous power, the influence of each branch was increased through a process of mutual reinforcement. The unanimity among the various branches was believed by the outside world to be the result of the influence of a single Truth, while really it was result of a single group." (Note: for clarity Quigley's text has been broken into smaller paragraphs.)

Once the new idea, which invariably increases the power of the elites, is in the air, backed by prestige and money, the elected politicians under the sway of the various ruling-elite organizations like the Council on Foreign Relations, the Trilateral Commission and the others described in the rest of this chapter put it into law. And the deal is done. And more ideas begin to bubble up by the same reliable process.

One can see this conspiratorial process routinely working today, molding and shaping public opinion and public policy.

During his 1992 acceptance address before the Democratic National Convention upon receiving his party's nomination for president of the United States, Bill made this statement:

"As a teenager I heard John Kennedy's summons to citizenship. And as a student at Georgetown, I heard the call clarified by a professor I had, named Carroll Quigley, who said America was the greatest country in the history of the world because our people have always believed in two great ideas: first, that tomorrow can be better than today, and second, that each of us has a personal moral responsibility to make it so."

When Bill spoke these words, most of the many millions of Americans listening no doubt thought it was just the usual political claptrap. But for some who were aware of Carroll Quigley and his Tragedy and Hope, a chill ran up their spines. For this seemed like a public declaration to the Powers That Be that Bill was acknowledging his awareness of the Rhodes conspiracy and its modern-day manifestations – and his intentions as a willing agent of that conspiracy.

Bill continued to publicly praise Quigley after that speech.

Was it mere coincidence that Bill Clinton, seemingly fast-tracked to become president of the United States, studied under Carroll Quigley at Georgetown after his Rhodes Scholarship?

Which brings us to examine the first American branch of the Rhodes/ruling elite conspiracy: the Council on Foreign Relations – to which both Bill and Hillary are deeply connected.

Bill and Hillary's Relations with the Council on Foreign Relations

"The Trilateral Commission doesn't secretly run the world. The Council on Foreign Relations does that." – Winston Lord, president of the Council on Foreign Relations

"The granddaddy of the modern American secret societies." – New York Times bestselling author Jim Marrs, Rule By Secrecy (2000)

"The think tank of monopoly-finance capital, the Council on Foreign Relations, is the world's most powerful private organization. The CFR is the ultimate networking, socializing, strategic-planning, and consensus-forming institution of the U.S. capitalist class. It is the central 'high

command' organization of the plutocracy that runs the country and much of the world." – historian Laurence H. Shoup, Wall Street's Think Tank: The Council on Foreign Relations and the Empire of Neoliberal Geopolitics, 1976-2014 (2015)

"The majority of leaders and advisers in national politics are CFR members." – Joan Roelofs, Professor Emerita of Political Science, Keene State College, New Hampshire.

"The ultimate aim of the CFR is to create a one-world socialist system, and to make the U.S. an official part of it." – Dan Smoot, former member of the FBI Headquarters staff.

"The Council on Foreign Relations is 'the establishment.' Not only does it have influence and power in key decision-making positions at the highest levels of government to apply pressure from above, but it also announces and uses individuals and groups to bring pressure from below, to justify the high level decisions for converting the U.S. from a sovereign Constitutional Republic into a servile member state of a one-world dictatorship." – former Congressman John Rarick 1971

"There is no building that says 'Establishment' on the door, but there is a century-old institution made up of wealthy and influential representatives of business, Wall Street, corporate law, academia and government. It is a creation of the elite ruling class to ensure their control over shaping policy for their own benefit." – journalist Matt Peppe on the Council of Foreign Relations, CounterPunch, February 24, 2016

"Since 1944 every American secretary of state, with the exception of James F. Byrnes, has been a member of the CFR. Almost without exception the members of the CFR are united by a congeniality of birth, economic status, and educational background." – Senator Barry Goldwater, With No Apologies (1980)

"The main purpose of the Council on Foreign Relations (CFR) is promoting the disarmament of U.S. Sovereignty and national independence and submergence into an all-powerful, one-world government." – Admiral Chester Ward,

CFR member for 16 years and judge advocate general of the U.S. Navy.

"[T]he common interests very largely elude public opinion entirely, and can be managed only by a specialized class whose personal interests reach beyond the locality." – journalist Walter Lippman, former CFR board member, 1922

"Whenever we needed a man [for a position in the Roosevelt administration], we just thumbed through the roll of Council members and put through a call to New York [to CFR headquarters]." – John J. McCloy, chairman of the CFR, adviser to nine U.S. presidents.

"In the next century, nations as we know it will be obsolete; all states will recognize a single, global authority. National sovereignty wasn't such a great idea after all." – Strobe Talbott, President Bill Clinton's deputy secretary of state, Council on Foreign Relations and Skull and Bones member, Rhodes Scholar, and Bill Clinton college roommate, TIME magazine, July 20, 1992.

"We shall have world government, whether or not we like it. The question is only whether world government will be achieved by consent or by conquest." – James P. Warburg, Council on Foreign Relations member, speaking before the U.S. Senate Committee on Foreign Relations, February 17, 1950

In a July 15, 2009 speech to the Council on Foreign Relations (CFR) at their new Washington headquarters, Hillary – then serving as U.S. secretary of state – revealed just how much influence the CFR wields over America – and herself:

"I am delighted to be here in these new headquarters. I have been often to, I guess, the [CFR]'mother ship' in New York City, but it's good to have an outpost of the Council right here down the street from the State Department. We get a lot of advice from the Council, so this will mean I won't have as far to go *to be told what we should be doing and how we should think about the future...*" (Emphasis added.)

Hillary is a strong supporter of the Council on Foreign Relations (CFR), the granddaddy of all U.S. globalist organizations, notorious among conspiracy watchers for relentlessly driving American policy towards a "New World Order" or a supranational world governing body. Indeed, Hillary's very first appointment as secretary of state was former CFR head George Mitchell as special envoy for Middle East peace.

Though Hillary is not a CFR member, both Bill and daughter Chelsea are, she loaded her State Department with CFR members, and her views and actions are deeply intertwined with the CFR agenda.

Earlier in this chapter we saw how the Cecil Rhodes secret society was behind the founding of America's Council on Foreign Relations, which evolved from Britain's Royal Institute of International Affairs. Now a bit more detail.

The CFR emerged from secretive meetings during World War I of ambitious American globalist and statist scholars. This group called itself "the Inquiry," and their meetings were organized and directed by the mysterious and shadowy figure Col. Edward Mandell House. The Inquiry was established in September 1917 to plan for the negotiations that would come at the end of World War I, and went on to discuss and prepare options for remaking and controlling the entire postwar world. After the war, the Inquiry merged with an earlier but dormant group entitled the Council on Foreign Relations, composed of, as House's top aide put it, "high-ranking officers of banking, manufacturing, trading and finance companies, together with many lawyers." Now these powerful political and financial elites had a gaggle of scholars and other opinion-shapers to provide intellectual backing for the global internationalist schemes that, not coincidentally, benefited them enormously.

Colonel House, sometimes called "the Texas Sphinx," is almost completely forgotten today. But as Dr. Robert Higgs of the Independent Institute notes, House was "was one of the most important Americans of the twentieth century... he arguably had a greater impact on the past century than all but a handful of other actors."

Indeed, his long-dead finger still reaches from his grave to poke and manipulate our age.

House worked hard to get Woodrow Wilson elected president, and once that happened, he became President Wilson's confidential adviser for years, and the very embodiment of the concept of "the power behind the throne."

In 1912 House wrote and published, anonymously, a dull but very strange and provocative novel entitled Philip Dru: Administrator, A Story of Tomorrow, 1920-1935. The novel concerns the exploits of a political operative who, enthralled by the idea of establishing "socialism as dreamed of by Karl Marx" in the U.S., violently seizes power in a revolution, becomes dictator, creates a kind of Federal Reserve banking system, institutes an income tax, controls all political parties, and engages in an imperialistic foreign policy to, among other things, conquer Mexico and rearrange Europe to his liking.

Most of those things would in fact come true in one way or another in the decade or so after House's novel was written, and House would be directly and deeply involved in making them happen.

Dru, it should be noted, is no fan of the U.S. Constitution and legal system: "Our Constitution and our laws served us well for the first hundred years of our existence, but under the conditions of to-day they are not only obsolete, but even grotesque." Dru achieves his ends by violence and dictatorship.

House considered Philip Dru a manifesto. In 1917, while advising Wilson, he wrote in his diary:

"Philip Dru expresses my thought and aspirations, and at every opportunity, I have tried to press rulers, public men and those influencing public opinion in that direction. Perhaps the most valuable work I have done in this direction has been in influencing the president. [Wilson.] I began with him before he became president and I have never relaxed my efforts. At every turn, I have stirred his ambition to become the great liberal leader of the world."

Some have argued that Col. House was associated with occult organizations. Some even say House had occult powers.

Author and radio host Dr. Stanley Monteith wrote: "I believe Colonel House was involved in occult practices, and I believe he used occult power" to exert control over those in power. Dr. Monteith noted House's ties with various organizations that Monteith believed had occult backgrounds, including the Grand Orient Masonic Lodge, Cecil Rhodes' secret society, and the Milner Group (named after Cecil Rhodes' close associate and member of various secret societies created to push the Rhodes agenda).

President Wilson was no stranger to the occult himself. In a move remarkably reminiscent of Hillary's occult-tinged experiments with the mystic Jean Houston, Wilson purportedly had secret consultations with the renowned American psychic Edgar Cayce after suffering a debilitating stroke following his split from Colonel House in 1919. Cayce, known as the "Sleeping Prophet," went into trance states from which he gave predictions of the future and insights on the ancient past. In his biography Edgar Cayce a Seer Out of Season: The Life of History's Greatest Psychic, Dr. Harmon Hartzell Bro – who knew Cayce personally and worked with him – says Cayce met with Wilson twice to give psychic readings on the future of the League of Nations. If true, we have yet another example, one of many mentioned in this book, of trance-dictated thoughts influencing American politics – and supporting the idea of a supranational New World Order-type world governing body.

But back to Colonel House. American historian and journalist Arthur D. Howden Smith (1887–1945) knew Colonel House personally and wrote a worshipful 1918 biography of House in which he noted:

"Colonel House would come into an office and say a few words quietly, and after he had gone you would suddenly become seized by a good idea. You would suggest that idea to your friends or superiors and be congratulated for it; it would work first rate, beyond your wildest dreams. You might forget about it. But some time, as sure as shooting, in cogitating profoundly over it, you would come to an abrupt realization that *that idea had been oozed into your brain by Colonel House* in the course of conversation." (Emphasis added.)

In similarly strange and provocative language, President Wilson described House as "my second personality. He is my independent self. His thoughts and mine are one."

Such bizarre descriptions – ideas secretly "oozed into your brain" by Colonel House – to some will sound occultish, or on a lesser level, indicative of hypnotic powers. Indeed, Smith's biography is so gushing and hagiographical that one wonders if House did not "ooze" some of into Smith's mind. (For a remarkably similar example of such seemingly occult psychic "oozing" by Hillary, see the worshipful British article on Hillary described in Chapter 11.)

In his book Changing Esoteric Values, Theosophist leader Foster Bailey refers to Colonel House as a "disciple" of the occult entities guiding the Theosophists, and refers to the servile President Wilson as a "sixth ray disciple" of the same, though Bailey provides no verification for this except telepathic transmissions he received from those same otherworldly entities. Foster Bailey was husband of, and partner with, Alice Bailey, one of the twentieth century's most influential occultists and the founder of the Lucifer Publishing Company (named in honor of, yes, *that* Lucifer), described elsewhere in this book.

Senator Thomas P. Gore of Oklahoma remarked to a colleague that House could "walk on dead leaves and make no more noise than a tiger."

House manipulated Wilson into entering World War I, a war in which the American people were not threatened and had no interest at stake. The consequences, as we shall see, were disastrous for America and the world – but very rewarding for the ruling elite.

Colonel House, as we have noted, was an agent of J.P. Morgan, who he knew well enough to call "Jack," and was closely associated with other financial and political elites, all of whom realized the financial benefits that would come to them via the war.

Economist and historian Murray N. Rothbard points out the role powerful business interests played in pushing for war – and why:

"The extensive economic ties of the large business community with England and France, through export orders and through loans to the Allies – especially those underwritten by the politically powerful J.P. Morgan & Co. (which also served as agent to the British and French governments) – allied to the boom brought about by domestic and Allied military orders, all played a leading role in bringing the United States into the war. Furthermore, virtually the entire eastern business community supported the drive toward war."

Morgan, in a personal letter dated September 4, 1914, bluntly told President Wilson: "The war should be a tremendous opportunity for America." And indeed it was – for some Americans, namely bankers, politicians, and other members of the ruling elite, who made what can truthfully be called "a killing."

Further, the beginnings of the tyrannical U.S. national security state are also found in House's work. As his biographer Godfrey Hodgson notes: "While the president dreamed of saving the world, House was beginning to contemplate the implications for the American state of being a world power. In this activity between 1915 and 1917 it is not fanciful to see a first, sketchy draft of what would become the national security state."

House's manipulation of Wilson was treasonous, Rothbard writes: "House shamelessly manipulated Wilson, in secret and traitorous collaboration with the British, to push the president first into entering the war and then into following British wishes instead of setting an independent American course. ... Advising British Prime Minister Arthur Balfour on how best to handle Wilson, House counseled Balfour to exaggerate British difficulties in order to get more American aid, and warned him never to mention a negotiated peace. Furthermore, Balfour leaked to Colonel House the details of various secret Allied treaties that they both knew the naive Wilson would not accept, and they both agreed to keep the treaties from the president."

The new Federal Reserve Act signed into law in 1913 by

President Wilson – following the plan for national domination outlined in House's novel cum blueprint Philip Dru, Administrator – created the Federal Reserve System and gave the U.S. the funds to engage in this gratuitous war of convenience. The Fed was the result of years of plotting and scheming by the ruling elites, including the Morgans, the Rockefellers, and Kuhn, Loebs. This culminated in the now-infamous super-secret 1910 ten-day meeting of senior government officials and private banking interests at the private resort of Jekyll Island, Georgia, where plans for the Federal Reserve System were cemented. Colonel House was there at Jekyll Island, no doubt "oozing ideas" into attending minds as required.

Rothbard tells us how the secretly formed Fed made World War I – and future wars – possible: "The massive U.S. loans to the Allies, and the subsequent American entry into the war, could not have been financed by the relatively hard-money, gold standard system that existed before 1914. Fortuitously, an institution was established at the end of 1913 that made the loans and war finance possible: the Federal Reserve System. By centralizing reserves, by providing a government-privileged lender of last resort to the banks, the Fed enabled the banking system to inflate money and credit, finance loans to the Allies, and float massive deficits once the United States entered the war."

This enormous extension of the conflict brought the unnecessary deaths of huge numbers of soldiers and civilians. World War I, before it was over, had become one of the deadliest conflicts in human history, with casualties estimated at over 17 million military and civilian deaths and 20 million wounded. Roughly 120,000 young Americans died in this utterly unnecessary war in which America's safety and borders were never remotely threatened. Ironically, the country was led into the war by a president who had narrowly won re-election just a few months earlier on the slogan "He kept us out of war."

But that is just the beginning of the horrific impact of this war. The disastrous settlement of World War I negotiated by House and his comrades created the conditions that subsequently gave birth to most of the worst political nightmares of the twentieth century (all of which benefited various elites that House served). These include the rise of Hitler in Germany, the rise of communism in Russia, the rise of authoritarianism in Japan, arguably the Ho Chi Minh revolution that became the Vietnam War, and the radical destabilization of the Middle East which led to today's Islamic conflicts including the Israeli-Arab conflicts. Thus World War II, the Korean War, the Cold War, the Vietnam War and many Middle East wars and conflicts of the past few decades all arguably spring from House's efforts to rebuild a world to the likings of his New World Order colleagues. Had the U.S. not intervened, World War I, like other European wars, would probably have fizzled out with a negotiated settlement, and the global horrors that followed it might well have never occurred. It is impossible to calculate how many tens of millions of people died in the wars, conflicts and by the hands of the totalitarian governments that resulted directly from this hideous settlement. Historian R.J. Rummels has estimated that 262 million people were killed by their own governments in the twentieth century, which he says is six times the number of people killed by war in the twentieth century. Whatever the ultimate number of those who died in the world that arose from the Treaty of Versailles, it is unimaginably huge and tragic.

James Brown Scott of the U.S. delegation said of the treaty that "the statesmen have ... made a peace that renders another war inevitable."

Wilson had boasted the U.S. would lead a "war to end all war," but as British General Archibald Wavell wryly noted, the result was more like a "Peace to end Peace."

After the treaties were negotiated, President Wilson became horrified at what House and his cabal had wrought. Wilson split from House in 1919 and shortly thereafter suffered a massive stroke that preceded his painful lingering death.

The destabilized world created by the settlement of World War I continues, a century later, to justify many U.S. interventions around the globe, including Secretary of State Hillary's interventions in the Middle East and elsewhere, and to enrich the pockets of many of the corporations, banking firms, and munitions manufacturers that pour millions into Bill and Hillary's multifaceted political empire.

After the war ended, Colonel House's "Inquiry" found Americans sick of wars of convenience and suspicious of globalists and financial elites. To correct this and advance the globalist cause, the Inquiry went on to form the Council on Foreign Relations in 1921. The CFR was the U.S. version of the Royal Institute of International Affairs, which was established to promote and advance the ideas of the Cecil Rhodes conspiracy.

The CFR was designed to operate as a secret society. As the CFR itself notes at its website, "From its inception, the activities of the Council on Foreign Relations were private and confidential." The bylaws declare that anyone revealing details of CFR closed meetings can be tossed out. As the CFR's 1992 Annual Report put it, "At all meetings, the Council's rule of non-attribution applies. This assures participants that they may speak openly without others later attributing their statements to them in public media or forums, or knowingly transmitting them to persons who will."

The "rule of non-attribution" was devised in June 1927 by the CFR's British model, the Royal Institute of International Affairs, and is also known as "Chatham House Rules," Chatham House being the headquarters of the Royal Institute of International Affairs. Variations of the "rule of non-attribution" operate in other gatherings of the ruling elite, some discussed later in this chapter.

CFR founders included the sinister Allen Dulles, later to become head of the CIA; his brother John Foster Dulles, later secretary of state and collaborator in his brother's crimes; Averell Harriman, the "godfather" of the secret society Skull and Bones; and Colonel House. The first president of the CFR was John W. Davis of the J.P. Morgan banking empire. Beginning in 1927, the Rockefeller family began funding the Council. The CFR today is funded by several sources including major global corporations and large foundations. In return, the CFR gives these giant corporations access to immense political power.

The CFR has dominated the American foreign policy political debate and the governing of America since it was founded. Virtually every major foreign policy of modern times has been generally favored by the CFR.

British political figure Philip H. Kerr (Lord Lothian) was a longtime activist in the Cecil Rhodes conspiracy. In 1922 Kerr published an article in the fledgling CFR journal Foreign Affairs, in which he passionately argued for world government as a means of extending the original aims of the British Empire, a blatant indication of how the CFR and related institutions were to be used to advance the Rhodes scheme for world domination:

"The real problem today is that of world government. ... Obviously there is going to be no peace nor prosperity for mankind so long as it remains divided into 50 or 60 independent states..."

This focus on the Rhodes/world government idea is made clear in a 2006 article in the highly regarded journal The Round Table: The Commonwealth Journal of International Affairs, a policy journal that grew from the Round Table efforts. Entitled "World War I and Anglo-American relations: The role of Philip Kerr and the Round Table," the article by Priscilla Roberts features this abstract:

"As the 19th century drew to a close, an alliance between the USA and the British Empire dominated the thinking of a political elite in the UK [who were] attracted to the idea of the USA as a potential ally with whom Britain could establish an Anglo-American world hegemony, and during World War I, Philip Kerr, first editor of the Round Table, was in the vanguard of efforts to make this vision reality. Later, as ambassador to the USA, Kerr was at the center of efforts to bring the U.S. into World War II and to ensure its continuing involvement in international affairs once fighting had ended. This outcome owed much to moves during and between both world wars by influential British figures and institutions, including Kerr and the Round Table, to persuade the American elite that their country should take on a far greater international role."

In a remarkable article in the Washington Post entitled "Ruling Class Journalists," by top-ranking Washington Post editor Richard Harwood, published October 30, 1993, Harwood laid out the nature of the CFR for all to see –

including the often-overlooked fact that key journalists are among the ruling elite:

"Council on Foreign Relations [members] are the nearest thing we have to a ruling establishment in the United States.

"The president is a member. So is his secretary of state, the deputy secretary of state, all five of the undersecretaries, several of the assistant secretaries and the department's legal adviser. The president's national security adviser and his deputy are members. The director of Central Intelligence (like all previous directors) and the chairman of the Foreign Intelligence Advisory Board are members. The secretary of defense, three undersecretaries and at least four assistant secretaries are members. The secretaries of the departments of housing and urban development, interior, health and human services and the chief White House public relations man, David Gergen, are members, along with the speaker of the House and the majority leader of the Senate.

"This is not a retinue of people who 'look like America,' as the president once put it, but they very definitely look like the people who, for more than half a century, have managed our international affairs and our military-industrial complex. ...

"Allen Dulles, first [civilian] head of the CIA, was a Council director for 42 years and was its president from 1946 until 1950. David Rockefeller succeeded McCloy, serving as chairman from 1970 until 1985. ...

"Captains of industry and finance, the big universities, the big law firms and the big foundations are heavily represented. That is the way it has always been.

"What is distinctively modern about the Council these days is the considerable involvement of journalists and other media figures, who account for more than 10 percent of the membership. ... The membership of these journalists in the Council, however they may think of themselves, is an acknowledgment of their active and important role in public affairs and of their ascension into the American ruling class. They do not merely analyze and interpret foreign policy for the United States; they help make it. ...

"They [journalists and the media] are part of that establishment whether they like it or not, sharing most of its values and world views."

Indeed. Concerning the media and the CFR, in 2013 author G. Edward Griffin noted: "In the media there are past or present members of the CFR holding key management or control positions – not just working down the line – but in top management and control positions of Atlantic magazine, The Army Times, American Publishers, American Spectator, Atlanta Journal-Constitution, Associated Press, Association of American Publishers, Boston Globe, Business Week, Christian-Science Monitor, Dallas Morning News, Detroit Free Press, Detroit News, Dow Jones News Service, Farm Journal, Financial Times, Financial World, Forbes, Foreign Affairs, Foreign Policy, Harper's, Industry Week, Insight, London Times, Los Angeles Times, Medical Tribune, National Geographic, National Review, Naval War College Review, New Republic, New York Post, New York Times, New Yorker, New York Review of Books, Newsday, News Max, Newsweek, Pittsburgh Post-Gazette, The Progressive, Political Science Quarterly, Public Interest, Random House, Reader's Digest, Rolling Stone, Rupert Murdoch News Corp, San Diego Union-Tribune, Scientific American, Time, Times Mirror, Time-Warner, US News & World Report, USA Today, Wall Street Journal, Warner Books, Washington Post, Washington Times, The Washingtonian, Weekly Standard, World Policy Journal, Worldwatch, W.W. Norton & Co., ABC, CBS, CNN, Fox News, NBC, PBS, RCA, and the Walt Disney Company.

"Media personalities include David Brinkley, Tom Brokaw, William Buckley, Katie Couric, Peter Jennings, Kathryn Pilgrim, Dan Rather, Diane Sawyer, Leslie Stahl, Barbara Walters, Brian Williams, Judy Woodruff, Paula Zahn, and Andrea Mitchell, wife of Alan Greenspan (former chairman of the Federal Reserve System, also a member of the CFR)."

We could also add Facebook, Google, Bloomberg and Microsoft.

Both the Democratic and Republican parties tend to

advance domestic and foreign policies in line with the views of the CFR. Indeed, often it seems as if there is really just one political party in America: the CFR Party.

CFR members dominate U.S. presidential politics. presidents who were members: Barack Obama, Bill Clinton, Jimmy Carter, Richard M. Nixon, John F. Kennedy, Gerald Ford, George H.W. Bush, Herbert Hoover.

The CFR has dominated every U.S. administration since it was formed. There is a long list of vice presidents, secretaries of state, secretaries of war/defense, secretaries of the treasury, CIA directors, members of Congress, presidential and vice-presidential candidates, Supreme Court justices, and so forth. The enormously influential neoconservative Project for the New American Century, considered by many to be the "power behind the throne" of the George W. Bush administration, was strongly connected to the CFR, with 17 of its 25 founding members also being CFR members.

Historian Laurence H. Shoup, author of two books on the CFR, has calculated that between 1976 and 2014, 80 percent of top government policy positions were held by CFR members.

As journalist Jonathan Vankin sums up: "Since its founding... the CFR has been the preeminent intermediary between the world of high finance, big oil, corporate elitism, and the U.S. government. Its members slide smoothly into cabinet-level jobs in Republican and Democratic administrations. The policies promulgated in its quarterly journal, Foreign Affairs, become U.S. government policy."

A 2016 list of CFR Corporate Members includes such world-famous entities as Alcoa, American Express, AT&T, Bank of America, Bank of New York Mellon Corporation, Barclays, Boeing, Bridgewater Associates, Chevron, Citi, Coca-Cola, Exxon Mobil, FedEx, General Electric, Goldman Sachs, IBM, JPMorgan Chase & Co, Lockheed Martin, Merrill Lynch, Morgan Stanley, Nasdaq OMX Group, PepsiCo, Pitney Bowes, Shell Oil, Toyota Motor North America, the U.S. Chamber of Commerce, Walmart, Wells Fargo, Western Union, and Xerox... to name just a few.

A few other prominent current and recent past members: Trilateral Commission founders Zbigniew Brzezinski and David Rockefeller, William F. Buckley, Bill Bundy, Paul Warburg, George Soros, Colin Powell, Bill Moyers, Rupert Murdoch, David Rockefeller, Henry Kissinger, Peter G. Peterson, Maurice Greenberg, Robert Rubin, George P. Shultz, Alan Greenspan, John Sweeney, Jessie Jackson, Katrina vanden Heuvel (The Nation), and Daniel Schorr. Notorious war criminal Henry Kissinger, accused by critics of complicity in the illegal killings of millions of innocent civilians around the globe, got his start in politics via the CFR.

The Bill Clinton administration had dozens – by some reports, over 100 – CFR members, despite the fact that the CFR's total membership at the time was only 3,000, and many of those, as shown earlier, were deeply engaged in other full-time careers in their fields. Doubtless Hillary will continue the tradition. For example her presumptive choice for secretary of defense is the hawkish CFR member Michele Flournoy, who was Obama administration undersecretary of defense for policy.

Some prominent CFR members have interlocking connections to virtually every major ruling-elite secret society. Indeed, roughly half of the CFR board of directors are also members of the Trilateral Commission.

Which brings us to...

The Trilateral Commission

"[The Trilateral Commission] is intended to be the vehicle for multinational consolidation of the commercial and banking interests by seizing control of the political government of the United States. ... "[The Trilateral Commission is] a skillful, coordinated effort to seize control and consolidate the four centers of power: political, monetary, intellectual, and ecclesiastical. "What the Trilateral Commission intends is to create a worldwide economic power superior to the political governments of the nation-states involved. "As managers and creators of the system, they will rule the future."

– U.S. Senator and 1964 presidential candidate Barry Goldwater, With No Apologies (1979)

"The Trilateral Commission [is] a secretive association of the world's most powerful private citizens... The Trilateral Commission's annual meetings...have inspired conspiracy theories of powerful puppeteers who secretly pull the strings of world powers as they seek to establish a new world order. The theories are based partly on fact." – journalist Joseph Curl, The Washington Times, April 18, 2005

"...an end run around national sovereignty, eroding it piece by piece, will accomplish much more than the old-fashioned frontal assault." – Richard Gardner, member of the Trilateral Commission and the Council on Foreign Relations (CFR), "The Hard Road to World Order," Foreign Affairs (published by the CFR), 1974

Bill is a longtime member of the Trilateral Commission, notorious among conspiracy watchers as a key organization in the ruling elite's efforts to establish a world government and New World Order. Like numerous other conspiracy organizations, the Trilateral Commission brings together heads of state, banks, multinational corporations, media magnates and other elements of the global elite.

Hillary is not a member, but is obviously deeply connected to the Commission's agenda and leadership.

The Trilateral Commission was founded in July 1973 by David Rockefeller, at the time also chairman of the Council on Foreign Relations and involved in innumerable other ruling elite organizations. "Trilateral" refers to the three global regions the organization focuses upon: North America, Europe, and Asia.

Like its big sister the Council on Foreign Relations, the Trilateral Commission is essentially a secret society, conducting its meetings in private. As its website states, "All proceedings of the Commission are held under the Chatham House rule, i.e., no attribution of remarks is allowed without the permission of the speaker."

Aiding Rockefeller in creating the Trilateral Commission was Harvard University professor and first Trilateral Commission executive director Zbigniew Brzezinski.

Four years earlier, Brzezinski had written: "[The] nation state as a fundamental unit of man's organized life has ceased to be the principal creative force. International banks and multinational corporations are acting and planning in terms that are far in advance of the political concepts of the nation state."

Shortly after the founding of the Trilateral Commission the globalist Brzezinski would be named national security assistant to president (and fellow Trilateralist) Jimmy Carter, making Brzezinski arguably the most powerful man in the Carter administration. Carter's running mate, Walter Mondale, was also a Trilateralist. The odds of three previously mostly unknown men, out of a small group of 60-odd American Trilateralists, becoming president, vice president and national security leader are astronomical. Yet the odds extend further. Under Carter, fully 19 of the sixty-odd U.S. members of the Trilateral Commission – nearly one in three of the total Trilateral U.S. membership – would be on President Carter's staff.

Brzezinski would later write in his memoirs that "all the key foreign policy decision makers of the Carter administration had previously served in the Trilateral Commission." Indeed, this process started well before the nomination. Carter's ascendancy to the White House was aided by Trilateral-connected media and Trilateral-connected rich donors and fundraisers.

Ironically, top Carter aide Hamilton Jordan, reflecting growing concern among Americans that the country was being ruled by elites and insiders working in secret to take over the government, said before the Carter inauguration: "If, after the inauguration, you find a Cy Vance as secretary of state and Zbigniew Brzezinski as head of National Security, then I would say we failed. And I'd quit." Yet Carter selected Vance as secretary of state and Brzezinski as National Security adviser. (And Jordan did not quit.)

In 1980 Ronald Reagan, campaigning against Carter,

made a remarkably similar statement: "I don't believe that the Trilateral Commission is a conspiratorial group, but I do think its interests are devoted to international banking, multinational corporations, and so forth. I don't think that any administration of the U.S. Government should have the top nineteen positions filled by people from any one group or organization representing one viewpoint. No, I would go in a different direction."

Yet after winning, Reagan picked ten Trilateralists for his transition team, and included prominent Trilateralists in his administration including Vice President George H.W. Bush, Defense Secretary Caspar Weinberger, U.S. Trade Representative William Brock, and Fed Chairman Paul Volcker.

Founding members of the Trilateral Commission quickly found their way into key government positions: Harold Brown, secretary of defense under President Carter; Caspar Weinberger, secretary of defense under President Reagan; Paul Volcker and Alan Greenspan, former heads of the Federal Reserve. All these men, incidentally, were also CFR members. Almost all World Bank presidents and U.S. trade representatives have been Trilateralists. The Federal Reserve has likewise been mostly headed by Trilateralists: Arthur Burns (1970-1978), Paul Volcker (1979-1987), Alan Greenspan (1987-2006). Most secretaries of state have largely been Trilateralists since 1973 as well: Henry Kissinger (1973-1977), Cyrus Vance ((1977-1980), Alexander Haig (1981-1982), George Shultz (1982-1989), Lawrence Eagleburger (1992-1993), Warren Christopher (1993-1997), Madeleine Albright (1997-2001), Hillary Clinton (2009-2013).

Bill Clinton, elected in 1992, was the third member of the Trilateral Commission to be elected president since the Commission was founded in 1973. Non-Trilateralist Ronald Reagan had Trilateralist founding member (and CIA, Skull and Bones, Council on Foreign Relations, Bohemian Grove, etc., etc. member) George H.W. Bush as vice president, and filled his administration with other CFR and Trilateral Commission members. Bush went on to be president, of course, as did his son. Bill Clinton also appointed Trilateralists to key administration posts.

Indeed, every administration since Carter has had Trilateral Commission members as either president or vice president, or both, with the exception of the Obama administration – and Obama filled his administration with Trilateralists.

Trilateral Commission co-founder Zbigniew Brzezinski groomed Obama for the White House, just as he did with Carter. In 2007 Obama selected Brzezinski as a top foreign policy adviser, calling him "somebody I have learned an immense amount from... one of our more outstanding thinkers..." Within the first few days of his administration, President Obama appointed eleven of the 87 members of the Trilateral Commission living in America to posts in his administration. Obama-appointed Trilateralists included such key figures as Tim Geithner, treasury secretary; James Jones, National Security adviser; Paul Volker, chairman, Economic Recovery Committee; Dennis Blair, director of National Intelligence. Vice President Joe Biden, though not a Trilateralist, is a member of the sister organization Council on Foreign Relations, a Bilderberg attendee, and self-declared proponent of a "New World Order."

Further, notes Trilateral expert and critic Patrick Wood, "There are many other links in the Obama administration to the Trilateral Commission. ... Secretary of Treasury Tim Geithner's informal group of advisers include E. Gerald Corrigan, Paul Volker, Alan Greenspan, and Peter G. Peterson, all members. Geithner's first job after college was with Trilateralist Henry Kissinger at Kissinger Associates.

"Trilateralist Brent Scowcroft has been an unofficial adviser to Obama and was mentor to Defense Secretary Robert Gates. And Robert Zoelick, current president of the World Bank appointed during the G.W. Bush administration, is a member."

Between 1977 and 2008:

- Every president and/or vice president of the United States was a member of the Trilateral Commission (TC).
- Six of the eight presidents of the World Bank were members.

- Eight of the ten U.S. world trade representatives were members.
- Seven of the twelve secretaries of state were members.
- Nine of the twelve secretaries of defense were members.
- Three of the five chairmen of the Federal Reserve Board were members.

Why isn't there more public awareness and criticism of this domination of American government by a small, self-appointed elite? Patrick Wood, coauthor of Trilaterals Over Washington, answered that in 2010:

"Why have the American people been kept in the dark about a subject so great that it shakes our country to its very core? The answer is simple: The top leadership of the media is also saturated with members of the Trilateral Commission who are able to selectively suppress the stories that are covered."

Further, Wood noted, "There are many other top-level media connections due to corporate directorships and stock ownership."

Incidentally, the Trilateral Commission logo is composed of three stylized arrows that quite clearly form a 666 – the infamous Number of the Beast.

The Atlantic Council: "Crowning" Hillary for President

"[T]he Atlantic Union movement and the Atlantic Council of the United States...believes national boundaries should be obliterated and one-world rule established." – Senator Barry Goldwater, With No Apologies (1980)

The Atlantic Council is a think tank and public policy group whose mission is to promote "constructive leadership and engagement in international affairs based on the Atlantic Community's central role in meeting global challenges."

Less known than many such organizations, it shares a similar ideology and cross-membership with the more familiar conspiratorial groups like the Council on Foreign Relations (CFR), Trilateral Commission, etc.

The Atlantic Council was inspired by the Cecil Rhodes conspiracy of uniting Britain and the U.S. It has its intellectual origins in the work of Clarence Streit, a Rhodes Scholar and prominent advocate of one-world government. In his 1939 book Union Now, Streit advocated a gradual (Fabian strategy) approach to world government, to start with the Rhodes scheme of uniting the U.S. and Britain.

Streit's book was strongly promoted by the Carnegie Endowment for International Peace, which put hundreds of copies into U.S. libraries and over one thousand copies into the hands of elite opinion shapers in both countries. The Carnegie Endowment was founded by billionaire Andrew Carnegie in 1910. Carnegie was one of the leading supporters of a Cecil Rhodes-type U.S.-British reunion, writing confidently to his friend, the renowned journalist and fellow one-worlder W.T. Stead, that "We are heading straight to the Re-United States."

Incidentally, Stead, like quite a few others involved in conspiratorial schemes and organizations, had what he called an "interest in occult studies." He claimed that he regularly received messages from the spirit world, spoke with the dead, attended séances, and received and transcribed messages from other worlds via automatic writing; indeed, at one point he was proclaimed by fellow spiritualists as the future "St. Paul of Spiritualism." Stead met occultist and Theosophy founder Madame Blavatsky in 1888, and introduced his friend, the occultist Annie Besant – who would become Blavatsky's successor – to Blavatsky's occult system; Besant would in turn inspire Alice Bailey, the one-world occultist who founded Lucifer Publishing. Besant would go on to become one of the most important occultists of the century, and is further discussed elsewhere in this book. Besant opposed what she called the "barbarous doctrines of the Christian faith" which she saw as "but the dreams of ignorant and semi-savage minds." Besant claimed to have developed clairvoyance (ESP) under the guidance of controversial Theosophist leader Charles Webster Leadbeater, who also claimed ESP powers. Author of some three dozen books, she was a leading socialist activist, a member of the extraordinarily successful socialist Fabian Society, and a member of the Marxist Social Democratic Federation (SDF), Britain's first socialist party. She was an early and extremely vocal advocate of anti-population policies based on Malthusian theory, another theme one finds repeatedly in the twentieth century ruling elite organizations. (In the early 1900s some Fabian Society members supported eugenics and sterilization. For example, H.G. Wells wrote of "lethal [gas] chambers for the insane" and wrote that the "swarms of black, brown, and dirty white, and yellow people ... have to go." His fellow Fabian George Bernard Shaw George argued that "the only fundamental and possible socialism is the socialization of the selective breeding of man" and like Wells suggested the defective and undesirable be eliminated via a "lethal chamber.") Today the idea of progressive support for such barbarism seems incongruous to some. Yet eugenics and state socialism were a natural fit, explained British journalist Jonathan Freedland in the UK Guardian in 2012: After all, "what could be more socialist than planning, the Fabian faith that the [government] really did know best? If the state was going to plan the production of motor cars in the national interest, why should it not do the same for the production of babies?" Such early Fabian enthusiasm for eugenics, along with many U.S. ruling elites' similar advocacy, inspired both the Nazis and the Soviet Union, who created massive death camps to test these ideals on a large scale. Given this, those today who are aware of the roots of such things can be forgiven for looking upon today's elites and central planners, the intellectual descendants of the original purveyors of these ideas, with some suspicion and concern.

Clarence Streit was not involved in the actual founding of the Atlantic Council, in part because some of the founders thought he was too closely publicly associated with the one-world-government scheme, and they feared this would bring unwelcome controversy to the new organization. But his ideas and ultimate goal were well known to the founders. According to Melvin Small of Wayne State University, a leading expert on the Atlantic Council, some of the group's founders believed "that Streit is right as to the ultimate answer... [but] a lot of long hard work will be necessary before it comes over the horizon of practicability."

Thus the Atlantic Council was founded with the hope by at least some of its founders that it would lead to nothing less than the end of U.S. sovereignty and the abolition of the Declaration of Independence. More blandly, members saw its mission as continuing, expanding and defending post-World War II political relations between North America and Europe, including support for post-war NATO.

Small noted that the Council's real strength lies in the relationships it fosters among influential policy makers. It functions, he writes, as a "center for informal get-togethers" of leaders from both sides of the Atlantic, fostering "networks of continuing communication." Rather like Bilderberg, Davos, the Clinton Foundation's annual meeting, and others described in this chapter.

In 2013, at an Atlantic Council dinner, the notorious war criminal Henry Kissinger, member of the Atlantic Council and many other globalist organizations, essentially crowned Hillary for president, according to the Washington Post:

"At least four secretaries of state became president," Kissinger said. "I want to tell Hillary that when she misses the office, when she looks at the histories of secretaries of state, there might be hope for a fulfilling life afterwards."

The Aspen Institute

Both Bill and Hillary have long been associated with the Aspen Institute, both as speakers and supporters.

The Aspen Institute was founded in 1950 as The Aspen Institute for Humanistic Studies. It says it is dedicated to "fostering enlightened leadership and open-minded dialogue" and providing "a global forum" which "seeks to improve the condition of human well-being by fostering enlightened, responsible leadership and by convening leaders and policy makers to address the structural changes of the new century."

This seemingly innocuous phrasing, of course, echoes that of numerous other meeting grounds and recruiting grounds of the rich and powerful.

Conservative writer Berit Kjos, writing in May 2000, rephrases that mission statement: The Aspen Institute, he writes, is "one of the world's foremost training centers for global re-learning and collective thinking."

The Institute is headquartered in Washington, DC and is funded by the usual suspects, including the Carnegie Corporation, the Rockefeller Brothers Fund and the Ford Foundation. Among the Honorary Trustees of its Board of Trustees are people who have dedicated their lives to one-world government and rule by powerful secretive elites, such as the ubiquitous Henry Kissinger and the treasonous Secretary of Defense Robert S. McNamara, whose lies to President Lyndon Johnson about the Tonkin Gulf incident in 1964 led Johnson to dramatically escalate the disastrous Vietnam War.

UN Under-Secretary Maurice Strong was a Trustees Emeriti of the Aspen Institute. Strong, who described himself as "a socialist in ideology, a capitalist in methodology" (an excellent description of many the crony capitalist ruling elite), was a Canadian multi-billionaire and one of the most connected of the one-world globalists. He was secretary general of the United Nations Conference on the Human Environment and the first executive director of the United Nations Environment Programme. He was founder of the globalist World Economic Council and Planetary Citizens organizations, director of the World Future Society, trustee of the Rockefeller Foundation, a longtime foundation director of the World Economic Forum (aka Davos), a member of the radical Malthusian globalist Club of Rome – among many, many other globalist/elite positions he held. He was founder and head of the Earth Council and helped draft that organization's controversial Earth Charter, criticized by some as a call for state socialism and one-world government. Strong also drafted a document calling for the creation of a powerful United Nations army to enforce global law. During the Bill Clinton administration he kept an office just a few blocks from the White House.

Dr. Saul Mendlovitz, a prominent advocate of one-world government, was a director of Maurice Strong's Planetary Citizens. Mendlovitz declared that there "is no longer a question of whether or not there will be world government by the year 2000. The questions are how it will come into being (cataclysm, drift, more or less rational design), and whether it will be totalitarian, benign, or participatory (the possibilities being in that order)." His prediction was premature, but few would argue that world powers are not moving relentlessly towards that goal.

In 2004 the New Yorker published a startling article about a "clandestine meeting" held at the Aspen Institute. Five billionaires met with Democratic Party political activists to discuss how their billions could be used to influence America's presidential elections.

"No one was supposed to know about this," an assistant to one participant told the reporter when he called for confirmation. "We don't want people thinking it's a cabal, or some sort of Masonic plot!"

Now who would think anything like that?

The Fellowship (aka The Family, The International Foundation): "You guys are here to learn how to rule the world"

It is rather startling to realize that Hillary – to the world at large a poster child of liberalism – has been for many, many years an active participant with the Fellowship: a highly controversial, secretive, and enormously influential right-wing Christian political organization headquartered in Washington, DC that has worked with some of the bloodiest dictators in modern times, including despots who have murdered many thousands of people.

Yet it is true. In fact, in 2007 Mother Jones magazine noted Hillary had been a participant in some Fellowship activities for 15 years.

The Fellowship is so secretive that little is known about it, even to researchers. Former Republican Senator William Armstrong has said the group "made a fetish of being invisible." The group has also gone by other names: The Family, The Foundation, C Street Center, and International Christian Leadership.

Yet the Fellowship numbers among its members a host of U.S. congressmen, senators, CEOs of major corporations, senior U.S. military officers, members of the Supreme Court, at least one president of the United States, and heads of religious and humanitarian aid organizations – all of whom take a vow of secrecy – as well as similarly powerful leaders, ambassadors and high-ranking politicians from around the globe. According to Jeff Sharlet, author of the definitive book on this group, U.S. senators and members of Congress associated with the Fellowship have worked together to pass legislation.

Sociologist D. Michael Lindsay, an expert on the U.S. evangelical movement, says the Fellowship "has relationships with pretty much every world leader – good and bad..."

David Kuo, a special assistant in George W. Bush's Office of Faith-Based and Community Initiatives, said "The Fellowship's reach into governments around the world is almost impossible to overstate or even grasp."

Sharlet reports a Fellowship leader telling members living in the group's Arlington, VA quarters: "You guys are here to learn how to rule the world."

Judging from its past and present membership, the group is well on the way to that goal.

According to Sharlet's book The Family: The Secret Fundamentalism at the Heart of American Power, the Fellowship was created in 1935 to oppose aspects of FDR's New Deal and the spread of trade unions. It was started by Abraham Vereide, an immigrant Methodist preacher who organized a small group of businessmen, some of whom, Sharlet says, were sympathetic to European fascism (not as unusual as one might think in pre-World War II America). After the war the U.S. State Department sent Vereide and some of friends on a kind of mini-"Operation Paperclip" mission to find captured Nazi war criminals willing to switch allegiance to avoid persecution.

Over time Vereide, says Sharlet, "counseled presidents and kings and was spiritual adviser to more senators and generals than Billy Graham has prayed with and all his days of bowing to power" while deliberately remaining unknown to the public.

Since then, the Fellowship has organized well-attended weekly prayer meetings for members of Congress and annual National Prayer Breakfasts attended by every president since Eisenhower. Further, Sharlet says, the Fellowship's international reach ("almost impossible to overstate") has "forged relationships between the U.S. government and some of the most oppressive regimes in the world."

The Fellowship has paid the travel expenses of sympathetic members of Congress to visit areas of political turmoil around the world, including Darfur, Lebanon, the Balkans and Belarus.

Sharlet considers the Fellowship's politics to be "authoritarian" and "ultimately worse than fascism ... The Family is an imperial ideology, which is why I think it's ultimately worse than fascism. Since the Second World War, fascism hasn't been a very powerful ideology, but imperialism has."

Hillary would seem to be an odd fit here, yet, as Mother Jones (2007) noted: "Through all of her years in Washington [as first lady], Clinton has been an active participant in conservative Bible study and prayer circles that are part of a secretive Capitol Hill group known as the Fellowship."

"[S]he regularly met with a Christian 'cell' whose members included Susan Baker, wife of Bush consigliere James Baker; Joanne Kemp, wife of conservative icon Jack Kemp; Eileen Bakke, wife of Dennis Bakke, a leader in the anti-union Christian management movement; and Grace Nelson, the wife of Senator Bill Nelson, a conservative Florida Democrat.

"[Hillary] Clinton's prayer group was part of the Fellowship (or 'the Family'), a network of sex-segregated cells of political, business, and military leaders dedicated to 'spiritual war' on behalf of Christ... The Fellowship believes that the elite win power by the will of God, who uses them for his purposes. Its mission is to help the powerful understand their role in God's plan."

Hillary first met Fellowship leader Doug Coe – founder Abraham Vereide's successor – in 1993.

Says Mother Jones: "When Time put together a list of the nation's 25 most powerful evangelicals in 2005, the heading for Coe's entry was 'The Stealth Persuader.'

"'You know what I think of when I think of Doug Coe?' the Rev. Schenck (a Coe admirer) asked us. 'I think literally of the guy in the smoky back room that you can't even see his face. He sits in the corner, and you see the cigar, and you see the flame, and you hear his voice – but you never see his face. He's that shadowy figure.'"

Continued Mother Jones: "The Fellowship's long-term goal is 'a leadership led by God–leaders of all levels of society who direct projects as they are led by the spirit.'

"According to the Fellowship's archives, the spirit has in the past led its members in Congress to increase U.S. support for the Duvalier regime in Haiti and the Park dictatorship in South Korea. The Fellowship's God-led men have also included General Suharto of Indonesia; Honduran general and death squad organizer Gustavo Alvarez Martinez; a Deutsche Bank official disgraced by financial ties to Hitler; and dictator Siad Barre of Somalia, plus a list of other generals and dictators."

In Slate magazine, Jeff Sharlet noted: "Such interests have led the Family into some strange alliances over the years. Seduced by the Indonesian dictator Suharto's militant anti-communism, they described the murder of hundreds of thousands that brought him to power as a 'spiritual revolution,' and sent delegations of congressmen and oil executives to pray to Jesus with the Muslim leader. In Africa, they anointed the Somali killer Siad Barre as God's man and sent Sen. Grassley and a defense contractor as emissaries. Barre described himself as a 'Koranic Marxist,' but he agreed to pray to Grassley's American Christ in return for American military aid, which he then used to wreak a biblical terror on his nation."

Sharlet told NBC News that when he was an intern with the Fellowship "they were being taught the leadership lessons of Hitler, Lenin and Mao" and that Hitler's genocide "wasn't an issue for them, it was the strength that he emulated."

In one videotaped lecture series in 1989, Coe said:

"Hitler, Goebbels and Himmler were three men. Think of the immense power these three men had... But they bound themselves together in an agreement.... Two years before they moved into Poland, these three men had... systematically a plan drawn out... to annihilate the entire Polish population and destroy by numbers every single house... every single building in Warsaw and then to start on the rest of Poland."

Coe adds that it worked; they killed six and a half million "Polish people." Though he calls Nazis "these enemies of ours," he compares their commitment to Jesus' demand for total commitment: "Jesus said, 'You have to put me before other people. And you have to put me before yourself.' Hitler, that was the demand to be in the Nazi party. You have to put the Nazi party and its objectives ahead of your own life and ahead of other people."

Coe also used the Red Guard terrorism during the Chinese Cultural Revolution as a tool to explain Jesus' teachings on covenants:

"I've seen pictures of the young men in the Red Guard of China... they would bring in this young man's mother and father, he would take an axe and cut [his mother's] head off... They have to put the purposes of the Red Guard ahead of the mother-father-brother-sister – and their own life! That was a covenant. A pledge. That was what Jesus said."

To be fair, Coe's defenders say such examples are simply metaphors, used to dramatize and illustrate the power of commitment in small groups; and further, they are not typical of his subject matter, that most of the time he talks about Jesus, not Hitler, bloodshed, mass murder and so on. But even the most forgiving critic of the Fellowship must surely acknowledge that this is a strange and disturbing way to present the teachings of Jesus to some of the most powerful men and women in the world. Especially when those people include tyrants and dictators and their henchmen.

In Slate, Sharlet noted: "They're followers of a political religion that embraces elitism, disdains democracy, and pursues power for its members the better to 'advance the Kingdom.' They say they're working for Jesus, but their Christ is a power-hungry, inside-the-Beltway savior not many churchgoers would recognize."

The Fellowship operates at the very highest levels of government in the U.S. and abroad. Fellowship prayer cells exist in governments around the world, according to Mother Jones. Sharlet notes that the Fellowship's international reach is "almost impossible to overstate."

"Davos Man": Davos World Economic Forum

Bill and Hillary are frequent attendees at the Davos World Economic Forum, an annual meeting of about 2500 of the world's most powerful business leaders, international political leaders, selected intellectuals, and journalists.

Indeed, Huffington Post reporters Ryan Grim and Daniel Marans note that "Hillary and Bill Clinton are stars of the Davos set."

Each winter these elites meet together in Davos, Switzerland to discuss various important issues facing the world. The World Economic Forum also hosts other similar events around the world.

Though there are some open meetings at Davos, much that goes on – especially the most important matters – is secret. As the BBC noted in 2016:

"There are lots of meetings, surrounded by varying degrees of secrecy. The public ones – which anyone can attend. The closed ones – which only those participants with a white badge can attend (i.e., they've paid to attend the conference or have been invited), and then the private ones that you don't even know have happened. *Those are where the big deals are discussed, behind closed doors.*" (Emphasis added.)

Among the topics on the agenda at the 2014 meeting was "The Reshaping of the World: Consequences for Society, Politics and Business." Yes, the reshaping of the world.

Samuel Phillips Huntington, a highly influential American political scientist, presidential adviser and Harvard professor, is credited with inventing the phrase "Davos Man" to describe the global elites who gather there: they "have little need for national loyalty, view national boundaries as obstacles that thankfully are vanishing, and see national governments as residues from the past whose only useful function is to facilitate the elite's global operations."

By now, this should sound very familiar to readers.

Harvard's Steven Strauss is highly regarded as an expert on public policy and management, regularly cited by such news organizations as: CNBC, the Guardian, the New York Observer, Mother Jones, Al Jazeera, the Dallas Morning Post, the Jerusalem Post, and other media outlets.

In a 2014 article provocatively titled, "Why Do U.S. Politicians Meet with 'Criminal' Entities in Switzerland?" Strauss notes that Davos is funded by 1,000 global multi-billion dollar businesses. These huge multinational corporations (called "Partners" by Davos) pay $500,000 per year and more to fund this event, while the world's political leaders attend for free.

It's hard to imagine these mega-corporations paying $500,000 per year just to thank the world's hardworking "public servants" for all the good work they're doing and to kick around some ideas for making the world a better place.

So what's really happening? This annual $500,000 buys these multinational corporations privileged secret access at Davos to more than a thousand carefully selected and invited political leaders from around the world – including members of the U.S. Congress, ambassadors, heads of state, and other world leaders. These corporations also set the agenda for what these political leaders will discuss.

It's very cozy. Strauss notes: "…many of these Partners have criminal records, are under investigation for potential criminal activity (e.g., bribery), are mired in significant legal/ethical issues, or have blatant conflicts of interest while setting the agenda for a supposedly 'non-partisan' event."

Strauss, in his 2014 article, gave some examples (bulleted statements are his words):

- J.P. Morgan, which is under criminal investigation for possible bribery in China, operates under a deferred prosecution agreement relating to two felony violations in the Madoff scandal, and much else. Recent fines and settlements paid, so far, for various criminal and civil violations exceed $40 billion.

- HSBC, which admitted to criminal activities, paid $1.9 billion in fines, and currently operates under a deferred prosecution agreement.

- Standard Chartered, which admitted to willful acts of criminal money laundering, operates under a deferred prosecution agreement and paid a $660 million fine.

- Saudi Aramco, controlled by the Kingdom of Saudi Arabia – a country that doesn't allow women to drive, uses public flogging as a form of judicial punishment, and ranks 163rd (bottom 10 percent) in the world for press freedom.

There are many similar examples.

Strauss concludes: "U.S. politicians shouldn't attend Davos. Unless, of course, the real purpose of Davos is to provide politicians with opportunities for off-the-record meetings with questionable characters."

The conservative National Review's Kevin D. Williams has denounced Davos as a gathering of "our putative betters and would-be rulers" and noted that at Davos "Bill Clinton makes the case for wealth redistribution while sporting a $60,000 platinum Rolex."

Williams also noted that Davos offers the irritation of hearing "puritanical little homilies on how we need to learn to live with less from guys wearing shoes that cost more than the typical American family earns in a quarter."

Davos, like other global elite secret gatherings, is coming under growing criticism. In recent years thousands have gathered to protest the carving up of the world in secret and other dirty deals that seems to be going on there.

The New World Foundation/ Institute for Policy Studies

The little-known New World Foundation, of which Hillary was director and chair of the board of directors in 1987 and 1988, and a board member for years before that, has an extraordinary and fascinating history with many threads that tie deeply into this book's narrative of the occult, the political, and Hillary.

It was formed in 1954 by Anita McCormick Blaine, an heiress to the fortune of Cyrus Hall McCormick, inventor of the mechanical reaper. The mixture of the occult and political radicalism that one finds in the life of Hillary is almost eerily foreshadowed by the life of Blaine, her associates, and the Institute for Policy Studies (IPS).

Anita McCormick Blaine was born on July 4th, 1866. As an adult she began hearing "voices" instructing her do to various things. She began spells of automatic writing, eventually filling hundreds of pages with sayings and instructions from the mysterious otherworldly voices speaking to her. Following the death of her son in 1918, her interest in spiritualism, the occult, and psychic phenomena intensified. At one point she had a medium imported from England to have on hand for consultation, hiring her a secretary and putting her up at hotels for a full decade, paying all her bills down to tips and hairdos.

Politically, Blaine seems in many ways to resemble Hillary. She was a strong financial supporter and personal friend of Henry A. Wallace's socialist, communist-infiltrated Progressive Party's 1948 presidential campaign.

Henry Wallace is yet another strange figure, yet another link in the lengthy political-occult elite chain that leads ultimately to Hillary. Wallace was secretary of agriculture 1933–1940 and U.S. vice president under President Franklin D. Roosevelt, 1941–1945. Wallace was a 32nd-degree Freemason – as was President Roosevelt – and led the effort to put the All-Seeing Eye On the Pyramid – a major symbol to occultists – on the U.S. dollar bill. He was a Theosophist between 1925 and 1935, resigning two years after becoming secretary of agriculture. He was a devoted student of the remarkable Russian painter, poet, mystic, Theosophist, and yoga teacher – and founder of Agni Yoga – Nicholas Roerich, who Wallace addressed in a series of private letters as "my guru." (Later these private letters would be made public, embarrassing Wallace and leading to his political downfall.) Roerich was yet another person receiving messages from otherworldly entities via channeling, in this case the Ascended Masters El Morya and Koot Hoomi, who had also directed Theosophy leader Madame Blavatsky in forming the Theosophy Society decades earlier (according to Blavatsky).

In 1933, while Wallace was head of the U.S. Department of Agriculture (and still a Theosophist) he funded an expedition by Roerich and USDA scientists to Inner Mongolia, Manchuria, and China. Ostensibly the expedition was to collect plant seeds that might be useful in stopping soil erosion. However, given Roerich's and Wallace's intertwined occult interests, many have wondered if far more esoteric objectives than halting erosion were in mind. Roerich and Wallace were very aware of beliefs held by Theosophists and many others that this mysterious region contained the mystical city of Shamballa and the underground land of Agharta. Wallace, in fact, purportedly wrote Roerich and/or his associates: "May the Light of Northern Shamballa lead you and the Guru and *the true expedition* toward the eternal glory of the New Age." (Emphasis added.)

Indeed, Nicholas and Helena Roerich had earlier led an dangerous and arduous 1924-1928 expedition of 15,500 miles across little-known parts of India, China, Russia, Mongolia and Tibet seeking (among other things) a glimpse of Shamballa and Agharta. Many Theosophists, Buddhists and others believe Agharta is a vast complex of caves beneath Tibet populated by... malevolent serpent/reptilian beings. To this day many occultists and occult researchers believe these tunnels exist and are home to such things as secret organizations that attempt to guide the world; UFOs, aliens and/or beings from other planets or other dimensions; and the afore-mentioned reptilians.

During his first expedition Roerich described seeing what may have been a UFO, in this passage from his travel diary on August 5, 1926:

"We were in our camp in the Kukonor district not far from the Humboldt Chain. In the morning about half-past nine some of our caravaneers noticed a remarkably big black eagle flying above us. Seven of us began to watch this unusual bird. At the same moment another of our caravaneers remarked, 'There is something far above the bird.' And he shouted in his astonishment. We all saw, in a direction from north to south, something big and shiny reflecting the sun like a huge oval moving at great speed. Crossing our camp this thing changed in its direction from south to southwest. And we saw how it disappeared in the intense blue sky. We even [had] time to take our field glasses and saw quite distinctly an oval form with a bright surface, one of which was brilliant from the sun."

Roerich's guide told him the flying disc was from the ancient underground city of Agartha.

The influential occultist Alexandre Saint-Yves d'Alveydre (1842-1909) is widely credited with introducing Agartha to the Western world. Saint-Yves believed that Agartha was the site of an ancient world government which moved there around 3,200 B.C. He claimed to have received information about Agartha in the early 20th century via, yet again, telepathic transmissions from the spirit world.

Agartha was also mentioned in the writings of Ernst Robert Dickhoff, discussed in the reptilian-hypothesis section of this book. The concepts of Agartha, immense and lengthy tunnels winding and joining around the globe, and reptilian beings are frequently found in UFO and esoteric literature.

Interestingly, Nazi leaders Heinrich Himmler and Rudolf Hess also sent expeditions near this area, Tibet and Mongolia, in 1930, 1934-1935, and 1938-1939. These, too, were ostensibly for cultural and agricultural reasons, but some argue there were occult reasons behind the trips: the same desire to find Shamballa-Agartha, the secret tunnels, mystic powers, and perhaps the original Eden of the human race. Perhaps even... reptilians, whose vast knowledge and power could be harnessed to the cause of the Third Reich.

If they indeed found such beings, what they uncovered may have been terrifying. Hitler is widely quoted as telling Hermann Rauschning, the Nazi governor of Danzig: "The new man is living amongst us now! He is here! ... I will tell you a secret. I have seen the new man. He is intrepid and cruel. I was afraid of him."

Was this frightening "new man" a visitor from strange worlds beneath the surface explored by the Nazis?

But back to Anita McCormick Blaine. In 1948, she pledged $1,000,000 to create the Foundation for World Government, under a World Constitution drafted by the group. (As we have seen earlier in this chapter, one-world government, or a supranational world governing body, is a leading obsession of many elite organizations and individuals today.)

Blaine also supported other leftist and globalist causes, publications, and political figures. At her death, a share of her inheritance was used to save the struggling globalist progressive publication The New Republic – originally funded by J.P. Morgan agent Willard Dickerman Straight and the authoritarian progressive Herbert Croly to, according to historian Carroll Quigley and others, serve as a tool for the ruling elite to monitor and control the emerging progressive movement and shape it into a tool for the advancement of their goals; her grandson-in-law Gilbert Avery Harrison became its owner and editor from 1953 until 1974.

This exotic, extraordinary stew of socialism, Marxism, Fabianism, authoritarianism, elitism, globalism, occultism, secret societies, UFOs, reptilian beings, underground cities and vast tunnels beneath the earth, ESP, communion with strange spirits, and so on, eventually leads us to... Hillary.

Who, as we earlier noted, was director and chair of the board of directors of the New World Foundation, 1987-1988. (She was on the board from 1982 to 1988.)

In this role Hillary gave funding to several key far-left organizations. Among them was the Institute for Policy Studies (IPS).

Conservative congressman Larry McDonald (R-GA) said the following about the IPS, quoted in the Congressional Record, September 26, 1977: "The Institute for Policy Studies is a consortium of Marxist New Leftists organizing for a 'new economic and political world order'..."

In his book The KGB and Soviet Disinformation: An Insider's View, Ladislav Bittman, a former Communist police agent from Czechoslovakia, wrote that the IPS was pro-Soviet and part of the Soviet intelligence and propaganda network.

Conservative Joshua Muravchik wrote in 1988: "IPS literature abounds in praise of Ho and Mao and Fidel and the Sandinistas, not to mention all manner of still more obscure Leninists like Angola's ruling MPLA, the People's Front for the Liberation of Oman, the governments of Mozambique, Laos, and even Somalia..."

Conservative author and professor John J. Tierney of the Institute of World Politics is a harsh critic of IPS: "The political outlook of the Institute for Policy Studies (IPS) is classically Marxist. .... In classic Leninist design it is a revolutionary 'cell' of politically motivated activists. ... During the Cold War IPS spouted a far left anti-capitalist ideology, and it fostered close ties to communist and socialist parties around the globe. ... IPS believes American society will be transformed in a new world order. Combining the ideas and rhetoric of Marxism/socialism and liberal internationalism, the report calls American society the chief obstacle to a 'just' and 'fair' world."

As president, Bill Clinton carried on Hillary's support of IPS by appointing many IPS members to high government positions.

IPS was not the only controversial group Hillary funded through the New World Foundation, according to Antony Sutton and Patrick Wood: "In addition to IPS, Hillary sent money to other pro-communist groups which themselves have strong ties to IPS – indicating a collaborative attempt for donations to serve similar purposes."

As head of the New World Foundation, Hillary gave funding to Grassroots International, which, according to a Washington Times investigation, at the time funded two groups with connections to the terrorist Palestinian Liberation Organization (PLO). (This was given before PLO leader Yasser Arafat renounced terrorism and accepted Israel's right to exist.) For much more on Hillary's connections to communist and terrorist individuals and organizations, see Chapter 14.

Clinton Global Initiative (CGI) Annual Meeting

"This is a close as you will get to global government." – three-time Pulitzer Prize-winning New York Times columnist Thomas Friedman

As if the Trilateral Commission, CFR, Davos, Bilderbergers and all the rest don't offer enough meet-and-greet time for world politicians, Establishment journalists, and global multinationals, the Clinton Foundation – Bill and Hillary's controversial worldwide nonprofit foundation – has its own such gathering, the Clinton Global Initiative.

The Clinton Global Initiative (CGI) is just one of many program of the Clinton Foundation, which Bill founded in 2001. The Washington Post has called it "the public face" of the Clinton Foundation.

The Clinton Global Initiative's Annual Meeting is invitation-only and attended by the same categories and many of the same individuals as participates in other organizations in this chapter: heads of state, business leaders, nonprofit directors, prominent members of the media, etc. Past attendees have included President Barack Obama, Her Majesty Queen Rania Al Abdullah, UN Secretary-General Ban Ki Moon, Mayor Michael Bloomberg, Warren Buffett, Bill Gates, former vice president Al Gore, Rupert Murdoch, Bono, Mick Jagger, Brad Pitt and Angelina Jolie.

It is distinct from other similar gatherings in that it seeks to create discussions to generate specific plans and action pledges to solve specific world problems. As the Washington Post summarizes, it attempts to "Woo the world's most powerful interests to help the powerless."

Thomas Friedman, three-time winner of the Pulitzer Prize for his journalism (and, it should be added, member of the Council on Foreign Relations and the Trilateral Commission, Bilderberg Club attendee, and so forth) was wildly enthusiastic after attending a Global Initiative meeting.

"This is a close as you will get to global government," Friedman said. "[H]ere you have these leaders from all over the world. And let's say [Richard] Branson pledges $3 billion to fight global warming – that is really a government-level, government-size commitment. That is a form of transnational governance and it is filling a void. ... The Clinton Global Initiative was enlisting government-level commitments from individuals in order to provide governance, in this case social safety nets."

Prominent members of the media regularly participate in Clinton Global Initiative events. For years the Foundation in turn listed these participants as "Members" or "Notable Past Members." Increasingly, however, concerns were raised about the appearance – or substance –of media impropriety, since these same media Members sometimes interviewed or otherwise interacted as journalists with persons involved with the Clinton Foundation without disclosing their status as Members.

In response to such growing criticism the Foundation in 2012 re-classified CGI media participants as "Guests" rather than "Members."

For example, the October 2015 Democratic presidential debates – featuring Hillary and four other Democrats – was moderated by CNN host Anderson Cooper, listed proudly by the Clinton Foundation Global Initiative at their website as a "Notable Past Member." (Cooper is also, by the way, "ex" CIA.)

After CNN's Cooper was criticized for this, he denied he had done anything improper, and further said that he actually had no relationship with CGI other than having one time hosted a panel at a CGI event.

"...this is total bunk," Cooper said of such accusations of undisclosed conflicts of interest. "Honestly, I can't even remember what the panel was. There were no Clintons on the panel. I think it was on, like, international development aid or, honestly, I have no memory of what it was. But I was [a] panelist. I was the moderator of a panel of handful of people. I walked in, I did my moderation, I left, I wasn't paid. I've never been back to the Clinton Global Initiative."

Similarly, George Stephanopoulos is chief anchor and the chief political correspondent for ABC News, a co-anchor of "Good Morning America," the host of ABC's "Sunday Morning This Week," and regular substitute anchor for ABC's "World

News Tonight." Busy guy! The New York Times has called him "the most recognizable political journalist at the most-watched news network in the country."

Stephanopoulos received considerable criticism in 2015 for reporting on the Clinton Foundation for ABC's "This Week" without disclosing his large financial donations to that organization and his past membership in the Clinton Global Initiative. His involvement was considerably deeper than Anderson Cooper's. Unknown to viewers watching his report, between 2006 and 2013 he was a featured attendee, panel moderator, judge, and played other roles at the annual meeting; in 2015 it came to light that he had donated $75,000 to the Clinton Foundation between 2012 and 2014, without telling ABC News.

(Stephanopoulos is also a former Democratic Party political adviser, worked as communications director for Bill Clinton's 1992 U.S. presidential campaign, became White House communications director and then senior adviser for policy and strategy. He is also a member of the Council on Foreign Relations.)

Other media stars who are Clinton Foundation Global Initiative "guests" (including some formerly listed as "Members") include: CNN's Christiane Amanpour, NBC's Matt Lauer and Tom Brokaw, New York Times' Nicholas Kristof, Yahoo's Katie Couric, the Economist's Matthew Bishop, PBS's Judy Woodruff, Newsweek's Fareed Zakaria and Financial Times' Lionel Barber. And the New York Times' Thomas Friedman, formerly listed by the Foundation as a "Notable Past Member," who wrote the glowing tribute/endorsement quoted at the start of this section.

Their relationships with the Clinton Foundation Global Initiative, whether real or, as Anderson Cooper implies, a lie concocted by the Foundation, are seldom, if ever, mentioned when they cover Global Initiative-related stories, according to critics.

Washington Post media blogger Erik Wemple agreed that the relationships are exaggerated, writing: "those [media] 'members' are more like CGI 'guests.' They come in and moderate a panel session or two, as Cooper noted, and then go on their merry way. That the Clinton Foundation once touted them as 'members' stands as a testament to the Foundation's interest in conveying intimacy with modern media giants."

So: is Wemple saying that the Clinton Foundation is exaggerating – or, perhaps more accurately, lying – about its media connections to puff up its profile? And perhaps also using that exaggerated profile to gain more credibility and possibly donations? That would seem an interesting story in itself, to say the least.

However, Wemple goes on to note: "CNN and its competitors in TV news – while not serving as real 'members' of CGI – have indeed provided rather generous publicity and exposure for the Clinton Foundation/CGI in exchange for access to former president Bill Clinton and other newsmakers who attend CGI events. This blog has written a great deal about these transactions, *calling into question why independent news organizations would agree to broadcast what are, in effect, extended infomercials for CGI*." (Emphasis added.)

Hmmmmm... so CNN and other media giants that participate with CGI are not "members" and are not compromised by their association. They just give "generous publicity and exposure ... extended infomercials" for CGI events in order to have "access" to Bill and other CGI "newsmakers," something the Washington Post itself believes is worth "calling into question." Okay... And many also share relationships with the Clintons in such secretive off-the-record organizations as the Council on Foreign Relations, the Trilateral Commission, Bilderberg, Davos and so on.

Move on, folks, no conflict of interest to see here...

It's also worth noting that as of August 3, 2015, individuals associated with Time Warner, the parent company of CNN, had given half a million dollars to Hillary's presidential campaign.

All of this, of course, is similar to other surprisingly close relationships between big media and the power elite documented in this chapter.

The Clinton Global Initiative is just one of many programs of the controversial Clinton Foundation. Close

Clinton advisers and family have been involved since its creation, leading some to accuse the Foundation of, among other improprieties, serving as a convenient vehicle to fund numerous Clinton activities and to temporarily park and/or reward close Clinton associates and political operatives.

"It seems like the Clinton Foundation operates as a slush fund for the Clintons," bluntly declared Bill Allison, a senior fellow at the Sunlight Foundation, a nonpartisan, nonprofit government watchdog group that advocates for open government.

The Clinton Foundation "has always been a vehicle to promote the careers of the Clintons. ... in recent years it has functioned more like an unofficial campaign headquarters for Hillary Clinton's 2016 presidential bid," observes the Capital Research Center, a nonprofit group that investigates charities and foundations from a free-market, limited-government perspective.

And the Washington Examiner noted "many longtime Clinton political associates who have found lucrative positions with the Foundation since the former president founded it in 2001."

For example: As of 2016, Donna E. Shalala, Bill Clinton administration secretary for health and human services, was president. Clinton Foundation CEO from 2003 to 2013 was Bruce Lindsey, who served the Bill Clinton presidency in numerous high-level roles and was national campaign director of Bill's 1992 presidential campaign. John Podesta, longtime Clinton ally and chief of staff to President Bill Clinton, also has served as Foundation CEO. Vice president of the Foundation is Chelsea Clinton. Chelsea's friend and colleague Eric Braverman was made CEO of the Foundation in 2013. After Braverman stepped down, Maura Pally, a Hillary Clinton confidante and a deputy assistant secretary during Hillary's time at the State Department, became interim CEO. Stephanie Streett, the Foundation's executive director was assistant to President Bill Clinton and was his White House director of scheduling. Dennis Cheng, a former Hillary Clinton campaign official and State Department deputy chief, headed a 2013 endowment drive. Ira Magaziner, the senior adviser for policy development for President Bill Clinton, is head of the Foundation's Health Access Initiative. Douglas J. Band, former personal assistant and counselor to President Bill Clinton, and who personally negotiated with the Obama administration for Hillary to become secretary of state, was a co-creator of the Clinton Global Initiative. Craig Minassian, the Foundation's chief communications officer, was assistant press secretary and director of television news for President Clinton. Katie Dowd, digital director of Hillary's presidential campaign, worked for Clinton at the State Department and for the Clinton Foundation. Amitabh Desai, the Foundation's foreign policy director, was a legislative aide Hillary while she was a U.S. senator. Laura Graham, who has served as the Foundation's senior adviser on global programs and as chief operating officer, was deputy assistant to President Bill Clinton from 1995 to 2001.

In 2009, Huma Abedin, wife of Democratic U.S. Representative Anthony Weiner, was appointed deputy chief of staff to Clinton in the State Department. The State Department crafted a "special government employee" arrangement that let her work as a consultant for private sector clients at the same time. One of those clients (again, while working for Secretary of State Hillary) was the Clinton Foundation itself; another was Teneo, a strategic consulting firm founded by Doug Band, who had worked for the Clinton Foundation and for President Bill Clinton (see paragraph above), and by Declan Kelly, who raised several million dollars for Hillary's first presidential run and had worked with Hillary's State Department; Bill Clinton was honorary chairman of Teneo; Teneo employed "numerous Hillary Clinton associates" (Politico.com); Teneo's clients included Foundation donors. Abedin later worked as director of Hillary's transition team to assist Hillary's return to private life while at the same time continuing her work for the Clinton Foundation. In 2015 Abedin became vice chairwoman for Hillary's campaign for president.

Such coziness and big money has raised ethical concerns. As this book goes to press, newly revealed emails have raised concerns about possible improper connections between the Foundation and Hillary's role as secretary of state.

"There is no doubt of the connections between Clinton Foundation staffers and State Department staffers," reported CNN in August 2016.

To give one example of that: Cheryl Mills is yet another longtime Clinton operative. She was President Bill Clinton's deputy White House counsel, and defended him during his impeachment proceedings. In 2008 she was Hillary's senior legal campaign adviser. In between these roles she was on the board of the Clinton Foundation. When Hillary became secretary of state, Mills left the Clinton Foundation board to became Hillary's chief of staff.

In 2012, Mills, still chief of staff for Hillary at the State Department, interviewed potential CEOs for the Clinton Foundation. The executives Mills interviewed worked at Pfizer and Walmart. Both companies had given massive donations to the Clinton Foundation, and worked with the Clinton Global Initiative. After Hillary resigned as secretary of state, Mills returned to the Clinton Foundation board.

To many critics, such dizzying and ongoing intermingling of political and private charity activities – within an international foundation with millions of dollars to spend, the majority of which comes from corporations or foreign citizens, groups or governments – has at least the appearance of impropriety.

Indeed, from its 2001 founding through early 2015 the Foundation raised "close to $2 billion from a vast global network that includes corporate titans, political donors, foreign governments and other wealthy interests," reported the Washington Post in February 2015.

A major share of the Clinton Foundation's income comes from foreign donors who are prohibited by law from contributing to political candidates in the U.S. The Washington Post noted that "many of the Foundation's biggest donors are foreigners who are legally barred from giving to U.S. political candidates. A third of Foundation donors who have given more than $1 million are foreign governments or other entities based outside the United States, and foreign donors make up more than half of those who have given more than $5 million."

As we shall see, many of these donor nations are authoritarian regimes, some of whom have received political benefits from the U.S. government after making their donations to the Clinton Foundation.

Peter Schweizer, author of the bestselling book Clinton Cash: The Untold Story of How and Why Foreign Governments and Businesses Helped Make Bill and Hillary Rich, says bluntly that the Clintons, by creating the Foundation, have "created an apparatus that allowed them to get around prohibitions on foreign entities influencing our political process."

As we go to press the Foundation is undergoing increased scrutiny and criticism.

The Bilderbergers: "Bilding" a New World Order

"...the most influential group in the world... former leaders of the Bilderberg conferences say they were the most important events they ever went to... the discussions that took place decisively shaped modern Europe." – UK Telegraph

"It's officially described as a private gathering, but with a guest list including the heads of European and American corporations, political leaders and a few intellectuals, it's one of the most influential organizations on the planet. ... Not a word of what is said at Bilderberg meetings can be breathed outside." – BBC

"To say we were striving for a one-world government is exaggerated, but not wholly unfair. Those of us in Bilderberg felt we couldn't go on forever fighting one another for nothing and killing people and rendering millions homeless. So we felt that a single community throughout the world would be a good thing." – Denis Healey, Bilderberg group co-founder and steering committee member for four decades.

Imagine a meeting where 150 or so of the world's greatest professional athletes gathered in total secrecy with world-famous coaches, scientists, team owners and promoters.

Now imagine that the planet's most influential sports writers also were in attendance – but had sworn in advance not to print or say a word about anything that was discussed.

Plus, add to the above that there would be additional unnamed figures of great power, wealth and importance in secret attendance. And the entire meeting would be guarded by a small army of trained security guards.

Needless to say, there would be a media frenzy. The meeting would be talked about nonstop around the world. Speculation would run rampant. Hordes of journalists would do in-depth research, storm the meeting and seek interviews with anyone who had any idea at all as to what might be happening. Governments might well demand an investigation.

Yet every year some of the richest and most powerful people on earth meet in total secrecy with political leaders, renowned academics, and owners and luminaries of the most influential mass media in the world – and they have done so for more than half a century. And eerily, little is said about it in the mainstream media, which seems curiously uncurious.

Indeed, for decades virtually no mainstream U.S. media reported anything of any significance on these extraordinary meetings – even though some of the world's leading media power players were in attendance themselves, sworn to secrecy. And what few mentions there were were mostly written in a dismissive, joking manner, as if the whole thing were of no concern or importance whatsoever.

Only fairly recently, when the Internet made it impossible to pretend that these meetings did not occur, was there much coverage in the mainstream media, and even now most of it remains trivial and condescending.

Welcome to the strange, controversial, top-secret world of the Bilderbergers, also known as the Bilderberg Group, Bilderberg conference, Bilderberg meetings or the Bilderberg Club.

As journalist Daniel Estulin writes in his 2009 book The True Story of the Bilderberg Group, it is like "a private club where presidents, prime ministers, international bankers and generals rub shoulders, where gracious royal chaperones ensure everyone gets along, and where the people running the wars, markets, and Europe (and America) say what they never dare say in public."

"Bilderberg is not a conspiracy theory. It's a conspiracy reality," Estulin told the UK Telegraph in 2013. "It was [created as] a vehicle through which private financier oligarchical interests were able to impose their policies on nominally sovereign governments. The idea is the creation of a global network of cartels, more powerful than any nation on Earth, destined to control the necessities of life of the rest of humanity."

"Even a cursory comparison between the guest list and the conference agenda raises red flags," said journalist Charlie Skelton in the UK Guardian in 2016. "All those finance ministers sitting round discussing the 'geopolitics of energy and commodity prices' with the group chief executive of BP, the vice chairman of Portuguese petroleum giant Galp Energia, and the CEO of Royal Dutch Shell. And then afterwards saying nothing to their respective parliaments about what they discussed. It's so off-the-chart inappropriate that it beggars comprehension."

Bilderberg participants as the "high priests of globalization," said writer and economist Will Hutton, a former attendee.

The Bilderberg Club was formed in 1954. The first meeting was held at the Bilderberg Hotel in Oosterbeek, Netherlands, thus the name. Bilderberg co-founder and promoter Prince Bernhard was an ex-Nazi, though he strenuously denied this all his life: "I can swear this with my hand on the Bible: I was never a Nazi." However, various family members were enthusiastic Nazis; and after his death, documents were found proving he was in fact a member of the Nazi Party until 1934, having joined a Nazi student association at Berlin's Humboldt University while studying there, training to become a fighter pilot, and also becoming a member of the "Reiter-SS," a mounted unit of the SS. (Bernhard's past remains contentious. Supporters argue he joined the Nazi Party out of political necessity at the time, but that he did not agree with their politics, and point out that in World War II he fought against the Nazis.) To help with the founding of the Bilderberg Club in 1954 Prince Bernhard brought in the CIA – which, as we shall see in Chapter 9, was certainly not averse to working with ex-Nazis, reformed or not. Prince Bernhard was Bilderberg chairman until 1976, when he was embroiled in an international scandal for taking a $1.1 million bribe from U.S. firm Lockheed to guarantee contracts for that firm's military aircraft. Prior to the exposure of this bribe the Prince had been a busy fellow, serving on more than 300 corporate boards or committees around the world.

As an example of some of the topics covered at Bilderberg, here is an excerpt from the 2016 agenda:

"The key topics for discussion this year include: current events; China; Europe: migration, growth, reform, vision, unity; Middle East; Russia; U.S. political landscape, economy: growth, debt, reform; Cyber-security; Geo-politics of energy and commodity prices; Precariat and middle class; technological innovation."

Quite a full plate. But then, the world is a big place.

Bilderberg attendees constitute a virtual who's who of the ruling elite, the most powerful and influential people in the world. Many are connected to just about every conspiracy theory and power elite organization one can imagine. Attendees have included U.S. senators, governors and future U.S. presidents; kings and queens and other royalty; prime ministers; military leaders; journalists; representatives of tax-exempt foundations; corporate leaders and CEOs; and other representatives of pure, raw political and economic power.

A sampling of attendees: David Rockefeller, Henry Kissinger, Alan Greenspan, Ben Bernanke, Larry Summers, George Soros, Donald Rumsfeld, Paul Volcker, Colin Powell, David Petraeus, Robert Murdoch, Edmond de Rothschild, Robert McNamara, Tony Blair, Jeff Bezos of Amazon, Eric Schmidt of Google, Bill Gates of Microsoft, Chris Hughes of Facebook… and so forth. As for journalists, 2016 alone featured well-known figures from the Washington Post, NBC News, Bloomberg, and the Wall Street Journal.

And those are just from the official list of attendees. In 2013 the UK Daily Telegraph quoted a source connected to the

Bilderbergers who said there are other, secret attendees, whose names are kept from the public.

The 1991 Bilderberg meeting in Baden Baden, Germany was supposedly attended by the then virtually unknown governor of Arkansas, Bill Clinton. A few years later Bill became, seemingly out of the blue, president of the United States. George H.W. Bush attended Bilderberg conferences before being elected to the White House. Tony Blair attended in 1993 before becoming prime minister of England. Romano Prodi attended in 1999 and later that year became president of the European Union Commission.

In 2014 Hillary said, in answer to a question at a book signing, she had never attended a Bilderberg meeting. The questioner then tried to show her a picture he said looked like her that was taken at the 2013 event. It could not be her, she said, because she wasn't there. However, a previously classified document later released under the Freedom of Information Act indicates that she did in fact attend.

Nor is it likely that it was her first Bilderberg meeting.

In 1997 Bilderberg watchers reported seeing Hillary attending, though her name was not listed among attendees.

In June 2008, in the midst of their heated race for the Democratic Party's presidential nomination, Barack Obama and Hillary held a private meeting in Virginia at an undisclosed location. Obama left his plane when it landed at Dulles International Airport to meet with Hillary. Dulles was just a short walk from where the 2008 Bilderberg was underway. Was their secret meeting held at Bilderberg?

In 2015 observers reported that both Hillary and Bill were seen entering the Bilderberg meeting.

One of Hillary's top advisers, Jim Messina, nicknamed "The Fixer," attended Bilderberg in 2015. (Messina was White House deputy chief of staff for operations under President Obama from 2009 to 2011 and was campaign manager for Obama's 2012 re-election campaign. White House communications director Dan Pfeiffer called him "the most powerful person in Washington that you haven't heard of.")

Longtime Clinton adviser and ally Vernon Jordan – who took Bill to the 1991 Bilderberg conference – was one of over a dozen Clinton allies and supporters known to have attended in 2016.

The financial blog and news site ZeroHedge also notes that many Bilderberg attendees have paid Hillary millions of dollars in speaking fees.

Skull and Bones: Death, Depravity and Power Among America's Ruling Elite

"It's a secret." – U.S. Senator John Kerry, when asked by a journalist during his 2004 presidential campaign about his membership in Skull and Bones

"It's so secret, we can't talk about it." – George W. Bush on NBC television's "Meet the Press," February 2004, when asked about the fact that both he and the Democratic front runner, Senator John Kerry, are members of Yale University's Skull and Bones

"The life which we invite you to share in our society is based on such intangible factors that we cannot meaningfully convey to you either its nature or quality." – from a document to prospective members of Skull and Bones

"For nearly a century and a half, Skull and Bones has been the most influential secret society in the nation..." observed journalist Ron Rosenberg in 1977 in a ground-breaking article for Esquire magazine.

We would be amiss in skipping over the notorious Skull and Bones in a chapter devoted to the secret societies and meeting places of America's ruling elites.

Though Bill and Hillary are not Skull and Bones members (as far as we know) some of their most trusted associates are Bonesmen who network with other Bonesmen. Further, a great many of both Bill and Hillary's key advisers have come from Yale, home to the Skull and Bones headquarters, so there are other significant Clinton contacts with Skull and Bones members as well.

In the dark secret chambers of the near-windowless tomb-like Skull and Bones building at Yale, members are surrounded by dozens of skulls, bones and skeletons, human and animal, hanging from the walls; they drink from cups in the shape of skulls, under light streaming from skull-shaped fixtures. Attendees have reported seeing swastikas arranged in a shrine to Nazism. Members assume secret names, sometimes the names of demons and devils. They sneer at non-members, who they call "barbarians."

The symbol the group chose for itself, the skull and crossbones, is the age-old symbol of death, once used by pirates, used today to indicate deadly poison. It was also the emblem of the Nazi SS.

"Satanism loves and courts death," notes occult researcher David Bay. "Thus, Satanists love death symbols like skeletons, skulls, and coffins."

Indeed, at one time the organization was known as the Brotherhood of Death.

Membership initiation rites have been described as essentially Satanic Black Masses, in which Christian rites are mocked and reversed. The name of Judas Escariot is invoked; the Pope is mocked; a parody of the sacrament is enacted in which symbolic blood is drunk from a human skull. Initiates reportedly must masturbate in a coffin while describing to members their complete sexual history, and must kiss a human skull and the feet of a Black Mass pope, all in the company of members dressed as skeletons and Satan, as foul curses and invocations to monstrous spirits are shouted. There is a faux throat-slitting ritual murder.

It is through such bizarre and blasphemous ceremonies that some of the most powerful people in the world – the ruling elite, the men who govern nations, command armies, and dole out as they desire destruction and riches – meet and forge lifelong bonds.

For Skull and Bones members are not ordinary citizens. They are carefully chosen from among the elite of the elite, top students at one of the world's most prestigious universities, Yale. And they are handpicked to assume roles as members of the ruling elite: the future shapers and makers of American domestic and foreign policy.

"It's an initiation ceremony that has bonded diplomats, media moguls, bankers and spies into a lifelong, multi-generational fellowship far more influential than any fraternity," says journalist Rosenbaum, who has spent over a quarter century investigating the shadowy group. "It was – and still remains – the heart of the heart of the American Establishment...

"The rituals are less important than the relationships – the bonds of power and influence that develop between Skull and Bones initiates after they graduate. But the relationships are first forged by the rituals...

"...the fact that the founders of Time Inc. and the CIA, as well as several secretaries of state and national security advisers – the men who made the decision to drop the Hiroshima bomb, invade the Bay of Pigs and plunge us into Vietnam, the Tafts, the Bundys, the Buckleys, the Harrimans, the Lovetts – all took part in this initiation ritual, may have something to do with the real world power of those bonds. The unspoken understanding, the comfort level with the clandestine, the nods and winks with which power is exercised."

Yes, incredibly, this orgy of blood and blasphemy, this celebration of death and darkness, is how hundreds of the most powerful and influential figures in America's ruling class – including future U.S. presidents, Supreme Court justices, other holders of powerful national office, and some of the wealthiest of America's financial elite – have met and joined together to form secret lifelong partnerships.

Skull and Bones members include president and Supreme Court Justice William Howard Taft; presidents George H. W. Bush and George W. Bush, and their father Prescott Bush; Supreme Court Justices Morrison R. Waite and Potter Stewart; James Jesus Angleton, a founding officer and dominant figure within the CIA; McGeorge Bundy, national security adviser to presidents Kennedy and Johnson and major architect of the Vietnam War; Henry Stimson, U.S. secretary of war (1940-1945); U.S. Secretary of Defense Robert A. Lovett; tycoon and ultimate political insider Averell Harriman; Henry Luce, immensely influential publishing magnate; over twenty U.S. senators; and congressmen, governors, CIA officials, Fortune 500 CEOs, authors and other similarly powerful figures spread throughout American society...

And there are darker connections as well, according to Alexandra Robbins, author of Secrets of the Tomb: Skull and Bones, the Ivy League and the Hidden Path to Power:

"One doesn't need to scratch deeply to uncover accusations of sinister ties with the CIA, the Trilateral Commission, the Illuminati, the Council on Foreign Relations, even the Nazis."

Skull and Bones was founded in 1832, after founder William Huntington Russell spent a year studying in Germany. Many researchers say Skull and Bones was modeled on the ultimate secret society, the infamous Illuminati of Germany, and perhaps even was – or is – a branch of that group.

That connection may seem unlikely to some. Indeed, the Illuminati, or Bavarian Illuminati, is often assumed by many people to be mere fiction. But it was very real. It was formed on May 1, 1776 by Adam Weishaupt. The Illuminati was designed to operate secretly behind the scenes to control government and society; in this way it can be seen as a forerunner of other conspiratorial groups discussed in this chapter. At its peak the Illuminati's secret membership is estimated to have been between 600 and 2,500 members, including some of the most powerful and influential persons in Germany and surrounding areas. As the Illuminati gained more power, including numerous political offices, and used that power for their own mysterious ends, alarms were raised. Karl Theodor, Elector of Bavaria, banned the Illuminati in 1785, and founder Weishaupt fled the country and disappeared from history.

Here the trail gets murkier. Some scholars say the Illuminati ended. Others, however, say Illuminati did not break up after the ban, but rather went further underground and infiltrated numerous organizations around the world, and remains powerful today – perhaps even the most powerful force in the world. Some say the Illuminati incorporated Satanism and other black occult practices.

Whatever the full story of Skull and Bones' origin, from the very beginning the connection between Skull and Bones membership and political power is clear: Skull and Bones co-founder Alphonso Taft became attorney general of the United States; his son, William Henry, became a Bonesman and then president of the United States.

And, when they feel threatened, Skull and Bones members have used their immense power to protect the mysteries of the organization.

"They don't like people tampering and prying," an anonymous Skull and Bones alumni told journalist Ron Rosenbaum, warning him of the dangers of digging into the secrets of the cult. "The power of Bones is incredible. They've got their hands on every lever of power in the country. You'll see – it's like trying to look into the Mafia."

That power and influence was obvious in 2004. The U.S. presidential race consisted of two Skull and Bones members running against each another: Democrat John Kerry (Skull and Bones 1966) versus George W. Bush (Skull and Bones 1968, son of president and fellow Skull and Bones member George H.W. Bush). Your vote was thus cast for a Skull and Bones member regardless of which major party candidate you chose.

Yet both men refused to answer questions – including questions from the national media – about their membership in the super-secret occult society.

The winning Bonesman, President Bush, went on to appoint numerous Bonesmen to high-level positions; among his first social gatherings at the White House was a Skull and Bones reunion.

Kerry had to wait a few years before being appointed secretary of state by President Barack Obama, where he served alongside fellow Bonesman Austan Goolsbee, chief economist of President Obama's Economic Recovery Advisory Board.

But what of Bill and Hillary?

Both earned law degrees in 1973 from Yale Law School. At the time Skull and Bones was supposedly exclusively for male undergraduates at Yale, so it is presumed that Bill and

Hillary, both graduate students, were not members. (Though it is easy enough to imagine ways in which they could have, if they and the society wished, been involved.)

But there are significant links to Hillary and the Skull and Bones power elite. Bonesman Strobe Talbott, who roomed with Bill for a time when both were students) was deputy secretary of state under Bill Clinton (1994 to 2001) and was a key architect of U.S. foreign policy during that time; the globalist Talbott also had been a Rhodes Scholar, director of the Council on Foreign Relations, a trustee of the Trilateral Commission, and a member of the Aspen Strategy Group. Bill's ambassador to China and assistant secretary of state was Winston Lord, a Skull and Bones member who was also – busy man – chairman of the Council on Foreign Relations, a Bilderberger, and a Trilateralist. Jake Sullivan, Hillary's top policy adviser, was a Bonesman. All of these were able in turn to draw on a vast network of Skull and Bones members, giving Bill access and connections.

Going back further, one of Bill's mentors and biggest financial supporters was the notorious Pamela Harriman, a lifelong courtesan of numerous rich, powerful and/or famous men. When Bill lost his campaign for Governor of Arkansas, Harriman made him chairman of her PAM-PAC – the single largest fundraising source for the Democratic Party, a tremendously powerful and influential position. When running for president Harriman saw to it that Bill received a million dollars at a critical campaign moment, and she ultimately raised a whopping $12 million for him. It is very possible that Bill could not have become president without her assistance and financial support. Speaker of the House Tom Foley bluntly said, "No one in this country can take greater credit for winning the White House than Pamela."

The source of Pamela Harriman's wealth? Her last of three husbands was Averell Harriman, whom she married when he was over 80 years old. A leading member of the U.S. Establishment, Averell Harriman (who died in 1986) was extremely wealthy, powerful and influential. He inherited the largest fortune in the country upon graduating from Yale in 1913. He held elected and appointed offices and served Democratic presidents from Franklin Roosevelt onward in numerous powerful roles. And he was a member of many ruling elite cabals such as those described in this chapter – including Skull and Bones.

In fact, Averell Harriman was widely considered the "patriarch" of Skull and Bones, the organization's godfather and a top funder. Harriman was a founding partner in the wealthy Wall Street firm Brown Brothers Harriman & Co., which was heavily linked to Skull and Bones. During the 1931 merger that formed the company, fully 8 of the company's 16 founding partners were known members of Skull and Bones. A Brown Brothers Harriman & Co. leader managed Skull and Bones' financial affairs for many years.

So Pamela Harriman's massive donations of millions of dollars to Bill's presidential campaign, her near-infinite connections to the rich and powerful which she made available to Bill at critical times, and her fundraising rescue of the Democratic Party in the late 1980s, were all the fruits of the political arch-insider who was arguably the number one Skull and Bones member in America.

After Bill became president, Pamela Harriman had constant access to the White House. Indeed, says her biographer Christopher Ogden, she "put the Clinton administration together."

Led, no doubt, by the ideas of the late Averell Harriman, now a bones-man for real, still guiding America's future even from the grave.

Bohemian Grove: Devil Worship and Symbolic Child Sacrifice Ceremonies of the Rich and Famous

Bohemian Grove, or the Bohemian Club, was formed in 1872. Membership is extremely exclusive and expensive, and by invitation only. Members constitute a ruling elite, a sort of One Percent of the One Percent: roughly 2,500 of America's richest, most powerful, most influential males.

Most of the organization's activities take place at the Bohemian Grove, a privately owned forest compound 75 miles north of San Francisco.

As the Washington Post writes: "Every July, some of the richest and most powerful men in the world gather at a 2,700 acre campground in Monte Rio, Calif., for two weeks of heavy drinking, super-secret talks, Druid worship (the group insists they are simply 'revering the Redwoods'), and other rituals."

The highlight is an extraordinary and, to some, extremely disturbing occult ceremony entitled The Cremation of Care. In this ceremony Bohemian Grove members – again, drawn from America's ruling elite – assemble to conduct a symbolic sacrifice of a child to a strange, gigantic, some say Satanic, idol.

There are differing descriptions of the ceremony, but we know the essentials. Bohemian Grove members, surrounded by skulls dangling above them, gather in the darkness of night to chant ritualistically as priests dressed in dark robes, their faces garishly painted, accompanied by the Grim Reaper Death, carry the bound effigy of a child symbolically named "Dull Care." The child is placed in a small boat tipped with a carved skull. The boat is sent across a lake, where it arrives as a sacrifice to a grim and terrifying 40-foot stone owl with a black alter at its base. Some have noted the disturbing resemblance of the owl idol to the ancient demon Moloch; more on that below. (The owl of Minerva, we should note in passing, was the first symbol adopted by the Illuminati when it formed in Bavaria in the late 1700s.)

The giant owl is dramatically lit by spotlights. The child begs for its life, but the owl idol commands the priests to continue the sacrifice. The priests set the child afire, and it dies screaming in agony as the enraptured ruling elite roar their approval. The high priest says he will "read the remains" of the child after its death for clues to the future – "a deep occult tradition," says conspiracy researcher Alex Jones, who notes that such reading of the cremated corpse of an innocent child is representative of the blackest kind of black magic.

Some have raised the possibility that actual living children are sacrificed in this and other Bohemian Grove ceremonies. Brian Romanoff of the Bohemian Grove Blog notes that "persistent rumors and reports from various sources, tell of bizarre rituals, child snuff films, (films in which a child is murdered) and other horrors taking place within the confines of The Grove."

Alex Jones, who in 2000 became the first person to infiltrate and film the occult ceremony, says the child sacrifice took place behind large black drapes and notes: "Whether it was an effigy or real, we do not know...

"The body continued to scream in pain. Suddenly, all of those little metal crosses that we had seen along the bank during the day burst into flame. So, I was there witnessing something right out of the medieval painter Hieronymus Bosch's Visions of Hell: burning metal crosses, priests in red and black robes with the high priest in a silver robe with a red cape, a burning body screaming in pain, a giant stone great-horned owl, world leaders, bankers, media and the head of academia engaged in these activities. It was total insanity. ...

"If my neighbor was worshiping a 40-foot stone owl and burned children on a fire, I wouldn't let that neighbor walk my dog or babysit my children. Instead these people are babysitting the big red button... This is some sick stuff."

Self-proclaimed former Project MONARCH mind-controlled sex slave Cathy O'Brien – see Chapter 9 for more on her – writes in her book TRANCE Formation of America: The True Life Story of a CIA Slave: "Slaves of advancing age or with failed programming were sacrificially murdered at random in the wooded grounds of Bohemian Grove..." (though she does not provide evidence for this claim).

In his book The Franklin Cover-Up, which explores an alleged national child sex trafficking ring centered in Omaha, Nebraska, author John DeCamp tells of one alleged kidnapping victim who says he was forced to participate in the making of a snuff film in which another child was murdered. After the first edition of the book DeCamp identified the location as Bohemian Grove. This was said to have happened in 1984 or 1985.

To be sure, such charges of murder and human sacrifice remain unverified.

Alex Jones sums up the horrific spectacle: "This is not the Hollywood devil with red pajamas – this is the real deal, Babylon mystery religion-style."

Journalist Mark Walter Evans, an early critic of Bohemian Grove, makes this point about the ceremony and its symbolism: "The Masters of War at the Bohemian Grove are nasty customers, and all their works are evil. ... It would make sense to immolate caring, conscience and the consequences of their business transactions, lest they take responsibility for millions of souls around the globe whose lives have been affected by wars of Yankee Imperialism in the twentieth century."

What does the Bohemian Grove owl idol symbolize?

Some say the horns make it appear startlingly like the head of Baphomet, the goat-headed satyr-like figure that has been used in occult ceremonies and secret societies for a thousand years, deeply associated with occultism and dark magic. Often Baphomet is considered a representative of Satan. Indeed, Baphomet is the official symbol of the Church of Satan. The notorious British occultist Aleister Crowley, popularized as "the most evil man in the world," was known to fellow occultists by one of his nicknames: Baphomet.

If the Bohemian Grove owl is indeed representative of Baphomet, then the symbolic child sacrifice ceremony could be worship of Satan.

However, other researchers say the Bohemian Grove owl and/or the accompanying service most closely represent Moloch (sometimes spelled Molok, Molech or Molek), a monstrous ancient deity worshiped for centuries in Northern Africa and the Middle East. Moloch is normally portrayed as having the head of a bull, but the design of the statue and sacrificial altar resembles the altars of Moloch, and the sacrificial ceremonies and ritual sacrifice closely mimic those performed for Moloch.

Like the Bohemian Grove owl, Moloch demanded child sacrifices. Parents would sacrifice their children to this hideous thing to be burned alive – just like the child-effigy sacrificed in flames to the Bohemian Grove owl.

John Milton in Paradise Lost (1667) described sacrifices to Moloch that eerily mirror the Bohemian Grove ceremony:

> ...Moloch, horrid king, besmeared with blood
> Of human sacrifice, and parents' tears;
> Though, for the noise of drums and timbrels loud,
> Their children's cries unheard that passed through fire
> To his grim idol.

If the owl idol of Bohemian Grove is indeed Moloch, the annual ritual sacrifice is anti-biblical blasphemy on the level of a Satanic Black Mass, if one considers these Old Testament verses which denounce Moloch by name:

"Do not give any of your children to be sacrificed to Moloch, for you must not profane the name of your God. I am the Lord." (Leviticus 18:21)

"Say to the Israelites: 'Any Israelite or any alien living in Israel who gives any of his children to Moloch must be put to death. The people of the community are to stone him. I will set my face against that man and I will cut him off from his people; for by giving his children to Moloch, he has defiled my sanctuary and profaned my holy name." (Leviticus 20:2,3)

"So Solomon did evil in the eyes of the LORD ... On a hill east of Jerusalem, Solomon built a high place for Chemosh the detestable god of Moab, and for Moloch the detestable god of the Ammonites." (1 Kings 11:6,7)

Every Republican president since Calvin Coolidge (president 1923–1929) has attended Bohemian Grove. Nixon, Reagan and George W. Bush all attended shortly before winning their presidential races.

Here's a sampling of other prominent political, corporate, news media and cultural leaders believed to be or have been members or invited attendees: Henry Kissinger, Alan Greenspan, Arnold Schwarzenegger, James A. Baker III, William F. Buckley, Dick Cheney, Robert and Joseph Kennedy, Walter Cronkite, Franklin Murphy (Times Mirror CEO), Charles Scripps (Scripps-Howard newspaper chain), Tom Johnson (CNN president), Bing Crosby, John E. Dupont, Clint Eastwood, Barry Goldwater, Merv Griffin, Alexander

Haig, Charlton Heston, Jack Kemp, Colin Powell, David Rockefeller and Nelson Rockefeller (of course), Karl Rove, Donald Rumsfeld, Charles Schwab, Earl Warren (of the Warren Commission), Ray Kroc, Prince Bandar Bin Abdul Aziz, Mikhail Gorbachev, James Woolsey, William Randolph Hearst... and that's just a small sampling.

As we have seen with the Council on Foreign Relations, the Trilateral Commission, the Bilderberg Club, and others, the media moguls and star journalists who attend swear not to report what they witness; indeed, over the years, stories on Bohemian Grove scheduled to appear in major publications, including NPR, Time, and People have been quashed by Bohemian Grove-friendly media forces.

As Vanity Fair contributing editor Alex Shoumatoff, who briefly infiltrated the secretive Grove until discovered and arrested, puts it: "Over the years all the usual suspects have made appearances: Rumsfeld, Kissinger, two former CIA directors (including Papa Bush), the masters of war and the oilgarchs, the Bechtels and the Basses, the board members of top military contractors – such as Halliburton, Lockheed Martin, Northrop Grumman, and the Carlyle Group– Rockefellers, Morgans, captains of industry and CEOs across the spectrum of American capitalism. The interlocking corporate web – cemented by prep-school, college, and golf-club affiliations, blood, marriage, and mutual self-interest – that makes up the American ruling class.

"Many of the guys, in other words, who have been running the country into the ground and ripping us off for decades."

Although officially the aim of Bohemian Grove is relaxation and enjoyment of the arts, with deal-making prohibited or strongly discouraged, in reality, critics charge, domestic and foreign policy are inevitably discussed.

Indeed, the Washington Post notes that "in 1942... planning for the Manhattan Project took place at the Grove, leading to the creation of the atom bomb."

According to the Bohemian Grove Action Network, "At these gatherings men representing the government, military-industrial, and financial sectors meet and make major policy decisions."

The discussion and making of foreign policy in secret under such circumstances, particularly if private or classified information is discussed, is at the least, highly unethical, and arguably criminal. But as we have seen, it goes on at many of the ruling-elite confabs.

Officially, no women (except a small number of female cooks and maids, forced upon the Grove by federal anti-discrimination law) are allowed in this meeting of some of the most powerful political and economic leaders on the planet. In a country where ladies' nights at bars and nightclubs have been ruled illegal gender discrimination in some states, and where men-only clubs are picketed, outlawed and denounced as being sexist, America's ruling elites play by a different set of rules and standards, insulated, it would seem, by their wealth and power.

The deliberate exclusion of women has raised some eyebrows in other ways.

"Sometimes the homoerotic themes can get weird," one Bohemian Grove member told Vanity Fair's Shoumatoff. Many members perform skits in female clothing; some allegedly wear kilts with nothing underneath.

President Richard M. Nixon, who sometimes attended, vulgarly said (on the infamous Nixon tapes): "The Bohemian Grove – which I attend, from time to time – it is the most faggy goddamned thing you could ever imagine…"

Even the highly regarded mainstream publication Foreign Policy notes that the secretive nature of this occult gathering of the world's elite raises legitimate suspicions:

"Whether or not the club, founded in 1872, is an attempt by the Illuminati to steer global events, or just a gathering of powerful people doing rich people things, depends on your appetite for conspiracy. But though its existence has been acknowledged by club members, it's undeniably secretive, which makes it a bit suspect."

Of the rituals filmed by Alex Jones, Foreign Policy says: "it's hard to deny something bordering on the occult is taking place."

Bill Clinton has publicly denied he has ever attended Bohemian Grove, though according to some watchers, Bill did in fact attend in 1991 – the year before he became president, making him yet another commander-in-chief anointed by a visit to Bohemian Grove. If Bill did attend, denying it would hardly be the first lie he ever told.

Was this yet another Bohemian Grove crowning, as seems to have happened with Nixon, Reagan, and Bush? Given his known memberships and relationships in virtually every other New World Order world-control group, it is hard to imagine Bill Clinton could resist this one.

Regardless of whether Bill (and/or Hillary – after all, what is there to prevent her from slipping in disguised, if the elites wish?) ever attended, some of their closest associates, appointees and friends are verified members, among them Warren Christopher, secretary of state in Bill's first term; David Gergen, presidential adviser to Bill and longtime Clinton ally; Clinton adviser, confidant and fellow Trilateralist and Bilderberger Vernon Jordan; and of course Bill and Hillary's close personal friend and adviser, and annual Christmas companion, the infamous Henry Kissinger.

In August 2016, the whistleblower organization WikiLeaks released a batch of secret Hillary emails.

Among them was one from Lewis Amselem, a senior U.S. Foreign Service officer, at the time head of the U.S. delegation to the Organization of American States (OAS).

On August 29 2008, Amselem wrote Hillary:

"With fingers crossed, the old rabbit's foot out of the box in the attic, I will be sacrificing a chicken in the backyard to Moloch . . . "

An abrupt reference to Moloch in a mail from a senior U.S. Foreign Service officer to a U.S. secretary of state is... startling.

As journalist Baxter Dmitry put it, "Nobody randomly uses Moloch in a conversation. Most people don't even know what Moloch is."

That Amselem can refer to Moloch so casually in an email to Hillary, even if it is only in jest, shows at the very least what some might consider an unsettling familiarity among Hillary and her associates with this ancient idol of bloody human sacrifice.

Of course, there is also the chilling possibility, backed up by other chapters in this book, that this was no joke at all – that Amselem was simply reporting to his superior that he had made a bloody sacrifice to this ancient evil deity, and performed other ritual magic, in order to fulfill some unstated but foul and occult Hillary assignment.

That might not be as unlikely as it might sound. According to some journalists, Amselem is no stranger to human death and sacrifice. Journalist Jeremy Bigwood, who covered Central America civil wars while Amselem was stationed there, said Amselem "would put a positive spin on the extermination of a couple hundred thousand Guatemalan Indians. The guy should be sent to the International Criminal Court for abetting war crimes."

Doesn't sound like someone who would have a problem with sacrificing a chicken to win favor from Moloch...

And we are reminded, too, that Hillary is no stranger to ritual blood sacrifice. Indeed, it was the bloody sacrifice of a *chicken* – exactly what Amselem pledges to do – during a 1975 Haitian voodoo ceremony that marked the beginning of Hillary and Bill's sudden rise into political power. (See Chapter 2.)

Finally, one last startling public connection between Hillary, Bohemian Grove, and the power elite dream of one-world government.

In 1999, Bohemian Grove regular and world-famous CBS anchor Walter Cronkite appeared at the United Nations to accept the Norman Cousins Global Governance Award from the World Federalists Association, which, as you might gather from the name, has as its goal the creation of a world government, a world law, and the military might to enforce it.

Upon accepting the award, Cronkite, who for 19 years was a major shaper of the American citizenry's political opinions, made some startling pronouncements:

"It seems to many of us that if we are to avoid the eventual catastrophic world conflict we must strengthen the

United Nations as a first step toward a world government patterned after our own government with a legislature, executive and judiciary, and police to enforce its international laws and keep the peace.

"To do that, of course, we Americans will have to yield up some of our sovereignty. ... We need a system of enforceable world law – a democratic federal world government – to deal with world problems."

This and similar declarations were met with vigorous applause from the assembled globalists.

Near the end of his speech Cronkite noted that some people oppose the notion of world government as deeply and profoundly evil, even Satanic.

He then chuckled: "Join me, *I'm glad to sit here at the right hand of Satan.*"

Immediately after this remarkable speech, Hillary spoke to Cronkite and the World Federalists via video, congratulating Cronkite:

"Thank you for inspiring all of us... we are still listening to your every word... with your continuing leadership we can sail across these un-navigated seas into the 21st century – and there's no better captain I can imagine than you."

By the way, in our discussion above of the strange occult rites at Bohemian Grove we mention the (presumably) mock human sacrifice of children before a huge idol of a demonic owl creature.

Well, the voice of this terrifying child-eating monster, booming out via electric amplification to the rapt and cheering crowd of ruling elites, is none other than... Walter Cronkite.

Yes, Walter Cronkite, the beloved good gray newscaster, often cited as "the most trusted man in America" after being so named in a (rather dubious) opinion poll, was a red-blooded advocate of one-world government – and a key figure in (again, presumably) mock ritual child sacrifices and other occult rituals performed before a howling drunken crowd of the richest and most powerful men in the world.

Strange world, isn't it?

To borrow Cronkite's famous closing: "And that's the way it is."

CHAPTER FOURTEEN

Hillary's Disturbing Politics: Fascism, Communism, Terrorism, Statism, War Crimes and…?

"Hillary Clinton is a hardcore liberal." – OnTheIssues.com

"Clinton is staking out liberal positions to start the 2016 campaign." – Harry Enten, "Hillary Clinton Was Liberal. Hillary Clinton Is Liberal," FiveThirtyEight.com, May 19, 2015

"Hillary is a pragmatic progressive." – Vermont Governor Peter Shumlin.

"Clinton looks an awful lot like a mainstream progressive." – Jonathan Cohn, "Hillary Clinton Is A Progressive Democrat, Despite What You May Have Heard," Huffington Post, May 8, 2016

"…I guess she is not a progressive." – Bernie Sanders, TIME magazine, Feb. 2, 2016

"Hillary Clinton is a neoliberal building on the legacy of Ronald Reagan and Bill Clinton." – Benjamin Studebaker, "Why Bernie vs Hillary Matters More Than People Think," February 5, 2016

"Clinton is the conservative option … she's the clear conservative choice." – James Kirchick, "Hillary Clinton Is 2016's Real Conservative – Not Donald Trump," The Daily Beast, June 9, 2016

> "Hillary Clinton is ... closer to being a conventional Republican than Trump is." – Andrew O'Hehir, "After Trump, the deluge," Salon.com, May 4, 2016

> "In Thursday's debate Hillary Clinton showed how much she has become a neocon [neoconservative] true-believer." – Robert Parry, "Yes, Hillary is a Neocon," Consortium News, April 16, 2016

> "Hillary is a staunch neocon." – Jeffrey Sachs, "Hillary Is the Candidate of the War Machine," Huffington Post, February 5, 2016

> "She intends to fully support the two pillars of elite American imperialism: Transnational corporations and the military-industrial complex." – The Daily Bell, "No Liberal: Hillary Is Pro Multinational and Pro Military-Industrial Complex," July 14, 2016

> "What most energized Mrs. Clinton's speech were her populist attacks." – New York Times, May 27, 1993.

> "You know, I get accused of being kind of moderate and center. I plead guilty." – Hillary, September 10, 2015.

Right? Left? Center? Moderate? Populist? Neocon? Neolib?

Hillary's politics seem awfully hard for even seasoned political observers to pin down and label.

But if we are willing to step outside the conventional (and deeply flawed) left vs. right model of politics and peer behind the curtain a bit... we may be surprised at what we discover about Hillary's true political beliefs.

Hillary: A "Liberal Fascist" and "Theocrat" with "Totalitarian" Ideas

Conservative author and former National Review editor Jonah Goldberg's controversial book Liberal Fascism: The Totalitarian Temptation from Mussolini to Hillary Clinton argues that fascism as it emerged in the first half of the 20th century was a left-wing movement, connected significantly with America's turn of the century progressive movement.

Goldberg gives us a definition of fascism early in the book:

"Fascism is a religion of the state. It assumes the organic unity of the body politic and longs for a national leader attuned to the will of the people. It is totalitarian in that it views everything as political and holds that any action by the state is justified to achieve the common good. It takes responsibility for all aspects of life, including your health and well-being, and seeks to impose uniformity of thought and action whether by force or through regulation and social pressure. Everything, including the economy and religion must be aligned with its objectives. Any rivalry identity is part of the 'problem' and therefore defined as the enemy."

And Hillary, he says, is the very embodiment of, the leading spokesperson for, that modern fascist view in America.

"If [conservative/classical liberal commentators] Waldo Frank and J.T. Flynn were right that American fascism would be distinct from its European counterparts by virtue of its gentility and respectability, then Hillary Clinton is the fulfillment of their prophecy. But more than that, she is a representative figure, the leading member of a generational cohort of elite liberals who (unconsciously of course) brought fascist themes into mainstream liberalism. Specifically, she and her cohorts embody the maternal side of fascism – which is one reason why it is not more clearly recognized as such. *...Hillary and her friends [are] the leading proponents and exemplars of liberal fascism in our time.* (Emphasis added) ...

"The economic ideas in Hillary Clinton's It Takes a Village are breathlessly corporatist. ...the economic ideas of Bill and Hillary Clinton, John Kerry, Al Gore, and Robert Reich are deeply similar to the corporatist 'Third Way' ideologies that spawned fascist economics in the 1920s and 1930s. ...

"No more thorough explication of the liberal fascist agenda can be found than in Hillary Clinton's bestselling book, It Takes a Village. All the hallmarks of the fascist enterprise reside within its pages. Again, the language isn't hostile, nationalistic, racist, or aggressive. To the contrary, it brims with expressions of love and democratic fellow feeling. But this only detracts from its fascist nature if fascism itself means nothing more than hostile or aggressive (or racist and nationalistic). The fascistic nature of It Takes a Village begins with the very title."

As for Hillary's famous phrase "the politics of meaning," Goldberg says: "The politics of meaning is in many respects the most thoroughly totalitarian conception of politics offered by a leading American political figure in the last half century. ... at the most substantive level, the politics of meaning stands on Mussolini's shoulders. ...

"Hillary's vision holds that America suffers from a profound 'spiritual crisis' requiring the construction of a new man as part of a society-wide restoration and reconstruction effort leading to a new national community that will provide meaning and authenticity to every individual."

Indeed, the "politics of meaning" encompasses not only fascism but theocracy, Goldberg argues:

"The politics of meaning is ultimately a theocratic doctrine because it seeks to answer the fundamental questions about existence, argues that they can only be answered collectively, and insists that the state put those answers into practice. Under the politics of meaning, all of society's institutions are wrapped around the state like sticks around the fascist blade."

Goldberg also notes that "Hillary Clinton's writings on children show a clear, unapologetic, and principled desire to insert the state deep into family life – a goal that is in perfect accord with similar efforts by totalitarians of the past."

Goldberg further notes the fascist elements in Hillary's close mentor Saul Alinsky's thought: "...vast swaths of [Alinsky's] writings are indistinguishable from the fascist rhetoric of the 1920s and 1930s. His descriptions of the United States could have come from any street corner Brownshirt denouncing the corruption of the Weimar regime. His worldview is distinctly fascistic."

Incidentally, it's not just the right that notices more than a whiff of fascism around Hillary. Dr. Norman Pollack, a

Guggenheim Fellow, writing in the left-wing publication CounterPunch, September 5, 2016, describes Hillary as "fascistically inclined" with "contempt for working people and minorities" and having "chauvinistic militarism in [her] blood."

Leading Liberal Magazine:
Hillary Is No Liberal, She's a "Statist"
Who Is Hostile to Civil Liberties – And Could Send Critics to "Re-Education Camps"

The July 22, 1999 issue of The Nation – America's leading journal of liberal-left politics since the early twentieth century – featured a scathing article entitled "Hillary's No Liberal" by author, feminist, lawyer and ACLU board member Wendy Kaminer.

Kaminer's article dynamites the idea that Hillary is any kind of tolerant civil liberties-oriented liberal. Instead, Kaminer says, Hillary is first and foremost a "statist": indifferent – if not downright hostile – towards liberty.

Kaminer writes that Hillary has "little regard for civil liberties, especially free speech. ...*Clinton, I suspect would commit her critics to re-education camps.* (Emphasis added.)

"She has no apparent concern for freedom of speech on the Internet. The Clinton Administration has championed clearly unconstitutional restrictions on online speech, such as the now-defunct Communications Decency Act and its successor, the Child On Line Protection Act, currently being challenged in federal court. ...

"She spouts the subtly repressive principles and platitudes of communitarianism, envisioning a majoritarian society in which collective concerns almost always prevail over individual rights. ...

"Clinton seems likely to sacrifice rights – like freedom from religion – to her notion of social goods. ... [She exhibits] the sanctimony of people who believe they know what's best for the rest of us – less liberty, more order and values imposed by the state or our neighbors. ...

"...her liberalism...tends to take the form of statism. She is a statist first and a feminist only half-formed -- sympathetic to women's demands for civil rights but often indifferent if not hostile to liberty."

Echoes of Tyranny in Hillary's "It Takes a Village"

After their controversial White House experiments, which some deem occult in nature (see Chapter 3), the mystic Jean Houston would go on to help Hillary write her highly contentious 1996 book It Takes a Village: And Other Lessons Children Teach Us.

The title of that book ostensibly comes from an African proverb, though no proverb of that exact wording has been found.

However, some have noticed that the phrase "it takes a village to raise a child" rather eerily parallels sayings attributed to the worst dictators of the twentieth century:

> "When an opponent declares, 'I will not come over to your side,' I calmly say, 'Your child belongs to us already. . . . What are you? You will pass on. Your descendants, however, now stand in the new camp. In a short time they will know nothing else but this new community.'" – Adolph Hitler, November 6, 1933.
>
> "This new Reich will give its youth to no one, but will itself take youth and give to youth its own education and its own upbringing." – Adolph Hitler, May 1, 1937.
>
> "Chairman Mao is your new father and mother." – allegedly printed in school textbooks in communist China after Mao's revolution, which eventually took the lives of as many as 50 million people.
>
> "Give me four years to teach the children, and the seed I have sown will never be uprooted." – attributed to Lenin.

There is no missing the authoritarian tone of Hillary's views on education, or her elevation of the state over the child and family, which matches the statism found in all of her political positions.

As the distinguished historian and social critic Christopher Lasch wrote of Hillary in the October, 1992 issue of Harper's Magazine: "her writings leave the unmistakable impression that it is the family that holds children back, the state that sets them free."

Hillary's Early Days: Seduced by Radical Politics in the Guise of Theology

Hillary's militant, statist radicalism may have taken root, strangely enough, in her early days as... a Methodist youth.

As Jonah Goldberg notes in Liberal Fascism, "religious leaders in the 'mainline' churches were seduced by radical politics. The Methodist youth magazine 'motive' – a major influence on the young Hillary Clinton – featured a birthday card to Ho Chi Minh in one issue... 'motive' was an indisputably radical left-wing organ..."

Rev. Donald Jones, her youth minister and mentor, bought Hillary a subscription to "motive" (the title was lowercase) and it was a major influence on her early life. "I still have every issue they sent me," she told Newsweek in 1994.

Among the writers who appeared in "motive" were Playboy's Hugh Hefner, future Trilateral Commission founder Zbigniew Brzezinski, and radical labor leader and left-wing political activist Sidney Lens. The magazine's letter section was called "The Picket Line."

Jonah Goldberg notes that Rev. Jones was "a radical pastor who eventually lost his ministry for being too political." Indeed, Rev. Jones took his youth group, including Hillary, to meet with the notorious radical organizer Saul Alinsky, who became another major influence on Hillary as discussed elsewhere in this book.

According to Barbara Olson's Hell to Pay: The Unfolding Story of Hillary Rodham Clinton, Rev. Jones "drew explicit parallels between the utopia of Karl Marx and the heavenly kingdom."

The New York Times noted that "Dr. Jones's methods proved controversial in Park Ridge, and he resigned his minister post after two years." But his influence on young Hillary had already taken hold, and would last throughout her life.

According to the Boston University School of Theology, "motive" ceased publication in 1972 when the Methodist Church stripped it of funding because its overt radicalism "became more than [the denomination] could take."

The final issue of "motive" ended with a lengthy list of addresses of organizations for its young Methodist readers to contact, among them "Sodom Radical Bisexual Free Communist Youth" in Hayward, California and the "Psychedelic Venus Church" in Berkeley.

Hillary's Communist Summer Internship

While at Yale Law School, Hillary Clinton spent the summer of 1971 interning as a law clerk at the firm Treuhaft, Walker and Burnstein, which had a reputation as one of the most radical law firms in America.

The head of the firm, Robert Treuhaft, was a former active member of the American Communist Party. During the House Un-American Activities Committee hearings in the 1950s, Treuhaft was described as one of the 39 most "dangerously subversive" lawyers in America.

Treuhaft and his wife Jessica Mitford left the Communist Party in 1958, long before Hillary started her internship with the firm. Treuhaft and Mitford remained ideologically communists, however. They simply felt the CPUSA was no longer a viable vehicle for creating a communist America.

Indeed, Treuhaft and Mitford were known to sing the Internationale, the international anthem of communism, long after leaving the CPUSA.

"Anyone who went to college or law school would have known our law firm was a communist law firm," Treuhaft told journalist Gail Sheehy in 1999.

Mary Nichols, who worked as a clerk at the firm the summer before Hillary arrived, said Treuhaft "was proud of having been a communist at one time. This was not something that they hid in any way."

The New York Sun further notes: "Indeed, those at the firm assumed that reputation [as a left-wing, radical, 'Movement' law firm] drew [Hillary] in."

Not all of the partners of the firm had abandoned the Communist Party USA. Doris Walker was a Party member at the time Hillary interned. Walker was asked by the Party to defend Communist revolutionary Angela Davis against charges of murder, kidnapping and conspiracy stemming from a 1970 shootout "I was asked by the Party to participate in Angela's case," Walker told the Sun. (Walker claims no one else at the law firm, including the young Hillary, worked on the Angela Davis case.)

In his 2004 book on Hillary, Rewriting History, Dick Morris – who served as Bill Clinton's political consultant for twenty years, guiding him to a successful reelection in 1996 – states for the record that he doesn't believe Hillary is a communist. However, he notes:

"But the fact that she chose this job out of all the summer jobs that might have been available, traveling 3,000 miles for it, tells something about her orientation at the time. Just as the fact that she does not describe the firm's work or reputation says something about her today."

In her book Hell to Pay: The Unfolding Story of Hillary Rodham Clinton, Department of Justice prosecutor and New York Times bestselling journalist Barbara Olson wrote:

"Hillary has never repudiated her connection with the communist movement in America or explained her relationship with two of its leading adherents. Of course, no one has pursued these questions with Hillary. She has shown she will not answer hard questions about her past, and she has learned that she does not need to – remarkable in an age when political figures are allowed such little privacy."

Post-College Radicalism

As described in Chapter 13, from 1982 to 1988 Hillary was on the board of the New World Foundation; she was head of the organization in 1987 and 1988.

During Hillary's time with the Foundation, it gave money to controversial left-wing organizations that some critics say had links to Marxism or terrorism.

Pardoning Violent U.S. Communist Terrorists

The Weather Underground was a domestic communist terrorist group, formed in 1969, that set off bombs across America in a years-long attempt to launch a violent communist revolution in the U.S. In a signed statement the Weather Underground declared their goal to be "the achievement of a classless world: World communism" and to "achieve the dictatorship of the proletariat."

As they wrote in their 1974 manifesto Prairie Fire: The Politics of Revolutionary Anti-Imperialism (which they dedicated to, among others, Robert F. Kennedy's convicted killer Sirhan Sirhan):

"We are a guerrilla organization. We are communist women and men... The only path to the final defeat of imperialism and the building of socialism is revolutionary war. ...

"Revolutionary war will be complicated and protracted. It includes mass struggle and clandestine struggle, peaceful and violent, political and economic, cultural and military, where all forms are developed in harmony with the armed struggle. Without mass struggle there can be no revolution. Without armed struggle there can be no victory."

To this end the Weather Underground conducted a literal guerrilla war against the U.S. government. Beginning in 1970, and continuing for years, the Weather Underground set off hundreds, possibly thousands, of bombs across America and made perhaps thousands of bomb threats. Among the buildings bombed: the U.S. Capitol, the Pentagon, the State Department, police stations. Weather Underground members are known to have killed two police officers and a Brinks guard, are suspected in other unsolved murders, and made plans to kill high-ranking government and military leaders.

According to the conservative New American magazine: "[T]he Weather Underground received funds, training, weapons, false identification documents, passports, safe houses, and other assistance from our enemies: the communist governments of China and the Soviet Union, as well as their minions – Cuba, East Germany, North Vietnam, Czechoslovakia, and North Korea. We know this from the many admissions of Weathermen in their own writings and interviews, as well as from defectors and the numerous documents released by the FBI of intercepted communications, surveillance photos, testimony of undercover operatives, and captured records."

The conservative media watchdog organization Accuracy in Media (AIM) says "The group received terrorist training in Communist Cuba and was advised by Soviet and Cuban intelligence agents."

The New American also claims that the Weathermen may have been responsible for "Hundreds of bombings... dozens killed, and millions terrorized by their tens of thousands of bombing threats."

Some of the bombs that failed to explode as planned seemed intended to kill hundreds of people. Harvey Klehr, the Andrew W. Mellon professor of politics and history at Emory University in Atlanta, told the New York Times in 2003, "The only reason they were not guilty of mass murder is mere incompetence. I don't know what sort of defense that is."

At a "War Council" public gathering of radicals in 1969, Weather Underground leader Bernardine Dohrn praised and congratulated the Manson Family for their infamous murders – including the eight-months pregnant Sharon Tate and her unborn child.

Said Dohrn, admiringly: "Dig it! First they killed those pigs, then they ate dinner in the same room with them. Then they even shoved a fork into the victim's stomach. Wild!"

Indeed, Dohrn and fellow Weather Underground radicals so admired the Manson murders that they sometimes greeted each other with their fingers spread wide – symbolizing the fork stabbed into Sharon Tate's womb.

At the same 1969 "War Council" Weatherman John Jacobs declared, "We're against everything that's 'good and decent' in honky America. We will loot and burn and destroy. We are the incubation of your mothers' nightmares."

In 1970 Dohrn said: "We've known that our job is to lead white kids into armed revolution. ... Revolutionary violence is the only way."

(In a surreal twist, after an unrepentant Dohrn was released from prison, she went on to teach law at Northwestern University and direct that institution's Children and Family Justice Center, thus becoming... an advocate for the legal needs of children and adolescents. Presumably she didn't greet her new clients and colleagues with her old forked-hand gesture.)

Dohrn's husband Bill Ayers, a Weather Underground founder and later colleague of President Obama, reportedly described the group's aim as "Kill all the rich people. Break up their cars and apartments. Bring the revolution home, kill your parents. That's where it's really at."

FBI undercover operative Larry Grathwohl – described by TIME magazine as "the only FBI informant known to have successfully penetrated the Weather Underground" – reported a meeting in which the Weather Underground discussed their plans for the new communist America they were working to create. After their successful revolution, Grathwohl said, they planned to rule America and, with the help of the Cuban, Chinese, Russian, and North Vietnamese communist governments, execute 25 million Americans in concentration camps, modeled after similar communist "re-education" camps in Vietnam, Cambodia, Laos, and elsewhere.

Ah, the peace and love sixties. Guess you had to be there...

The Clintons and the Weather Underground

The above background is necessary to grasp the significance of the Clinton connection with the Weather Underground.

On January 20 2001, his last day in office, President Bill Clinton unexpectedly pardoned Weather Underground terrorists Susan L. Rosenberg and Linda Evans.

Evans had been sentenced in 1987 to 40 years in prison for purchasing firearms using a false identification and for harboring Marilyn Jean Buck, a fugitive in a 1981 Brinks armored truck robbery, in which two police officers and a guard were murdered. In 1990 she was sentenced to five years in prison for conspiracy and malicious destruction in connection with eight bombings – including the U. S. Capitol – in the 1980s.

Rosenberg was arrested in 1984 while unloading 740 pounds of explosives, which she said she intended to give to others for terrorist bombings, and for possessing weapons including a submachine gun, along with evidence of plans to attack the U.S. Capitol Building, the National War College, the Navy Yard Computer Center, the Navy Yard Officers Club, Israeli Aircraft Industries, the FBI and the New York Patrolman's Benevolent Association. She was suspected of involvement in other crimes, including bank robberies and the highly publicized 1981 Brinks robbery that left a guard and two police officers dead. She was sentenced to 58 years in prison.

These two Weather Underground terrorists' pardons were widely denounced by leading political figures including New York Mayor Rudolph W. Giuliani, U.S. Senator Charles E. Schumer (D-NY), and Bernard B. Kerik, New York City's police commissioner.

"She [Rosenberg] was convicted of having in her possession 740 pounds of explosives, a submachine gun, weapons," Mayor Giuliani told the New York Times at the time of the pardon. "She admitted she had these weapons to give to someone to use in a bombing, and she had been involved in a significant number of robberies, bank robberies."

Hillary publicly stated her disagreement with some of President Clinton's long list of controversial pardons at the end of his second term – but not these.

Rosenberg's lawyer Howard Gutman was a friend of Bill

and Hillary, as well as a Bill Clinton donor and Democratic fundraiser and activist (and later donor to Hillary's presidential runs).

After Hillary became secretary of state, President Obama, for whom Gutman had raised over $750,000, appointed Gutman U.S. ambassador to Belgium.

The Mainstreaming of the Weather Underground Terrorists?

After Clinton's pardons, Weather Underground terrorists moved into mainstream politics.

Linda Evans received a criminal justice fellowship from the Open Society Institute, funded by the billionaire progressive Clinton supporter George Soros. She began working to restore civil rights to felons.

Susan Rosenberg continued to work as an anti-prison activist.

Four former Weather Underground terrorists – founder Bill Ayers and Bernardine Dohrn, Mark Rudd, and Jeff Jones – began working through an organization called "Movement for a Democratic Society," affiliated with the newly revived Students for a Democratic Society (SDS); Movement for a Democratic Society in turn spun off "Progressives for Obama" which raised money and recruited activists for Obama.

"Guilty as hell, free as a bird – America is a great country!" Ayers laughingly told conservative journalist David Horowitz years later. Other Weather Underground terrorists, including the two pardoned by Bill Clinton, could have said the same.

Pardoning Yet More Communist Terrorists

On August 11, 1999 President Clinton pardoned 16 members of the FALN, a Puerto Rican Marxist-Leninist terrorist organization that sought to make Puerto Rico a communist dictatorship and promoted "clandestine armed struggles" against the United States.

The FALN was responsible for over 130 bombings that killed six people and injured dozens more in the U.S. Their bombings included the New York office of the FBI, military recruiting headquarters, and former President Jimmy Carter's Chicago campaign office.

The sixteen Clinton pardoned had been convicted for conspiracy to commit robbery, conspiracy bomb-making, and sedition, as well as for firearms and explosives violations. (None had been convicted of personally harming or killing anyone.) Some were believed to be preparing to rob an armored car when arrested; three were believed by the FBI to be preparing to bomb military facilities in Chicago. At one point a group affiliated with the Weather Underground attempted to help some of them escape prison.

These pardons were opposed by the U.S. Attorney's Office, the FBI, and the Federal Bureau of Prisons, and were criticized by former victims of FALN terrorism and the Fraternal Order of Police.

President Clinton refused requests by Congress for documents relating to his decision to offer clemency to the FALN terrorists, citing executive privilege. Congress condemned the pardons, with votes of 95-2 in the Senate and 311-41 in the House.

Hillary at first publicly supported the pardons. She did, however, say she had "no involvement in or prior knowledge of the decision."

Of this denial, longtime Clinton operative turned critic Dick Morris laughs: "Her statement is ridiculous. Two days before the announcement of the pardons, New York City Councilman Jose Rivera personally presented Hillary with a packet of materials including a letter asking her to 'speak to the president and ask him to consider granting executive clemency to the prisoners.' What a coincidence – the sentences were immediately commuted!"

It was widely believed that Bill pardoned the FALN terrorists because he thought doing so would increase support among New York's large Puerto Rican community for Hillary's upcoming race for U.S. senator from New York.

As outrage mounted, Hillary reversed her support of the pardons, but only because, according to Hillary spokespersons, the prisoners had waited too long to accept one of the conditions for the pardon – the renunciation of any future violent activity.

Still More Terrorist-Related Pardons from President Clinton

The pardons of wealthy felon billionaires Marc Rich and Pincus Green – who violated U.S. law by trading with terrorist and rogue states and who were hiding from U.S. arrest when President Bill Clinton pardoned them – caused special outrage among U.S. political, law enforcement, and media figures.

The U.S. House Committee on Government Reform issued a scathing critical report on the pardons entitled "Justice Undone: Clemency Decisions in the Clinton White House" on March 14, 2002.

Excerpts:

"Marc Rich and Pincus Green have a history of illegal and corrupt business dealings contrary to the security interests of the United States. ... Rich and Green have had extensive trade with terrorist states and other enemies of the United States. Despite clear legal restrictions on such trade, Rich and Green have engaged in commodities trading with Iraq, Iran, Cuba, and other rogue states which have sponsored terrorist acts. By engaging in these activities, Marc Rich and Pincus Green demonstrated contempt for American laws, as well as the well-being of Americans who were harmed or threatened by these states. ...

"Because of the strength of the case against them, Marc Rich and Pincus Green fled the country rather than face trial. Rich's own lawyer told him that by fleeing the country, Rich had 'spit on the American flag' and that 'whatever you get, you deserve.' For the 17 years leading up to his pardon, Marc Rich was one of America's 10 most wanted international fugitives. ..."

"Rich and Green's crimes were so serious that for seventeen years, the U.S. government devoted considerable resources to apprehending them and closing down their business activities."

Even longtime Clinton friends, associates and supporters condemned these pardons, including former President Jimmy Carter (who denounced the pardons as "disgraceful," Clinton strategist James Carville (leader of Clinton's 1992 campaign) and Terry McAuliffe (co-chairman of Clinton's 1996 re-election campaign and chairman of Hillary's 2008 presidential campaign).

Amidst this national firestorm of protest, Hillary denied knowing anything about the Rich and Green pardons or why Bill had granted them.

The pardon certainly had a big pay-off financially for both Bill and Hillary, coincidentally or not. Journalist Peter Schweizer – author of Clinton Cash: The Untold Story of How and Why Foreign Governments and Businesses Helped Make Bill and Hillary Rich – noted in the New York Post that, prior to the pardon, Rich's ex-wife Denise donated $450,000 to the fledgling Clinton Library and over $1 million to various Democratic campaigns.

And since the pardon, Schweizer notes, Rich's "business partners, lawyers, advisers and friends have showered millions of dollars on the Clintons in the decade and a half following the scandal."

Hillary and the Clinton Foundation: Helping the Russians Acquire Uranium?

In July 2015 international news magazine The Week noted disturbing indications that the Clinton Foundation helped arrange the sale of American uranium mines to the Russian government – and Hillary as secretary of state authorized the deal to make it legal:

"In 2005 … Canadian mining magnate Frank Giustra joined Bill Clinton on a trip to Kazakhstan. There, Giustra and Clinton dined with the country's dictatorial president, Nursultan Nazarbayev. Within days, Giustra acquired uranium interests in Kazakhstan that he later turned into a financial bonanza. The next year, he donated $31 million to the [Clinton] Foundation. Eventually, Giustra sold off his uranium company to Russia's nuclear agency, Rosatom. The sale included some American uranium mines, which meant Hillary Clinton, by then secretary of state, was one of the people who had to sign off on the deal."

Bill received a whopping $500,000 for a Moscow speech from a Russian investment bank with links to the Kremlin that was promoting Uranium One stock – one of the largest amounts he had ever received for a speech. The New York Times noted that the audience for his speech included "leading Russian officials" and a Russian government news service reported that Russian president Vladimir Putin personally thanked Bill for his speech.

A headline in an April 23, 2015 New York Times story nicely summed it up: "Cash Flowed to Clinton Foundation Amid Russian Uranium Deal."

This deal made Russia one of the world's largest uranium suppliers. Because the U.S. produces only a small amount of the uranium it needs for nuclear energy (which supplies 20 percent of U.S. electrical needs), some critics claim this deal threatens to make the U.S. (and possibly Europe) energy dependent upon Russia.

Furthermore, thanks to this deal, the Russians – who have thousands of nuclear weapons and are producing new ones – now control one-fifth of all uranium production capacity *in the United States.*

Hillary: Helping Arm Terrorists, Despots and Authoritarian Regimes?

The State Department is supposed to consider human rights records when deciding whether to permit foreign governments to purchase military equipment from American companies. Algeria is classified as an authoritarian regime by the Democracy Index, a project of The Economist Magazine that attempts to rank countries by the amount of democratic freedom they offer. Hillary Clinton's own State Department in its 2010 Human Rights Report denounced Algeria's government for imposing "restrictions on freedom of assembly and association" … "arbitrary killing" … "widespread corruption" ... "lack of judicial independence" and other abuses.

Yet, shortly after a $500,000 donation to the Clinton Foundation, Algeria received permission to import military weapons including deadly chemical and biological substances – a deal that shocked many observers as unethical.

According to The Week: "The Clinton Foundation boasts a lengthy list of foreign donors. Under an ethics agreement Hillary Clinton made with the Obama administration, that cash flow was allowed to continue while she served as secretary of state, as long as donations were properly reported – a condition that was not met. One gift not reported was a $500,000 donation from Algeria. Shortly thereafter, the Algerians won a 70 percent boost in military export authorizations for items including chemical and biological agents."

According to International Business Times: "...the Algerian government donated $500,000 to the Clinton Foundation and its lobbyists met with the State Department officials who oversee enforcement of human rights policies. Clinton's State Department the next year approved a one-year 70 percent increase in military export authorizations to the country. The increase included authorizations of almost 50,000 items classified as 'toxicological agents, including chemical agents, biological agents and associated equipment' after the State Department did not authorize the export of any of such items to Algeria in the prior year.

"During Clinton's tenure, the State Department authorized at least $2.4 billion of direct military hardware and services sales to Algeria – nearly triple such authorizations over the last full fiscal years during the Bush administration. The Clinton Foundation did not disclose Algeria's donation until this year – a violation of the ethics agreement it entered into with the Obama administration."

An article in The Hill portrayed the Algerian deal as part of a bigger possible scandal: "The State Department under Hillary Clinton authorized arms sales to countries that had donated millions of dollars to the Clinton Foundation, according to a new report. ... The Clinton Foundation received between $54 million and $141 million in donations from the foreign governments and defense contractors involved in those sales..."

The Hill article continues: The State Department "approved $165 billion worth of weapons sales to 20 foreign governments during Clinton's tenure, the International Business Times reports. Among the countries involved in the sales were Algeria, Bahrain, Kuwait, Oman, Qatar, Saudi Arabia and the United Arab Emirates."

More from International Business Times: "The State Department formally approved these arms sales even as many of the deals enhanced the military power of countries ruled by authoritarian regimes whose human rights abuses had been criticized by the department. Algeria, Saudi Arabia, Kuwait, the United Arab Emirates, Oman and Qatar all donated to the Clinton Foundation and also gained State Department clearance to buy caches of American-made weapons even as the department singled them out for a range of alleged ills, from corruption to restrictions on civil liberties to violent crackdowns against political opponents."

Indeed, Hillary's own State Department in 2010 expressed concern about such problems in Saudi Arabia as "torture and physical abuse ... arbitrary arrest and incommunicado detention; denial of fair and public trials ... restrictions on civil liberties ... Violence against women and a lack of equal rights for women ... trafficking in persons..." and much more. The weapons aid the regime in these atrocities.

Incredibly, some of these nations that Hillary was allowing to purchase billions of dollars' worth of weapons were, at the same time, being criticized by Hillary herself, and by Hillary's own Department of State, as failing to clamp down on terrorist funding and terrorist activities within their borders. This led the State Department to view them as threats to the United States and its allies.

In short, there is the appearance, at least, that, in exchange for huge donations to her Clinton Foundation, Secretary of State Hillary Clinton allowed repressive authoritarian regimes – including regimes considered to be potential terrorist threats to the United States because of their failure to clamp down on terrorist funding and activities within their borders – to purchase weapons that could be used against their neighbors and to oppress their own people.

Hillary: Friend of Tyrants and Despots Around the World

On March 10, 2016 renowned liberal investigative journalist Glenn Greenwald described Hillary as, to quote the title to his article, a "Stalwart Friend of [the] World's Worst Despots."

Among her despotic friends:

- Egyptian tyrant Hosni Mubarak: "I really consider president and Mrs. Mubarak to be friends of my family," said Hillary in 2009.

- Syrian president Bashar al-Assad: "Many of the members of Congress of both parties who have gone to Syria in recent months have said they believe he's a reformer." – Hillary on "Face the Nation," 2011.

- King Abdullah of Saudi Arabia: "Hillary and I are saddened by the passing of His Majesty Abdullah bin Abdulaziz. I had many dealings with His Majesty during and after my presidency, as did Hillary both inside and outside the State Department... Hillary and I are also grateful for his personal friendship and kindness toward our family..." – joint statement by Bill and Hillary Clinton on the death of King Abdullah, January 23, 2015.

  In 2008 Parade magazine listed Hillary's "personal friend" King Abdullah as one of the "World's Worst Dictators." Also in 2008 About.com listed him among "The 5 Worst Dictators in Asia," noting that "Saudi citizens live under a strict Wahhabist interpretation of Sharia law, which mandates amputation of hands as a punishment for theft and floggings for crimes like drunkenness. Execution by public beheading is common for murder, rape, drug trafficking, and witchcraft. Women have almost no rights – they can't work, vote, or drive a car. Women are forbidden from appearing in public without a male relative, and rape victims are often punished as harshly as the perpetrators. Religious freedom is non-existent..."

- Other Arab tyrannies: Writes Greenwald: "Algeria, Saudi Arabia, Kuwait, the United Arab Emirates, Oman, and Qatar all donated to the Clinton Foundation and also gained State Department clearance to buy caches of American-made weapons even as the Department singled them out for a range of alleged ills, from corruption to restrictions on civil liberties to violent crackdowns against political opponents."

- Arch-war criminal Henry Kissinger, responsible for perhaps 3-4 million or more deaths around the globe: "Kissinger is a friend ... [I] relied on his counsel ... [he] checked in with me regularly, sharing astute observations about foreign leaders..."; and "I was very flattered when Henry Kissinger said I ran the State Department better than anybody had run it in a long time." – Hillary Clinton February 4, 2016.

    Regarding the widely reviled Kissinger, it should be noted that his relationship with the Clintons is far more personal and friendly than Hillary lets on. Journalist David Corn of Mother Jones pointed out that the Clintons and the Kissingers have for years spent their winter holidays together at the tony Dominican Republic beach front villa of fashion designer Oscar de la Renta (who died in 2014) and his wife, Annette. Guests joining them have included fellow Council on Foreign Relations members Barbara Walters and Charlie Rose. (Yes, it's a small world for America's elite.)

Reportedly it was during this annual vacation, around Christmas 2014, that Hillary decided to run again for president.

Final Note: Is Raising Such Issues Fair to Hillary?

For those concerned that raising unresolved issues of Hillary's past communist, radical, authoritarian, statist, dictatorial and possible terrorist associations is somehow unfair, we must turn to an argument made strongly by... Hillary herself.

During her 2008 presidential campaign, Hillary forthrightly attacked then-Senator Barack Obama for his allegedly close connections to Bill Ayers, the former member of the Weather Underground domestic terrorist group, who set off bombs across America and conspired to murder 25 million Americans in communist death camps on American soil (see earlier in this chapter).

Hillary said during one speech, "What they [the Weather Underground] did was set bombs. And in some instances, people died. So it is – I think it is, again, an issue that people will be asking about."

Obama responded: "By Senator Clinton's own vetting standards, I don't think she would make it, since President Clinton pardoned or commuted the sentences of two members of the Weather Underground, which I think is a slightly more significant act."

By Hillary's own 2008 words, then, it is not only completely legitimate but vitally important that Americans closely examine and consider Hillary's communist, fascist, radical, terrorist, conspiratorial and other unsavory connections – and yes, that includes even allegations of occult, reptilian, alien and demonic connections.

CHAPTER FIFTEEN

Hillary Is Coming for Your Guns

"Certainly one of the chief guarantees of freedom under any government, no matter how popular and respected, is the right of citizens to keep and bear arms. ...the right of citizens to bear arms is just one more guarantee against arbitrary government, one more safeguard against the tyranny which now appears remote in America, but which historically has proved to be always possible." – U.S. Senator (later Vice President) Hubert Humphrey, Feb. 1960

"All too many of the...great tragedies of history — Stalin's atrocities, the killing fields of Cambodia, the Holocaust, to name but a few — were perpetrated by armed troops against unarmed populations. Many could well have been avoided or mitigated, had the perpetrators known their intended victims were equipped with a rifle and twenty bullets apiece.... If a few hundred Jewish fighters in the Warsaw Ghetto could hold off the Wehrmacht for almost a month with only a handful of weapons, six million Jews armed with rifles could not so easily have been herded into cattle cars. ...

"The Second Amendment is a doomsday provision, one designed for those exceptionally rare circumstances where all other rights have failed — where the government refuses to stand for reelection and silences those who protest; where courts have lost the courage to oppose, or can find no one to enforce their decrees.

"However improbable these contingencies may seem today, facing them unprepared is a mistake a free people get to make only once."

– Judge Alex Kozinski, United States Court of Appeals for the Ninth Circuit, dissenting opinion,
Silveira v. Lockyer (2002)

In the landmark 2008 case District of Columbia v. Heller, the Supreme Court of the United States ruled that the Second Amendment is "premised on the private use of arms for activities such as hunting and self-defense, the latter being understood as resistance to either private lawlessness or *the depredations of a tyrannical government...*" (Emphasis added.)

If Hillary becomes president she will be commander-in-chief of a massive world-wide global military superpower, the most powerful military in all history.

Yet she has throughout her political career supported disarming honest, law-abiding Americans of the weapons that would enable the American people to defend themselves against that very army should Hillary or any other president attempt to use it to foist a tyranny upon America.

Further, while Hillary herself is constantly protected by heavily armed and highly trained professionals, she favors taking guns away from honest Americans, or otherwise restricting access to them, leaving them unarmed and at the mercy of criminals and government tyranny.

Hillary's Years of Anti-Gun Positions

From the website of the nonpartisan, nonprofit organization On The Issues, which provides information to voters about candidates, here are some of the positions on gun restrictions Hillary has taken since the mid-1990s (the wording is theirs):

- Support Brady Bill and closing the Charleston loophole. (Dec 2015)
- Reversal of gun manufacturer immunity; let them get sued. (Nov 2015)
- Don't shield gun manufacturers from lawsuits (Oct 2015)
- Rein in idea that anybody can have a gun anywhere, anytime. (May 2014)
- Advocate for national gun registry, 2000; backed off, 2008.

- Balance lawful gun ownership and keeping guns from criminals. (Apr 2008)
- Give local police access to federal gun tracking info. (Apr 2008)
- Let states & cities determine local gun laws. (Apr 2008)
- Against illegal guns, crack down on illegal gun dealers. (Jan 2008)
- Backed off a national licensing registration plan on guns. (Jan 2008)
- Get assault weapons & guns off the street. (Jul 2007)
- Background check system could prevent Virginia Tech massacre. (Apr 2007)
- Congress' failure at Littleton [Columbine High School shooting] response inspired Senate run. (Nov 2003)
- Keep guns away from people who shouldn't have them. (Sept 2000)
- Limit access to weapons; look for early warning signs. (Sept 2000)
- License and register all handgun sales. (Jun 2000)
- Tough gun control keeps guns out of wrong hands. (Jul 1999)
- Gun control protects our children. (Jul 1999)
- Don't water down sensible gun control legislation. (Jul 1999)
- Lock up guns; store ammo separately. (Jun 1999)
- Ban kids' unsupervised access to guns. (Jun 1999)
- Get weapons off the streets; zero tolerance for weapons. (Sept 1996)

- Voted NO on prohibiting lawsuits against gun manufacturers. (Jul 2005)
- Voted NO on banning lawsuits against gun manufacturers for gun violence. (Mar 2004)
- Prevent unauthorized firearm use with "smart gun" technology. (Aug 2000)

Hillary: Put American Citizens on Secret Watch Lists to Deny Them Their Constitutional Rights

In 2015 Hillary supported restricting American citizens on the highly controversial federal "no-fly" list from purchasing firearms.

"If you're too dangerous to get on a plane, you are too dangerous to buy a gun in America," Hillary declared.

Hillary thus favors denying people the right to exercise a constitutionally protected right because they have been, without explanation, without due process, placed on a federal list of dubious constitutionality – a list that restricts the freedom of some Americans because the government – without evidence, without anything more than a mere hunch – suspects they might commit a crime.

The ACLU explains why this is an outrage:

"The U.S. government maintains a massive watchlist system that risks stigmatizing hundreds of thousands of people –including U.S. citizens – as terrorism suspects based on vague, overbroad, and often secret standards and evidence.

"The consequences of being placed on a government watchlist can be far-reaching. They can include questioning, harassment, or detention by authorities, or even an indefinite ban on air travel.

"And while the government keeps the evidence it uses to blacklist people in this manner secret, government watchdogs have found that as many as 35 percent of the nominations to the network of watchlists are outdated and tens of thousands of names were placed on lists without an adequate factual basis.

"To make matters worse, the government denies watchlisted individuals any meaningful way to correct errors and clear their names. ...

"A bloated, opaque watchlisting system is neither fair nor effective. A system in which innocent people languish on blacklists indefinitely, with their rights curtailed and their names sullied, is at odds with our Constitution and values."

ACLU National Security Project director Hina Shamsi sums it up: "The standards for inclusion on the No Fly List are unconstitutionally vague, and innocent people are blacklisted without a fair process to correct government error."

In President Hillary's world, bedrock Bill of Rights freedoms will be taken away from American citizens by the federal government in secret, in secret courts, on what amounts to a mere whim, with no chance for them to find out why or challenge the process.

It is a nightmare vision of government. Such practices turn our legal system – where you are supposedly innocent until proven guilty – upside down. In fact, it is even worse than that, because you do not even have access to a process to prove your innocence.

Throughout their political careers, the Clintons have been accused of using private and government power to harass their critics. Imagine if the Clintons had the power to place someone on vague federal watchlists and deny them the right to buy arms, fly, and exercise other constitutional rights.

Indeed, one wonders what constitutional liberties President Hillary will restrict next, using the same principle? After all, terrorists use cell phones and the Internet to recruit and to exchange plans. Arguably this is far more dangerous than purchasing guns.

Will President Hillary thus also ban the First Amendment rights of millions of Americans on the "no-fly" list – restricting their freedom to speak, write and use cell phones and the Internet?

Hillary-Supported "Buy-Backs" Could Launch a Bloody U.S. Civil War

Hillary speaks favorably of the massive and coercive gun roundups in Australia and Britain that, while failing to prevent violence according to some studies, have left citizens unarmed and helpless against criminals (and government), and have created a violent black market in firearms.

At a 2015 New Hampshire town hall meeting, a voter asked her: "Recently, Australia managed to get away, or take away tens of thousands, millions, of handguns. In one year, they were all gone. Can we do that? If we can't, why can't we?"

In her response Hillary described the Australian programs as "buy-backs" instituted as a response to shoot-outs, and implied they were similar to the Obama administration's "Cash for Clunkers" program in which Americans were offered tax credits for trading older cars for newer more fuel-efficient models.

"The Australian example," Hillary said, "that was a buyback program." She said the Australian government "offered a good price" for "buying hundreds of thousands of guns, and then they basically clamped down going forward..." They were thus able, she explained, "to curtail the supply" of guns and "to set a different standard for gun purchases in the future."

"I think it would be worth considering doing it on the [U.S.] national level if that could be arranged." (Emphasis added.)

However, the Australian and UK "buybacks" were nothing like she described. The Australian government's 1996 and 2003 programs were compulsory and coercive, and they involved mass confiscation of common firearms. They included *mandatory* buybacks for newly banned weapons and severe penalties for failure to give up guns, even if owners felt they desperately needed them for protection.

As the NRA summarized:

"The misnamed 'buybacks' of Australia and Great Britain were nothing like the failed 'Cash for Clunkers' program, which simply sought to update the cars Americans drove, not to ban them. They weren't even comparable to local gun buybacks, which attempt to incentivize the voluntary surrender of guns that their owners are free in most cases to replace as they see fit.

"No, the Australian and UK 'buybacks' were merely an attempt to mollify firearm owners whose property had been declared contraband and subject to seizure. They were, to paraphrase Vito Corleone, an offer gun owners could not refuse. The owners had the 'choice' to accept the money and turn in the guns they had previously been forced to register... or they could risk the government forcibly confiscating the guns and being sent to prison for possessing them (supposing, of course, that they survived the confiscation attempt itself).

"If you own a gun now, take heed. ...Hillary Clinton finally made clear what [she is] really after – national gun confiscation."

There are well over 300 million guns in America, according to the Congressional Research Service. Between a third and a half of Americans own guns. About one-third of households in America have one or more guns.

Australian-style confiscation in the U.S. would thus require the government to seize those 300 million guns – kept in every third household in this vast county. As Varad Mehta of the Federalist notes: "If proponents of gun control are serious about getting guns out of Americans' hands, someone will have to take those guns out of Americans' hands.

That will not be easy.

In a country founded upon a successful revolution made possible by an armed citizenry, with a long and proud history of constitutionally protected private gun ownership, where "You'll Get My Gun When You Pry It From My Cold Dead Fingers" is a popular bumper sticker, it is highly unlikely that these millions of Americans will give up their guns voluntarily.

Indeed, notes Mehta, any massive Australian-style gun confiscation in the United States "would require violating not only the Second Amendment, but the Fourth and Fifth as well, and possibly even the First. ... Armed men would be dispatched to confiscate guns, they would be met by armed men, and blood would be shed. Australia is a valid example for America only if you are willing for that blood to be spilled in torrents and rivers. To choose Australia is to choose civil war."

Such a full-blown bloody civil war – a war of American versus American – would, if the Hillary administration won, necessarily end in nothing less than a Hillary dictatorship.

Hillary Promises "Administrative Action" to Overturn the Second Amendment

In 2015 Hillary declared "*the Supreme Court is wrong on the Second Amendment.* And I am going to make that case every chance I get."

Presumably she was referring to the landmark U.S. Supreme Court decisions in District of Columbia v. Heller (2008) and McDonald v. Chicago (2010). Heller established that the Second Amendment protects an individual right to keep and bear arms for self-defense. The McDonald decision found that the right to keep and bear arms was fundamental and applies to all Americans.

Astoundingly, Hillary is thus proposing to use all the powers of her office to attack what the U.S. Supreme Court has declared to be a constitutional right every bit as bedrock as the rights to free speech or freedom of religion.

"If Congress refuses to act, Hillary will take administrative action" on firearm ownership restrictions, her campaign boasts.

Similarly, the Washington Post says that President Hillary would be "relying on the executive power of the presidency to further gun restrictions" that would have little to no chance of getting through Congress.

Hillary Proposes Thought Control on Gun Issues

In 2014 Hillary even said that people shouldn't be allowed to even hold a strong pro-Second Amendment opinion:

"We cannot let a minority of people – and that's what it is, it is a minority of people – hold a viewpoint that terrorizes the majority of people."

To say that people cannot even be allowed to hold a differing viewpoint is the very definition of totalitarianism. It is a call for the creation of "thought crime" like that in the nightmare world of George Orwell's 1984, in which a totalitarian government seeks control not only of the speech and actions but also the very thoughts of its subjects.

Further, Hillary's equating gun rights activists with "terrorists" is a dangerous step towards demonizing gun rights advocates and stripping them of fundamental civil liberties and Bill of Rights freedoms and protections.

It's the same kind of thinking that has given us such unconstitutional nightmares as the above-described "no-fly" list – and that guides Hillary's desire to expand that plainly unconstitutional mechanism.

Hillary's Private Top Secret Army Will Remain Armed

In the next chapter we explore the arguments, made by many critics over the years, that Hillary has a private police and espionage force she uses to covertly advance her political agenda, using threats, harassment, physical violence and blackmail against critics.

One thing is certain: while Hillary is eager to seize guns from millions of law-abiding Americans, she will not disarm this alleged Clinton secret police.

Unless, of course, with the CIA, FBI, NSA, IRS and other alphabet soup police and espionage agencies at her command as president, she won't feel the need for her private police and spy team any longer.

Readers are probably familiar with the famous bumper sticker slogan: "If guns are outlawed, only outlaws will have guns."

If Hillary becomes president, that may have to be altered:

"If guns are outlawed, only outlaws – and President Hillary – will have guns."

CHAPTER SIXTEEN

Hillary's Secret Army: Terrorism, Harassment, Blackmail and More

For years, some of Hillary's critics have accused her of having secret forces at her command to harass, spy upon, threaten, blackmail, intimidate and – some say – even murder those who stood in her way.

This chapter examines those charges.

"The Shadow Team": Hillary's Secret Police Force

Richard Poe is an award-winning journalist, New York Times bestselling author, screenwriter and filmmaker. His nonfiction books on science, history, business, and politics have sold nearly a million copies in the U.S.

He is author of Hillary's Secret War: The Clinton Conspiracy to Muzzle Internet Journalists (2004).

From the publisher's description of that book: "From her own 'war room' in the White House [during Bill's presidency], Hillary Clinton commanded a secret police operation dedicated to silencing dissent, muzzling media critics, intimidating political foes, whitewashing Clinton scandals, and obstructing justice.

"Hillary's operatives infiltrated every level of the news media, federal law enforcement, intelligence agencies, and the federal court system. ...Hillary's secret police persecuted Internet dissidents with special ferocity."

Poe describes this secret police agency, the "Shadow Team," in a FrontPageMagazine.com interview, May 07, 2004:

FrontPage: "Hillary's Secret War tells us that Hillary personally led a secret police force from her office in the White House. Tell us about your proof and evidence."

Poe: "The operations of Hillary's secret police have been copiously documented, to the point where the topic can hardly be called controversial any longer.

"During the [Bill] Clinton years, journalists who probed too deeply into Clinton scandals ran terrible risks. Journalists were beaten, wiretapped, framed on criminal charges, fired and blacklisted. They experienced burglaries, IRS audits, smear campaigns and White-House-orchestrated lawsuits."

"Some may have paid the ultimate price. In February 1998, just as the Clinton impeachment was gathering steam, Sandy Hume, the 28-year-old son of Fox News anchorman Brit Hume, suddenly turned up dead of a gunshot to the head. He was covering the U.S. Congress for the magazine The Hill and was known for his excellent sources among Republican insiders. Sandy Hume supposedly committed suicide, but friends and associates have questioned the official story."

"Some of the White House 'secret police' were private detectives, such as Terry Lenzner, Jack Palladino and Anthony Pellicano. Others were Clinton loyalists embedded in federal intelligence and law enforcement agencies such as the FBI, the CIA, the IRS, the NTSB and so on. Many of these people are still in place, and still doing the Clintons' dirty work. I call them the Shadow Team."

FrontPage: "How does Hillary fit into all this?"

Poe: "Hillary is the muscle end of the Clinton mafia. It was she who organized and led the Shadow Team. Her role as White House enforcer was first revealed by the late Barbara Olson.

"Mrs. Olson was a former federal prosecutor who served from 1995 to 1996 as chief investigative counsel for the Clinger Committee – Rep. William F. Clinger Jr.'s House Government Reform and Oversight Committee, which probed the Filegate and Travelgate affairs. The evidence Mrs. Olson uncovered convinced her that Hillary Clinton had, among other things, conspired to use the Federal Bureau of

Investigation unlawfully to intimidate, punish, harass, frame and otherwise harm innocent people who stood in her way.

"In her 1999 book Hell to Pay, Mrs. Olson wrote, 'Hillary is not merely an aider and abettor to this secret police operation. She has been its prime instigator and organizer. ... In one White House scandal after another, all roads led to Hillary. To investigate White House improprieties and scandals, the evidence necessarily led to her hidden hands guiding the Clinton operation.'"

More on Hillary's Secret Police

Christopher Andersen is the critically acclaimed award-winning author of more than 30 books – more than a dozen of which have become New York Times bestsellers – which have been translated into more than 25 languages worldwide. A former contributing editor of TIME magazine and senior editor of People magazine, Andersen has also written hundreds of articles for a wide range of publications, including Life magazine, the New York Times, and Vanity Fair.

In his 2004 book American Evita, Andersen writes:

"[During Bill's presidency] Hillary built up a secret police for the purposes of conducting a systematic campaign to intimidate, frighten, threaten, discredit and punish innocent Americans whose only misdeed is their desire to tell the truth."

In October 2013 Dick Morris – former intimate Clinton associate turned Clinton critic – wrote of what he, too, called Hillary's "secret police" and noted it was in operation long ago: "During the 1992 presidential campaign, she [Hillary] approved hiring private detectives (paid with campaign funds) to amass compromising information on women who claimed to have been sexually involved with her husband.

"Suddenly, reports surfaced of abortions, bankruptcies, messy divorces and high school and college misconduct in the lives of women who got in her husband's way. The detectives she hired – who we've called the 'secret police' – were doing their work. And the women went away."

And it is still going on. On March 27, 2015, ProPublica presented an article entitled "Private Emails Reveal Ex-Clinton Aide's Secret Spy Network: Emails disclosed by a hacker show a close family friend was funneling intelligence about the crisis in Libya directly to the secretary of state's private account starting before the Benghazi attack."

The authors, Jeff Gerth of ProPublica and Sam Biddle of Gawker, made it clear that Hillary's secret police is alive and well:

"Starting weeks before Islamic militants attacked the U.S. diplomatic outpost in Benghazi, Libya, longtime Clinton family confidante Sidney Blumenthal supplied intelligence to then Secretary of State Hillary Clinton gathered by a secret network that included a former CIA clandestine service officer, according to hacked emails from Blumenthal's account."

Renowned leftist journalist Christopher Hitchens testified from personal experience about the cult-like attitude of many of those doing dark deeds for the Clintons, a mindset which sounds disturbingly like some form of Clinton mind control:

"I have known a number of people who work for and with, or who worked for and with, this man [Bill]. They act like cult members while they are still under the spell, and talk like ex-cult members as soon as they have broken away."

For much more on Hillary's alleged use of her private police force to cover up Bill's sex crimes, see Chapter 9.

Hillary's "Private NSA"

Hillary also has her own high-tech private spy agency, in the guise of an innocent-sounding political action committee (PAC), according to some journalists.

An article entitled "Special Report: Hillary's Private NSA; Privacy of CPAC attendees, GOP delegates targeted" by journalist Jeffrey Lord in the March 2014 American Spectator began with this shocking revelation:

"Hillary Clinton has her own private NSA."

Lord – a respected conservative journalist who has contributed to CNN, The Weekly Standard, The American Spectator, National Review Online, the Wall Street Journal, the Washington Times, the Los Angeles Times and numerous other publications, as well as serving in the Reagan administration – went on to describe Hillary's American Bridge Super PAC, founded by former Clinton critic turned pro-Hillary hatchet man David Brock. The largest individual funder to the American Bridge PAC is the ubiquitous billionaire and longtime Hillary supporter George Soros.

(Soros, incidentally, is yet another of the mega-rich globalist elites, from both the left and right, discussed in Chapter 13, who want to put Americans under the yoke of international organizations. As far back as 1998, Soros wrote: "Insofar as there are collective interests that transcend state boundaries, the sovereignty of states must be subordinated to international law and international institutions." Readers of the conservative publication Human Events voted Soros "the single most destructive leftist demagogue in the country" for supporting numerous controversial left-wing organizations.)

Hillary's American Bridge PAC employs dozens of spies, called "trackers," who are equipped with high-tech recording gear, then sent to follow and record Republican candidates across the country.

ABC called the trackers "essentially Democratic spies."

The New York Times said the organization "aims to record every handshake, every utterance by Republican candidates... looking for 'gotcha' moments that could derail political ambitions or provide fodder for television advertisements by liberal groups."

Hillary's private espionage force also compiles detailed dossiers on the Republican candidates they are surveilling. Their dossier on Republican Mitt Romney was a startling 2,500 pages long.

Journalist Jeffery Lord noted the PAC had actually bragged of "spying on the private conversations of attendees at the [2014] Conservative Political Action Conference (CPAC)."

American Bridge PAC president Brad Woodhouse boasted that Hillary's "trackers" at CPAC had been "in the hallways capturing conversations and that kind of thing. ... We're tracking whatever Republicans are saying, wherever they're saying it."

Says Lord: "The group has been transformed from an ordinary political action committee into the political version of the NSA, its staffers working out of a room littered with computer monitors that will flash the latest privacy invasion for dissemination."

Lord warns of "a room filled with Hillary allies, computer monitors, and 'trackers' spying on the private lives of everybody from CPAC attendees to the as-yet-unselected delegates to the 2016 Republican National Convention in an as-yet-unselected city. ... All of this in the name of electing Hillary Clinton president – where [she] would be in charge of the IRS, the NSA, the FBI, and the CIA."

Did Hillary Steal FBI Files – and Use Them for Blackmail?

"Filegate" is the nickname of a Clinton Administration scandal that arose in June 1996. Filegate centered around allegations that Bill and Hillary and other senior Clinton administration figures in 1993 and 1994 illegally sought and gained access to as many as 900 highly confidential FBI security-clearance documents. Many of the files covered White House employees from previous Republican administrations, including top presidential advisers. The files, by their nature, contained extremely private and personal information about these hundreds of White House employees.

"According to sworn witness testimony, Clinton aides entered the data from these files into a computer database," wrote New York Times bestselling author Richard Poe in Hillary's Secret War. "This information presumably remains in Clinton hands to this day."

There were allegations made that the Clintons had obtained these files to use them for political purposes, i.e., blackmail.

The Filegate charges were investigated by the House Government Reform and Oversight Committee, the Senate Judiciary Committee, and the Whitewater Independent Counsel. In 1998, Independent Counsel Kenneth Starr exonerated President Bill Clinton and First Lady Hillary Rodham Clinton of any involvement in the matter. In 2000 Independent Counsel Robert Ray issued his final report on Filegate, finding no credible evidence of any criminal activity by any individual.

However, critics charge that there is far more to Filegate that the government failed to address. Judicial Watch, a conservative watchdog group with an anti-Hillary bias, filed a lawsuit on behalf of several members of the Reagan and George H. W. Bush administrations arguing that in fact the FBI files had been illegally sought and read by the Clintons. The lawsuit went on for nearly 14 years, finally dismissed by a federal judge in 2010. The judge agreed that the privacy of the White House employees had indeed been violated, but said it was due to "a bureaucratic snafu." "Bureaucratic snafu" was the exact phrase that Bill and Hillary had used years earlier while claiming innocence in the matter.

Judicial Watch founder Larry Klayman strongly disagreed, insisting that it was deliberate and that "Hillary Clinton was the mastermind of Filegate."

Critics charge that the Clinton administration would not hesitate to use blackmail against political opponents, citing allegations that the Clintons had used the IRS to attack critics. Conservative groups critical of the Bill Clinton administration who were audited during the Bill Clinton presidency included the Heritage Foundation, the National Rifle Association, Concerned Women of America, Citizens Against Government Waste, National Review, the American Spectator, the National Center for Public Policy Research, the American Policy Center, American Cause, Citizens for Honest Government, Progress and Freedom Foundation, David Horowitz's Center for the Study of Popular Culture, and the Western Journalism Center.

Individuals audited during the Bill Clinton presidency included Paula Jones and Juanita Broaddrick, who claim they were sexually assaulted by Bill; Gennifer Flowers and actress and former Miss America Liz Ward Gracen, who claim they were sexually involved with Bill; Bill O'Reilly of Fox News, Clinton critic who says he was audited three times; numerous religious-right broadcasters; journalists; and many more persons critical of the Clintons.

However, according to the conservative World News Daily: "A 1996 survey by the Washington Times could not identify a single liberal public policy organization that had been audited during the entire Clinton administration."

Clinton Hit Man Confesses to Murders, Castration for Bill and Hillary

In 2013 the world received shocking further support for the claim that Hillary has a private police force – one that includes paid murderers.

Larry Nichols is a former Green Beret and was a close associate of the Clintons during part of Bill's term as Arkansas governor.

On the Pete Santilli radio show of September 24, 2013, Nichols bluntly declared he had murdered "up to 20 people" for the Clintons, in his role as hit man for the Clinton machine.

Larry Nichols: "I have actually beat up women and beat up husbands to protect the Clintons.... Not only have I killed people for [Bill Clinton], I've [never been in] jail. ...

"...let's call a spade a spade. I've been all over the world killing people for this country, some deservedly, some not. Ain't matter to me. Just what I was paid to do.... When Ronald Reagan sent me to Nicaragua, when Ronald Reagan sent me to El Salvador, I did it for God and country. ...

"I didn't give a shit. ... I mean, hey, some of these people...needed to be dealt with... [I did it for] just money. ...One minute and I'm doing something for the government, next minute I'm doing something for the Clintons. What difference was it?"

Asked how he was sent to kill, Nichols responded:

"Whenever I got an F2 call, that meant go and kill. .... I had an F2 call, that meant go in and kill a guy. I didn't give a shit.... When it came from Clinton, hell, I didn't give a damn. I'd just go kill somebody..."

Such accusations sound incredible. Yet, coupled with decades of stories of women who claim they had sex with Bill or were sexually abused by Bill – and then severely threatened and harassed – such charges may be, at the least, worthy of further exploration. Add to that the lengthy lists of allegedly mysterious deaths some critics have long connected with the Clintons... (More on the Clinton Death Lists in the next section of this chapter.)

Nichols has also claimed he castrated a man named Wayne DuMond for the Clintons. Certainly someone did. While Bill was governor DuMond was convicted of the 1984 rape of Ashley Stevens, a 17-year-old Arkansas cheerleader who was a distant cousin of Bill's. On March 7, 1985, after DuMond's arrest but before his trial, two masked men broke into his bedroom, hog-tied him, forced DuMond to have oral sex with one of them, and then castrated him. Incredibly, for a while the sheriff proudly kept DuMond's severed testicles on display in his office, floating in a formaldehyde-filled fruit jar; eventually he flushed them down the toilet. Later DuMond's house was burned down.

Said Nichols: "I didn't give a shit. Some of these people, like Wayne DuMond, needed to be dealt with. So I went to the jail, cut his nuts off, put them in a jar, put formaldehyde in it and left it there," Nichols said.

It should be noted that later, in an article in the May/June 2015 issue of the progressive magazine Mother Jones, Nichols, according to the writer of the piece, "now says he didn't mean [that he had been a Clinton hit man] and wouldn't have said [so] if he hadn't been on painkillers."

Perhaps, then, there is nothing to Nichols' horrific claims. But some may wonder if Nichols had been threatened after his confession, perhaps by a new-generation Clinton hitman, into recanting.

Especially when one considers a bizarre turn the Mother Jones interview abruptly takes: Nichols, for many years one of the most outspoken opponents of the Clintons, is quoted as saying he now supports Hillary for president.

"I'm not saying I like Hillary, you hear me?" Nichols says of this peculiar and startling endorsement. "I'm not saying anything I've said I take back."

Nonetheless, he says, "God help me" but Hillary is needed as president because of the threat of terrorism – and, he says, from his long personal experience he knows that Hillary has the iron will, the ruthlessness and the sheer meanness necessary to do any ugly deeds needed to protect America.

"[W]e have no choice but to give Hillary her shot. ... I know she won't flinch. That's a mean sonofabitch woman..."

But in May 2016 Nichols reversed this, telling award-winning journalist Greg Hunter at usawatchdog.com that he was endorsing Donald Trump, fearing that Hillary is part of a sinister scheme by the power elite to transform the U.S. into a tyranny:

"We are at the beginning of a velvet or silent coup. It's been going on for years. There's been a slow subtle takeover of our form of government, starting years and years ago, but it is coming to an end. That's why there is this power play now. It's more aggressive than you have seen before.

"If we don't stop Hillary, it's over."

The Clinton Death Lists

If the Clintons indeed have private armies, private police, private investigators and private killers-on-call, then one might expect to find numerous strange murders, mysterious disappearances, charges of threats and blackmail, and other such allegations of criminal behavior floating around the Clintons.

And that is precisely what many researchers claim to have documented.

For years there have been many versions of a "Clinton Death List" floating around the Web. They are also sometimes referred to as "The Body Count" or "The Clinton Body Count." Some are more carefully researched than others.

The lists include a startling number of people who have been involved, in one way or another, with alleged Clinton scandals and controversies.

A surprising number of these deaths have been described as "execution-style" killings. There are many mutilations: skulls crushed, bodies dismembered and burned. Critics charge that many possible murders were simply ruled accidents or suicides by Arkansas medical examiners for political reasons. Critics also say this was so widespread that such deaths were often referred to as "Arkancide" or "Arkansas Suicide."

Journalist Deroy Murdock noted in 1994 that "...an apparent pattern of violence and intimidation has befallen a number of men and women with ties to Bill and Hillary Clinton, their partners in business, law and politics, and people investigating their affairs."

Reporter David Bresnahan of the conservative World News Daily claims that he originated the granddaddy of all such lists in 1997 while researching his book Cover Up: The Art and Science of Political Deception.

"I started looking into all the various deaths of people that were involved in various Clinton scandals," Bresnahan in told World News Daily in 1999. "I started to investigate the entire picture instead of just one focused event. ...

"When you investigate all Clinton scandals, you find similarities, you find common tactics, you find common actions and you find dead people."

Early versions of the list carry his byline, he says.

Furthermore, Bresnahan devised other startling lists regarding the Clintons.

"Not only did I find a list of dead people, but I also found that there are over 100 people who have refused to testify," Bresnahan said in 1999.

"There is also a list of people who have gone to jail. There are 45 people who have gone to jail, some of them White House staff, Cabinet members as well as people from the Justice Department. So many of those [lists] developed when I started to pursue the big picture."

Since then, many others have expanded on Bresnahan's Clinton Death List. Many versions can be found online.

There are also lengthy lists of women who have allegedly been Bill's extra-marital sexual partners or who are allegedly victims of sexual abuse or rape by Bill.

And then there are the Clinton suicides. In 2016 journalist Guy Somerset compiled a list of 15 suicides committed by people connected in some way with Hillary. While noting that many of them had acceptable explanations, the sheer numbers astounded him:

"Generally speaking an ordinary individual will have personal connections to approximately one or two suicides over the course of many decades. ... [W]hat should we make of a woman who in less than seventy years on this planet has had particular relations with five, ten or as many as fifteen people who committed suicide? Would we question whether there might be some explanation behind this startling high amount? Indeed, would it be incorrect to consider such a woman anything less than the Typhoid Mary of suicidal epidemics? ...

"Any personality who has the effect on their confrères of making them habitually kill themselves is by definition highly suspicious, almost laughably so.

"Yet it is one of the two national candidates for the presidency of the United States who seemingly has the odd effect on those who know her of causing them to die by their own hand. Moreover, such deaths are often carried out in the most bizarre ways; such as numerous execution-style gunshot wounds."

Investigating the veracity of the numerous allegations on the Clinton Death Lists is outside the scope of this book.

However, it is important that anyone considering these accusations should also be aware that many writers have made well-researched efforts to refute these lists and say they have proved the various "Death Lists" to be inaccurate, misleading, and in other ways invalid.

The liberal fact-checking site Snopes.com, for example, has examined many of the charges on some Clinton Death Lists and dismisses the allegations as "claptrap."

"Any unexplained death can automatically be attributed to President Clinton by inventing a connection between him and the victim," says Snopes.com. "The longer the list, the more impressive it looks and the less likely anyone is to challenge it. By the time readers get to the bottom of the list, they'll be too weary to wonder what could possibly be relevant about the death of people such as Bill Clinton's mother's chiropractor."

Because of the controversy surrounding these lists and their incendiary charges, anyone attempting to examine the Clinton Death List allegations should also check Snopes.com and other easily found online challenges to these lists.

Writers and Investigators Fear for Their Lives After Researching Clintons; Journalist Charges Hillary Is "Paranoid" and Has "Penchant for Doing Illegal Things"

In 2016 Peter Schweizer, author of the acclaimed book Clinton Cash, which documents Clinton money scandals and corruption regarding the Clinton Foundation, was asked by Bloomberg News during a televised interview *if he had received any death threats because of his book.*

Readers should take note: the mere fact that this astounding question was even asked by a respected news organization speaks volumes about mainstream journalists' knowledge and concern about the Clinton machine.

"I'll just say we have [full-time] security," Schweizer replied. "And that security is not something that just came because we decided to have security. And we'll just leave it at that."

This was nothing new. Word News Daily reported that Dick Morris, the former Clinton aide and intimate turned Clinton opponent, told Matt Drudge on his Fox News TV show in 1999 that Senate impeachment investigators he personally met with said they feared IRS retaliation by the Clinton administration.

Morris also said three veteran investigators – with FBI, IRS and other law-enforcement experience – working on the case told him they were aware of the Clinton Death List and actually feared for their lives.

"[M]ost people are afraid of invoking the wrath of Hillary Clinton, and so they will talk about her only on condition of anonymity," said Edward Klein, author of The Truth About Hillary: What She Knew, When She Knew It, and How Far She'll Go to Become President (2005), in a 2005 interview with National Review.

Klein, it should be noted, is a former editor-in-chief of the New York Times Magazine and a widely respected and published journalist (Newsweek, the New York Times, Vanity Fair, Parade, etc.)

"Like Nixon, Hillary is paranoid and has an enemies list. Like Nixon, Hillary has used FBI files against her enemies.

"Like Nixon, Hillary believes the ends justify the means. Like Nixon, Hillary has a penchant for doing illegal things."

Hillary vs. the Internet and Free Speech

"We are all going to have to rethink how we deal with [the Internet], because there are all these competing values. Without any kind of editing function or gatekeeping function, what does it mean to have the right to defend your reputation?" – Hillary Clinton, February 11, 1998, when asked by reporters if she favored restrictions on the Internet.

The Clintons have long wanted to control the Internet, where so much criticism and exposure of them has occurred, as well as other forms of electronic communication.

As far back as 1993 the Clinton administration announced its support for the infamous Clipper Chip, an encryption chip that would be put into every digital voice communication device to give the government a "back-door" to let them intercept any conversation.

In 2016 the libertarian magazine Reason, in an article "Hail to the Censor! Hillary Clinton's Long War on Free Speech," noted Hillary's long support for unconstitutional government control of the media.

"She has consistently backed government intrusions into communications devices, from content-filtering V-chips on television sets to anti-encryption back doors on iPhones. She has established as her litmus test for Supreme Court nominees a commitment to overturn 2010's Citizens United v. Federal Election Commission, in which a 5–4 majority overturned on grounds that 'the censorship we now confront is vast in its reach' a federally enforced cable TV ban of a documentary film attacking a certain politician named Hillary Rodham Clinton. Several other laws that Clinton championed, including the Communications Decency Act (CDA) and the Child Online Protection Act (COPA), were opposed by the American Civil Liberties Union (ACLU) and struck down by the Supreme Court as violations of the First Amendment."

In a January 2010 speech she argued that "free expression has its limits" and attacked "hate speech." Said Hillary: "The same networks that help organize movements for freedom also enable Al Qaeda to spew hatred and incite violence against the innocent. ... Now, all societies recognize that *free expression has its limits*. [Emphasis added.] We do not tolerate those who incite others to violence, such as the agents of Al Qaeda who are, at this moment, using the Internet to promote the mass murder of innocent people across the world. And hate speech that targets individuals on the basis of their race, religion, ethnicity, gender, or sexual orientation is reprehensible. It is an unfortunate fact that these issues are both growing challenges that the international community must confront together."

Not even the right to anonymous speech – one of the hallmarks of political free speech and one of the strengths of the Internet – is safe from Hillary's lust for control. From the same speech: "And we must also grapple with the issue of anonymous speech."

In Hillary's world, citizens will be marked, ID'd, monitored and controlled at all times.

Of course, "terrorism" and "hate speech" are open-ended excuses for any politician justifying an attack on free speech.

On December 26, 2015 she repeated her frequent call for tech companies to work with the government to find ways to shut down speech by terrorists and their sympathizers. While the idea of hampering terrorists in this way may sound attractive to some on the surface, in practice this is a call for full-time government and private-sector monitoring of all online speech in order to determine which is "good" and which is "bad" so that the latter can be shut down. Hillary dismissed the obvious urgent First Amendment concerns with a sneer and a wave of the hand: "You're going to hear all of the usual complaints, you know, freedom of speech, et cetera..."

In the same vein, Hillary has condemned the heroic NSA whistleblower Edward Snowden, saying he should "not be brought home without facing the music," that is, he should be arrested and tried for attempting in 2013 to defend American freedom from criminal assault by the rogue National Security Agency (NSA), whose crimes he exposed. Hillary argues Snowden should have gone public and asked for legal protections for whistleblowers – which, in fact, were not legally available to him as a contractor for the NSA.

Hillary has also attacked encryption, the very basis of privacy in electronic communication and, as experts point out, a form of speech itself:

"It doesn't do anybody any good if terrorists can move toward encrypted communication that no law enforcement agency can break into before or after," she said during the December Democratic debate. "I just think there's got to be a way, and I would hope that our tech companies would work with government to figure that out. ...*we always have to balance liberty and security*, privacy and safety, but I know that law enforcement needs the tools to keep us safe."

Of course, "balancing liberty and security" is authoritarian-speak for taking away civil liberties. Benjamin Franklin, famously, had the best answer for such proposals:

"Those who would give up essential Liberty, to purchase a little temporary Safety, deserve neither Liberty nor Safety."

CONCLUSION

"What rough beast, its hour come round at last...?"

*The blood-dimmed tide is loosed, and everywhere
The ceremony of innocence is drowned;
The best lack all conviction, while the worst
Are full of passionate intensity. ...*

*And what rough beast, its hour come round at last,
Slouches towards Bethlehem to be born?*

– "The Second Coming," William Butler Yeats, 1919

In the 2016 presidential elections, marred by hatred, belligerence, ignorance, hubris, corruption and venality, you can feel it: something indeed evil has been born, is coming into power.

Its hour has come round at last, and it slouches, no, strides confidently, to Washington to be born.

And to clutch us all in its grasp.

Is Hillary Clinton a blood-drinking reptilian shapeshifter? An alien conspirator? The Antichrist? A witch, a consorter with demons, a worshipper of Satan?

In this book we have examined the best evidence for these and other widely believed accusations. In doing so, I have been startled and surprised many times, and I hope you have been, too.

Now it is up to you to make up your own mind. If this book has stimulated you into fresh thinking on important issues, it has accomplished its chief task.

We have explored other vital questions, too: whether Hillary is an agent of a ruthless global elite, a dangerous authoritarian, a congenital liar, a warmonger.

On these the record is crystal clear.

There simply can be no doubt that Hillary is, in political terms, a monster: a willing tool and partner of ruthless global elites conspiring to ransack and pillage the planet, a statist, a war-hungry super-hawk whose polices are a threat to the existence of all life on the planet.

Jeffrey David Sachs, the renowned economist and director of the Earth Institute at Columbia University, is one of the world's leading experts on economic development and poverty alleviation. A liberal Democrat, he has said he will probably vote for Hillary. Yet here is his description in 2016 of her foreign policy:

"Hillary's record as secretary of state is among the most militaristic, and disastrous, of modern U.S. history. ... Hillary was a staunch defender of the military-industrial-intelligence complex at every turn, helping to spread the Iraq mayhem over a swath of violence that now stretches from Mali to Afghanistan. ...

"It is hard to know the roots of this record of disaster. Is it chronically bad judgment? Is it her preternatural faith in the lying machine of the CIA? Is it a repeated attempt to show that as a Democrat she would be more hawkish than the Republicans? Is it to satisfy her hard-line campaign financiers? Who knows? Maybe it's all of the above. But whatever the reasons, hers is a record of disaster.

"Perhaps more than any other person, Hillary can lay claim to having stoked the violence that stretches from West Africa to Central Asia and that threatens U.S. security."

Let that sink in. *A million or more people are dead directly because of policies enthusiastically advanced by Hillary*. Millions more are today desperate refugees fleeing shattered homelands. Much of the world is in flames because of policies she advocated and instituted. ISIS was born as a consequence of her ghastly and illegal interventions in the Middle East, and it now spreads violence and terror around the world. Even worse plagues wait in the wings.

Not only did Hillary set the Middle East ablaze. She aggressively meddled in the internal affairs of nations bordering Russia, prodding and provoking and threatening Russia until she actually has restarted the Cold War. She similarly championed aggressive U.S. interference in China's sphere of influence and engaged in saber-rattling with North Korea. As a result we now face the very real threat of nuclear war with Russia, China and North Korea – war that could conceivably destroy all civilization, end all human life.

The door for global peace that opened up so briefly, so promisingly with the collapse of the Soviet Union and the end of the Cold War has long since been slammed shut by the ceaseless warmongering that followed that epochal moment. And Hillary continues on, poking hornets' nests, stirring up alarm and outrage in nations around the world. One day soon, some of those hornets will sting. Hard.

The neoconservatives who formulated today's monstrous bipartisan foreign policy of endless global intervention have largely joined her side in 2016. She is the personification of their unholy, unhinged schemes. The military-industrial-surveillance Moloch is rubbing its bloody hands in gleeful anticipation of the additional riches and power soon to tumble into its endlessly greedy maw.

> Generals gathered in their masses,
> just like witches at black masses.
> Evil minds that plot destruction,
> sorcerer of death's construction.
> In the fields the bodies burning,
> as the War Machine keeps turning.
> Death and hatred to mankind,
> poisoning their brainwashed minds...
>
> – "War Pigs" by Black Sabbath

If Hillary is not a flesh-eating reptilian shapeshifter, or a demon-mongering witch, or the Antichrist, she might as well be. Could sinister reptilian invaders from another planet cause more destruction than Hillary has already conjured? Could the Antichrist conceive of a more calamitous foreign policy, or a more sinister shattering of fundamental rights to worldwide privacy and liberty, than she is calling for?

This is the nightmare Hillary has planned for you and me, dear reader. She has been moving toward it her entire political life.

Hillary boasts that, when she shared the power of the White House with Bill, "I urged him to bomb" Serbian forces in Yugoslavia in 1998 that posed no conceivable threat to the U.S.; up to 1500 civilians were killed. The bombing allowed a ghoulish regime to take power that instigated, among other things, savage ethnic cleansing and the murdering of civilians in order to sell their organs abroad. Journalist Alexander Cockburn wrote that "Hillary Rodham Clinton was an enthusiastic advocate for the cluster bombs that now litter the Serbia and Kosovo landscapes, set to kill or cripple for the next half century."

With Hillary presumably cheering him on, Bill bombed again and again and again, entering in eight wars or interventions in Afghanistan, Bosnia, Colombia, Haiti, Iraq, Somalia, Sudan, and Yugoslavia, none authorized by Congress.

Three of those bombings were in 1998, at critical moments during Bill's sordid impeachment battle. The night before House impeachment proceedings were to begin Bill ordered a shelling of Iraq; many critics openly wondered if the Iraq bombing was an attempt to have the impeachment proceedings halted or delayed, and indeed, many of Bill's allies in Congress called for exactly that. The same day Monica Lewinsky made her second grand jury appearance, Bill ordered a U.S. missile strike against a pharmaceutical factory in Sudan accused, on flimsy and since discredited evidence, of processing nerve gas. The charge was as false as the later charge that Iraq possessed weapons of mass destruction. But the factory, which produced a huge amount of critical medical supplies for a poor country wracked by famine and civil war, was destroyed; by some estimates thousands of people died as a result. In December, as the Clinton impeachment proceedings reached their peak, missiles were again hurled at Iraq.

Handmade signs were seen at demonstrations throughout the Arab world: NO WAR FOR MONICA!

Was the timing of these strikes all just a coincidence? Or was this yet more of Hillary protecting – at any cost – Bill and her own political ambitions from the consequences of his reckless sexual behavior?

As senator Hillary famously voted for and loudly supported the Iraq War. That war in turn set off much of the violence and destruction that has engulfed the Middle East. Legal experts from around the world argue that not only was the invasion of Iraq disastrous, it was illegal and criminal. United Nations Secretary General Kofi Annan said in September 2004: "From our point of view and the UN Charter point of view, it [the Iraq War] was illegal." Renowned foreign policy critic Noam Chomsky calls the U.S. invasion of Iraq "the worst crime of this century."

As Bill's equal partner in the Clinton Inc enterprise, and as New York senator, Hillary endorsed the savage sanctions against Iraq, imposed by the UN in 1990 and continuing through Bill's two terms and afterwards, until 2003. Decent people around the world gasped in horror when Bill's secretary of state Madeleine Albright was asked in a 1996 television interview whether the killing of half a million utterly innocent Iraqi children – the grand achievement of the sanctions – was justified, and Albright responded coolly: "We think it was worth it."

Those who scoff at the idea that our ruling elites would sacrifice living children on strange altars at such events as Bohemian Grove might ponder this casual dismissal by those same elites of the lives of half a million such innocents. Here is documented proof that our rulers do indeed sacrifice children to fearsome and unholy gods.

None of us should expect any more mercy from her than was shown to these poor victims.

In 2006 both Hillary and Bill endorsed torture. Bill suggested a secret court be created to issue torture warrants "when the only way they can get a reliable piece of information is to beat it out of someone or put a drug in their body to talk it out of 'em..."

U.S. Senator Hillary suggested a law allowing the president to order the torture of any suspect so long as the president says there is an "imminent threat" to national security. But don't worry, she proposed a "check and balance": "reporting in a Top Secret context" to, presumably, a secret court or select members of Congress.

In 2014, while accepting the Robert F. Kennedy "Ripple of Hope" award, which "celebrates leaders who have demonstrated a commitment to justice [and] basic human rights," Hillary denounced torture to a cheering audience of human rights activists. Which Hillary are we to believe?

In this book we have showed Hillary's intricate connections with the rich and the powerful, the global elites that meet in secrecy to set the agenda for the world. We have seen her symbiotic relationship with the military-industrial-spy state that feeds upon us, stripping us of our liberty, our belongings, our privacy, to fuel an unconstitutional global war empire.

Hillary, we have seen, is cozy and comfortable with mass murderers, despots and torturers. As secretary of state she provided them with the very weapons they use to torture and crush those unfortunates suffering under their rule. Indeed, as we have noted, she calls some of the world's worst tyrants her friends. She even spends Christmas holidays with a widely reviled war criminal responsible for millions of deaths.

Do the Clintons and the Kissingers spend their Christmas time together as reptilians, Satanists, witches and warlocks, quaffing human blood and sacrificing babies in strange and bloody ceremonies, communing with hideous demons... or do they just sing carols and exchange yuletide pleasantries, happy fellow members of the one-percent ruling elite? Either way, blood, death, misery and mayhem are the fruits of their unholy labors.

Hillary and her associates drink blood metaphorically, if not literally. They sacrifice millions on their altars, whether those altars are dedicated to Satan, ghastly otherworld deities, or simply their own hubris, power lust and bank accounts.

Hillary worships death. Hillary *is* death for people around the globe.

Is Hillary a participant in some modern version of the CIA's infamous MK-ULTRA mind-controlled slave-creation project, as the alleged victims of the rumored Project MONARCH charge? Read the evidence in this book and make up your mind. But we do know beyond question that Hillary is a devotee and servant of the national security state that produced MK-ULTRA and countless other horrors. She will provide the CIA, the NSA, and the whole alphabet soup of murderous spook agencies with whatever they desire to keep on spying on us and everyone else, subverting the Constitution and overthrowing other governments, as they have done since the end of World War II.

We will have no way of knowing what horrific secret projects Hillary's surveillance-state partners are using against us, because their massive budgets will remain secret, and the agencies will continue to operate under secret laws created in secret courts presided over by secret judges. We will all be stamped with the Mark of the Beast, or something similar, and tracked and controlled like farm animals. Death will rain down, as it does today, from flying killer robot drones directed by secret government orders and guided by secret soldiers of secret armies. Dissent will be muffled by a subservient press run by elite media moguls in cahoots with the state; by propaganda campaigns and psy-ops directed against the American people in the guise of popular movies, TV shows, video games and other entertainment; by a spyocracy that can read our every online communication, listen to our phone calls, peer at us through own computers, and, perhaps soon, read and record our very thoughts; and by an education system that seems purposefully designed to churn out armies of ignorant, obedient citizen-slaves to serve as unquestioning worker drones or cannon fodder.

Do not expect anything but further assaults on fundamental rights and civil liberties should Hillary become our ruler.

Hillary spews death, destruction, delusion, disruption, poverty and bondage wherever she goes. Is she driven by demons or malevolent spirits from other dimensions? This book presents the best available evidence for such things. But by the historic record of her actions and results, she may as well be.

AFTERWORD

Is It Hopeless?

"We have it in our power to begin the world over again."
– Thomas Paine, Common Sense, 1776

Reading page after page about reptilian overlords, witches, demon possession, secret conspiracies, hideous government experiments, ruling elite conspiracies, despotic politicians and so on could lead one to wonder if things are hopeless. Maybe it's time to give up? Close the book on the American experiment?

The answer is no. Despite the horrors explored in this book, our situation is far from hopeless. In fact, there is great reason for optimism.

Americans are an immensely wealthy and powerful people. We are the inheritors of a great legacy of individual rights and limited government. Those rights remain enshrined in our governing documents, even if those who rule us have conducted an end-run around them in the past several decades.

We still have the power and the tools to peacefully change the government, and, by doing so, change the world.

This is not the place for detailing a plan for achieving that. You doubtless have ideas of your own.

But here are some brief thoughts:

1. Educate yourself. Always, change begins with you. The Internet has revolutionized political education. As in no other time in human history, you have the opportunity to hear alternative political views that challenge and rebut Establishment lies and false histories, as well as your own prejudices and errors. Seek out responsible dissenting voices from across the political spectrum, from the left, the right, and libertarians. Find common ground where you can.

Follow the old bumper sticker advice: Question Authority. Subvert the Dominant Paradigm.

2. Educate others. Share what you learn. For the first time in history, you have the ability to become the media yourself, through social media, websites and blogs, letters to publications, songs, movies, and much much more. Use that power.

3. The most important issue of our time is foreign policy, which is not only the cause of devastation abroad, but also the instigator of many of our worst domestic tyrannies. Our current militaristic foreign policy creates enemies around the world, brings blowback in the form of terrorism, drains our national income, and provides the excuse for the federal assault on our freedoms.

Happily, foreign policy is one area where good people from across the political spectrum can meet and agree and form coalitions for reform.

We must end the post-World War II neoconservative foreign policy of endless global intervention. We should replace it with the traditional American foreign policy of peaceful non-intervention: a capable defense for America, but non-interference in the internal affairs of other nations. No one ever put it better than Thomas Jefferson: "Peace, commerce, and honest friendship with all nations – entangling alliances with none."

We urgently need a massive, active and ongoing antiwar/pro-peace movement in America demanding non-interventionism. Bring the troops home. Cut military spending to the amount necessary to defend the country. Let the U.S. support peace and freedom in the world the way we do best: by serving as a shining example to the rest of the world of how to be peaceful and free, and of the abundance that flows from living those values.

4. We should uproot the whole spyocracy. Abolish the CIA, the NSA, and the rest of the gigantic, invisible, unaccountable, secret government.

Is this unrealistic? Not at all. The CIA has been documented as a failure and a human rights disaster since its 1947 inception. This book has detailed just a few of its innumerable crimes against the American people and the people of the world.

President Kennedy famously said he wanted to "splinter the CIA in a thousand pieces and scatter it to the winds.'"

President Harry Truman, who gave us the CIA, later wrote of his concern that the CIA had become "so removed from its intended role ... I never had any thought that when I set up the CIA that it would be injected into peacetime cloak and dagger operations. ... It has become an operational and at times a policy-making arm of the government..." He wanted to "see the CIA be restored to its original assignment as the intelligence arm of the President... and that its operational duties be terminated or properly used elsewhere."

Sen. Daniel Patrick Moynihan (D-NY), one of America's most influential senators and vice chairman of the Senate Intelligence Committee, introduced legislation in 1991 and again in 1995 to abolish the CIA and turn any legitimate functions over to the State Department or the military.

The great libertarian congressman and two-time Republican presidential candidate Ron Paul said he would "abolish the NSA, the TSA, the CIA and all spying on American citizens" and pursue a Jeffersonian foreign policy of peace and non-intervention. Surprise Democratic presidential contender Bernie Sanders said in 1974 that the CIA was "a dangerous institution that has got to go" (though he later moved away from that position – hopefully he or another Democrat with his influence will champion this again).

America's two largest third parties, the Libertarian Party and the Green Party, receive collectively millions of votes each election year and run candidates for office across America. And their vote numbers are increasing, especially among the young. Both of these fast-growing parties have called for abolishing the CIA and other spy agencies and ending U.S. military intervention abroad.

Ultimately the entire National Security Act of 1947 – which transformed our government from one at least nominally led and limited by the U.S. Constitution to one that operates in secret, with unlimited power in the hands of shadowy spy agencies – should be repealed. Legislation to do exactly that was also introduced in Congress in the past. It can happen again.

If enough Americans come to understand the importance of this, we will see such legislation introduced again – and candidates who support it elected – and the legislation itself ultimately passed.

It begins by talking about it – by pushing the issue back into the public debate.

America was free and safe without the CIA and the rest of the spookocracy for most of its history. We can be so again.

And deprived of access to political power, the kind of evil we have discussed in this book is largely disarmed.

Major political change can happen – and quickly. The Berlin Wall, seemingly as permanent as the pyramids, was abruptly torn down and vanished in a matter of days.

Our American ancestors fought the army of the most powerful king in the world and won their freedom.

Gandhi's peaceful protests forced the mighty British empire to stand down. Martin Luther King took Gandhi's example to heart and in a short time peacefully transformed the segregated American South and the world.

The oppressive agents of the world – whether reptilian, demonic, Satanic, or just plain old power-hungry human beings – thrive in secrecy and fear and darkness. Shine a light, remove their cover, expose their works, and they will quickly be powerless.

The ultimate power remains in the hands of the people, if we will use it.

James W. Harris
OccultHillary.com

SOURCES

Regretfully, in order to get this book published (barely!) before the 2016 elections, I was unable to include a list of sources. Please note, however, all quotes, dates, etc., were carefully researched for authenticity.

I have included in the text of the book itself many of the sources for quotes, dates and so on. Many of those that aren't included in the text can be found easily enough with a short Internet search.

A lengthy list of sources for each chapter, most with links, is posted at this book's website, www.OccultHillary.com.

I am compiling a complete source list and will add it to the ebook and print editions as soon as possible. If you purchased a Kindle ebook, the addition should update automatically when it is available. I will also update the references at the website.

ACKNOWLEDGEMENTS

Thanks to Sharon, who shared with me the astonishment, shock, and not-infrequent laughter as this book took shape. Without her loving support, encouragement, and assistance, this book would not have been possible, and writing it would not have been nearly as much fun.

Thanks to Susan Monahan and Zach Varnell for their invaluable assistance.

Please note that none of the above-mentioned people bear any responsibility for the concept or contents of this book.

ABOUT THE AUTHOR

Amazon bestselling author **JAMES W. HARRIS** has published over a thousand articles, op-eds and other writings. His work has appeared in some of America's most influential publications – including *The Nation, Reason,* the *Atlanta Journal-Constitution* and the *Orange County Register* – and in some of its strangest and most notorious, including Larry Flynt's *Hustler, FATE* magazine, and *The Splatter Times* ("The World's Most Violent Magazine").

He has been a Finalist in the Mencken Awards, given for Outstanding Journalism in Support of Liberty, and was a state winner of the "Freedom: Worth Fighting For" national First Amendment essay contest. He is co-author, with Sharon Harris, of the Amazon Number One bestseller *How to Be a Super Communicator for Liberty*.

He is an award-winning filmmaker whose short films have played at film festivals across America. He was singer and guitarist for Alabama's first punk rock band. *Crud Bomb* zine declared him "Bishop of the Gamera Flicks" for his enthusiasm for that renowned giant fire-breathing flying turtle of Japanese monster movie fame.

He can be reached at OccultHillary.com.

One Last Thing...

Thank you, dear reader, for reading this book!

If you enjoyed it, please take just a few minutes to go to Amazon, rate the book (5 stars would be great!), and write a brief (or lengthy) review.

I would appreciate this enormously, as you will help me reach a wider audience and contribute to the success of the book. Thank you!

James W. Harris

—

Printed in Great Britain
by Amazon